SECOND EDITION

Peoples and Cultures of the Middle East

Daniel G. Bates
Istanbul Bilgi University
and Hunter College, CUNY

Amal Rassam
Queens College, CUNY

Prentice
Hall

Upper Saddle River, New Jersey 07458

Library of Congress Cataloging-in-Publication Data

Bates, Daniel G.
    Peoples and cultures of the Middle East / Daniel G. Bates, Amal Rassam.—2nd ed.
        p. cm.
    Includes bibliographical references and index.
    ISBN 0-13-656489-5
    1. Middle East—Civilization.   2. Ethnology—Middle East.   I. Rassam, Amal.   II. Title.

DS57 .B34 2001
956—dc21
                                                                            00-41680

VP, Editorial Director: Laura Pearson
Publisher: Nancy Roberts
Managing Editor: Sharon Chambliss
Director of Marketing: Beth Gillette Mejia
Interior Design and Project Manager: Serena Hoffman
Prepress and Manufacturing Buyer: Benjamin Smith
Copy Editor: Mary Louise Byrd
Illustrations: Carto-Graphics
Photo Researcher: Toby Zaussner
Director, Image Resource Center: Melinda Reo
Image Specialist: Beth Boyd
Manager, Rights and Permissions: Key Dellosa
Cover Art Director: Jayne Conte
Cover Designer: Bruce Kenselaar

This book was set in 10/12 Adobe Palatino
by Stratford Publishing Services and was
printed and bound by Courier Companies, Inc.
The cover was printed by Phoenix Color Corp.

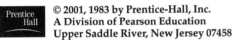

© 2001, 1983 by Prentice-Hall, Inc.
A Division of Pearson Education
Upper Saddle River, New Jersey 07458

Printed in the United States of America

10   9   8   7   6   5   4   3   2   1

ISBN   0-13-656489-5

Prentice-Hall International (UK) Limited, *London*
Prentice-Hall of Australia Pty. Limited, *Sydney*
Prentice-Hall Candad Inc., *Toronto*
Prentice-Hall Hispanoamericana, S.A., *Mexico*
Prentice-Hall of India Private Limited, *New Delhi*
Prentice-Hall of Japan, Inc. *Tokyo*
Pearson Education Asia Pte. Ltd., *Singapore*
Editora Prentice-Hall do Brasil, Ltda., *Rio de Janeiro*

*To Sophia, Nina, and Murat with love,
and to the memory of Eric R. Wolf,
whose scholarship still stimulates,
and whose many acts of kindness are not forgotten.*

Contents

6   Agriculture and the Changing Village   143

7   Cities and Urban Life   171

8   Kinship, Marriage, and the Family   201

9   Women and the Social Order   226

Preface

This is the second edition of a book that has gone through more than twenty printings since its original publication in 1983. The unexpected vitality of the original edition was as pleasant as it was unexpected. In the normal course of events, reports about regions and people have a relatively short shelf life. The fact that the first edition has continued to be read indicates, to us at least, that there is a sense in which social scientific findings have a cumulative quality that goes beyond the fads of the moment. It would also seem that there is a need for scholarly reporting that is broadly accessible and relatively free from an over-burden of scholarly jargon and theoretical minutiae. The first edition had this as an explicit goal, and to some extent at least, it seems that it was successful. We hope that this edition is equally useful.

This anthropological essay builds on nearly three decades of teaching and research by both authors in various countries of the Middle East and in neighboring regions in Africa, the Balkans, and Central Asia. As friends and colleagues of long standing, we have maintained an ongoing dialogue about the craft of anthropology and what it offers the student of Middle Eastern society. Our different but complementary points of departure and field experiences have helped, we feel, to make our discussions particularly fruitful. This book has no senior author. Indeed, it would not be possible to attribute any passage or section to any one of us; the venture was truly collaborative in all respects. In the first edition the actual, sometimes tedious, process of writing and revising was done in joint sessions; in this edition we had relatively brief but intensive sessions of joint work, but the actual crafting of chapters was necessarily done while working on separate continents, with Bates often in Turkey and Rassam in New York.

As the title suggests, we see this book as an exercise in social anthropology. To that extent, our objectives are to provide a synthesis of what we feel our discipline has been able to contribute to an understanding of this important area of the world. We have avoided theoretical polemics and specialized jargon in the hopes of avoiding a common social science tendency to mystify and thereby to explain less than is already known by common sense.

Our point of departure—in fact, the assumption underlying the analysis we provide—is that explanations of cultural institutions and social processes must be relatable to the behavior of individuals, their needs, values, and motivations. Individual decisions and actions, indeed, behavior of all sorts, take place in the context of particular social or cultural settings. These social and cultural settings are themselves shaped by the momentum of a specific history. Not only do the material constraints of the moment affect the strategies of individuals today, but the particular ways in which material problems or opportunities were handled in the past also influence current choices.

Systems of values, norms, and religious beliefs are also an integral part of social process. Not only does an ideational system give meaning to individuals' actions, but the system itself is a source of constraints facing the individual and society, as well as an arena in which people compete. Individuals and groups use ideologies of all sorts as they strive for power—to control resources, gain prestige, and influence outcomes. Although we have not paid great attention to national-level politics and economics, we have consistently kept this larger and important context in view as we developed our analysis. It would not be too much to say that a full understanding of the activities of people in the most remote village today requires an awareness of how that community fits into a national, indeed, a world economic and political system.

Many people are to be thanked for the assistance they have rendered us directly or indirectly. Both of us were students of William Schorger at the University of Michigan at critical junctures of our intellectual growth. To him we express that special thanks due to one's teachers. We also want to acknowledge our special intellectual debt to Eric Wolf, who as teacher, friend, critic, and colleague, stimulated and challenged us over many years. In fact, at the outset of this enterprise, we took as a model his early book, *Sons of the Shaking Earth*, which describes the cultural history of the valley of Mexico. To us, this book exemplifies a superb treatment of a complex historical and cultural tradition, a treatment at once elegant, sympathetic, and honest.

Of the many friends and colleagues who assisted us by the critical reading of parts of the present manuscript, we would like to thank Ayşe Akalın, Alan Duben, David Gilmore, Greg Johnson, Uğur Kömeçoğlu, Luci Saunders, Aseel Sawalha, Ali Murat Yel, Judith Tucker, and at least two anonymous but very constructive readers. Luci Saunders, a friend of long standing, was especially encouraging and thoughtful in urging this revision at a time when the undertaking was languishing. Ron and Nancy Adams, Goble Messer, and Joe Morris provided much needed help to Bates while he was ignoring his family and neighborly obligations. Ülkü Ülküsal, Marc de Clercq, Jonathon Shanon, Aseel Sawalha, Çağlar Keyder, and Harald Skogseid kindly made available photos for use. Three colleagues at Istanbul Bilgi University, Arus Yumul, Alan Duben, and

Uğur Kömeçoğlu, were especially generous in sharing their time and thoughts. Among other colleagues at Bilgi University, Didem Daniş, Duygun Erim, and Aybike Hatemi were unfailing in their practical and moral support.

One person deserves special acknowledgment. Judith Tucker read the entire manuscript not once but at several stages, and offered detailed suggestions for its intellectual coverage and for improvement of the manuscript both in terms of content and in presentation. Her contribution is greatly appreciated. Two other individuals worked closely with us during the final four months during which we struggled to bring many pieces together. Christina Mitrakos, our research assistant in New York working out of Hunter College with Bates and Rassam, sought out books and other sources, gathered data for several of the chapters, and prepared the figures and tables and the bibliography. Ayşe Akalın, working with Bates in Istanbul, also provided numerous sources, gathered a wealth of data and downloaded material from the Internet. Both, we are confident, will go on to fine careers in the social sciences. We also wish to acknowledge the helpful comments provided by the following individuals who reviewed the original manuscript for Prentice Hall: William Irons of Northwestern University and Charles L. Redman of Arizona State. Kathleen Borowik prepared all maps, for which we are grateful. All photographs not otherwise credited were supplied by the authors.

The system of transliteration generally used is that recommended by *The International Journal of Middle Eastern Studies*. However, we have deviated from it where purposes of clarity might be served.

Daniel Bates, Istanbul
Amal Rassam, New York City

Introduction

In this book we treat a particular region, the Middle East—its peoples and its cultural heritage—in light of what we feel to be the best available sources. Our principal objective is to impart as much information about the society and culture of this vast area as can be reasonably synthesized and interpreted in a relatively short volume. The goal we have set for ourselves is thus straightforward, even though the materials we work with are complex and refractory. Our emphasis on the synthesis of information and factual material is deliberate. Informed discussion and analysis necessarily start with a shared body of conceptualizations and facts, be they rooted in commonplace observations or in relatively esoteric knowledge. This venture, jointly undertaken by two anthropologists, is an attempt to provide materials and ideas suitable to informed discussion and debate, and thereby to provide the basis for further synthesis and analysis.

The term *Middle East*, however delineated, has become accepted in common usage, replacing such earlier references as the Near East, the Levant, the Holy Land, and so on. Although the term *Middle East* was not originally employed by the peoples of the area, it has been widely accepted and used by indigenous scholars, writers, and politicians and, in its broadest construction, refers to a part of the world that encompasses all of the Arab states, Turkey, Iran, Israel, and Afghanistan. As such, it forms the largest cultural area commonly taken as a field of study. Without entering into the unprofitable debate of what does and does not properly constitute the Middle East, for purposes of this book we use the term to refer to a geographic and cultural area that includes Egypt, Israel, Jordan, Kuwait, Iran, Iraq, Lebanon, Oman, Syria, Saudi Arabia, Turkey, Qatar, Bahrain, Yemen, and the United Arab Emirates. We have thus excluded the nation-states of North Africa, Central Asia, and Afghanistan.

When compared with the wider connotation of the term, the area we are concerned with might, with justification, be called the *Central Middle East*. The area of focus here is paralleled in a number of recent general syntheses in other disciplines; for example, by Colbert Held (2000) writing as a cultural geographer, Roger Owen and Şevket Pamuk (1999) as economists, and Naji Abi-Aad and Michel Grenon (1997) as political scientists. Even within this area, we are not concerned with a country-by-country discussion; the perspective we offer focuses on broader problems, patterns, and cultural processes. In preparing this edition, our reviewers were divided as whether we should expand our coverage, particularly with respect to North Africa. We seriously considered doing this, as one of us has had long experience in Morocco and both authors have traveled widely in the region. We also considered including Central Asia, as again Rassam has lived and worked in the Central Asian republics, and Bates among the Türkmen. We decided not to because, given our resources and time and the publisher's constraints of length, such expansion would have been more by way of lip service than substance.

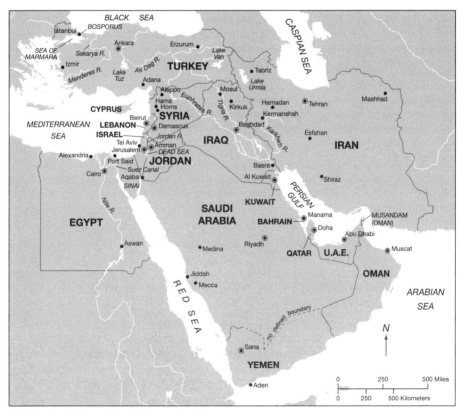

Political Map of the Central Middle East

The Central Middle East, as we have delineated it, acquires considerable coherence when considered from a number of perspectives. Historically this is the "cradle of civilizations," an ancient heartland of empires and cities that included those of Egypt and Mesopotamia. Urban life and state forms of political organization first arose here. For millennia, in ever-changing configurations, great stretches of this region have been politically and economically integrated. This is also the birthplace of the three major monotheistic religions: Judaism, Christianity, and Islam. All three were shaped in the context of Middle Eastern civilization and all contribute to its ongoing expression in the lives and activities of Middle Eastern peoples.

More immediate are a number of geopolitical facts. Since the eighth century, most of the great Islamic empires have had their centers located in this heartland area. In fact, the most recent of these, the Ottoman Empire, held sway over most of this region for almost 500 years, and even though its domains included much of North Africa, the latter area (except for Egypt) was peripheral to the empire. Such political facts, together with the presence of long-established routes of coastal and internal communication and trade, impart a high level of cultural integration to the Central Middle East. Today the oil wealth found in and near the Gulf area and the large concentrations of population in Egypt, Turkey, and Iran give this central zone great strategic importance.

One can easily argue that the French colonial experience and the presence of large Berber-speaking populations set Northwest Africa apart. Similarly, Afghanistan partakes more of the Central Asian cultural experience. But these are not our main reasons for focusing our discussion on the Central Middle East. We take this narrower geographic perspective because it allows us to draw on a relatively closely interrelated body of ethnographic and historical data, thus facilitating a more systematic body of generalizations. Even with this self-imposed limitation, we feel confident that much of the interpretive discussion we offer can be useful to those interested in North Africa, Central Asia, or Afghanistan. Much, too, of the synthesis applies to Israeli society, particularly to the Arabic-speaking population. No attempt is made here to explore systematically those cultural and political features that so sharply distinguish Israel from other Middle Eastern countries.

The Middle East, however defined, presents an almost unique challenge for anthropologists. Its long historical record, literate cultures, and established traditions of indigenous and foreign scholarship, while providing a wealth of material, make great demands on the individual scholar. Moreover, the rivalry between Christian and Muslim states for control of the Mediterranean and the Balkans, not to mention the more recent Western colonial and military ventures, add a polemical dimension to any discussion of the region. It is no surprise that there is, as Charles Lindholm puts it, a "deep crisis in Middle Eastern ethnography" (1995, p. 805). We will comment on this only to the extent that it might affect how the reader uses our book.

The core debate or controversy concerns the proper role of theory in guiding observation and empirical research and the utility or even validity of generalizations based on empirical studies. This is a reflection of what is occurring in anthropology generally, but it is given a special flavor in Middle Eastern studies by the sustained impact of devastating critiques, most notably by Edward Said, of generations of European-trained scholars—in particular, but not exclusively, historians and collectively labeled *Orientalism*. Efforts by Western scholars to describe Islam, features unique to Middle Eastern society, family life, urban spaces, and the like could, it is said, be seen at their worst as a form of intellectual aggression through the imposition of Western values and ideals, and at best exercises in "essentializing" or stereotyping. Said's critiques and those of others, dovetail nicely with the concerns of many current ethnographers that genuine objectivity is an impossible goal, and that to generalize is to dehumanize the population under study. They favor treating culture as a form of text, which might be read differently by different readers, thus making interpretation a very personalized goal.

The postmodern or interpretive approach, strongly articulated by Clifford Geertz, argues that since each culture has to be viewed "relativistically," the anthropologist should not strive to uncover general patterns of behavior or build theory through systematic observations and comparisons. Rather, "representation" is important, and to that end a common technique in presenting data is to use the narrative form—that is, to put the focus on key individuals and present them through their own words. Also, the anthropologist acting as an interlocutor is by necessity a crucial part of the report. While the shared humanity of the informants and the anthropologist emerges very eloquently in the better crafted of such studies, there are obvious limits to this approach. It privileges a small number of carefully selected informants and abandons generalization. In our opinion, reliance on this approach risks reducing the field to snippets of insight, often very interesting but curiously noncumulative.

While Orientalism, or specific authors of that genre, may have tended to view Islam and Muslim society as unique and esoteric phenomena, often sketched in sharp contrast to their European or Judeo-Christian experience, this scholarly tradition has, we feel, contributed much useful insight, and we make no apologies for using their observations where appropriate. Also, we see acquiring knowledge and generalizing about the world as not only feasible but important, the basic anthropological perspective that seeks to understand variations in institutions and cultures in terms of universal human imperatives and processes. As anthropologists, we draw heavily on the work of Orientalists as well as current post-modern scholarship, while retaining what we feel to be the most useful analytic tools of our own discipline. What gives us confidence that this is a fruitful approach is a very practical one. It is immediately obvious when reading current social scientific writing on the Middle East that we know more today than we did in the past about family life, religious beliefs and practices, local political processes, and countless other areas. Regardless of the very real problems of objectivity and measurement, a cumulative process of scholarship is possible and occurring.

Although this book is meant to be an essay in social anthropology, we have not limited ourselves to the traditional concerns of that discipline. We rely heavily on the work of historians, economists, sociologists, political scientists, and geographers in order to provide a comprehensive picture of an important part of the world. We have deliberately adopted a straightforward style and nontechnical vocabulary in an effort to facilitate a discussion with as wide and varied an audience as possible.

Even though we build on work that has gone before, the intellectual history of Western scholarship on the Middle East is beyond the scope of this book. Modern social science research in the area really began in the 1920s, and only well after World War II do we find a body of data and theory building cumulatively on systematic and comparative research. This is not to deny the immense value of such earlier observers of Islamic society as Edward Lane, Richard Burton, Charles Doughty, and others. In fact, ethnographic reports by trained social scientists often fall short of such works as Lane's *The Manners and Customs of the Modern Egyptians* or J. L. Burckhardt's *Notes on the Bedouins and the Wahabys,* both genuine classics of their genre.

The attention of earlier anthropologists working in the Middle East was most often focused on such topics as tribal organization, patterns of marriage and kinship, and community studies of nomads and peasants. These concerns remain important. Today, although much is still to be learned from the close observation of small communities, anthropologists increasingly formulate their research in terms of theoretical problems and concerns that lead them beyond the local community. For the Middle East, as for other regions of the world such as Latin America and Southeast Asia, the disciplinary boundaries among social historians, political scientists, cultural geographers, and anthropologists are hard to distinguish. All share an interest in understanding the human condition as they draw on a common pool of materials and conceptualizations. All, too, are concerned with the problems of the day and the shape of the future.

At this juncture, a brief synopsis of the material to follow serves to orient the reader to how we conceive of this book in terms of the selection of topics and the rationale for their organization. The book is organized into three general sections, each building on the preceding. The first section establishes what we feel to be the basis for any discussion of contemporary life and culture in the region. In the opening chapters we describe the geographic setting, and we sketch some of the ecological constraints and material resources on which the societies rely. These constitute the backdrop against which Middle Eastern society has to be understood. Considerable attention is then paid to Islam as an ideational structure—that is, Islam as a source of shared but always contested meaning and a system of cultural communication. As such, Islam also has to be understood as a vehicle for political action. Chapter 4 offers a general description of ethnic and communal differences, especially those of religion, sectarian affiliation, and language.

The three chapters that follow our discussion of ethnicity can be considered the second section. They constitute an ethnographic excursion treating rural and urban society in an effort to depict the ongoing social and economic processes that currently shape the social landscape. These chapters are concerned with nomadic pastoralism, village life and agricultural production, and urban society. They deal at length with how people acquire access to resources, exercise leadership, and contend for social status. The three chapters, although they share many concerns, are not meant to be entirely parallel. The chapter on pastoralism includes substantial sections dealing with the life and social or political organization of particular peoples. This is, we hope, a means of introducing the human aspect of ethnographic analysis. The chapter on village life and agriculture contains a lengthy analysis of changing patterns of land use and settlement as they pertain to the ongoing transformation of the Middle Eastern countryside as a result of commercial farming and mechanization. The chapter dealing with urban society is directed, in some measure, toward an understanding of the current patterns of urban growth as well as the problems associated with it. The objective throughout is not to present comprehensive ethnographic reviews of the literature but to depict the sources of continuity and the sources for change that are at work in all sectors of Middle Eastern society.

The third area around which we have organized our inquiry addresses a number of issues that, while least amenable to generalization and synthesis, are central to understanding the broad texture of Middle Eastern society and local politics. We pay considerable attention to what some have called primordial systems of social and political organization and interaction or, more simply put, kinship, family, and household. We try to see the individual in Middle Eastern society as an actor within an institutional and cultural context in which the actor's behavior unfolds. We treat changing sources of personal identity, changing gender roles, and the principles by which social groupings are constituted and transformed. We examine the nature of political leadership and the local organization of what, in essence, are relationships of power and contention. In this analysis, the tribal idiom of political action is viewed in terms of other, alternative vehicles of recruitment and mobilization, such as religion, the state, or even individual charisma. We conclude the book with a tentative sketch of what we regard to be the major transforming processes underway, their economic and social sources, and some of their consequences for national integration and the development of civil society.

1

The Setting: Human Geography and Historical Background

Sources of water are the sources of life itself in the Middle East. The distribution of people, the settlements they have created, and the ways they secure their livelihoods are closely shaped by the challenges of securing and controlling this vital resource. To be sure, access to water is only one among many environmental variables affecting the inhabitants of the region. Others include crop-threatening and life-threatening disease vectors, variable soil quality, seismic instability, extremes of temperature, and ever-diminishing sources of ligneous fuel. However, one need only compare a rainfall map of Europe with one of the Middle East to appreciate the significance of water. Indeed, geographers classify most regions of the Middle East as being rain deficient.[1]

Water, whether from rainfall, rivers, or subterranean aquifers, is the primary limiting factor governing human habitation. Beyond the frontiers of cultivation lies desolation, and the towns and villages of the Middle East closely hug the rainswept coasts and mountain valleys, the courses of major streams, and scattered oases. As the archaeologist Robert Adams writes with respect to the ancient heartland of Mesopotamia, the prevailing uncertainties about water underlie all the human adaptations, whether farming or pastoral, or urban (1981).

MAJOR ENVIRONMENTAL ZONES OF THE CENTRAL MIDDLE EAST

It is thus impossible to separate cultural or social processes from the environmental setting in which they occur. The geological or topographical configuration, the climatic conditions, the distribution of water and minerals, and the

---

[1] See, for example, Colbert C. Held (2000) for excellent cultural and physical geographic coverage.

occurrence of plant and animal life all affect the ways in which people live and, indeed, how society has developed. In addition, waterways, large lakes, seas, ports, and river systems shape lines of communication, trade, and even climate. Of course this is a two-way process, as human activity itself has had a profound impact on the natural habitat. Rivers are dammed or diverted, canals opened and occasionally closed, soil replenished or exhausted—in short, dynamic physical and cultural processes are at work. The physical environment and the landscape we describe for the Middle East are at once the setting for and the result of a long history of human adaptation. The face of the Middle East we see today is as much history as it is geography.

SEAS AND MARITIME WATERWAYS

The Central Middle East, as we are treating it, is ringed by five seas: the Mediterranean (including the Aegean), the Gulf (referred to variously as the Persian Gulf or the Gulf of Arabia), the Black Sea, the Caspian Sea, and the Arabian or Indian Sea. Thus, contemporary states and early empires were easily accessible by water; indeed, these waters saw some of the world's earliest maritime commercial and political powers emerge. The presence of these seas and connecting waterways has led to the region often being termed a "land bridge," one linking Europe, Asia, and Africa. With the exception of much of the Red Sea, these bodies of water offer very favorable habitats for human settlement and numerous ports in which trade has flourished since antiquity. All of these settled coastal areas are culturally distinct from their hinterlands as a result of the contact that inevitably accompanies trade.

Of the five major waterways, two deserve special note: the Suez Canal offers a short route to the lands of the Indian Ocean and Southeast Asia from Europe, and the Turkish straits of the Bosphorus and Dardanelles link the Black Sea with the Mediterranean. The Suez Canal was opened in 1869 and has been in continuous operation ever since, apart from an eight-year closure from 1967 to 1975 due to the war between Israel and Egypt. Currently, about 6 percent of the world's trade passes through each year (Abi-Aad & Grenon, 1997, p. 2). The status of the relatively narrow Bosphorus Straits, passing as they do through Istanbul, a city of over 12 million people, is an increasingly contentious issue, as Turkey is concerned that steadily rising tonnage, especially in oil, increases the potential for a major accident. Unlike the Suez, the straits have treaty agreements that guarantee free passage by all civilian vessels, and large numbers of heavily loaded but aging tankers carrying Russian and Azerbaijan oil make the difficult traverse without aid of pilots.

THE GEOLOGICAL FOUNDATIONS

Carleton Coon, an anthropologist who has worked extensively in the area, notes: "Geologically speaking, the world's oldest civilizations arose in some of the world's youngest lands"(1958, p. 10). The geological youth of the Middle East is evident in the steep, craggy mountain ranges that form an often spectacular backdrop to the flat plains and steppes. The process of recent mountain formation has determined the distribution of critical resources in the area, including the sources of water and minerals. The mountains of the Middle East consist of sea-deposited layers of sandstone and limestone. Consequently, these are, apart from the earth itself, the most commonly used building materials in the region today, and they were used to produce some of the best-preserved monumental architecture of antiquity. However, these recent deposits of sandstone and limestone do not contain metallic ores, and it is only where mountains have folded and faulted to expose underlying older layers that iron, copper, tin, silver, gold, and other minerals are found. These minerals are restricted to relatively few

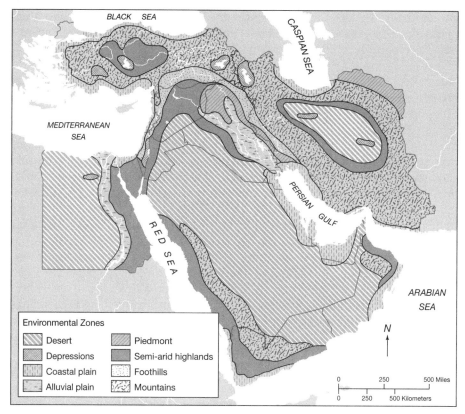

Major Environmental Zones of the Central Middle East

sites; the most important historically have been the iron and copper mines of eastern Anatolia, the copper of the Zagros and Sinai, and the silver of the Taurus. Few minerals are produced in exportable quantity today; indeed, with the important exceptions of oil and bauxite, the Middle East imports its industrial-grade minerals.

Regional and local topography are important in determining where people settle, how cities develop, the arrangement of trade and trade routes, and even political organization. For instance, the Nile Valley, by virtue of its topography and river-facilitated communications, lends itself to unified political control, whereas the rugged, crosscutting mountains of the Levant do not. Topography further directly influences local climatic regimes, which in turn determine the potential for human and animal life. If you were to fly over the area, your immediate impression would be of a landscape alternating between rugged mountains or plateaus and lowland areas where the boundaries between desert and cultivated land are often starkly etched. This impression reflects the way in which most geologists and geographers classify and describe the land forms in the area.

The geology of the area is often described as being made up of three different and colliding tectonic systems.[2] On the one hand, the vast lowland areas that make up the bulk of the Arabian Peninsula and part of Egypt are part of a large, geologically stable, and for the most part, highly arid shield or massif that extends from Africa to India. This massif is called the Arabian Plate or Shield. In contrast, the second plate system, to the east and north of the Arabian Shield, is a geologically active mountain zone subject to recurrent earthquakes. This encompasses the great Iranian and Anatolian plateaus. Lying between the Iranian Plateau and the Arabian Shield, the broad plains and marshes of Mesopotamia form a continuous depression subject to massive alluviations from the Tigris and Euphrates rivers that traverse it. It is extremely seismically active along the zone where it comes against the neighboring plate—the "fold-belt," as it is called—which contains the long and earthquake-prone North Anatolian fault. The third plate system is the Nubian or Egyptian Plate whose points of contact with the Arabian Shield run along the Red Sea and which is far less prone to quakes.

The unity of the first landform system, which may have formed one ancient continent, is interrupted by the recent faulting that created the Dead Sea, whose floor is 395 meters below sea level. This broad area is one where horizontal layers of sedimentary deposits lay largely undisturbed, and where hills rarely rise above 1000 meters. One place in which we can see ancient sedimentary deposits exposed is in Egypt, where the force of the river Nile, flowing from its headwaters in the highlands of Ethiopia, Lake Victoria, and Lake Turkana in Africa, to the Mediterranean Sea, has laid bare the various layers.

---

[2] Again, see Held (1994, 2000) for an excellent description of the geology of the region and its cultural implications.

Few visitors to Luxor, the ancient capital of Upper Egypt, ever forget the effect of the day's last light playing on the red-hued cliffs into which the Pharaohs carved their magnificent tombs. Egypt, which has been called "the gift of the Nile," has its productive heartland in this valley, which the Nile has carved out of the desert waste.

To the east, the great Arabian Shield is bounded by the major river system of the Tigris and Euphrates. Here, as in Egypt, we find the heartlands of other ancient civilizations. In contrast with Egypt, however, the Tigris and Euphrates Valley is broad, with regular shifts in the rivers' courses occurring each spring as they flow in a wide geologic depression to the Persian Gulf from their headwaters in the mountains of the north and west in Turkey. The Euphrates is, in Adams's words, "a brown, sinuous pulsing artery that carries the gift of life" (1981:1).

It is the sedimentary layers of the Arabian massif formed by ancient seas that harbor the petroleum wealth of the region. In 1995, it was estimated that over 65 percent of the world's proven oil reserves lay in the Middle East and that 31 percent of all oil produced originated in this part of the world; natural gas reserves account for about 31 percent of the world's total (Abi-Aad & Grenon, 1997, p. 3). The proven reserves of Saudi Arabia alone are a staggering 25 percent of the world's total. Iran, Iraq, and Kuwait jointly account for another 25 percent, with the result that this relatively small geographic region on the Arabian Peninsula and the Persian Gulf dominates the world's energy market.

A major topographic feature is an extensive and complex mountain zone, part of a large one that reaches from the Alps to the Himalayas. Perhaps the best way to picture this complex of craggy and often disconnected local ranges is to visualize two roughly parallel zones of transcontinental foldings. One stretches from the northern Alps through northern Turkey, Iran, and Afghanistan and culminates in the Himalayas. The second zone, rising with the southern Alps, extends along the southern Turkish coast, northern Iraq, and Iran, and it also culminates in the Himalayan ranges. The northern rim of mountains in Turkey includes the Pontic range, which runs along the Black Sea and continues in Iran as the Elburz Mountains. In eastern Turkey, the highest peak is Mount Ararat of biblical fame (elevation 16,946 feet). In Iran, the Elburz continues south of the Caspian Sea, with Demavend as its highest peak (elevation 18,934 feet). Demavend is the highest mountain west of the Hindu Kush, and like most of the other major mountains in the area, it is volcanic but dormant.

The southern mountain system in Turkey is represented by the twin ranges of the Taurus and the Anti-Taurus. Rising in the west where the Aegean meets the Mediterranean, they continue eastward, dominating the southern coastline of Turkey and leaving a relatively narrow coastal strip. The Taurus range is relatively unbroken until it reaches the northeastern extremity of the Mediterranean where the hitherto narrow coastal strip opens into an extensive plain surrounding Turkey's fourth largest city, Adana. Broken by a major pass, the Cilician Gates, which gives access from the plateau to the coast, the range then continues as the Anti-Taurus in southeast Turkey and as the Zagros in Iraq and Iran. Both the northern Pontic-Elburz and the southern Taurus-Zagros ranges are punctuated by many alluvial valleys, frequently with rich soil and relatively well watered, although separated from one another by terrain difficult to traverse.

The major mountain systems in Turkey and Iran enclose and isolate two large interior plateaus comprising most of the landmass of this geological zone. The Anatolian and Iranian plateaus vary in elevation from 1650 feet to 4950 feet and are bordered by ranges whose peaks frequently rise above 6600 feet. Rimmed by high mountains, these inland plateaus are characterized by internal drainage, resulting in a number of brackish or alkaline lakes, the most outstanding of which are Lake Van in Turkey and Lake Urmia in Iran. Lake Van, in particular, is a stunning gift of recent geological activity. It was formed as a result of volcanic activity that blocked a major highland river, resulting in a vast lake larger than Lake Geneva in Switzerland and rimmed by towering snowcapped peaks. The rich volcanic soils of the plains surrounding the lake supported the first kingdoms of the Armenians. Areas of central Turkey, Tüz Gölü, for example, are marshy salt flats, and still greater areas in Iran consist of salt flats or virtual deserts such as the Dasht-i-Kavir and Dasht-i-Lut.

Although it is perhaps possible to sketch the broad geographic outlines of the Middle East in terms of these contrasting geological systems, such a picture would be far from complete, as it ignores the most critical elements for human activity—namely, the distribution of surface water and vegetation. From this perspective, the interface of these geological systems constitutes a major area in itself, one that stretches from the Persian Gulf northward and westward along the Mediterranean and ends in the delta of northern or lower Egypt. This vast arc encompasses most of the areas of ancient civilization—Mesopotamia, the Levant, and Egypt—all sites of great agrarian societies in antiquity. This, too, is where it seems that the earliest human experimentation with the domestication of plants and animals took place.

CLIMATIC REGIMES AND WATER

Within this area of interface lies the so-called Fertile Crescent, a grassland steppe formed as a result of the annual regime of windborne rains caused by winter westerlies from the Mediterranean. However, no community in this area is far removed from nearby zones of considerable aridity. It is this marked local contrast between areas of cultivation and rangelands or deserts that is one of the most striking environmental characteristics of the Middle East. This contrast is often the result of what geographers term the *orographic effect:* the precipitation caused by mountains when they force moisture-bearing winds that seasonally move inland to cool suddenly, dropping the bulk of their water on the seaward-facing slopes. In fact, only Lebanon is without significant areas of extreme aridity.

In the southern part of the Arabian Peninsula, the summer monsoons coming across the Indian Ocean strike the green mountain, Jabal Akhdar of the Hadramawt, and the mountains of Yemen to make parts of the latter some of the most fertile areas of the peninsula—the fabled *Arabia Felix*. In the past, high rainfall here permitted local populations to grow fine coffee, an endeavor largely abandoned today. The spread of coffee as an international beverage can be traced back to its Yemeni origins and its export from the coastal town of Mocca. Immediately behind this monsoon-drenched, sea-facing escarpment, however, begins *Arabia Deserta,* the region that envelops the Empty Quarter, or Rub'al-Khali, a vast sand desert largely devoid of human settlements apart from a number of oases—some of considerable size—and oil stations and other recent settlements using drilled wells that tap deep aquifers.

In most of the Middle East, westerly rain-bearing winds coming from the Atlantic and across the Mediterranean sweep inland during the winter months. From the point of view of water loss in this region of high summer

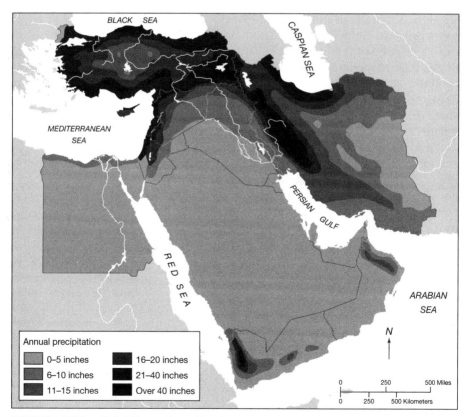

RAINFALL MAP: Rainfall, together with other sources of water, set the contours of agriculture and the distribution of settlements.

temperatures, winter rains arrive at the ideal time. Less water is lost through evaporation—always a problem in this arid zone—and many indigenous plants, such as barley, wheat, lentils, and chickpeas, are adapted to a winter growing season. Even so, conditions for plant growth are highly constrained because the winter cold impedes maturation, and the spring season of maximal growth is short. These westerlies are, moreover, extremely capricious, so that the amount and distribution of annual rainfall are not predictable. Villages experiencing severe drought one year may be contending with floods the next. As we have noted in the case of southern Arabia, mountain topography determines the strikingly uneven distribution of moisture. The spatial and temporal variability in both rains and river flooding constitutes fundamental uncertainties with which people must cope.

The often lush, well-watered western slopes and plateau edges of the mountains stand in marked contrast to the aridity and desiccation of the eastern-facing slopes and valleys. For example, the Sinai Peninsula and eastern Jordan, which lie within such a rain shadow, experience virtually no rainfall. On the other hand, the coastal strip of the Levant or eastern Mediterranean coast, with an annual rainfall of over 30 inches per year, due to the orographic effect, receives more rain than some parts of the British Isles. However, Damascus, an hour's drive inland through the Lebanon range, receives a mean annual rainfall of less than 10 inches. The Mediterranean and Aegean coastal plains of Turkey exhibit a similar pattern. Along the coast, rich soils support lush groves of orange trees, cotton, and even bananas in the region of Alanya. However, a short drive over the Taurus Mountains brings one to the Anatolian Plateau, where rainfall agriculture is limited to drought-resistant grain crops and legumes, and is in places precluded altogether due to either aridity or soil salinity.

Even though 10 inches of annual rainfall is considered to be the minimal requirement for dry farming of wheat, estimates of average rainfall in the area are virtually meaningless. For example, in the Damascus region, rainfall agriculture is impossible because the rains vary so greatly from year to year and much of the rainfall may come in the form of one or two cloudbursts. Thus, in the interior of the Middle East, wherever agriculture depends on rainfall it becomes a risky venture. The principal exceptions are restricted areas along the Black Sea coast of Turkey, the Caspian coast of Iran, and parts of highland Yemen. Most of Arabia and Egypt is rainless; in fact, not more than 10 percent of the total landmass of the Middle East is suitable for cultivation for this reason. The most pervasive and enduring strategy of land use in areas where rainfall agriculture is feasible is to pursue very extensive forms of field use, with long fallows and a variety of crops planted, in hopes that, despite poor rains, some will last until harvest. Cultivation is often combined with animal husbandry to further diversify the household's resources in the face of high risk. Animals are more than an alternative form of food production; they are also a means of storing food on the hoof. In fact the economists Roger Owen and Sevket Pamuk refer to the current widespread importing of meat and cereals as a form of "water substitution"—that is, imported foods are grown with water not available locally (1998, p. 242).

Although the distribution of peoples and settlements in the Middle East closely reflects the distribution of rainfall, this does not complete the picture of sown areas. Although agriculture depends on regular water supplies, these can be obtained in ways other than by rainfall. First perfected in the Middle East, irrigation agriculture was a major technological advance that allowed for the development of a very complex social order. The two great civilizations of antiquity—Egypt and Mesopotamia—owed their fluorescence to the irrigation systems developed along the river valleys of the Nile and the Tigris-Euphrates. Of the Euphrates, Adams writes that despite the vicissitudes of shifting courses, unpredictable annual flow, and periodically devastating floods, "It has provided the only possible foundation for an immense column of human achievement that has risen laboriously in a pivotal region over hundreds of generations" (1981, p. 1). Precisely how the development of irrigation influenced the course of early civilization is a complex question, but, without doubt, even early efforts at water control increased agricultural productivity and ultimately generated the food surpluses to sustain segments of the population not directly involved in cultivation.

Water control and management in general are ancient sciences in all of the area. As water is life, the people of the Middle East have ingeniously devised many and varied means of conserving it and extending its distribution. Water control in the form of dams and irrigation schemes is still undertaken as major public works projects by governments of the region. The massive Aswan Dam of Egypt is only one of many; others are the large Southeast Anatolia Project (GAP) of eastern Turkey, the Euphrates Dam of Syria, and the Kur River project of south-central Iran. All of these further illustrate that water is the single most important factor limiting agriculture in the Middle East and, perhaps, the most enduring source of political conflict.

The Nile River at 4145 miles (6669 km) is the longest river in the world, with most of its water coming from the White Nile, which drains the vast, vegetation-rich marshes of the Sudd in southern Sudan; but it is the torrential annual floods of the Blue Nile carrying monsoon waters originating on the plateau of Ethiopia that historically determined the agricultural season in Egypt. The annual floods brought nutrient-rich waters in a major summer pulse, varying slightly every year. Since the river flows through extremely arid lands, there is considerable loss due to evaporation. There was an effort in the 1980s to create a shortcut in the form of a canal, the Jonglee Canal in the Sudan, which would have reduced this loss. The scheme was never finished because of civil unrest.

While there have long been a number of dams on the river, the completion of the Aswan High Dam in 1970, which created the huge artificial Lake Nasser, some 297 miles (478 km) long, has altered the flow altogether. No longer are the lower reaches of the river and the delta in the north washed with silt-rich floods. Egypt has benefited on balance in greater agricultural production due to

Dam on upper Tigris River, part of the Southeast Anatolia Project in Turkey. The dam will control upland flood waters of the Tigris and Euphrates Rivers.

extension of farmlands and greater hydroelectric production, but there have been costs as well. Much valuable water that is impounded in Lake Nasser is lost each year to evaporation. The nutrients carried by the river are now left as lake sediments and have to be replaced by manufactured fertilizers, and the loss of these same nutrients has also killed an important fishery industry in the delta and adjacent Mediterranean.

Turkey has the most ambitious water-control program in the region, and its hydroelectric output follows only those of Sweden and Norway in Europe. The main component of this program is GAP, mentioned earlier, which involves 22 dams and 19 hydroelectric installations and is designed to irrigate 4.2 million acres (1.7 million ha) of land. All or most of this water is taken from the head-waters and tributaries of the Tigris (Dicle) and Euphrates (Fırat) rivers, and by 2006, GAP will control the bulk of the flow of these rivers to Iraq and Syria. Needless to say this is a major point of political contention (see Abi-Aad & Grenon, 1997).

DISTRIBUTION OF POPULATION IN THE CENTRAL MIDDLE EAST

Although the politics of large-scale hydraulic projects attract the most attention, of far greater importance to the peoples of the arid zones of the Middle East are the highly varied local techniques for water management. The *qanats* of Iran and the *aflajs* of south Arabia are underground tunnels that carry water from upland sources and thus create artificial oases and extend village cultivation into the desert. An entire string of communities may come to depend on one water source, and households may share use rights and responsibilities for its maintenance. Building a *qanat*, a dangerous undertaking requiring great skill, involves digging what amounts to a primary well at an upland water source, then connecting it by a gently sloping horizontal tunnel with another dry well farther down the slope, which is in turn connected to yet more down-slope wells. Thus, dozens of water points may be linked to one upland source. This technology developed in antiquity in Persia and spread westward as far as Arab-ruled Spain (and was transferred by the Spanish to the New World). These *qanat*s are rapidly being phased out of use and replaced by mechanized drilled wells and pipelines.

The ancient Egyptians developed three devices for lifting water from canals and basins to their fields: the *shadduf*, or weighted pole with a bucket on the end; the Archimedean screw; and the waterwheel powered by animal traction. These techniques, few among many, were early achievements of the

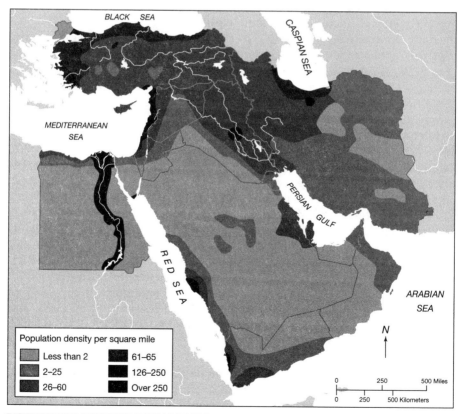

DISTRIBUTION OF POPULATION IN THE MIDDLE EAST

agricultural peoples of the region. Increasingly, traditional methods of securing and lifting water are being replaced by tube wells and motor-driven pumps.

Although techniques of irrigation have improved dramatically, sometimes opening new areas for cultivation, one age-old problem remains—that of soil salinity. Wherever the water table in this area of high evapotranspiration rises to about 1.5 meters (4.6 feet) from the surface, salts occurring naturally in the soil are drawn upward. This leaching of salts ultimately contaminates the soil to the point of diminishing yields, and may even preclude planting altogether. In Iraq and elsewhere, this problem has led over the centuries to the abandonment of much otherwise tillable acreage for which reclamation would be a costly enterprise. The use of modern pumps often exacerbates the problem of salinity because it encourages over-irrigation, particularly where river water is available. Where tube wells are used, another frequently encountered problem is the depletion of stored water reserves, which are not recharged by rains in this rain-deficient region.

Another factor affecting human life in the Middle East is temperature. The Middle East generally experiences hot, dry summers and cool, wet winters, making much of it generally Mediterranean in climatic regime. For example, the average winter temperature in Tehran (elevation 4000 feet) is 37°F (2.7°C), and the daily summer average for three months is 86°F (30°C). Some cities in arid, low-lying zones experience consistently higher temperatures throughout the year. In Baghdad, the capital of Iraq, the temperature may occasionally exceed 100°F (38°C) during a seven- month period, with a July extreme of up to 121°F (49°C). At one desert oil-producing center in eastern Saudi Arabia, the mean temperature in July and August is 98°F (37°C); however, the average afternoon high temperature is 113°F (45.5°C), and an absolute high has been recorded of 124°F (52°C) (Held, 1994, p. 49). In many parts of the Middle East summer temperatures are exacerbated by hot, dust-laden winds known variously as the *sirocco, sharqi,* or *khamsin.* These winds, blowing from the south and southeast, often reach gale force and contribute to desiccation by removing topsoil layers.

The climatic regime in the Middle East, with its extremes in temperature and precipitation everywhere, requires that urban and village inhabitants invest heavily in shelter. In traditional Iraqi homes, substantial basements offer cool, daytime summer refuges for members of the household, and the flat rooftops provide much-prized relief during the nights. In the upland regions of the Anatolian and Persian plateaus, winter blizzards of great severity are not uncommon, and mountain passes are often closed by snow. Each winter and early spring in the mountains of Iran, Turkey, and Iraq, thousands of villagers can be temporarily cut off from the world by heavy and long-lasting snowfalls and their subsequent meltwater.

Landforms, climate, and water combine to establish the distribution of natural vegetation. Even slight variations in altitude, precipitation, or range of temperature have great consequences for plant life and, by extension, for food production and even for the availability of fuel and building materials. Wood fuel and lumber are restricted today to relatively constricted high-level areas. However, these are receding rapidly in the face of pervasive overgrazing and heavy exploitation for household use. As the forest and brush cover diminishes, ever-increasing amounts of topsoil are carried off by the winter rains or spring melting of snows, which further limits the propagation of most tree species.

Along the Black Sea coast of Turkey and the southern shores of the Caspian, we see the last remnants of formerly extensive deciduous forests among the tea and hazelnut plantations. In the Taurus range, parts of the Zagros, and sporadically elsewhere, stands of conifers are found where enough moisture is available. Like the deciduous forests, they too are in retreat in the face of great demand for firewood, charcoal, and building material. Elsewhere, low-growing shrubs are predominant. In the much more extensive nonforest areas of the highlands, open areas support alpine or sub-alpine grasses, depending on altitude and rainfall. The vast reaches of Arabia, the Syrian steppes, and the more arid portions of the Anatolian and Persian plateaus are characterized by rugged plants that take advantage of brief, irregular rains by rapid growth and bloom, followed by long periods of dormancy. In the arid areas, trees are generally found standing as a ring of green sentinels around village settlements only where tended by humans for building or fuel purposes. Desert and steppe grazing cycles were formerly determined by the availability of water for the flocks. Today, with mechanized transport of animals and water, grazing pressures are far heavier. Overgrazing is causing the rapid reduction of desert flora, including brush cover in southern Arabia, Syria, and Jordan.

POPULATION AND SETTLEMENT PATTERNS

Given the diversity of landforms and climate, population is very unevenly distributed in the Middle East. Overall, the region remains one of the least densely populated in the world; some areas are virtually uninhabited, such as the desert depressions of Iran, the Rub'al Khali of Arabia, and the Saharan deserts of Egypt, Libya, and the Sudan. In contrast, as we have noted, the well-watered alluvial river valleys are characterized by high population densities, with the Nile Valley and its delta by far the most heavily peopled area. According to one estimate, it has a density of 1775 people per square kilometer (or 4600 per square mile) of arable land. Thus, 99 percent of Egypt's population is concentrated on about 3 to 4 percent of its territory!

Because most Middle Eastern countries possess large tracts of arid, uncultivable land, the ratio of agricultural population to arable land is thought to be a better index of density. Such figures contrast markedly with standard density measures (population to total area). In the case of Saudi Arabia, the ratio of agricultural population to arable land for 1999 gives a density of 540 people per square kilometer, whereas the overall density ratio is 4.0 per square kilometer—more than a 100-fold difference. The discrepancy would be even greater if we included the nonagricultural population per square kilometer of cultivable land, which is perhaps an even more accurate index of density. Even in the desert, oases are densely populated by cultivators and by petroleum workers as well. More than half the populations of Jordan and Iraq inhabit 14 to 16 percent of their respective land areas. Even in Turkey, which has a more evenly distributed population than the other countries, regionally calculated rural densities range from 7 to 127 people per square kilometer.

For the most part, population distribution is conditioned by the availability of water. However, economic, historical, and political factors need to be examined for an adequate explanation of why certain areas—for example, the lower Nile Valley, the hill country of northern Lebanon, northwest Jordan, the uplands of Syria to the east of the Orontes River and extending into south-central Asia Minor, and the uplands of Yemen—are all more densely populated than neighboring areas characterized by similar ecological conditions.

The sharp contrasts in local environments and ways of life that distinguish the Middle East and its human geography can be seen in terms of the diverse challenges and problems to which people have responded in different ways. Today, in places, nomadic herders still establish successions of isolated camps through the deserts and steppes in pursuit of pasture, and in the Nile delta, Egyptian peasants concentrate in large villages of as many as 6000 people each. Meanwhile, along the slopes of the Zagros, villagers eke out a living from small plots on terraces carved out at great expense in labor. These patterns, which may impress us today as timeless, have their origins in particular times and places. In other words, they have their history. And to understand the Middle East today, we must know something of this history, since human societies are shaped not simply by their responses to problems of the present but equally in terms of how they solved those of the past.

Part of this "problem solving" involves movement. While we think of farming and urban life as committing people to particular places, in fact , movement has always been very much a part of the Middle Eastern social landscape. It involves people settling in new villages, resettling previously abandoned sites, or leaving villages to take up urban residence (and the converse on occasion). Thus, every country has regions of rapid growth and others that seem to decline in comparison. In Turkey, for example, two-thirds of the villages of central Anatolia were village sites in the early period of Islamic rule, subsequently abandoned, only to be resettled in the nineteenth and twentieth centuries. Similar patterns of settlement and resettlement can be seen in Iran, the Syrian steppe, Palestine, and elsewhere. While population growth, per se, can be a factor, exogenous forces are also at work. For example, routes and modes of communications shift, markets change, and flows of investment capital vary and have implications for how people can best secure a livelihood. Personal security is another factor; approximately 5.6 million people in the Middle East (as we define it) today are refugees, about whom we will say more later. So security has to be considered as at least equal to economic forces in determining where people live and how they pursue their livelihoods.

Turning now to some basic population parameters, we can sum up a great deal with a few factual observations: overall, Middle Eastern populations evidence a relatively high rate of growth but one that is now declining, and they are young in terms of percentages of individuals under 15 years of age, although this, too, is changing as growth slows. Further, people are extremely mobile. Whether from the countryside to the city, seasonally as migrant laborers, as part of international labor flows, or involuntarily as refugees, people are on the move. Any more detailed discussion of demography for the Middle East has to begin with the important caveat that figures are estimates, with significant variance among sources. Remember that countries not only vary greatly in the accuracy of their census procedures but also in the frankness with which they report the results.

Taken as a whole, the region we are concerned with had a population of about 43 million at the end of the nineteenth century, which surged to about 325 million at the end of the twentieth; it is expected to double by 2050 (see Table 1.1). Most of this huge growth has occurred since 1950. The overall rate of annual growth is about 3.2 percent; and the region is second only to Africa in this regard (Abi-Aad & Grenon, 1997, pp. 149–150). Iran's population, now at 66 million, is growing at the extraordinary rate of 3.7 to 4.0 percent and is expected

TABLE 1.1   Mid-year Population and Estimates (in thousands)

	Year		
Country	*1998*	*2025*	*2050*
Bahrain	595	858	992
Egypt	65,978	95,615	114,844
Iran	65,758	94,463	114,947
Iraq	21,800	41,014	54,916
Israel	5,984	8,277	9,440
Jordan	6,304	12,063	16,547
Kuwait	1,811	2,974	3,527
Lebanon	3,191	4,400	5,169
Oman	2,382	5,352	8,310
Qatar	579	779	844
Saudi Arabia	20,181	39,965	54,461
Sudan	28,292	46,264	59,176
Syria	15,333	26,292	34,490
Turkey	64,479	87,869	100,664
United Arab Emirates	2,353	3,284	3,615
Yemen	16,887	38,985	58,801
Total	321,907	508,454	640,743

Source: Adapted from United Nations sources, 1998, 1999.

to reach 94 million by 2025. Egypt, Iran, and Turkey are the most populous countries, with almost two-thirds of the population of the entire region. Although population alone does not make for political influence, these three countries also dominate the regional international scene. Birth rates are generally high but variable and are now in decline, as reflected in the age structure of the populations. Iran, for example, since 1980 and until very recently, pursued a pro-natalist policy by providing incentives, as do Iraq and Israel, whereas Egypt and Turkey for many years have encouraged family planning. Every national population is well above North American and European countries in terms of those under age 15, but this clearly is changing as well. Any middle-aged visitor from Europe or North America to most Middle Eastern countries will be immediately struck by the number of young people on the streets. Even though the rate of growth is declining, absolute growth will continue to put enormous pressures on the infrastructure of all countries apart from the oil-rich ones. We will return to the political implications of the demography of the region in Chapter 11. For the time being, we move to the deep past.

PREHISTORIC PATTERNS OF ADAPTATION

Although humans have lived in the Middle East for tens of thousands of years, history in one sense begins with the period known as the Neolithic, or New Stone Age. The Neolithic, which roughly dates from about 10,000 years ago and extends until the rise of states and cities at approximately 3000 B.C., is often regarded as a watershed in the development of human culture. It was during this era that domestication of plants and animals took place, thus setting in motion profound changes in human society. In fact, some archaeologists have characterized this development as a revolution, analogous to the Industrial Revolution that so dramatically transformed the world in the last two centuries.[3] Other archaeologists, in view of the fact that the events of the Neolithic unfolded over a period of several thousand years, avoid the term *revolution*, while still acknowledging that the advent of food production, as opposed to hunting and gathering, established the preconditions for what we usually term *civilization*.

Domesticated grains, such as wheat and barley, and animals, such as sheep and goats, ultimately gave humans access to increased sources of food energy per unit of land. Perhaps of greater importance, as food production became more reliable, it allowed large numbers of people to live in areas hitherto unsuited for year-round habitation. No longer dependent on often widely

---

[3] For a very readable classic, see V. Gordon Childe (1951); for a contemporary discussion, see Joy McCorriston and Frank Hole (1991), who nicely summarize the issues and offer a specific hypothesis as to when and where the first efforts at planting occurred .

scattered wild plants and game, the human population in the Central Middle East increased. Village life rapidly emerged as a more regular pattern, a prelude for the soon-to-follow cities and states. In this sense, the Neolithic marks the point at which the Middle East culture as we know it began to take shape. Let us briefly examine these developments, which laid the basis for adaptations persisting today.

Anthropologists recognize that people do not usually "discover" something as complex as agriculture; instead, it has to be regarded as the culmination of a long series of interrelated events, even accidents. People slowly, and often without realizing it, react to specific problems in ways that only later will be seen as significant. The question we have to ask is why people in the Middle East changed their mode of subsistence to emphasize agriculture and domesticated animals. As prehistorians put it: "There had to be *opportunity* (that is, sufficient populations of the prerequisite plants), *technology* to use the plants effectively, a *social organization* that could cope with 'delayed return' economies, and *need* before people would alter their habits of acquiring food" (McCorriston & Hole, 1991, p. 46). Joy McCorriston and Frank Hole, in fact, go so far as to assert exactly when and where these conditions came together to produce agriculture—in the Jordan Valley around lakes that were receding due to increased aridity around 10,000 years ago, give or take only a few hundred years (ibid.).

The natural habitat for the wild ancestors of wheat and barley is not in the lowlands but seems to lie in the higher areas of the Levant and in the Taurus and Zagros, which might suggest that early experimentation with domestication took place far from the centers of early civilization in the riverine lowlands. In fact, wild barley and wheat can still be found in the Zagros uplands. Jack Harlan, a botanist, demonstrated in 1967 the great abundance and productivity of wild wheat in southeastern Turkey. Using a primitive stone sickle, he hand-harvested 6 pounds of wild wheat in an hour and estimated that a family of four could gather a year's supply of food in approximately three weeks.

Early foragers in the area must have found such wild grains a good source of food, and it is likely that a number of pre-Neolithic foraging populations came to depend on them as their staple. Recent archaeological evidence indicates a long preagricultural tradition of village life based on wild grain and animals. Archaeologists refer to this cultural period as the *Natufian,* and it was then that people began making and using pottery, living in fixed dwellings, at least for significant portions of the year, and using stone mortars to make flour from wild grains.

At the same time, it is likely that not all populations had equal access to these naturally abundant grain areas. Some must have been living in areas with limited or erratic food supply. McCorriston and Hole suggest that, in fact, it was among these marginally located populations which had settled in the Jordan Valley that early experimentation in domestication is more likely to have occurred. Because domesticated grain represents a genetic change from the original form, it is possible that the pressures that precipitated this change were inadvertently engineered by humans attempting to utilize grains where they normally did not grow. For example, Frank Hole, Kent Flannery, and James Neely (1969) describe the planting of wheat and barley close to the edges of swamps at Ali Kosh, an archaeological site in southwestern Iran.[4] Because these grains do not normally grow wild in marshy areas, the native vegetation must have been cleared away to make room for them. Here, suggests Flannery (1999), we see some of the first steps in the deliberate modification of the Middle East landscape by human hands. Early efforts such as these must have ultimately led to a full-time commitment to agriculture.

Even though our understanding of all the events leading to the domestication of plants and animals in the area is still very limited, it is certain that within 1000 years agriculture had spread widely, and that by 7000 B.C., villages based on domestic plants and animals were becoming increasingly common. Evidence from this period suggests that early agriculturalists practiced dry farming and utilized domesticated sheep and goats. Certainly, by 6000 B.C., village life replaced nomadic foraging as the dominant pattern throughout most of the Middle East. Jarmo, a site in northeastern Iraq excavated by Robert Braidwood and now considered to be of signal importance, was a village of approximately 25 mud-walled houses, each with its own courtyard, storage pit, and oven. Sickle blades and grinding stones, found together with barley and wheat, indicate an ongoing commitment to agriculture. Finds elsewhere, for example, in Turkey, Iran, Syria, Israel, and Jordan, suggest that the case of Jarmo is not unique.

Although a modern visitor to ancient Jarmo would find its inhabitants unlike any group living in the Middle East today, certain features of their general life would be familiar. The people of Jarmo, like many contemporary rural Middle Easterners, practiced a mixed economy, combining grain production with animal husbandry. In an environment of unpredictable climatic variability, it is advantageous for people to hedge their bets by diversifying their subsistence base. Moreover, the presence of individual domiciles and granaries in Jarmo suggests another similarity to modern farmers in that the household, then as now, was an extremely important social and economic unit. Everywhere in the rural Middle East the household is still the primary unit of production and consumption—a point we take up later.

Although dry farming, as evidenced in sites like Jarmo in Iraq and Jericho in Jordan (the latter is perhaps the oldest continually inhabited site in the world), became rapidly established, it did not solve all the problems of livelihood and security. As people came to rely heavily on cultivation, they placed themselves in an increasingly vulnerable position. Variation in rainfall, for example, usually affects farmers more severely than it does hunters and gatherers. Foragers exploit a very broad range of food sources and may find it easy to disperse and congregate according to local conditions. Village-dwelling farmers, on the other hand, invest labor in the land they till, and in their houses and

---

[4] See also Charles Redman (1999).

tools, and they are very dependent on localized solutions to problems of food production. They find it harder simply to pack up and move or change their basic pattern of procurement.

It is, therefore, not surprising that efforts were made to control the critical variable for agriculture—namely, water. These attempts probably involved the planting of crops along the courses of shallow rivers or in seasonally flooded valley bottoms. Eventually, means were perfected to control water with canalization. As this involved great commitment of human labor, we can assume that it arose more from necessity than from an attempt to increase production, because people, then as now, are more apt to expend labor in efforts to maintain a system rather than to alter it.

In the Middle East, techniques of water control became elaborated in the arid lowlands, where irrigation farming is the key to stable settled life. It was only with irrigation and the development of drought-resistant crops that the lowlands became settled in the patterns we know today. By 5500 B.C., there were large lowland villages dependent on irrigation agriculture; and interestingly, there was also evidence of some degree of craft specialization in pottery and metalwork. Paralleling this, settlements in upland areas increased in size, number, and complexity.

A wealth of archaeological material from one such site, Çatal Hüyük of central Anatolia, attests to the sophistication and complexity of life in this early period. Dating from around 6250 B.C., Çatal Hüyük was one of the largest settlements of its day (about 13 acres), possibly containing several thousand inhabitants who lived in well-constructed houses with partitioned rooms, windows, platforms for sleeping, hearths, and ovens. Many houses also contained burials, polychromatic wall paintings, domestic religious shrines, clay figurines, elaborately painted pottery, and even clay stamp seals. The evidence for basketry, woven goods, and tool manufacturing suggests that some households may also have engaged primarily in craft industry. The community displays signs of both internal social differentiation and a high level of religious and ritual elaboration. There are signs of extensive trade relations with other regions, including contact with the Sinai Peninsula some thousand kilometers away. The economy that sustained this cultural development was one that combined irrigation farming, animal husbandry, and trade.

The shift to irrigation agriculture in the lowland areas and river valleys, paralleled as it seems to have been by an increase in overall population and by the development of large, dense settlements, was the prelude to the evolution of urban centers and the earliest empires. Thus, by 3000 B.C., the cultural canvas of the Middle East took on the special texture of complexity and local contrast that still distinguishes it today. Also there is some evidence from this early period of a way of life often considered the most distinctive in the area—nomadic pastoralism.

It is impossible to document fully the rise of nomadic pastoralism in which humans came to rely on a highly specialized and often risky undertaking.

All we know for sure is that while animals were domesticated at about the same time as plants, specialized nomadic pastoralism is a later development, probably accompanying the shift to lowland settlement and urbanism. One possibility is that changes in agricultural practices, especially in increased emphasis on canal irrigation, created the preconditions for specialized herding. Canal irrigation increased productivity, which led to an increase in population and an expansion of settlements. This meant that, in a practical sense, many villages were increasingly established in arid locales, away from areas of lush grazing.

It is also possible that with the intensification of agriculture, the land available for grazing became more and more limited. To get adequate food for their animals, herders probably would have had to travel greater and greater distances. This involved an appreciable investment of time and labor, and could have conflicted with their agricultural pursuits, which with irrigation had become time-consuming. In addition to the work of planting and harvesting, canals had to be dug, cleaned, and repaired, and the allocation of their water monitored. These conflicting demands for time and labor could have encouraged certain households, and ultimately larger groups, to specialize in increasingly intensive agriculture, while others devoted most of their attention to animal husbandry. Even though this cannot be confirmed, we know that pastoralism in the Middle East is a strategy predicated on agricultural surplus and is closely linked economically with farming communities. Everywhere in the Middle East, for example, the diet of the pastoral household is based on grains, legumes, or dates as a primary staple.

THE RISE OF CIVILIZATION

The Neolithic period set the stage for the rapid transformation of the Middle Eastern cultural landscape. In fact, by 3000 B.C., we move from the domain of prehistory to the era of early civilizations, with their written records and monumental architecture.

When we read written accounts from Mesopotamia or Egypt, or when we look at the scenes depicting everyday life later painted on the temple walls of Luxor and other Egyptian sites, the impression we get may be exotic in its details, but it is remarkably familiar in overall tenor. What is depicted are different aspects of that cultural complex referred to as *civilization*—a way of life that was qualitatively different from anything else that had preceded it. We see evidence, for example, of such nonagricultural occupations as artisan, merchant, priest, soldier, and king. We also see the division of society into a number of social classes and the political dominance of a few large centers over an extensive hinterland. Long-distance trade involving luxury and subsistence foods increased in importance.

But of all the features that characterized civilization, the two most significant were the development of large, dense settlements—the basis for *urbanism*—

and the emergence of centralized political institutions—the basis for the *state*. Just as the city marks a new form of human settlement and social life in the Middle East, the state marks a transformation in the political order. The state as a form of political organization involves much greater concentration of political power and the presence of a specialized administrative hierarchy with more than three levels.

Kent Flannery suggests that the original or, as archaeologists put it, pristine, states were formed in the context of competing chiefdoms where one succeeds in incorporating rivals, thus creating a far larger polity (1999, p. 3). Should a complex chiefdom—that is, one in which there already existed significant distinctions of rank and power between the chief, his principal retainers or subchiefs, and the common tribesmen—expand to absorb additional chiefdoms, the degree of administrative control required could lead to statelike specialization in domains of control. It has been postulated that should a polity come to extend spatially more than a day's travel from the ruler, administrative control will be based on subordinates (Spencer, 1998). The evidence to support this line of thinking comes from both archaeological sources in the Middle East and historical accounts of recent state formation in Africa, the Pacific, and Central Asia. The point to emphasize here is that without the impetus of agriculture and associated sedentarism, such processual developments could not have occurred.

Although we may never fully understand the genesis of civilization in the Middle East, nor the specific developments that led to the formation of the state, what we do know is that by 3000 B.C., patterns of life in the area had acquired a form whose contours persist even today.[5] This complex can be described in terms of a number of central themes: the relationship between the rulers and the

(*left*) Drawings of guest houses from antiquity in Mesopotamia. (*right*) A guest house today in a village in southern Iraq.

[5] For recent reviews, see C. S. Spencer (1998), H. T. Wright (1998), and Kent Flannery (1999).

ruled, religion and the state, the family and the community, the farmer and the town dweller. What is remarkable is that we have documents from these early periods written on clay that give us a sense of the life at that time. Among these documents are letters—from father to son, governor to king, husband to wife, steward to overseer—all painting a vivid picture of social life. We have chosen the following excerpts because of their intrinsic interest and human touch.

The first excerpt, taken from a Sumerian text from approximately 2500 B.C., recounts a conversation between a father and son. The father begins by asking his son:

> *"Where did you go?"*
> *"I did not go anywhere."*
> *"If you did not go anywhere, why do you idle about? Go to school, stand before your 'school' father (professor), recite your assignment, open your school bag, write your tablet, let your 'big brother' write your new tablet for you. After you have finished your assignment and reported to your monitor, come to me, and do not wander about in the street. Come now, do you know what I said?"*
> *"I know, I'll tell it to you."*
> *"Come, now, repeat it to me."*
> *"I'll repeat it to you."*
> *"Come on, tell it to me."*
> *"You told me to go to school, recite my assignment, open my school bag, write my tablet, while my 'big brother' is to write my new tablet. After finishing my assignment, I am to proceed to my work and to come to you after I have reported to my monitor."*
> *"Come now, be a man. Don't stand about in the public square or wander about the boulevard. When walking in the street, don't look all around. Be humble and show fear before your monitor. When you show terror, the monitor will like you."*[6]

As is clear from this conversation, education, in this case probably for the post of a scribe, was already the responsibility of the school and specialized teachers. It also seems clear that city youth, then as now, did not necessarily appreciate the opportunities their fathers provided for them. We might also note that the respect and formal deference expected then of a pupil to a teacher is still very much in evidence in the Middle East today.

Like education, medicine too was a specialized craft, one for which the Middle East has long been famous. In Sumer, the physician was known as *a-zu*, or "water thrower," and one text from this time records the following treatment, thought to be for venereal disease:

> *Having crushed turtle shell and . . . , and having anointed the opening* [of the sick organ, perhaps] *with oil, you shall rub* [with the crushed shell] *the man lying prone* [?] *. . . After rubbing with the crushed shell you shall rub (again) with fine beer; after rubbing with fine beer, you shall wash with water; after washing with water, you shall fill (the sick spot) with crushed fir wood. It is (a prescription) for someone afflicted by a disease in the tun and the* nu.[7]

---

[6] Translated by Michel Civil, cited in Samuel Noah Kramer (1963, p. 244).

[7] Ibid.

The *tun* and *nu* have yet to be precisely identified, and the efficacy of the treatment is unknown. Beer, however, apart from its medicinal properties, was widely consumed and may have been the major impetus for grain production. The fermentation of beer from wheat and barley was a primary way of utilizing these cereals as food.

THE CULTURAL HERITAGE OF EARLY HISTORY

The two preceding excerpts refer to life in Sumer, but they could easily have come from Akkad, Babylon, Assyria, or even Egypt—all of which have left their indelible mark on the human and cultural makeup of the Middle East.

The history of dynastic Egypt is usually traced back to 3100 B.C., when Menes, the king of Upper Egypt, conquered Lower Egypt and ruled the united country from his new capital of Thebes. He, like subsequent Pharaohs, was believed to be the living embodiment of the falcon god Horus and was therefore considered divine. A succession of dynasties ruled Egypt until its conquest by the Romans. Presiding over an elaborate priesthood and a bureaucracy made up of officials, scribes, and clerks, Egyptian Pharaohs generally succeeded in preserving the unity of the country despite many invasions. These millennia of unity no doubt contributed to the Egyptians' strong sense of national identity, which transcends the claims of Islam and pan-Arab nationalism.

According to tradition, Christianity was first introduced into Egypt by St. Mark. It was not until the fifth century, however, that a separate Coptic national church was established as the result of a schismatic movement within the Byzantine church. The Muslim invasion of Egypt that began in A.D. 639 brought many Arab settlers to the country; it also resulted in massive conversions to Islam and the spread of the Arabic language. The result is that the Christian Copts constitute a minority in Egypt today—between 5 and 7 percent of the total population.

Unlike the Nile Valley, Mesopotamia experienced a far more varied cultural and dynastic history. Lacking the geographic unity and the easy communication of the Nile, Mesopotamia, the land between the Tigris and Euphrates rivers, was the scene of a succession of city-states, which included Sumer, Akkad, Babylonia, and Assyria. With the exception of the Sumerians, the inhabitants of these states spoke related languages classified as Semitic, a grouping that today includes modern Arabic and Hebrew.

Other Semitic-speaking populations, such as the Phoenicians and the Canaanites, settled in the eastern Mediterranean areas astride the cultural frontiers of the Egyptian and Mesopotamian civilizations. Seafarers and traders, the Phoenicians established their cities throughout the Mediterranean, and in time came to develop a system of writing based on a phonetic alphabet, which replaced earlier hieroglyphics and cuneiform.

The ancient Hebrews trace their origins to Mesopotamia, from which they migrated to the eastern Mediterranean and later to Egypt. Following their exodus from Egyptian bondage in the thirteenth century B.C., the Hebrews succeeded in conquering parts of the lands of Canaan where they settled. Under King David (1000 B.C.–960 B.C.), the various Hebrew tribes united, forming a state with its capital at the newly captured Jerusalem. Following the death of Solomon, however, the kingdom divided into two nations—Israel in the north and Judea in the south. Israel was destroyed by the Assyrians in 721 B.C., but the smaller kingdom of Judea survived until 586 B.C., when it fell to the Babylonians; they exiled Judea's leaders to their capital of Babylon in what is today southern Iraq. In 539 B.C., the Persian Emperor Cyrus conquered Babylon; a year later he allowed the Jews to return to Jerusalem and to rebuild their Temple. The Jews remained in Palestine, maintaining a semblance of independence under a succession of Persian, Greek, and Roman rulers until 63 B.C., when the Romans finally destroyed the Temple.

Another Semitic-speaking population is the Arabs. The term *Arab* first appears in an Assyrian cuneiform tablet dating from 853 B.C. and seems to have referred to nomadic pastoralists. With time, the term acquired its most common usage, designating the speaker of one of a group of closely related dialects of the Arabic language, which is itself divided into two major groupings, northern and southern Arabic. Dialects of southern Arabic survive today in scattered islands in the Indian Ocean, but few speech communities remain anywhere on the Arabian Peninsula.

From ancient days, Arab populations were active in land and sea commerce with trading communities as far away as China, India, and East Africa. Distributed over a broad area extending from the steppes of Syria to the highlands of Yemen, Arabic speakers exhibited great diversity in political and social organization. For example, one group, the Nabatean, established a prosperous trade center, Petra, whose elaborate buildings were carved into the pink sandstone of the cliffs in today's Jordan. To the east in the Syrian steppe, Palmyra was another important Arab city-state whose impressive architecture stands abandoned in the desert. Its last ruler, Queen Zenobia, managed to extend her realm until meeting final defeat at the hands of the Romans in A.D. 273.

In the period that preceded the Islamic conquest, a number of small Arab states were established along the buffer zones that separated the two dominant empires of the time—the Byzantines and the Persian Sassanians. As clients of one or the other, Arab kingdoms such as the Christian Ghassanids of Syria and the Lakhmids of southern Iraq survived until absorbed by the Persian Empire.

The Persians, who speak an Indo-European language, are heirs to a great civilization and a powerful empire that at one time stretched from Asia Minor to India. The Sassanian rulers of Persia, the last of the non-Muslim dynasties, had adopted Zoroastrianism as the national religion. It remained so for about 1000 years, until the Persian defeat by the Muslim Arabs. Even so, the conversion of Zoroastrians to Islam proceeded slowly in many places, and even today a small Zoroastrian community can be found in Iran. Zoroastrianism, which emphasizes the coexistence of good and evil and humanity's responsibility to uphold the good, is believed to have strongly influenced the development of early Judaism and Christianity and Islam in turn.

THE ISLAMIC CONQUEST AND AFTER

The Arab-Islamic conquests that began in the seventh century ushered in a new phase in the cultural history of the Middle East. These conquests initiated a process of cultural synthesis that culminated in the formation of an Arab-Islamic civilization. The synthesis was based on the spread of the Arabic language and the religion of Islam. In fact, we can say that while Christian and Jewish populations persisted, even flourished at times, Arab-Islamic culture provided much of the cultural matrix for people of all faiths, a point we shall explore in the next two chapters. The conquest itself proceeded very rapidly, sweeping through the Middle East in the course of very few years. What is particularly striking is the rapidity with which Islam as belief and polity established itself in the heartland of ancient civilizations. One way this can be understood is to realize that in the period preceding Muhammad's birth in A.D. 570, both the Byzantines and the Persians were greatly weakened and their claims on the local populace had eroded. Islam then arose and spread in what may be considered a political vacuum, at least inasmuch as one thinks of strong centralized state rule.

Of course, the advent of Islam, which originated in the Arabian Peninsula, did not result in immediate conversions of the masses of people who came in contact with the Muslim armies. The Arab conquerors themselves often discouraged the conversion of non-Arabs, seeking to preserve for themselves the privileged status of a conquering elite. However, Islam, as a universal religion, acknowledges no ethnic boundaries—a fact that in time encouraged the conversion of Aramaic-, Persian-, and Greek-speaking populations. With the exception of the Persians, the converted population fairly rapidly adopted Arabic, the language of government as well as religion. Even in Persia, the educated classes wrote in Arabic, and Arabic script came to be employed for writing Persian itself. At the same time, some populations, while adopting the Arabic language, nonetheless retained their separate religious identities; Christian and Jewish communities persisted within the Islamic order.

Another important population that, while embracing Islam, retained its language is the Turks, whose language belongs to the Altaic group (which also includes Mongolian). Chinese chronicles refer to groups of presumably Turkish nomadic pastoralists in central Asia as early as 1300 B.C. But the appearance of Turkish speakers in southwestern Asia is relatively recent, dating from about the ninth century A.D. Initially, Turkish mercenaries or warrior-slaves were recruited to the service of imperial houses of the Fatimids of Egypt, the Abbassids of Baghdad, and other dynasties. With time, these caste-like military contingents gained considerable power in their own right, and their ranks swelled as Turkish-speaking populations migrated westward from Central Asia in increasing numbers. It is usually thought that this movement of people was set in motion by the Mongol conquests. Although the processes by which the Turks established themselves as a major political and cultural presence are still unclear, historians often identify two main waves of conquest and political consolidation. Each period of consolidation was made possible because diverse Turkish-speaking groups or tribes had already migrated into the areas in question.

The first period of Turkish political rule over a major state or empire occurred when the Seljuk Turks of Persia gained ascendancy in the tenth century A.D. over most of the former Abbassid domains. By A.D. 1071, Seljuk rule and a Seljuk capital were soon established in the city of Konya, formerly Aykonium. Following 1071, when the Byzantines were decisively defeated in the east, Turkish settlers, both as nomadic tribes and warriors, arrived in large numbers in what is today Turkey. Ultimately, Seljuk rule was broken by the Mongols, and power was fragmented among numerous small Turkish emirates or mini-states, some no more than tribal confederations.

In the mid-thirteenth century, one of these emirates, the House of Osman, succeeded in establishing hegemony over its rivals and expanded its territory at the expense of the remaining Byzantine lands. This marked the onset of the second period of Turkish political and cultural expansion, that of the Ottoman Turks. By the fourteenth century, the Ottomans were masters of the whole of Asia Minor with the exception of Constantinople, and they had crossed the Bosphorus to acquire substantial territories in Europe. Where the early Arab armies failed in the seventh century, the Turks succeeded in capturing Constantinople in 1453. With the subsequent capture of Trabzond the last remnants of the Byzantine political presence were removed from the area.

At its apogee, the Ottoman Empire stretched from the great plains of Hungary in the west through the Balkans and around the Black Sea, continuing in a vast arc to encompass virtually the entire eastern and southern Mediterranean. With the exception of Iran, the countries we are concerned with in this book are recent successor states to the Ottoman Empire, whose legacy is still visible. For more than three centuries, the Ottoman Empire, one of the world's major imperial systems, was also the dominant power in Europe and remained a political force in the Middle East until its dissolution at the end of World War I.

In many ways the Turkish experience exemplifies the ideological appeal of Islam and its role in the political and cultural domains. Early Turkish warriors, adopting Islam, consecrated themselves to the task of extending its frontiers. Achieving power in their own right, Turkish dynasties utilized and adapted Islamic ideology and institutions to legitimize their rule and hold together a vast, multiethnic empire.

An almost parallel case is to be found with the longtime rivals of the Ottomans to the east, the Safavids of Persia. In 1501, a Safavid Shah proclaimed Shi'ism, a distinctive form of Islam, as the state religion, and consolidated power over a smaller but also an ethnically diverse empire. Despite long rivalry with the Ottomans, the Persians successfully resisted Ottoman encroachment to the east of the Zagros, and the current Turco-Iranian frontier dates from the seventeenth century.

While the successor dynasties and regimes to the Safavids continued to rule Iran within much the same frontiers as now, the breakup of the Ottoman Empire resulted in a vastly altered political landscape. Even before World War I, the European Great Powers were intervening in the empire in ways that still influence events today. Russia, instrumental in the collapse of the Ottomans in the west, assumed the role of protector of the Slavs and Orthodox Christians wherever they might be within the empire. As a consequence of the independence of Serbia, Greece, Romania, and Bulgaria at the end of the nineteenth century, over a million Muslim refugees from the Balkans fled eastward and were resettled in what is today Turkey, Iraq, Syria, and Jordan. British intervention established Egypt and the Sudan as protectorates in the late nineteenth century; the rise of Arab nationalism is closely associated with this colonial encounter. France assumed a role as protector of the Christians of Lebanon, on which basis it subsequently acquired direct rule over both Syria and Lebanon. Britain, operating out of British India, stationed political officers with great influence in all of the Gulf principalities, as well as directly administering Aden. Kuwait's claim today for nation-state status rests on the de facto British protectorate status it once had while nominally under Ottoman rule; Iraq's claim to Kuwait rests on the Ottoman legacy of it having been ruled from Basra.

In an era of intensive European nationalism, Arab nationalism developed in a fragmented and uncoordinated fashion, partly due to poor leadership and contradictory goals, but more because of its ambivalent place within a nominally Islamic empire. Jewish nationalism, or Zionism, which developed within the European experience of anti-Semitism, itself fueled by nationalism, grew rapidly after 1880. Its objective of forming a Jewish polity in Palestine rapidly attracted powerful backers with money to purchase land and, importantly, settlers. In 1901, one Zionist writer promoted settlement with the theme, since much repeated, "A people without a land for a land without people," at a time when Palestine had a population of over 400,000 Muslim and Christian Arabs (Held, 1994, p. 183).

During World War I, the Allies drew up specific plans for the postwar political makeup of the dying Ottoman Empire. In 1916, in order to encourage Arab rebellion against the Turks, the British entered into memoranda of agreement with various regional leaders that promised an independent Arab kingdom. This induced the Hashimite family, traditional rulers of Mecca and Medina, to rally tribal forces in revolt. At almost the same time, British and French ministers, meeting secretly, drew up the Sykes-Picot Agreement, which envisaged direct French rule in Lebanon, Syria, and what is today southern Turkey, and British rule in Iraq and Palestine. In 1917, after intense lobbying by influential Zionists, and in an attempt to gain the support of German and American Jews for the

British war effort, the British Foreign Secretary, Lord Balfour, issued a one-sentence declaration of support for a national home for the Jews in Palestine:

> His Majesty's Government views with favor the establishment in Palestine of a national home for the Jewish people, and will use their best endeavors to facilitate the achievement of this object, it being clearly understood that nothing shall be done which may prejudice the civil and religious rights of existing non-Jewish communities in Palestine, or the rights and political status enjoyed by Jews in any other country.

Known as the Balfour Declaration, this internally contradictory statement violated the spirit if not the wording of previous agreements with Arab leaders.

In what is today Turkey, the Allies planned the establishment of a Greek state in western Anatolia and in the Black Sea region, with Italian and French zones of administration in the south. They seemingly also encouraged Armenian and Kurdish aspirations; the French and Russians in fact gave material support to the Armenians in the immediate postwar years. In 1919, the Allies landed a Greek army in Izmir. However, the successful Turkish nationalist movement led by Mustafa Kemal (Atatürk) repulsed the Greeks in 1922, and the Allies subsequently withdrew support for Greek, Kurdish, and Armenian national or territorial claims on what is today Turkey . However, the French did establish a mandate government over Lebanon and Syria (lasting until 1945), and the British held a mandate over Jordan and Trans-Jordan in Palestine and very tight control over a nominally independent Iraq and Kuwait.

Although Jewish immigration from Europe, and particularly Russia, had begun in the 1880s, it was not until the First World War and its aftermath that conflicting Jewish and Arab claims to Palestine began to be expressed in internecine struggle. Until World War I, Palestine was part of the Ottoman Empire, but after the war, in 1922, the new League of Nations gave the British a mandate to rule the country. At the time of the Balfour Declaration in 1917 supporting the establishment of a Jewish homeland, there were in Palestine 84,000 Jews, 486,000 Muslims, and 71,000 Christians. During the period of the British mandate, the "Jews sought to strengthen their claim by attracting immigrants, purchasing land, and establishing settlements. The Arabs attempted to cut off immigration, to prevent Jewish land purchases, and to get rid of the British and establish their own national entity. All this led to a series of uprisings on the Arab side. . . . The final uprising . . . the Arab Rebellion of 1936–39, was a wide-scale revolt which raged over the whole of Palestine" (Gorkin, 1993, p. 9). In 1937, the Peel Commission, which had been set up in response to the revolt, recommended the partition of Palestine into two states, Jewish and Arab. The Jews accepted the plan (although not some details), but the Arabs rejected it outright, and it was scrapped. During World War II, the conflict intensified, and the United Nations once again recommended partition, which was once again accepted by the Jews and rejected by the Arabs. "On November 29, 1947, the United Nations voted to accept partition. The result was war" (p. 10).

Known to the Jews as the War of Liberation and to the Arabs as the Disaster (*Al nakba*), civil war raged between Jews and Palestinians until the British forces evacuated Palestine on May 15, 1948 (the state of Israel was proclaimed on May 14), when five Arab states entered the battle (Iraq, Lebanon, Syria, Jordan, and Egypt). Armistice agreements were finally signed between February and July of 1949. "As a consequence of the war, approximately 370 Palestinian villages and towns were destroyed, and between 600,000 and 760,000 Palestinians became refugees. The western portion of the territory that had been earmarked for a Palestinian state in the partition recommendation was absorbed into the new state of Israel" (Gorkin, 1993, p. 103); the eastern portion was annexed by Jordan.

Israel thus achieved independence in 1948 following a hard-fought war that vastly enlarged its territories beyond the original UN partition plan of 1947, and also precipitated the first great wave of Palestinian refugees. Today, approximately 5 million Palestinians live outside of Israel and the West Bank, forced to contend with their own diaspora.

2

Islam: The Prophet and the Religion

In a debate more than a little reminiscent of earlier ones in Europe, the specter of militant Islam, antithetical to Western civilization, has again been brought to the fore. Spurred in part by the challenge of a controversial thesis by the political scientist Samuel Huntington (1993), Western intellectuals and politicians alike have come to view Islam with apprehension. Huntington's thesis is that following the collapse of communism, a new phase of world politics is emerging in which culture will be the main source of great divisions and confrontations among people. In his view, "Western ideas of individualism, liberalism, constitutionalism, human rights, equality, liberty, the rule of law, democracy, free markets, and the separation of church and state often have little resonance in Islamic cultures." While he cites other so-called civilizations such as Hinduism and Confucianism as also alien to these values, it is Islam as the world's fastest growing religion that is the main target of his argument.[1]

While we do not agree with the implications of Huntington's thesis, it is important to note that in various forms its main assumptions are reflected in popular perceptions and media representations of Islam and especially the Middle East. In fact, similarly distorted representations with their implied threats are often used by local politicians in the Middle East to justify political ends where the support of Western public opinion is desired. In order to understand any ideology and historical tradition as complex and diverse as Islam, one has to begin with some very basic knowledge of its history and tenets. This chapter will sketch the main beliefs and early history of Islam. In Chapter 3 we shall explore the diversity in belief and practice that is also Islam and that

---

[1] See Roy P. Mottahedeh (1995) for a thoughtful and measured academic response. A very interesting Islamic response was the 1996 Istanbul "Dialogue of Civilizations," organized by a prominent religious leader, Felhullah Gülen, to which representatives of all faiths were invited (Uğur Kömeçoğlu [personal communication]).

justifiably can be termed Islamic culture. One point to remember is that the origin and spiritual roots of Islam are in the Middle East and, more than any other factor, it defines the area culturally.

> In the name of God, the Merciful, the Compassionate,
> Praise be to God, Lord of the Universe,
> The Merciful, the Compassionate,
> Ruler on the Day of Judgement.
> Thee alone we worship, Thee alone we ask for aid.
> Guide us in the straight path,
> The path of those whom thou has favored,
> Not of those against whom thou art wrathful,
> Nor of those who go astray.

This prayer, the *fatiha* or opening chapter of the Quran, the Holy Book of Islam, is one of the world's most often recited sacred verses. Of the billion or so people who profess Islam, a great number direct this praise to God four times before each of their five daily prayers, as well as before embarking on any important task or journey. Uttering these words, a traveler setting out from Fez in Morocco on a journey eastward to Afghanistan will pass through countries that differ in climate, language, and customs, but everywhere he or she will be

View of the Dome of the Rock mosque in Jerusalem, built in 691 A.D. It is considered the third holiest site to Muslims.

identified as a member of the universal community of the faithful, the *umma*. In each of the countries on the way the traveler will hear the public call to prayer chanted by the *muezzin* from the minarets of mosques, and nowadays almost always amplified through loudspeakers. The call that beckons the believers to prayer proclaims the central article of faith for all Muslim peoples: "I profess that there is no god but God and that Muhammad is his Messenger." This simple statement is regarded as the most fundamental part of the Islamic creed. Its threefold public recitation in Arabic is, for all intents and purposes, sufficient to make one a convert to Islam. Having spoken these words in seriousness, one becomes a member of the vast community of the *umma,* subject to its laws and recipient of its support.

THE SCOPE OF ISLAM

Despite evident diversity in both expressed belief and observed practice, those individuals who profess Islam thereby proclaim their membership in a community that transcends ethnic and national boundaries. The shared sense of one Islam, eternal and immutable, is itself a distinguishing and fundamental characteristic of the faith, for it irrevocably sets apart those who have accepted God's final prophecy from those who have not. Islam is a universalist religion like Christianity and Buddhism to which every person can belong. It is one of the great ideological movements in world history. It has created a community and endowed its members with a distinct identity; at the same time, it is an ideology projecting an ideal society and a utopian vision.

Viewed historically, it is evident that Islam draws on many sources of belief and practice. It is, of course, futile to attempt an acceptable universal definition of the beliefs and practices of any living religion, and Islam, like all religions that claim universal validity, is best viewed as an ongoing, ever-changing, living tradition. One aspect of this complex tradition in Islam is the set of beliefs and history recorded in scriptures that are passed on and reproduced from generation to generation. This aspect cannot be overstressed if one is to understand the role of Islam in Middle Eastern societies. This written repository of belief and history is, by and large, the domain of religious scholars who thus come to exercise considerable power and authority as well as providing a major source of cultural continuity. Islamic scripture and its scholarly interpretations might be thought of as constituting the formal expression of the Islamic tradition.[2]

In analyzing complex literate societies, it is often useful to distinguish the systems of belief and practice of the learned or the elite from the understandings of the common people. While the perceptions of Islam by the learned

---

[2] For a good introduction to Islam and Islamic institutions, see Fazlur Rahman (1979). See also John Esposito (1988) and Ahmed Akbar (1999).

and religious specialists will vary by region and sect, perhaps even making it impossible to establish a single shared dogma, still the Islam (or Islams, as some have said) of the learned displays less variation than do the beliefs and practices of the common people. This analytic distinction is often described as one between the Great or Universalistic Tradition and the Little or Local Tradition. Muslims themselves continue to debate orthodoxy and what constitutes true belief and practice, but the analytic fact remains that variation in practice and interpretation is inevitable in a living religion. How people understand, interpret, and act upon Islamic principles defines what Islam is at any given time for a particular community.[3]

Clearly, each of these two aspects or traditions of Islam informs the other. Formal or scriptural Islam can be seen at the same time as both the source of an ideal code and as a set of notions against which the reality of human behavior can be measured. It is, in fact, as we shall see later, a primary source for the establishment and exercise of law. Equally, this ideal code or formal system of belief itself reflects an ever-changing experience.

THE RISE OF ISLAM

One of the three great monotheistic religions of the world, Islam arose in the full light of history. Developing six centuries after Christianity, it rapidly achieved astounding success. At the time of his death, in A.D. 632, its founder, the Prophet Muhammad, was the undisputed ruler of most of Arabia. In fact, a mere decade after his death, the state he had founded had met and defeated the armies of the two great empires in the region, the Byzantine and the Sassanian. The Arab Muslim and the Persian Sassanian armies first met in A.D. 626 in southern Iraq at the battle of Qadisiyya in which the Persian emperor was defeated and forced to retreat. A second and decisive battle took place in A.D. 651 which effectively put an end to the Sassanian Empire and opened up Persia and beyond to the Muslim Arabs. By A.D. 732, one hundred years after the death of Muhammad, the Muslim Empire of his successors extended from France to India.[4] Continuing to gain adherents, Islam is still the most rapidly expanding religion in the world, especially on the African continent.

In order to understand and appreciate Islam as a religious, political, and social force, we turn our attention briefly to sixth-century Arabia, the birthplace of Muhammad. Like other ideological systems, religions evolve in specific economic and political contexts. They not only reflect the social tensions of the moment but also themselves shape ongoing processes of change. Islam has its

---

[3] See D. F. Eickleman and J. Piscatori (1996); see also Reinhold Loeffler (1988).

[4] For an interesting, if somewhat idiosyncratic, general historical treatment of the origins, spread, and development of Islam, see Marshall Hodgson (1974). Bernard Lewis (1993) is an invaluable concise handbook.

origins in the pervasive social and economic transformations that were taking place in Arabian society in the sixth century. At the same time, as a social and political force in its own right, it contributed to the transformation of Arabian society and eventually of societies beyond.

The Arabian Peninsula connects the lands of the Levant with the Indian Ocean, and from antiquity has served as the crossroads between the great empires of the Mediterranean and the Far East. Although little is known about the early inhabitants of central and northern Arabia, it appears that many were nomadic pastoralists and that they were organized in tribes and confederations that sometimes united nomad and oasis dweller together. Local resources alone were probably not sufficient to sustain the development of larger polities like the small-scale states and kingdoms that had developed earlier in southern Arabia.

The Romans, who dominated the Levant in an earlier period, never bothered to establish their direct rule over Arabia, but were generally content to exert their influence indirectly through control of the many small client states or chiefdoms that arose, prospered, and declined with regularity along the desert frontier of northern Arabia. Two of the more famous of these Arabian kingdoms were Petra and Palmyra, in today's Jordan and Syria, respectively.

The Romans were superseded by the Byzantines, but the general political pattern in the area remained much the same until the fourth century A.D. By this time a number of Arab tribes had converted to Monophysitic Christianity, although the majority retained their earlier polytheistic beliefs. In the next two centuries there appears to have been wide-scale economic deterioration and general political upheaval in the Arabian Peninsula. The exact causes remain obscure, but around this time the monarchies of southern Arabia collapsed and their agrarian economies fell into ruin. Some of these kingdoms succumbed to Persian invaders, and others to Abyssinian invasions. Southern Arabian tribes subsequently embarked on a series of migrations to the north that brought them into conflict with each other and with the northern tribes. As a result, the once-prosperous trans-Arabian trade languished, and the routes fell into disuse.

By the sixth century A.D., this long period of economic deterioration and intertribal warfare had worked itself out and a relatively stable pattern had emerged. Many of the Arabian nomads had settled down in oases, some founding new towns in the process. Other oases were inhabited by Arabic-speaking Jewish populations, and Christians were not uncommon among some of the nomadic tribes. Christian monasteries were scattered throughout the northern part of the peninsula, where some, such as St. Catherine's in the Sinai, remain today.

Trade was again becoming important, and the local populations played important roles as caravaneers, middlemen, and merchants. Towns along the major caravan routes grew wealthy. Among the most prosperous of the new towns was Mecca, which had been founded around A.D. 100 by the Quraish, a northern Arabian tribe, around the well of Zamzam. By the fifth century, Mecca had become the major trade town along the western coast of Arabia (a region known as the Hijaz), and its merchants maintained commercial relations with both the Byzantines and the Persians. The town itself seems to have been ruled by an oligarchy made up of the leading merchants, most of whom were members of the Quraish.

Besides long-distance trade, another source of revenue for the Meccans was the local shrine, a large, pan-tribal sanctuary that housed the images of the many gods and goddesses worshiped by the Arabs before Islam. It is said to have contained even some Christian and Jewish relics as well. The most sacred object in the shrine was the sanctuary of the Ka'ba, a cube-like structure that had in its center the sacred black stone (part of a meteorite) that was considered holy by the different tribes who came to Mecca to worship at the shrine and to attend the busy market nearby. The fame and success of this market, known as *suq 'ukaz*, was in no small measure due to the presence of the sanctuary. The sanctuary of Mecca, one of several in the peninsula, was considered a sacred place—*haram*, a consecrated area where no blood could be shed and where oaths could be taken. The sanctity of the shrine extended to the market area to ensure trust in business transactions and to guarantee a temporary truce among the chronically feuding tribes. The Quraish elders, in their capacity as the elite of Mecca, controlled and derived revenues from both the sanctuary and the market.

MUHAMMAD: THE MAN AND THE PROPHECY

Muhammad was born around A.D. 570 into the Quraish tribe. His father had died before his birth, and his mother, who came from Medina, a town to the northeast of Mecca, died when he was six years old. He was brought up first by his grandfather and then by his paternal uncle, Abu Taleb, a wealthy merchant and a respected member of the Quraish oligarchy. Abu Taleb evidently discerned intelligence and initiative in the boy and employed him to accompany his caravans as they traded in the north. It was probably on these journeys that Muhammad came to meet the elders or scholars from the several Arabic-speaking Jewish and Christian communities in Syria and Arabia, and learned something about their beliefs.

There are few stories considered authentic by a majority of scholars about Muhammad's early years. One does tell of the encounter between Muhammad and a man named Zayd, who apparently was banished from Mecca for preaching some form of monotheistic belief. The story is related by Muhammad's first biographer, ibn-Ishaq:

> I was told that the Apostle of Allah said as he was talking: "I had come from Al- Ta'if . . . when we passed Zayd son of 'Amr who was in the highland of Mecca. The Quraish had made a public example of him for abandoning their religion, so that he went out from their midst. I sat down with him. I had a bag containing meat which we had sacrificed to our

idols . . . and I offered it to Zayd—I was but a lad at the time—and I said 'Eat some of this food, my uncle.' He replied, 'Surely it is part of those sacrifices of theirs which they offer to their idols?' When I said that it was, he said, 'Nephew of mine, if you were to ask the daughters of 'Abd al-Muttalib they would tell you that I never eat of these sacrifices, and I have no desire to do so.' Then he upbraided me for idolatry and spoke disparagingly of those who worship idols and sacrifice to them, and said, 'They are worthless; they can neither harm nor profit anyone,' or words to that effect." The Apostle added, "After that I never knowingly stroked one of their idols nor did I sacrifice to them until God honored me with his apostleship." (in Guillaume, 1956, p. 26)

By the time he was 20, Muhammad had acquired a reputation for wisdom and trustworthiness. These qualities apparently brought him to the attention of a wealthy widow, Khadija, who hired him to manage her caravans and supervise her business. She eventually proposed marriage, and at age 25 Muhammad married Khadija, who was 15 years his senior. The marriage seems to have been a happy one; Khadija bore him a number of children, including a favorite daughter, Fatima, who later married Muhammad's first cousin 'Ali. The descendants of this latter marriage, called *sayyids,* are greatly revered by Muslims the world over today. After Khadija's death, Muhammad married a number of women, far exceeding, in fact, the four that came to be established in Islamic law, an exception granted him by divine dispensation. His last and favorite wife, 'Aisha, has a unique place in Muslim history in that she is believed to have passed on more than 2000 traditions (or sayings) attributable to the Prophet.

Although little is known about the period immediately preceding the apostleship of Muhammad, nevertheless scholars have attempted to understand the development of Muhammad's prophecy and career in terms of the socioeconomic transformations of his day. Of the early modern Western scholars, we single out W. Montgomery Watt (1961) and Maxime Rodinson (1971), who were concerned with showing the relationship between Muhammad's mission, the success he had in acquiring a following, and the prevailing social and economic conditions in western Arabia. In their view, once Islam was launched as a distinct religion, its transformation into a political movement was historically inevitable. Although it developed in the context of a tribal society rent by factions, Islam, as a universal movement, managed to transcend these cleavages and restructure the society along new lines.

In Rodinson's interpretation, Muhammad's early dissatisfaction with the pagan practices of his fellow Arabians and with the wide differences in wealth within Meccan society are closely related. At the time the population of Mecca included not only the wealthy merchant families of the Quraish but also their dependent clients, slaves, and the newly settled nomads who made up the majority of the inhabitants. The disintegration of tribal cohesion and the growth of social differentiation must have become particularly accelerated. As individuals became wealthy from trade, the traditional tribal norms of mutual aid and protection increasingly fell into disuse; the poor and the powerless began to be abandoned by the clan and were left out of its protective network. The old values that operated in a fairly egalitarian, tribal group were being superseded by values that stressed individualism, material display, and competition. In fact, rich merchants in Mecca joined together to form commercial associations whose objectives were to monopolize trade and keep away rivals. Loosely organized along clan and tribal subdivisions, these mercantile associations also functioned as political factions as they competed for the right to manage and control the pilgrimages, fairs, and trading activities of the city.

Unhappy with the increasing social differentiation within Mecca and sensitive to the plight of its needy and neglected groups, Muhammad took to retreating from the city to the nearby mountains to meditate—not unusual behavior in Arabia, and his action seems to have aroused no curiosity or concern, at least not initially. It was in one of the caves on the nearby mountain of Hira that Muhammad first underwent a profound religious experience in which he believed he was called to become God's messenger, charged with revealing the truth to humanity. The year was A.D. 610, when Muhammad was already 40 years old. That experience marked the beginning of his prophetic career.

Tradition has preserved the details of this first experience. Alone in the cave, Muhammad began to hear voices and see visions. Later he saw an apparition that he identified as the Archangel Gabriel. The Heavenly Messenger commanded the frightened man to speak, but Muhammad refused. Gabriel repeated the command three times, and at the third command, Muhammad spontaneously recited the following verses:

> Recite, (*iqra'*): In the name of Thy Lord who Created,
> Who created man from a blood-clot,
> Recite: And thy Lord is the most generous, who taught by the pen
> Taught man that he knew not.

Such was the beginning of Islam and the Quran, or Holy Book, which contains Muhammad's revelations spanning a period of approximately 22 years. The word *Quran* is derived from the first word of the first revelation, *iqra'*, which is from the Arabic root *qra'a*, meaning "to read or to recite." The early revelations were received by Muhammad in rhymed prose, a form of recitation widely used in Arabia by poets and soothsayers.

This religious or mystical experience was followed by others, and Muhammad slowly came to accept his role as God's apostle, the one chosen to receive and preach God's word. As both messenger, *rasūl*, and prophet, *nabī*, Muhammad falls clearly in Max Weber's typology of an "emissary prophet." The emissary or messenger prophet transmits or reveals a divine message—in this case, codified in the verses of the Quran. At the same time, Muhammad's own life became a perfect model to be emulated by Muslims. As such, he also came to represent an "exemplary prophet."[5]

---

[5] For a discussion of these concepts, see Charles Lindholm (1996, pp. 36–40).

The first to believe in his divine calling were members of his immediate family, notably his first wife, Khadija, and his first cousin, 'Ali. For three years Muhammad limited his preaching and conversions to a small group of intimates who met in secret. Then he decided to preach in public, and his group met daily to hold prayers, an activity that quickly brought them to the attention of the Meccan elite. By this time, Muhammad's followers included a number of young wealthy men, but the majority were from among the weak, the poor, and the powerless of the city. At first, the dominant Quraish simply mocked Muhammad and his followers, but when it became apparent that more and more people were joining his circle, they took steps to put an end to a movement that they perceived threatened their position as guardians of the holy sanctuaries and their political authority in the city. Their sanctions included harassment of the Muslims and the boycott of Muhammad's clan of Hashem, so that the other Quraish clans refused to intermarry with the Hashem or to have any business dealings with them.

In 619, Abu Taleb, Muhammad's uncle and protector, died and was succeeded as the clan's leader by another relative. This relative was not well disposed toward Muhammad and withdrew the clan's protection from him and his followers. This made it dangerous for them to stay in Mecca, and in 622, Muhammad with some 70 of his followers migrated to Yathrib (later, Medina), the birthplace of his mother, an oasis town some 200 miles to the northeast of Mecca.

UMMA: THE ORIGINS OF THE ISLAMIC POLITY

The migration, known as *Hijra,* marks a new phase in the evolution of the Islamic community. In Medina the religious movement was soon embodied in a political form, that of the *umma,* or community. In fact, the migration was considered so important by the Muslims that the first day of the year in which it took place, July 16, 622, marks the start of the Islamic calendar, in which a year is based on 12 lunar months.

Unlike Mecca, which depended on commerce for its livelihood, Medina was an agricultural town where dates and grains were grown. It was inhabited by a number of pagan Arab as well as Jewish tribes who lived in scattered settlements and maintained an uneasy accommodation among themselves. The Jews seem to have been dominant earlier, but their power had slipped away; and at the time of the migration, Medina was experiencing a difficult period of chronic feuding among the different groups. In fact, it was mainly in an effort to put an end to this anarchic and unstable state of affairs that a group of Medina notables invited Muhammad to their town. They wanted him to act as an arbiter and peacemaker, and in return promised him freedom to preach and asylum for his followers. Apparently, they were not greatly concerned with his prophecy and religious mission.

In Medina, the Islamic movement assumed a new shape—that of a community organized on political lines under the leadership of a single chief. Whereas in Mecca Muhammad and his followers had formed a new religious sect, in Medina they forged a polity. From this point on, to be a Muslim meant at once to adhere to a faith or religion *and* to be a member of a political community. The dual nature of Islam was thus established early, and is expressed in the saying, "*al-Islam din wadawla*," meaning "Islam is at once a religion and a state." As Talal Asad, among others, has noted, Islam has elaborated a tradition and discourse different from those of Europe, where secularism, both as an ideology and practice, evolved. In the Islamic tradition, the moral and political orders are intertwined and divinely rooted.[6] In fact, one prominent scholar, the late Ernest Gellner, has written to the effect that Islam is impervious to secularization for just these reasons (1994, p. 14). In his view, Islamic institutions have no difficulty in accommodation with new forms of technology, communication, and production.[7]

Muhammad's first act was to regulate Medina's political life by drawing up an agreement in which the emigrants who came with him and the eight groups already in the town who accepted his teachings were defined as Muslims. These groups were all conceived as being coequal, their rights and duties were listed, and they were pledged to mutual defense. The pact outlawed bloodshed among Muslims and specified the status of the neighboring Jewish tribes in the area, who as non-Muslims were excluded from the *umma*. What emerges from this remarkable document is the image of a new confederation of unrelated groups, all primarily united in their common allegiance to Islam, with Muhammad acknowledged as their prophet and leader. This new polity, based on ties of religion rather than kinship, formed the nucleus of what later became the earliest state in Arabia. We should not, of course, lose sight of the fact that however novel this polity and its ideology was, it had of necessity links to earlier traditions. Obviously, one is with the tribal organization of early followers, but other links are most vividly evidenced in the continuity with Jewish and Old Testament prophecy and rules. For the Muslim, nevertheless, the stress is on the absolute nature of the break with preceding eras, represented as "*al Jahiliyya*" or "Age of Ignorance." The metaphor of *jahiliyya*, meaning ignorance, confusion, and darkness, has over the centuries been repeatedly invoked to inveigh against perceived lapses and threats to the community and it features in current debates on "moral decay" and "social deviance."

Once established in Medina, Muhammad turned once more to winning Mecca over to his cause. Mecca was the undisputed trading and political center of western Arabia, and its capitulation would greatly enhance the status of

---

[6] Talal Asad (1993); see also Charles Lindholm (1996) for an insightful discussion of this issue.

[7] For a contrary viewpoint, see İlkay Savaş (1997, pp. 9–16) and Saad Eddin Ibrahim (1997, pp. 33–44). We return to this subject in Chapter 11.

Islam as well as guarantee its survival. It took seven years of a skillful combination of military and economic pressures before the Prophet forced Mecca to capitulate. The armed struggle began as the emigrants to Medina started to finance their own trade caravans, which immediately brought them into conflict with the Quraish. In 624, over 300 Muslims led by Muhammad ambushed a large Meccan caravan coming back from Syria. The ensuing battle, the Battle of Badr, marked the first military operation by the Muslims. It signaled the transformation of the Muslim converts into a potent military force, and confirmed the political status of the new religious community.

The Battle of Badr was followed by a number of skirmishes and engagements with the forces of the Quraish. The consistent military success of the Muslims enhanced their reputation among the tribes of Arabia, whose delegations converged on Medina to offer their allegiance to Muhammad and to share in the growing wealth and influence of the Muslim community. By 630, Muhammad had become the de facto master of most of Arabia, and he was able to enter Mecca with 10,000 of his men. He proceeded to destroy all the idols at the sanctuary save for the black stone, the Ka'ba, which he incorporated into the pilgrimage ritual that makes Mecca the most important of the holy cities of Islam.

Muhammad devoted the remaining two years of his life to consolidating the community. It was a period of intense political activity, as he tried to extend his influence further in Arabia while mediating disputes and rivalries among his followers. He must have succeeded, however, in imparting to his followers his own religious fervor and moral commitment, because following his death, in 632, his closest companions quickly became the center of a committed movement that carried his message beyond the frontiers of Arabia and promoted Islam to one of the world's great religions. The *umma* that Muhammad created is today a global phenomenon truly viewed by its adherents as a universal community. A contemporary scholar of nationalism, Benedict Anderson, describes the modern notion of "nation" as an imagined community. Imagined not because it is not real but because its members feel as though they are intimately linked and interdependent, just as they would be in a real community based on face-to-face relationships. This sentiment is created by the manipulation of myths, history, symbols, education, and of course, the media. Islam is in effect a "transnational community" in much the same sense; its adherents have a sense of shared mutual responsibility that goes beyond mere ideology.

THE REALM OF ISLAM AFTER MUHAMMAD

Muhammad died without naming a successor. His closest associates met in council and decided, following tribal custom, to choose one among them to be his deputy, or *khalifa* (caliph). The majority (now referred to as Sunni) chose Abu Bakr, an old and trusted companion of the Prophet and one of his first converts.

But a minority, supporting 'Ali, Muhammad's first cousin and son-in-law, insisted that the leadership of the community must remain within Muhammad's family. This group became known as *shi'at* 'Ali, or the partisans of 'Ali. The episode heralded the beginning of disunity and factionalism that came to plague Islam and only a few years later precipitated its first civil war.

The schism also reflects a fundamental tension between two competing principles of political legitimacy in Islam. On the one hand, legitimacy is believed to reside in the will of the community; on the other, it is seen as inherent in rights of descent. In time the minority group of the Shi'a, as they came to be known, evolved into the major schismatic division within Islam (discussed in Chapter 3).

Abu Bakr's first challenge as caliph was to deal with the wave of apostasy that followed the death of the Prophet. Some of the Arab tribes felt that their allegiance to Islam ended with Muhammad's death, and they reneged on their pledges and ceased to observe rituals or to pay taxes. There is also evidence to suggest that following Muhammad's death, a number of so-called false prophets appeared in Arabia claiming the right to lead the Muslim community. The best known was Musaylima, who with an army of about 40,000 men succeeded in defeating the orthodox Muslim armies on a number of occasions before being himself finally defeated.

Abu Bakr was succeeded in 634 by the second caliph, Omar, who presided over the successful expeditions that took the Muslim armies beyond the Arabian frontiers and into battle with Persian and Byzantine armies. Omar was an extremely able administrator, and is generally credited with the formation of the system of government that became a model for later Islamic dynasties. Once a Byzantine or a Persian province was conquered, Arab military commanders took over existing governmental institutions, which were kept relatively intact. New cities were founded at some distance from existing population centers to serve as garrisons. This was done in order to consolidate Arab influence in the newly conquered lands, a problem because the Muslim rulers and armies initially were a small minority.

The new Arab state appropriated Byzantine and Persian crown lands and the property of important enemy leaders, while explicitly recognizing the property and personal rights of most non-Muslim subjects. In so doing they quickly obtained the acquiescence, if not the active support, of the populace for their new rule. These non-Muslims were, however, required to pay special taxes. This payment evolved into a system of differential taxation for Muslims and non-Muslims that persisted until quite recently in some countries. Thus, although the Muslim state recognized the rights of non-Muslims (*dhimmis*), the system of taxation greatly encouraged conversion, which proceeded rapidly in most of the conquered areas. One early question that had to be resolved was that of the status of converts to Islam following the conquests. Were they to be recognized as obtaining equal status with the original warriors or not? While the universalistic tendency prevailed, the distinction between the original conquerors' followers and subsequent converts is used today in Iraq to justify continued Sunni domination.

Omar was assassinated in 644, and a council he appointed chose an unlikely successor, 'Uthman, a member of the Quraish ruling oligarchy. 'Uthman, a man of pious reputation, is recognized today by Muslim historians as responsible for reestablishing the influence of the Meccan aristocracy. He regularly placed his relatives in positions of power and ignored the resentment that resulted within the Muslim community at large. 'Uthman was murdered in 656 and was immediately succeeded by 'Ali, the Prophet's first cousin and son-in-law. 'Ali's reign as the fourth caliph marks the end of the caliphate as the expression of consensual leadership of the *umma*; he is, in fact, the last caliph recognized by most Muslims as justly elected. His three-year rule (656–659) was marked by intercommunal dissension and tribal and civil war. One important consequence of this conflict and 'Ali's ultimate defeat was that the caliphate became dynastic and political power moved out of Arabia.

Mu'awiya, a nephew of 'Uthman and a longtime political opponent of 'Ali, became the first Muslim ruler to found a dynasty: the Ummayads. By 661, two years after the military defeat of 'Ali, the center of power shifted from Medina to Damascus, which became the new capital of the Ummayad Empire, the first successor state to the early caliphate. With this shift, Islam ceased to be a purely Arab phenomenon limited to the peninsula; it established itself in Damascus at the heart of the Mediterranean world, becoming a successor to the classical Roman empires of the West and East. The religion founded by Muhammad in a remote corner of the Middle East had now become the guiding principle and raison d'être of a vast, ethnically heterogeneous and urban-dominated empire. Greatly diminished and practically limited to the city of Constantinople and its immediate environs, the Byzantine Empire managed to linger on until its final defeat by the Muslim Ottomans in 1453.

We have dwelt on Muhammad's biography and the historical events following his death because these particulars form the basis for contemporary sectarian divisions in Islam, a topic we take up shortly. Moreover these events of early Islam, differently interpreted, are continually invoked to explain and legitimize behavior. In Iraq, for example, the term *shu'ubiyya* has been used by the ruling regime to cast doubt on the loyalty of the Shi'ite Iraqis toward the Arab Sunni-dominated state. The term *shu'ubiyya* dates back to the eighth century, when groups of Persian converts to Islam who had become influential at the court in Baghdad demanded equal rights and the same status as the more privileged Arab groups in the Muslim Empire (Jawad, 1997).

In the same vein, the late Shi'ite leader Ayatollah Khomeini of Iran referred to his opponent, the late Shah of Iran, as the "Yazid" of his day, a most powerful Shi'a idiom for expressing tyranny and deceit. The caliph Yazid was the Ummayad ruler charged by the Shi'a with having ordered the murder of Hussein, son of 'Ali and perhaps the most revered martyr of the Shi'a sect. Pageants and passion plays, as well as many of the basic rituals of Islam, including pilgrimages, tend to reproduce these early historical events, giving them great symbolic importance to the believer as part of the living tradition of Islam.

Against the backdrop of Muhammad's life history and the political developments thereafter, we can now turn to some of the major beliefs and rituals that distinguish Islam.

ISLAM AS FAITH

The word *Islam* means "submission," that is, the submission of the self to the will of God; it was adopted by Muhammad himself to refer to the distinctive faith he preached, and it appears repeatedly in the Quran. A believer in that faith is a Muslim. Needless to say, the ideological system that was initially laid down by Muhammad and later interpreted and elaborated by Muslim theologians is too vast and complex to treat in this summary presentation. What follows, therefore, is simply a sketch of the basic principles of Islamic religion, particularly those that distinguish it from the other two monotheistic religions of the area, Christianity and Judaism. At the same time, it must be remembered that Islam draws upon a common Semitic tradition that had earlier produced and nurtured these two predecessors.

Islam has as its central tenet the Oneness of God, *al-Tawhid:*

Say . . . He is God, One,
God, the Everlasting Refuge,
Who has not begotten, and has not been begotten,
And equal to Him is not anyone.
(Sura 112, Quran)

Over and over the Quran preaches strict monotheism; in fact, the worst sin in Islam is to associate other deities or partners with God. God is conceived as being eternal, omnipresent, and inscrutable; however, this omnipotence is believed to be tempered with justice and compassion. The two basic and most frequent attributes of God in the Quran are the Merciful, *al-Rahman,* and the Compassionate, *al-Raheem.*

While espousing a strict monotheism, Islamic scriptures also acknowledge the presence of angels; these are pure, sexless beings who dwell in Heaven and who sometimes act as God's messengers transmitting the Divine Message to humans. The devil, *al-Sheitan,* is believed to have been an angel who was banished from heaven for refusing to obey God's commands. Ranking below the angels and separating them from humanity are a group of male and female spirits, *jinn,* who were created by God from "smokeless fire." These inhabitants of deserts and dark lonely places are mischievous creatures who delight in causing trouble; various charms are employed to ward them off.

Muslims believe that God makes his will known to humans through the agency of the prophets who have revealed his commands. He gave the Jews the Torah, the Christians the Gospels, and Muhammad the Quran. The first of the prophets was Abraham and the last Muhammad, one of whose titles is "the Seal of the Prophets." Muslims consider Muhammad to be the Messenger and Prophet of God and the most perfect of all people, but they do not attribute any divinity to him. However, some mystics consider the Prophet to be saintlike and practically divine, a line of reasoning generally more pronounced among the Shi'a.

Another basic belief is in the Day of Judgment, *yawm al-qiyama,* when God will appear on his throne to judge the deeds of humanity. The Quran reminds the faithful that "those who believe and who do good works and establish worship and pay the poor their due, their reward is with their Lord and there shall be no fear come upon them, neither shall they grieve." These beliefs enjoin a number of specific duties or obligations that are incumbent upon all adherents.

DUTIES AND RITUAL IN ISLAM

Islam tends to classify most human activities into two categories: those that are permissible or "lawful," *halal,* and those that are forbidden, *harām.* In a general sense this contrast can be likened to the distinction between acts that contribute to a state of spiritual grace or purity as opposed to those that pollute or taint. The context of the act is all important in determining whether it is *halal* or *harām.* For example, an animal slaughtered in accordance with certain prescriptions is considered *halal* and fit for consumption; if not, it is *harām* and should not be eaten by a believer. For the practicing Muslim, all actions should be performed in obedience to God's law as revealed to his Prophet Muhammad. This makes it almost meaningless to distinguish between the moral and legal aspects of an action; a sin is at once a crime.

Although it is recognized that no believer can completely achieve the full demands of the code of *halal* in behavior, among Muslims, dress, the manner in which food is prepared and presented, attention to such details of physical appearance as beards, nails, and so on—all carry considerable symbolic importance. Minimally, they announce the membership of individuals in the Islamic community; their more careful observance signifies a deeper commitment. In this sense even daily and mundane activities take on the significance of ritual.

The Five Pillars of Islam

The most important duties of a believer are the following acts, which together express the Muslim creed. They are often referred to as the Five Pillars of Islam (*arkan*):

The **shahada,** *or profession of faith.*   As mentioned earlier, the recitation of the simple formula "I profess that there is no god but God; Muhammad is his messenger" constitutes the formal conversion of the reciter to Islam. The phrase usually constitutes the first words spoken into the ears of a newborn baby and should be the last on the lips of the dying.

The simplicity of the *shahada* makes conversion an easy matter, a process that readily accommodates great variations in local custom and heritage. Dogma and catechism are secondary, and in many areas of the world new converts to Islam appear to know little about the faith beyond these few words. Once a convert to Islam, however, it becomes incumbent on the individual to learn its precepts and rituals; instruction thus usually follows rather than precedes the adoption of the faith.

The **salat,** *or prayer.*   The *salat* is enjoined on the Muslim five times a day: at dawn, midday, midafternoon, sunset, and nightfall. Worshipers face the direction of Mecca and go through the prescribed positions of the prayers, which they may perform anywhere after undergoing ritual ablutions. The Quran mentions two morning and two evening prayers; the noon one was added later by jurists in emulation of the practice of the Prophet. Muslims are also encouraged to attend the Friday communal prayers, which take place at midday. "O you who believe! When the call is proclaimed for *salat al jumm'a* (Friday prayer), come to the remembrance of Allah and leave off business (and every other thing). That is better if you did but know" (Quran 62:9).

Many Muslims do not observe the obligatory daily prayers. However, once an adult undertakes to pray daily, it is considered derelict for him or her to stop. Prayers should be offered wherever one finds oneself at the appropriate hours. Thus, intercity buses and trucks may stop by the roadside and passengers may get out to pray, with men and women in separate clusters. Farmers halt their plowing to pray in the fields. The ostentatiously pious may carry a

Interior view of a seventh-century mosque in Cairo, Egypt.

prayer rug, but most simply place a clean handkerchief on the ground before them to which they touch their foreheads during the prayers. A number of men may pray together, but they do not coordinate their prayers unless they are in sufficient numbers to form a congregation with a prayer leader. The formal prayer, although ritually fixed, does not preclude the individual from offering personal beseechments or prayers of thanksgiving.

The main communal prayers take place at the mosque at midday on Friday. The men of a congregation stand in straight lines facing a semicircular recess called the *mihrab*, which indicates the direction of Mecca. The *imam*, or prayer leader, stands in front with his back to the group. At the time of Muhammad, women attended the Friday prayers but stood behind the men; later, they prayed behind a screen. Today, women do not generally participate in the public prayers.

Many men who do not pray daily nevertheless may regularly attend the Friday mosque services. In many small towns or villages not to attend would be to withdraw from the public life of the community. Although the mosque and its congregation are thought by many to exemplify the unity of Islam and equality before God, in practice the congregations of urban mosques, and sometimes even those of small towns and villages, reflect social and economic divisions within the society. In heterogeneous communities, members of different ethnic groups, tribes, and even occupations may well have their own mosques. Furthermore, within any one congregation, an implicit social hierarchy is expressed because men of prominence and power tend to pray in the front rows along with the learned of the community.

The Friday prayers are significant for other reasons. Following the prayers, the leading religious functionary or scholar present usually delivers a sermon, *khutba,* which frequently goes beyond simple moral exhortation. The sermon is likely to deal with those topical issues that affect the community. At times, sermons may also serve as the vehicles for political announcements; they may even call for insurrection against rulers perceived to be unjust. This has occurred frequently in history, most recently and notably in Iran and in Egypt.

The zakat *and the* sadaqat, *or almsgiving.*   The Quran asks believers to give alms as an expression of piety and as an aid to salvation. The *zakat* began as a voluntary act of piety and sharing within the small Muslim community. After the emigration to Medina, it became obligatory, a tax levied on all Muslims that was regularly collected by appointed agents and administered by the state. Today, in most Muslim countries, the *zakat* has again become voluntary.

Almsgiving is an important means by which even those who do not closely adhere to other Islamic observances emphasize their identification with the community. In most communities, the *zakat* is calculated at the rate of 2.5 percent of a believer's annual net worth. In addition to the *zakat*, the Quran and the Traditions of the Prophet also encourage the believer to give the *sadaqat*, a voluntary charitable contribution to help the community in building hospitals, schools, and orphanages. Today, *zakat* contributions, where collected by governments, are regularly channeled to Islamic relief agencies, both state-sponsored, as in the case of the International Islamic Relief Organization headquartered in Jeddah, Saudi Arabia, and those operated by Islamist groups that provide local welfare services (see Benthall, 1998, p. 13).

The **sawm**, *or fasting.* Muslims are enjoined to fast during Ramadan, the month in which the Quran was first revealed to Muhammad; Ramadan is the ninth month of the Muslim lunar calendar. In the years when Ramadan falls in summer, its observance may entail a great deal of strain and self-discipline, especially in very hot regions like the Gulf area and Arabia. Even though some individual Muslims may choose not to fast, there exists strong public sentiment, even overt pressure, to observe Ramadan. The strength of this sentiment to conform publicly varies from one community to the other and from one country to the next. In Turkey, restaurants remain open throughout Ramadan, and many Turks continue to eat, drink, and smoke in public without fear of censure; in the Gulf states, all restaurants are closed.

The fast is observed from dawn until sunset, during which time one may not eat or drink. Everyone is enjoined to observe the fast except children under the age of puberty. Pregnant women, the sick, military personnel on active duty, and those on a journey are exempt, but they should make up the missed days later. Those fasting, however, are free to eat anytime after sunset, and Ramadan nights usually turn into happy social occasions, with much visiting and exchanges of hospitality. The end of the Ramadan fast is celebrated by a feast, *'id al-fitr*, which lasts for three days. People celebrate by buying new clothes, mutual entertaining, and visiting their dead at the cemeteries.

Ramadan is also a time for reaffirmation of the faith; readings from the Quran and religious sermons are broadcast daily over radio and television, and people are exhorted to pray and to renew their faith. The shared experience of community members in observing the discipline of the fast further enhances the feeling of solidarity. Ramadan, as a time of renewal of faith and as a uniquely Muslim celebration, acquires a special significance in countries under secular or non-Muslim rule. Under such circumstances, fasting becomes an expression of cultural pride and, implicitly, a statement of opposition to foreign rule. When unpopular colonial or native secularist regimes are in power, Ramadan is similarly of potential political significance, as it proclaims at once Islamic unity and strength of belief, which could serve as vehicles for political opposition.

The **hajj**, *or the pilgrimage to Mecca.* A pilgrimage to Mecca is required of every adult Muslim once in his or her lifetime, provided the person is capable of doing so. It takes place during the first half of the twelfth lunar month, when pilgrims from all over the world converge on Mecca to join in the complex ritual that includes circumambulating the Ka'ba seven times. Women undertake the pilgrimage provided they can be accompanied by their husbands or some other

View of the Ka'ba surrounded by pilgrims during the annual *hajj*.

adult male who could serve as their protector. Under certain conditions, individuals may delegate a substitute to undertake the *hajj* for them.

In the past, great caravans would form in Egypt, Syria, and Iraq for the difficult desert passage to Mecca.[8] Way stations stocked with food were placed along the routes, but the trip was often hazardous anyway. Today most pilgrims arrive by jet, stay in clean accommodations, and benefit from the modern facilities provided by the Saudi government, which is responsible for handling over a million pilgrims a year.

Those who would be pilgrims temporarily withdraw from their own society and routine activities; they embark on a journey of the spirit as much as a trip abroad. Even before leaving home, they undergo purification and consecration as they suspend their everyday roles and acquire the special status of a departing pilgrim. The ceremonies that begin the *hajj* are performed in a personal state of ritual purity achieved by the observance of certain taboos and restraints, including sexual abstinence. The pilgrims wash ritually, are shaved, and have their beards trimmed and nails cut. Each one then puts on a special robe that consists of two seamless white sheets, known as the *ihram*. This simple

[8] For a fascinating personal account of a pilgrimage undertaken in the mid-nineteenth century by the famous British explorer-scholar Richard Burton, see his *Personal Narrative of a Pilgrimage to al-Madinah and Meccah* (New York: Dover, 1964).

garb is considered by Muslims today to exemplify the unity of Islam and the equality of all believers before God.

Upon entering Mecca, the pilgrims may take local guides who lead them through the ritual of the pilgrimage and otherwise assist them, particularly when the pilgrims know no Arabic. The first duty consists of circumambulating the shrine; later, following attendance at instructional sermons in the Great Mosque, pilgrims leave Mecca for Mount 'Arafa, where Muhammad received his prophecy. The next several days are filled with prescribed ceremonies, sermons, and prayers that recapitulate events in Muhammad's life.

The pilgrimage ritual culminates on the tenth day of the month, when the pilgrim sacrifices an animal (usually a sheep or a goat) that he or she had consecrated. This ceremony of the sacrifice is reenacted on the same day throughout the Muslim world as the head of each family sacrifices an animal. The feast is known in the Middle East as *qurban bayram, 'id al-kabir,* or *'id al-adha,* the Feast of Sacrifice. All who can afford an animal, including women who own property in their own name, are expected to make the sacrifice. Part of the meat is consumed in family feasting, but some is given to the poor of the community. In this manner, even those who are not in the most sacred site of Islam participate in this major ritual associated with the annual *hajj.* Muslims may also perform the pilgrimage out of cycle, if their circumstances permit it. This form of *hajj* is referred to as the *'umra.*

Wall drawings depicting the pilgrimage to Mecca adorn a house in an Egyptian village.

The *hajj* has always had practical economic significance, as did its pre-Islamic predecessor, which was closely associated with trade. Traditionally, many pilgrims brought with them goods for trade, and a fair-like atmosphere attended the city of Mecca. Today, although few bring trade goods, many avail themselves of the numerous shops that sell all manner of imported luxury goods. More important, however, is the fact that the pilgrimage has always served to bring individual Muslims in touch with the fountainhead of their religion and to expose them to the theologians and savants who live and teach in Mecca. Inspired by the *hajj* experience, many pilgrims from Africa and Asia as well as the Middle East have launched political careers as Islamic reformists.

Having fulfilled the required ritual in Mecca and its environs, the pilgrim returns home bearing a new, respected title, *hajj* or *hajji* (feminine: *hajiyya*). In Egypt, and elsewhere, a village *hajji* might well hire a painter to depict in colorful pictures on the white wall of his house the various places he visited, his mode of travel, and, above all, the Great Mosque and the Ka'ba. For some time after the pilgrimage, the *hajji's* house becomes the focal point of much visiting by friends and neighbors, all seeking to share in the *baraka*, or blessing, of his experience. Pilgrims bring back prayer beads, perfumed oils, and mementos from the sacred city that they give out to visitors, especially those who had helped them prepare for the journey. The average *hajji*, while enjoying a special status, soon returns to normal pursuits. For some, however, undertaking the *hajj* gives special impetus to already established careers in public life, whether in religious or political arenas.

A lesser pilgrimage than the one to Mecca is to Jerusalem, site of the famous shrine-mosque, the Dome of the Rock. The mosque was initially built by the caliph Omar to consecrate the spot from which it is believed that Muhammad took off on a nocturnal journey to Heaven. This legend is well known throughout the Islamic world and is the subject of poetry and art. One version has it that one night the Prophet was carried from Mecca to Jerusalem on a white-winged horse with a human face. In Jerusalem he saw Abraham, Moses, and Jesus at prayer together. Later he ascended the different heavens until he reached the seventh one, after which the horse took him back to Mecca. Sunni Muslims consider the Dome of the Rock to be their second holiest area after the Ka'ba.

Food

As does Judaism, Islam imposes a number of dietary rules and taboos; among foods considered taboo are pork, blood, and all alcoholic beverages. Forbidden also is the flesh of dead animals; only animals that have been ritually slaughtered by having their throats cut are considered fit for consumption.

The handling and serving of food take on ritual significance in many circumstances. The believer is enjoined, for example, to treat bread, water, and salt with special respect and to avoid using the left hand for passing food or drawing from a common cooking pot or serving bowl; the left hand is associated with the performance of ablutions and unclean acts. Meals begin and end with words of praise to God, and the manner in which food is publicly offered, shared, and consumed has a significance that is more than simple etiquette.

Circumcision

Another ritual act that is not prescribed or even mentioned directly in the Quran but that is treated as a basic requirement of the faith is circumcision of males before puberty. This practice, which is universal among Muslims, is legitimized by the Quranic verse that recommends adherence to the practices of Abraham: "Follow, then, the community of Abraham, a man of pure faith, who was not a polytheist" (Quran 3:95). Although the Quran does not mention any specific practice, Abraham's account of his covenant with the Lord and the ritual of male circumcision are acknowledged and accepted by all Muslims. This rite is carried out with as much public celebration and feasting as the family can afford.

Circumcision, usually done between the ages of four and seven (and now, increasingly, a few days following birth), constitutes a rite of passage; it marks the transition of the boy from the private domain of the household to the public one of the community. Simultaneously, it signals the separation of the young boy from his mother and his joining the world of the males. At this point he is likely to begin his formal religious education and is increasingly expected to identify with and observe the male codes of behavior.

Death

Duties to the dead are elaborate and closely prescribed by religious law and custom. Although practices vary from one locale to another, certain rites are nearly universal. The body is washed by members of the same sex, shrouded in a single cloth, and interred by nightfall, if possible, and never later than the second day after death . Graves are dug so that the body can lie on its side facing Mecca, and care is taken that earth does not fall directly on the face of the individual. There is general agreement that the grave should be simple, and if adorned by a headstone or other marker, the ground immediately above the corpse should be left unobstructed. Under no circumstances are the dead brought inside a mosque, although the body may be carried in a coffin into a mosque courtyard for a final prayer. A frequent sight alongside an inner wall of a mosque courtyard is a wooden litter that serves to transport the dead to the graveyard.

We could elaborate further on belief and ritual practice, but what we hope has emerged from our brief discussion of Islamic Middle Eastern society is a view in which Islam the religion, its ritual, and its ceremony are seen to be enmeshed in the daily activities of the individual. The way one holds one's hands while washing, styles of dress and hair, the manner of presenting food, the prayers on the lips of a traveler at the onset of a journey—all are acts that weave Islam into the living culture of the people.

SOURCES OF ISLAMIC LAW: SHARI'A

Islam is often portrayed by its own scholar-jurists and by Western-trained orientalists as a severely formal, even rigid legal tradition. Although Islam is the source of law and as such has generated a scholarly tradition emphasizing its jural relevance to virtually any situation, it is also much broader and richer. It is the basis for a moral order. It answers the questions of what constitutes right and wrong, a moral person, a "good Muslim." Like all scriptural religions with codified ritual, it fundamentally distinguishes between the observant believer and the moral person whose life is informed by the ethical structure of Islam. We now turn to a consideration of the sources of this system of beliefs, ritual, and duties that regulate a Muslim's relation to God and to fellow humans.

There are basically two sources: the Quran and the Hadith, the Traditions of the Prophet. For Muslims, the Quran is the word of God; the term *Quran* means "recitation" and underscores the belief that it was revealed verbatim to Muhammad, who simply "recited" God's words: "The Koran (Quran) is the record of those formal utterances and discourses which Muhammad and his followers accepted as directly inspired. Muslim orthodoxy therefore regards them as the literal Word of God mediated through the Angel Gabriel" (Gibb, 1958, p. 36).

The Quran is believed to be a direct transcript of a tablet divinely inscribed and preserved in Heaven. Thus, as the literal word of God, the Quran may not be translated into any tongue other than Arabic and still retain the same validity.[9] This explains the phenomenon observed in non-Arab Muslim countries, where some worshipers learn the Quran phonetically by heart and recite it without necessarily understanding the meaning of the words they utter. Considered holy and miraculous, the Quran is used by many as a talisman to ward off the evil eye. Verses from it are sealed in metal or leather containers and carried on the body to ward off evil and sickness and to ensure health and good luck.

Most of the Quran was committed to memory or written down on pieces of parchment or bone during Muhammad's lifetime. The text was collected in its entirety by the first caliph, Abu Bakr, but it was not until the reign of the third caliph, 'Uthman, that a committee authorized a final version of the Quran. This standardized version is the only one that exists today, all others having been destroyed.

---

[9] There are few who would call themselves Muslim but not accept the standard version of the Quran. Some Alevi and Alawi (see Chapter 3) assert that the Quran merely reflects the powers that were in place following the death of Muhammad and that numerous passages that should have referred to 'Ali and the Prophet's family were expurgated in the time of the caliph 'Uthman. See Farouk Bilici (1998, pp. 54, 62). This view is considered heretical by both Sunni and Shi'a.

The chapters of the Quran, known as *suras,* are arranged according to length by descending order, with the exception of the *fatiha,* which comes first. In all, there are 114 suras, the first half of which tend to be inspirational and exhortative in content and poetic in style; the latter half are more concerned with legislative and prescriptive matters. The Quran is written in beautiful, poetic, rhymed prose that, when recited publicly, is intoned slowly in a melodic chant that is considered aesthetically pleasing to the listener. Special training is given in the art of Quranic recitation.

In addition to the Quran, Muslims are guided by the example of the life of Muhammad. The sayings and deeds of the Prophet form a system of social and legal usages collectively referred to as the Sunna of Muhammad (course of conduct or path). The Sunna is preserved in the form of short stories and anecdotes all dealing with what Muhammad said and did at various times. These anecdotes form an extensive but uncodified literature in Islam known as the Hadith, sayings or Traditions.

The Quran and the Hadith are the major sources of the Islamic legal system known as Shari'a, or Divine Law. "As in other Semitic religions, law is thought of not as a product of human intelligence and adaptation to changing social needs and ideals, but of divine inspiration and immutable" (Gibb, 1958, p. 73). But because neither the Quran nor the Traditions provided a comprehensive and unified legal system, it was left for Muslim theologian-jurists, *'ulama,* to interpret and elaborate the relevant texts and to construct the body of law, the Shari'a.[10]

The Shari'a joins faith and practice as a comprehensive code establishing Islam as a way of life. As Nathan Brown notes, the Shari'a is central to Islam in the minds of most Muslims, and its importance as a social and legal point of reference is, in fact, increasing, not decreasing, although the subject of contention and dispute (1997, p. 360). The Shari'a is not simply a finite legal code in the Western jural sense but is a set of institutional processes and practices that potentially govern all aspects of a believer's life. While there are standard texts and treatises, Shari'a law is not codified and not derived from state legislated texts. Shari'a courts were historically without lawyers and were "essentially for private disputes between and among parties" (Brown, 1997, p. 363). Even murder was not a crime against the state.

Although the interpretation and application of the Shari'a have been transformed in every country in the Middle East in recent years, the debate continues as to the proper balance between state-legislated law and the Shari'a. The consensus, according to Brown, is that while there is a need for state-instituted legislation, such legislation should be within the larger boundaries of the Shari'a. The very centrality of the Shari'a to an Islamic moral and social order has challenged every secular political movement in the Middle East. It has

---

[10] For two recent books on Islamic law, see R. Gleave and E. Kermeli (1997) and Rodolphe de Seife (1995).

raised problems for those who would legislate without reference to it; this is particularly true in the area of personal status or laws affecting marriage, divorce, and inheritance. But, with the exclusion of the laws of personal status, reform in every country in varying degrees and on differing schedules has led to the introduction of civil and criminal laws based on European models. Only the government of Turkey has completely repudiated the Shari'a as a source of legal guidance, and, indeed, a public appeal to the Shari'a is a criminal offense.

At the beginning of Islamic rule, the Shari'a developed in a period of lively debate and discussion about the sources of law that would govern the rapidly expanding and heterogeneous Muslim community. The debates focused on the relative weight to be given to experience, rationality, and local custom. In time, four different schools of law (*madhabs*) crystallized within the dominant division of Islam known as Sunni; each of these schools respects the "orthodoxy" of the other. The Shi'a, the other major division in Islam, has its own interpretations.

The four Sunni schools, or *madhabs,* do not constitute separate sects, as they are in agreement on matters of doctrine and creed. Each was named after its jurist-founder and predominates in a different region. The Hanafi is found primarily in areas formerly governed by the Ottomans: Turkey, Iraq, Syria, Lebanon, and Lower Egypt, as well as parts of Central Asia and India. The Maliki predominates in northern and western Africa, Upper Egypt, and the Sudan. The Shafi'i is represented in parts of Syria, Iraq, and Turkey, but especially in Indonesia. The Hanbali, which predominates in Arabia, is considered the most conservative in that it allows little scope for the use of "reason" or local custom.

Although purporting to be the universal basis for law, the Shari'a in practice today is evident primarily in matters pertaining to personal status. These are cases that we might think of as falling within the jurisdiction of family and probate courts. Only Turkey, as we have said, has altogether rejected the Shari'a as a basis for national legal codes. Even there, though, there is a movement instigated by the religiously motivated far right for the return of a Shari'a-guided court system. Elsewhere, Shari'a-based laws serve to adjudicate matters of marriage, divorce, child custody, inheritance, adoption, and public decorum. In most countries, commercial and criminal legislation tacitly ignores the Shari'a, and such codes are derived from European sources. Two major exceptions are Iran and Saudi Arabia, where, in principle at least, the Shari'a is adhered to in both civil and criminal matters. Today, one important controversy concerning the Shari'a throughout the Middle East is its relationship to the rapidly changing relative status of the sexes and to changing patterns of family life, topics we take up in later chapters.

RELIGIOUS LEADERSHIP: THE *'ULAMA*

Our cursory discussion of the Shari'a and its central place in Islam might suggest that the ideal Muslim state or society would be a theocracy. This, however, would be an inaccurate conclusion and one not supported by history. One paradox of Sunni Islam is that its great emphasis on the all-pervasive scope of the Shari'a disavows any fundamental distinction between religious and nonreligious domains. What a Christian might consider secular and religious domains of life are indistinguishable in Islamic thought; from this perspective, the terms *secular* and *theocratic* become meaningless. In fact, if one were to use them to describe the ideal Islamic society, it would have to be as a *secular theocracy*. For even though all legitimate power belongs to God, since Muhammad's death God has had no earthly spokesperson, nor is he served by a special caste or priesthood. In principle, each Muslim is equally capable of communicating with God without any mediation, and each may aspire to any position within the community. The Shi'a situation is rather different, and we take it up in the following chapter.

For Sunni Middle Eastern society, the many distinctions of religious rank, learning, and even institutional authority do not form one unified hierarchy, let alone a church. The most exalted religious office, for example, the Sheikh al-Azhar in Cairo, head of the most prestigious mosque-university of Sunni Islam, has no jural authority over the humblest village sheikh. In the absence of a church, the definition of "orthodoxy" becomes problematic. For example, senior *'ulama* can issue *fatwas*, or "responses," to specific questions that may involve legal ambiguity. Varied and often contradictory *fatwas* have been issued in recent years on such topics as abortion, birth control, female circumcision, suspected blasphemy, and even the appropriateness of state policies, such as the *fatwa* issued by the Sheikh al-Azhar to the effect that President Anwar Sadat's visit to the Israeli Knesset in 1977 did not violate the Shari'a. In general, the weight of the *fatwa* is directly proportionate to the authority and status of the issuer. A highly controversial *fatwa* was issued in 1989 by the late Iranian Shi'a Ayatollah Khomeini, declaring the Indian Muslim author Salman Rushdie, a British citizen, to be a blasphemer for his book *Satanic Verses*.

This situation is complicated by the fact that there is no final arbiter of the Shari'a. This results in another paradox. While viewed as eternal and fixed, the Shari'a is also constantly changing. Within this contradiction lies fertile ground for the development of reformist ideologies, mystical movements, and schismatic rebellions, all of which have been part of Islamic history.

Given the absence of church and priesthood, how is religious life structured within the society? Who instructs the young, interprets the Shari'a, and leads the congregation in prayer? And how does one account for the obvious disparities in rank and influence among different religious personages?

Until quite recently, as in medieval Europe, most formal teaching was in a religious context. Learned individuals, the *'ulama*, were by definition religious scholars whether they were concerned with the Quran and its exegesis or with astronomy or medicine. They could be self-taught or the student-disciples of one or another well-established scholar. With time, the *'ulama* came to form a special group, with its own insignia of distinctive turbans and robes and with more or less agreed-upon ranking procedures and rules for recruitment. Status differentiation was based on a combination of factors, which included scholarly achievement, the personality of the individual, peer recognition, and general support of the local community. Particular scholars emerged as authorities in particular areas, acquired reputations, and attracted followings. The lack of a formal hierarchy is reflected in the terminology. The same term, *sheikh,* may be used for *'ulama* of all levels. This is in contrast to the Shi'a practice in which clerics are more carefully distinguished by rank.

The *'ulama* as a group trained the teachers, preachers, and bureaucrats of the society, and in some periods they themselves constituted a powerful patrician class. Their students spent variable periods of time in places of learning, *madrasas,* where they would study individually under the tutelage of a particular master. Those who were successful themselves became the future *'ulama*— theologians-cum-jurists, judges, government advisers, and even ministers. The *'ulama* were, and still are, the self-appointed guardians and executors of the Shari'a. In the past, and in some countries today, it was they who ultimately legitimized a ruler, a role that conferred on them considerable power, even if indirectly. In some countries, they were incorporated into state bureaucracies, primarily as *qadis,* judges, and school administrators.

Traditionally, the *'ulama* derived their income and sometimes considerable power from their role as administrators and beneficiaries of trusts in land and urban property (called *waqf*) set up by wealthy donors. In some areas a sizable portion of the arable land was *waqf,* and the great mosque complexes of major cities were *waqf* supported not only by the donations of the faithful but by the income derived from renting the many shops and other properties they owned in the city, as well as from their rural holdings.

The spread of European-style education and the expansion of scientific curricula in the nineteenth century presented the *'ulama* with a serious challenge to their historic monopoly on education. Today the term *'ulama* refers exclusively to those trained in the religious tradition, and recruitment to this group in most countries reflects the *'ulama*'s increasingly restricted role in modern society. The governing elite and the well-to-do almost always educate their children in Western-style schools and universities. Quranic schools today are primarily attended by the very young, who come to learn the rudiments of religion and to memorize parts of the Quran. Virtually every large village aspires to its own Quranic school supported by the community, and failing that, families get together to hire a religious teacher (*mullah, fqih,* or *hoja*) for their children. This, however, is usually in addition to secular education.

The relationship between the *'ulama* and the state, both in Sunni and Shi'a Islam, is a very complex subject and is outside the scope of our presentation. Suffice it to say here that, generally speaking, in Sunni countries the *'ulama* have tended to work closely with the ruling establishment. Under the Ottomans, for example, the sultan came to appoint or ratify major religious posts and even attempted to centralize and control religious leadership through the creation of the post of *sheikh al-Islam,* a paramount sheikh. In Iran, the Shi'a *'ulama'*s position has generally been, at least since the eighteenth century, in opposition to the state. Following the revolution of 1979, however, the *'ulama* in Iran have come to constitute a major locus of power and authority in the state.

The *'ulama* themselves are subject to constantly shifting boundaries of religious knowledge. In an era prior to popular literacy, they enjoyed a near monopoly on text-based knowledge in almost every domain. In the nineteenth century, as they attempted to counter European influences spread with printed matter for the masses, they inadvertently weakened their own control. Today, Islam and the *'ulama* confront the digital age of Islam. CD-ROMs and electronic cassettes disseminate both reformist and conservative rhetoric, and there are numerous Islamic Web sites on the Internet. The impact of these changes on the worldwide Islamic community and on Islamic religious discourse remains to be seen, but in general the masses have direct individual access now to textual or scriptural Islam.

Our emphasis in this chapter has been on the origin and development of Islam, its basic tenets and rules. In the following chapter, we take up the doctrinal and historical bases for the important sectarian divisions, especially Shi'ism, as well as the development of mysticism in Islam and its different popular expressions today.

3

Islam as Identity, Islam as Culture

At this juncture, every country in the Middle East is witnessing serious, often strident, debates about how to reconcile Islam as culture, a set of guiding values and a source of personal identity, with existing or desired political structures and institutions. This is not a new phenomenon but continues an unresolved dilemma that began immediately after the death of Muhammad in A.D. 632 and that is, in a sense, being played out today in brutal confrontations in Algeria and Afghanistan. We also see it as shaping the ongoing struggle for power in the Islamic Republic of Iran, pitting an entrenched conservative clerical group against those seeking broader, participatory rule. In Turkey, another variant of this conflict can be seen in a struggle among a determinedly secular military establishment, Islamist political parties, and various parties of the left and right. One contested issue, whether explicit or not, is the balance between individual autonomy and group or communal responsibilities and social control. This chapter will focus primarily on the unfolding of Islam as both a nexus of values, norms, and expectations and as a source of identity.

The Prophet's vision of a community of believers united in their common faith in one God was embodied during his lifetime in the Islamic state. The unity of this polity was, however, more apparent than real, masking as it did great social and economic tensions and fundamental disagreements. In short, the early Islamic community, like any religious or ideological movement, had to accommodate existing social and political realities. The early Muslim movement had, in fact, brought together quite disparate societies from northern and southern Arabia, people pursuing different ways of life and speaking different dialects, but all seeking expression and even contending for power within the nascent Islamic state. Immediately upon Muhammad's death, the community was confronted by a number of political challenges, including the secession of some tribes who attempted to follow other, so-called "false prophets." The first caliphs, however, succeeded in keeping the community together and in forging a vigorously expanding empire. The borders of this empire soon reached the Pyrenees in the west and Afghanistan in the east. The conquest of this vast area, much greater than that conquered by Alexander, was rapidly accompanied by the conversion of its diverse peoples to Islam, a fact that must attest to the power of the new Islamic order.

Only the heartland of Byzantium in Asia Minor and its capital Constantinople withstood the forces of the early Arab armies. The great Sassanian Empire of Persia disintegrated rapidly as its armies were defeated and its capital, Ctesiphon, destroyed by 651. Perhaps it is because of the Islamic movement's great and rapid success that correspondingly powerful forces soon came to threaten it. Within a quarter of a century after Muhammad's death, dissenting political movements, using the idiom of Islam, had broken away from the main body of Muslims. Throughout subsequent Middle Eastern history, Islam as a revolutionary force has counterbalanced Islam as an established political and social order.

Islamic movements from the earliest periods have had their origin in political protests whose claims to legitimacy were always expressed in a religious idiom. This is consistent with a view that permits no theoretical distinction between religion and politics. Thus any political challenge to the state invariably assumes religious overtones, and any doctrinal disagreement can easily imply a potential political threat.

SCHISMS IN ISLAM: THE SHI'A

The single most important schismatic movement in Islam is the Shi'a, whose adherents predominate today in Iran, southern Iraq, and in parts of Turkey, Syria, and Lebanon. Until recently, in Syria and Lebanon the rural Shi'a communities constituted a poor and depressed population, dominated in feudal fashion by large landlords, including Sunni and Christian as well as Shi'a families.

As we described earlier, the Shi'a split arose from a dispute over who should succeed the Prophet after his death. A minority of Muslims championed 'Ali, the Prophet's first cousin and his son-in-law; this group, which became known as the Shi'a (that is, "partisans of 'Ali"), in effect, restricted legitimate succession to the direct line of descent from Muhammad through 'Ali and his wife Fatima, Muhammad's daughter. This position conflicted with that of the majority who believed that a successor *khalifa*, caliph, must be elected. The majority position prevailed, and Abu Bakr, an old, trusted companion of Muhammad was chosen as the first caliph and leader of the community. 'Ali did, in time, become the fourth caliph, but he was immediately opposed by an already entrenched Muslim leadership and, most importantly, by the new governor of Syria, who was a member of the powerful Ummayad clan. The ensuing civil war in which 'Ali was ultimately defeated and killed rent the Muslim community. In many respects the successful opposition to 'Ali on the part of the

Ummayads reflected the fact that the center of political power had, by now, shifted out of Arabia to Syria and Iraq. From then on, Mecca ceased to be a center of political power, a role assumed by Damascus and later Baghdad.[1]

The civil war and 'Ali's defeat had many important consequences for the Middle East. Quite apart from the emergence of Shi'ism as a separate political movement, it also affected the geographic and ethnic distribution of the population. For example, a large number of the supporters of 'Ali were Yemeni tribesmen who came to settle in the region of Kufa in southern Iraq. The Yemenis considered themselves culturally superior to the northern Arabian tribes and felt that they had been politically shunted aside by the ruling Ummayad aristocracy. They were among the first to rally to 'Ali's party, thus marking the beginning of a significant Shi'a presence in Iraq.

Another sectarian movement founded at this time was that of the Kharijites, or "seceders," who withdrew from 'Ali's camp during his war with the Ummayads. The Kharijite movement acquired considerable significance as the vehicle for local rebellions in Syria and Iraq, but its political importance declined after the eighth century. Descendants of the Kharijites are found today in Oman, Zanzibar, and parts of East and North Africa, where they are known as 'Ibadis. They represent a moderate branch of the original movement that espoused the simplicity and democracy of the original Muslim community at Medina. In Oman, the 'Ibadis constitute the ruling oligarchy, as they did in Zanzibar until the mid-1950s. Nevertheless, the Kharijites did establish a divisive precedent that has come to characterize much of Islamic dissidence. By defining those Muslims who do not espouse their beliefs as "apostates," they challenged the very definition of what constitutes an Islamic community.

Losing their challenge to the Ummayads and persecuted throughout the Islamic world, the Shi'a were soon forced to go underground. Secret but active, they began to rally dissidents with a proselytizing zeal that made them grow in number and influence. Increasingly, segments of the non-Arab populations of Iraq, Syria, and Persia joined their ranks. Some historians feel that the Shi'a movement represented a populist ethnic reaction to the exclusiveness and discrimination practiced by the conquering Arab tribes, who tended to form a privileged caste of warriors ruling over the indigenous people. Even though the latter had converted in large numbers and were, at least in principle, the equal of the Arabs, the social and political distinctions between the Arab conquerors and the converted population remained important. Quite apart from being a vehicle for political dissent, Shi'ism also allowed the perpetuation of local beliefs and practices that were contrary to Sunni formulations. Shi'ism flourished as a folk or popular cult, much as do the mystic orders and cults today, which are still often viewed as anti-establishment.

Although a Shi'a dynasty was to achieve power in Egypt during the tenth and twelfth centuries, the most significant and lasting political success of the

---

[1]For an excellent introduction to Shi'ism, see Richard Yann (1995).

Shi'a came in 1502, when Shah Ismail seized the throne of Persia and made Shi'ism the state religion. The formal attainment of power in Persia after a long period of struggle further shaped the dogma and organization of Shi'a Islam in ways quite distinct from that of Sunni Islam.

SHI'A BELIEFS: A CULTURE OF MARTYRDOM AND DISSENT

The Shi'a hold that the family of Muhammad, and specifically 'Ali and his male descendants from his marriage to Fatima, the daughter of the Prophet, possess supernatural powers and are uniquely qualified for the caliphate and the leadership of the Islamic community. Thus, the first three caliphs and all succeeding ones are viewed as usurpers, having displaced the only legitimate successor to Muhammad, namely, 'Ali, who is considered to be the first imam. Whereas to the Sunni, the term *imam* simply designates the leader of the Friday mosque prayers, to the Shi'a it has a very special meaning. In fact, for the Shi'a, belief in the imam constitutes the sixth tenet or pillar of religion, in addition to the five described in the previous chapter.

The doctrine of the imamate holds that the imam is the agent of Divine Illumination and the medium of Divine Revelation. Shi'a imams are considered to be sinless and infallible, and thus are empowered with authority to pronounce dogma. This authority, plus a body of "esoteric knowledge" that is believed to have been originally bestowed on 'Ali, have since been passed down to a select number of his male descendants. Nonetheless, the various Shi'a sects differ over the order of succession to the imamate, some championing one over another of the various descendants of 'Ali.

This doctrine, regarding 'Ali and his descendants as special beings, is in sharp contrast with the insistence of mainstream Sunni on the humanity of Muhammad, the Messenger, and his role as the last of the Prophets. It further makes of all descendants of 'Ali a caste-like group who even today enjoy a special status among the Shi'a, where they are collectively known as *sayyid*.

The sayyid (pl. sadda) tend to marry among themselves and are usually subject to special consideration in that violence should not be directed against their person or property; to do so, even inadvertently, is considered a sacrilege. Some sayyid are thought of as holy, and pious believers may give the sayyid money as a tithe. Even in Sunni communities, descendants of the Prophet's family are accorded special recognition. It should be emphasized here that the status of sayyid does not in itself confer wealth, power, or even significant social influence on the individual. In some communities, the sayyid may even form a loosely defined group of landless and socially marginal mendicants sustained by charity. Elsewhere, for example in southern Arabia until recently, the sayyid as a group constituted a wealthy, ruling oligarchy who jealously preserved their control over property and power at the same time that they perpetuated their genealogical claim to holy status.

Another distinguishing theme in Shi'ism is that of martyrdom centered on the figure of the third imam, Hussein, one of two sons of 'Ali, who succeeded to the imamate after the short-lived reign of his older brother. In 680, Imam Hussein, along with members of his family, was ambushed and massacred by Ummayad troops near the city of Karbala in southern Iraq. This tragedy, which closely followed the assassination of 'Ali by a Kharijite fanatic, gave Shi'a Islam a specifically tragic cast and a definite proclivity toward a cult of martyrdom. The devotion of the Shi'a to the tragic figure of Hussein and his descendants, many of whom also met with violent death, adds a dimension to Shi'ism not found in Sunni Islam.

The betrayal and martyrdom of Imam Hussein is dramatically enacted yearly on the tenth day, 'ashura, of the month of Muharram, with rites that portray the tragedy with much emotion and grief. These rites, known as the ta'ziyya, the mourning ritual, vary greatly among Shi'a communities and even within Iran. Probably no other public display so impresses the nonobserver as does the intensity of feeling expressed in the processions and passion plays, which culminate with the 'ashura performance. The murders of Hussein and family members are then enacted, often with local sayyid playing leading roles in dramatizations in which the severed head of the murdered Hussein addresses the community. Public parades and demonstrations of grief are joined by spectators who sometimes engage in violent self-flagellation. The predominant message concerns the injustice of this world, oppression by its illegitimate rulers, and the ultimate triumph of truth and justice. The plays dramatically portray the perfidy and tyranny of rulers, especially Arab and Turkish caliphs. Christians and Jews are sometimes represented as collaborators with the oppressors. Unpopular current leaders and governments may be reviled by being associated in the plays with the foes of Hussein. Thus, Hussein's betrayal and murder are transmuted into a sacrifice made on behalf of the community which ever since has become emblematic of martyrdom with its concomitant promises of a reward in Paradise.

The tomb of Hussein in Karbala and that of 'Ali in Najaf, like those of subsequent imams located in Baghdad, Qum, Meshhed, and elsewhere, are venerated as shrines and regularly visited by pilgrims. The sanctuaries of Karbala and Najaf are considered holy ground, and the pious make efforts to bring the bodies of their dead for burial in their environs. Pilgrims bring donations of gold, fine jewelry, carpets, and other valuables to the major shrines, which historically have been endowed with great wealth. Shahs, sultans, emperors, and other rulers have all made gifts in demonstration of piety and perhaps in pursuit of legitimacy. Even the not overly pious former empress of Iran, Farah Pahlavi, saw fit to donate two massive gold and jewel-encrusted doors to the sanctuary of Karbala.

The cupolas of prominent shrines are leafed in gold, and colored mosaics, mirrors, and gold and silver calligraphy embellish the inside walls. The effect on the pilgrim can be overwhelming. As the nineteenth-century German traveler-scholar Nöldeke wrote about the sanctuary of Hussein in Karbala:

the general impression made by the interior must be called fairy-like, when in the dusk—even in the daytime it is dim inside—the light of innumerable lamps and candles around the silver shrine, reflected a thousand and again a thousand times from the innumerable small crystal facets produces a charming effect beyond the dreams of imagination. In the roof of the dome, the light loses its strength; only here and there a few crystal surfaces gleam like the stars in the sky.[2]

The majority of the Shi'a today belong to the Imami, or Twelver sect. They believe in an unbroken chain of 12 imams, beginning with 'Ali and ending with Muhammad al-Mahdi, who, while still a child, disappeared in the mosque of Samarra in Iraq in 874. He was rumored to have been secretly murdered by the 'Abbasids, the dynasty then in power. Al-Mahdi is believed to be hidden or invisible, in a state of occultation, or noncorporeal existence, and one day he is expected to return as the *Mahdi,* the Rightly Guided One, to usher in a reign of justice and peace in a world full of sin and injustice. The Shi'a thus share a messianic concept with the Jews and the Christians, a concept that may have antecedents in the early Zoroastrian religion of Persia.

The cult of martyrdom and the messianic belief in the return of the Hidden Imam are at the core of the Shi'a ethos. Moreover Shi'a Islam has developed a form of mysticism lacking almost altogether in Sunni Islam in that esoteric knowledge (*nass*) is believed to have been passed from Muhammad to 'Ali, and hence down the chain of subsequent imams. Further, Shi'a are allowed to use dissimulation or denial (known as the doctrine of *taqiyya*) to preserve secret religious knowledge in the face of persecution. The idea of arcane or esoteric sacred knowledge, passed from expert to acolyte, is an important basis for religious rank (Lindholm, 1996).

The concept of the *Mahdi* has its echo in a widespread folk belief among Sunni people as well that a *Mahdi*-like leader will emerge to restore "True Islam" and obliterate injustice and oppression. This is a variant on what anthropologists call *millenarianism,* a belief in the restoration of an ideal but lost social order. Millenarian movements are often triggered by severe cultural dislocations, such as those occasioned by foreign invasion or colonialism. One such Islamic case was the *Mahdi* revolt in the Sudan in the late nineteenth century, which protested Anglo-Egyptian rule. Although put down after bloody fighting, the *Mahdiyya* movement marked the beginning of Sudanese nationalism.

THE SHI'A RELIGIOUS LEADERSHIP

In comparison with their Sunni counterparts, Shi'a clergy are more hierarchically and centrally organized; historically, they have also been much more prone to take oppositional roles in their relationship to government. Their claim

---

[2] A. Nöldeke, as quoted in H. A. R. Gibb and H. H. Kramers (1955, pp. 360–361).

to authority derives from their role as the deputies of the absent imam. In an influential article on the role of Iranian *'ulama* as opposition leaders, Hamid Algar prophetically foresaw their importance in rallying the populace against the unpopular regime of the Shah of Iran and even predicted the leadership of Ayatollah Khomeini (1972, pp. 211–231). As Algar pointed out, the very ideology of the imamate, with its emphasis on the return of the imam, renders all government, even those formally affiliated with Shi'ism, usurpatory. For generations, the Shi'a *'ulama* have reacted against the tyranny of autocratic rulers, using the martyrdom of Hussein as the exemplification of sacrifice in the attainment of temporal justice.

Higher levels of clergy, which in Shi'ism are distinguished by clear ranks, have propagated their role as arbiters of the imam's authority and interpreters of his will. Those holding the title of *mujtahid*, that is, those capable of interpreting the law, generally serve as community leaders. As spiritual teachers, especially those of high-rank called *ayatollahs*, they offer themselves as moral and spiritual guides. The rank of ayatollah (literally, the "sign of God") is achieved through piety, knowledge, and scholarship. From time to time, the ayatollahs induct new members to their ranks, which at any given time tend to number around thirty. In turn, they collectively recognize one from among them to be designated as *al-Uzma*, or Supreme. Some of Ayatollah Khomeini's more enthusiastic supporters took to referring to him as imam, a promotion to which in reality none can aspire. In theory, individual Shi'a select a particular *mujtahid* to emulate and to recognize as his or her personal authority on moral and religious issues. This obviously entails the submission of the layperson to the

A member of Hezbollah in south Lebanon. His wounds were self inflicted during *ta'ziyya* ceremonies commemorating the martyrdom of Imam Hussein.

Shi'a clerical students praying in a mosque in Qum, Iran.

opinions of the spiritual guide. Because *mujtahids* can be called upon to advise and make judgments on all aspects of life, their pronouncements are of obvious significance.

In Shi'a communities, both *mujtahids* and lower-ranking clerical functionaries called *mullahs* are in close touch with the masses as they are called upon to offer very personalized guidance, a role not usually played by Sunni *'ulama*. Still, even among the Sunni, spiritual guides—*sheikhs*—fill a similar role, albeit one not endorsed by orthodox doctrine. Individual men and women, the sick, the healthy, the rich and the poor alike regularly seek out their spiritual mentors with gifts, attend their prayer sessions, read their religious texts, and call upon them for solace when faced with misfortune. People gather in the presence of important *mujtahids* bearing petitions for help in dealing with government authorities—to get sons out of jail, to secure jobs, to rectify bureaucratic abuse—thereby reinforcing the clerics' prestige and influence.

In Iran, donations by the pious over generations have created vast holdings of property set aside for the support of clerics, shrines, mosques, and religious schools. Moreover the fact that followers give directly to their chosen mentors has traditionally given the *'ulama* an independent economic base. Both the Shah of Iran and his father before him attempted to seize those holdings and break the power of the *'ulama*—and both failed.

The Iranian *'ulama* perpetuate themselves much like their Sunni counterparts through their *madrasas* (school-seminary), to which students are drawn from all over the country. Students without means are supported by the endowments of the school-seminary. When deemed ready, they return to their communities; a select few may stay to pursue further study and themselves become *mujtahids*. Both the cities of Najaf in Iraq and Qum in Iran are considered to be major centers of Shi'a studies, attracting advanced scholars to their schools and libraries.[3]

SECTS WITHIN SHI'ISM

Shi'ism itself is fragmented in a way not encountered in the Sunni tradition. A number of sects disagree so profoundly on central issues of dogma that they scarcely recognize the legitimacy of each other's views. The dominant schismatic divisions have to do with the nature of the imamate and the order of succession. Divisions within Shi'ism are further complicated by the principle of *taqiyya*, "dissimulation of belief," which they all share. This pragmatic approach, which allows a believer to dissimulate or conceal his or her real belief when threatened or in a hostile environment, has also served to shield a proliferation of divergent rites and beliefs, even among sects that share the same name. It also raises difficult questions about the definition of "orthodoxy" in a religion that lacks a church.

Four Shi'a or Shi'a-derived groups deserve mention here because they illustrate some of the different directions taken by Shi'ism, as well as being of ethnographic importance in their own right. These four are the Isma'ili (or Seveners, as they are sometimes called), the 'Alawi in Syria and the Alevi in Turkey, the Druze, and the Zaidi.

The Isma'ili sect, perhaps the least important group in the Middle East today, originated in 765, when they broke off from mainstream Shi'a over the choice of a successor to the sixth imam. For them, the legitimate seventh imam should have been Isma'il (d. 760), whom they believe to be the last in the line of imams and the one who will reappear as the *Mahdi*. The Isma'ilis led a number of local revolts and even managed to establish short-lived states in Syria and Bahrain during the tenth century. But the apogee of their political success was the accession of the Isma'ili Fatimid dynasty to power in Egypt during the tenth and eleventh centuries. Later, in Persia, a strong and well-organized community of Isma'ilis was established around the mountain fortress of Alamut, near Qazvin. From their mountain stronghold, emissaries were sent out to perpetrate acts of political sabotage and assassination attempts against the rulers. As the sect was reputed to use hashish in their ritual, the Isma'ilis of Alamut came to be known as *al-Hashashin* (hashish smokers), whence the English word "assassin."

---

[3] For an excellent account of the *madrasas* of Qum and the culture of religious education in Iran, see Michael Fischer (1980).

After the Isma'ili stronghold in Persia was destroyed in 1250 by the Mongols, they ceased to be politically important in the Middle East. Today, Isma'ilis are found in India, Pakistan, Syria, the Persian Gulf area, and parts of Central Asia and East Africa. A group among them, the Nizaris, pays special homage to the Agha Khan, whose family claims descent from the seventh imam whom they consider to be the "living imam." What distinguishes the Isma'ili even today is their insistence on an allegorical and esoteric interpretation of the Quran. This practice separates the religious initiate from the layperson in a way not found among the majority of Muslims. The paradox in the case of the Isma'ili is clear. What began as a populist, near-revolutionary movement against the Sunni oligarchy and its ruling institutions has, in time, engendered an ideology that sustains a favored few in positions of leadership and mediation with God.

The Druze are an offshoot of the Isma'ili movement. The sect's origins date to the eleventh century, when a Persian Isma'ili theologian named Hamza began to preach a doctrine that later evolved into a new religion. Hamza's successor, al-Darazi (who gave his name to the movement), succeeded in establishing the new religion among the mountain-dwelling populations of southern Lebanon and Syria. The Druze, a secretive and tightly knit group, have distinct religious beliefs that, to a large extent, are also derived from an esoteric interpretation of the Quran. Their religion is held in secret and fully known only to a small number of people called the *uqqal*, those who are enlightened. The rest form a second category referred to as the *juhhal*, the ignorant , those who have not been fully instructed in the mysteries of their religion but who, nonetheless, are instructed to follow its strict moral and ethical code. Both men and women can choose to study and join the ranks of the *uqqal* . Each Druze community is regulated by a council, *majlis*, headed by an elderly sheikh; the *majlis* meets once a week on Thursday evenings for prayer and to review communal matters.

At the social apex of Druze communities as a whole is a handful of sheikhs who have achieved their rank through piety and scholarship and who act as moral guides for the community. The sheikhs, distinguished by their special crown-shaped wool turbans, lead a monastic life devoted to religious studies and to serving the spiritual needs of the larger Druze community, which today is found scattered in Syria, Lebanon, and Israel. Israeli Druze, unlike the Muslim and Christian Arab-Israeli communities, enjoy a privileged status with the Israeli government; Druze men, in fact, serve in the Israeli defense forces.[4]

The 'Alawis and Nusairis of Syria and Lebanon, the Alevis of Turkey, and the Shabak of Iraq are closely related Shi'a-derived sects.[5] The 'Alawi, who, like the others, are a predominantly rural population, practice a religion carefully concealed from outsiders; like the Druze, their doctrines and rituals are derived

---

[4] For a general study of the Druze, see Robert Brenton Betts (1988). For an ethnographic study of the Druze in Israel, see Aharon Layish (1982).

[5] The best source on the Alevi is Tord Olsson et al. (1998).

from an esoteric interpretation of the Quran. The 'Alawi, long a denigrated and marginal rural minority in Syria, today number among their members a majority of the political leaders who owe their initial power to their role in the Syrian army, to which they were recruited by the French.

In Turkey, the Alevi situation is rather different. In the past they were closely associated with the Bektaşi order of dervishes, itself closely associated with the Janissaries. Thus, while resembling the Alawi in many ways, their intellectual roots and recent history are quite distinct. Long regarded with suspicion and hostility by the Sunni 'ulama, they only recently have begun to mobilize politically. Frequently they are found in one or the other of the leftist parties and have been involved in armed communal conflict in at least two major towns in the east, Sivas and Maraş. The new visibility of the Alevis on the regional and national political scenes has occasioned a powerful backlash on the part of the Sunni 'ulama establishment, which had long both denigrated them and minimized their demographic presence. As recently as 1993, 37 members of a group celebrating the writings of *pir* Abtal, an Alevi saint and mystic poet, were killed in the southeastern city of Sivas by a mob that burned down the hotel in which they were meeting.

Alevis, speaking variously Turkish, Kurdish, or Arabic, depending on their region of origin, are widely distributed throughout Anatolia. While largely rural-dwelling in the past, there is at least one major Istanbul neighborhood of Alevi concentration and this is also the case in smaller cities. Alevis have to some extent been embraced by left-leaning intellectuals, as their rites and beliefs stress a communal and egalitarian ethos with less emphasis on sexual segregation. Further, they were represented by secular intellectuals as exemplifying a downtrodden population that chose religion as a vehicle of resistance. Some Alevi reject the primacy of the Quran and Shari'a; but one should be wary of any simplistic characterizations. In their own words, "We follow many paths." Alevi communal rituals involve men and women with an emphasis on group solidarity and the minimizing of intra-group dispute. Formerly socially invisible, today their spokesmen are increasingly prominent on the national scene.

A few local groups, however, are identified with orders considered too esoteric or heterodox to be included with either Sunni Islam or moderate Shi'ism. The Kurdish-speaking Shabak of northern Iraq are an extreme example of a religiously defined closed or encysted community, although there are parallels elsewhere (Rassam, 1974).

The Shabak were, until the 1960s, landless sharecroppers who worked on fields owned by urban Sunni landlords. Their religious leaders, called *pirs*, served as spiritual guides and leaders of the local community, while their ethnically distinct and powerful landlords served as general patrons and representatives in dealing with the national government. In common with other Muslim secret sects, the Shabak developed their own interpretations and ceremonials with distinctive features, including private and public confessions, tolerance of alcoholic beverages, and a general laxity in observance of Muslim ritual obligations. The primary mechanism of social integration within the community is the relationship between adult males and their spiritual guides, the *pirs*. The *pirs* are grouped into several ranked levels all under the leadership of the supreme head of the order, the *Baba*. The Shabak religious calendar is crowded with private and public ceremonies presided over by *pirs*, which bring together relatives and neighbors to participate in public sacrifice and the sharing of communal meals.

Their secretive beliefs, regarded as heretical by outsiders, their insistence on marrying within the community, and their rural isolation define the boundaries separating them from the larger society. Their secretive socioreligious system, which helped them maintain their identity over time, also kept them a weak and exploited minority and reinforced their dependency on their landlords. However, conditions for the Shabak began to change in the late 1960s as a direct result of land reform measures and literacy campaigns undertaken by the Ba'ath government of Iraq. Many Shabak now own their land, which was expropriated from their former landlords; some have moved to cities nearby, and still others work in newly established factories.

The Zaidi, who are found primarily in Yemen today, are perhaps the least heterodox of the Shi'a sects. While they restrict the imamate to descendants of Zaid, a grandson of Hussein, it is the community that chooses the imam among a number of qualified contenders. Zaidi imams are chosen on the basis of their religious knowledge, their political skills, and their ability to command. The Zaidi presence in Yemen goes back to the late ninth century, when Imam al-Hadi Yahya was invited by Yemeni tribes to come from Mecca to Yemen to resolve long-standing disputes among the warring tribal factions. From their beginning at the end of the ninth century until they were deposed in the 1960s, Zaidi imams ruled Yemen, providing a locus of political legitimacy and an avenue for reconciliation in a tribally segmented country. Even today, the Zaidi, a numerical minority, continue to dominate the political and economic scene in Yemen. The case of the Zaidi exemplifies how a small oligarchy using the claim of holy descent and religious leadership as a source for political authority and legitimacy succeeded in ruling an ethnically and tribally fragmented population.[6]

ISLAMIC MYSTICISM: THE SUFI WAY

The texture of Islamic religious experience is further enriched by mysticism. Middle Eastern people from all regions, rural and urban alike, have from the beginning of Islam been heirs to a long tradition of mysticism and asceticism in which personal piety and emotional catharsis combine. Sufism (Arabic: *tasawwuf*), as Islamic mysticism is commonly called, embraces a vast array of beliefs, rituals, and even formal institutions, such as orders and brotherhoods.

---

[6] For an informative discussion of the political role of Muslim sectarianism, including the Druze, the 'Alawi, and the Zaidi, see Fouad I. Khouri (1990).

In many respects, Sufism represents an aspect of Islam that adapts to the changing moods and exigencies of the moment. Through its openness and individuated character, Sufism has buffered Sunni and Shi'a orthodoxies from many of the challenges and pressures that might have engendered major reformation. In fact, many of the recurring revitalization and reform movements within Islam have sprung from Sufism and have expressed themselves through religious orders and brotherhoods that parallel, and sometimes even challenge, but do not replace, the structure of the formal religion. The significance of Sufism for facilitating the spread of Islam in India, central and Southeast Asia, and Africa cannot be underestimated. It is everywhere a vehicle for popular local beliefs and practices, and as such tends to be expressed differently in different areas, and its political role remains powerful as a potential mobilizer of mass sentiment. Sufism, therefore, has both its private dimension, rooted in intimate individual religious experience, as well as its public dimension in organizing politically significant movements.

The origin of the term *Sufi* is obscure. The general assumption is that it comes from the garments of rough, undyed wool (or *suf*) worn by the early mystics in Baghdad. As early as the eighth century, these men wandered from town to town preaching asceticism, spiritual discipline, and ecstatic communion with God. The Sufis emphasized emotional spontaneity and sought to free the religious experience from the legalistic demands of the Shari'a. By allowing each individual to seek his or her own spiritual path, *tariqa*, Sufism came to represent a popular reaction to the increasingly rigid and legalistic religious establishment.

In Sufism, the ultimate goal is loss of individual identity and complete union with "Truth" or "Ultimate Reality." This state, mystics believe, may be achieved through intuition and not through the exercise of reason. Mystics seek to achieve their goals by renouncing worldly concerns and through various spiritual and physical exercises. The Sufi path to God consists of a number of stages through which initiates have to pass. On the way, they are assisted by personal teachers—sheikhs, or *pirs.* Once the initiates successfully pass through all the stages, they will attain their ultimate goal, a new kind of consciousness consisting of *ma'rifa* (knowledge) and *haqiqa* (truth). This mystical progress is described in a Turkish saying:

> To know Shari'a is to know that yours is yours, and mine is mine.
> And to know the *tariqa* is to know that yours is yours, and mine is yours, too.
> But to know the *ma'rifa* is to know that there is neither mine nor yours.

From its inception and throughout its history, poetry has been an important medium for the expression of Sufi sentiment, and many of the leading mystics were also celebrated poets. Al-Hallaj, the ninth-century Sufi martyr, was born in Persia but spent most of his adult life teaching and writing in Baghdad. A great poet and a persuasive teacher, al-Hallaj attracted a large number of followers and grew so influential that he posed a threat to the established authority of the *'ulama*, who eventually conspired with the ruling dynasty to have him executed in 922. The charge against him was heresy. In what is perhaps the most celebrated statement of early Sufism, al-Hallaj had declared, "I am the Absolute Truth."

In his poetry, al-Hallaj celebrated mystical love and the harmony that follows the complete union with God:

> I am he who I love, and he whom I love is I,
> We are two spirits dwelling in one body.
> If thou seest me, thou seest Him,
> And if thou seest Him, thou seest us both.

Even before al-Hallaj, the theme of unbound, unconditional love for God had become an integral part of Sufi belief. Rabi'a al-'Adawiya (d. 801), a freed female slave who lived in Iraq, taught that love should replace fear as the motive for religious devotion. The story is told that once Rabi'a was seen walking in the streets with a torch in one hand and a pitcher of water in the other. When questioned, she answered: "I want to throw fire into Paradise, and pour water into Hell, so that these two veils may disappear and it becomes clear who worships God out of love, not out of fear of Hell or hope for Paradise" (Schimmel, 1975, p. 98).

One of the most popular folk characters in the Middle East, Mulla Nasrudin, is also a vehicle of Sufi teaching. The stories of Mulla Nasrudin, told as jokes or moral fables, form a distinct literary genre specifically used by Sufis to express the subtlety of mystical knowledge, as the seemingly simple tales can be interpreted at many levels. The following two examples, chosen from a vast repertoire, serve to illustrate a style of Sufi teaching and at the same time introduce one of the most famous figures of popular culture in the Middle East. They are taken from the work of Idris Shah (1964), a Pakistani Sufi who is largely responsible for the current popularity of Sufism in the West.

> *Mulla Nasrudin was walking along an alleyway one day when a man fell from a roof and landed on top of him. The other man was unhurt, but Nasrudin had to be taken to the hospital.*
> *"What teaching do you infer from this event, Master?" one of his disciples asked him.*
> *"Avoid belief in inevitability, even if cause and effect seem inevitable! Shun theoretical questions like: 'If a man falls off a roof will his neck be broken?' He fell, but my neck is broken."* (p. 59)

As Shah explains, this tale is used by Sufi masters to teach the initiate to question belief in simple cause and effect and to avoid taking things for granted.

Another tale illustrates the tendency of people to think in habitual patterns that may prevent them from grasping new points of view:

> *Nasrudin used to take his donkey across a frontier every day, with the panniers loaded with straw. Since he admitted to being a smuggler when he trudged home every night, the frontier guards searched him again and again. They searched his person, sifted the straw,*

steeped it in water, even burned it from time to time. Meanwhile, he was becoming visibly more and more prosperous.
Then he retired and went to live in another country. Here one of the customs officers met him years later.
"You can tell me now, Nasrudin," he said, "Whatever was it that you were smuggling, when we could never catch you at?"
"Donkeys," said Nasrudin. (p. 59)

SUFI ORDERS AND BROTHERHOODS

Sufism, which had its origins in isolated, individual religious experiences, by the thirteenth century had developed into a mass movement. It acquired an institutional structure within which full-time teachers instructed the lay or uninitiated. The different teachings of important mystics formed the basis for orders or brotherhoods that still exist today and that are usually known by the name of their founder. Each order revolves around a specific *tariqa* laid down by a famous mystic, who is often regarded as a saint because he is considered an intermediary between human beings and God. Allegiance to one or another of these orders may cut across different classes and ethnic backgrounds. Women may also participate, although they usually have their own separate groups. Some orders may be closely associated with segments of the ruling establishment, as, for example, in the case of the military during the early Ottoman period, who, as we mentioned earlier, were associated with the Bektaşi order of dervishes. Others may be limited in their membership to marginal groups in the society.

The sheikhs, or masters, meet regularly with their followers in lodges, *zawiya* (*tekke,* in Turkish), to study and to perform the spiritual exercises. Those who devote themselves full time to the order may themselves become teachers and establish their own *zawiya* within a loose association of the order. In this way, Sufi orders and brotherhoods come to link nomadic camp to village and village to city. Dispersed as they are, the orders constitute a vital network joining different regions and populations, even cutting across national boundaries. For example, the Qadiriyya order of Baghdad has lodges from India to Senegal, including some in countries such as Turkey where they function surreptitiously. In the past and in some parts of the Middle East today, *zawiyas* serve as hostels for pilgrims and travelers, as schools for children, and as community centers. *Zawiyas* that house the tombs of local saints are considered sanctuaries, sacred areas where oaths may be taken and where fugitives seek refuge.

POPULAR BELIEFS: "SAINTS," SHEIKHS, AND *BARAKA*

The success of Sufi orders was, to a large extent, no doubt due to their capacity to incorporate local beliefs and practices into an overall synthesis of popular Islam. Moreover, the close relationship between the *zawiyas* and the local community and the fact that the teachers in the *zawiyas* were most often of local origin and spoke the native dialect were of considerable help in integrating Islam into local community life. Two pre-Islamic beliefs that found their way into Sufism and that are retained in popular Islam are the cult of saints and the concept of *baraka*.

Valerie Hoffman, who has observed religious expression in Egypt over a long period, writes that belief in saints or people with supernatural powers is ubiquitous. The term *sheikh,* which literally means "elder," is also used to refer to men who possess religious authority and are regarded as teachers and masters. A sheikh of profound spirituality and charisma is called *"wali,"* meaning "friend of God," a term usually glossed as "saint" in English. Such individuals are believed to possess charisma, or *baraka,* divine blessing. In northwest Africa, they are commonly referred to as *marabout.* "The qualities typically deemed mandatory for saints include piety, observance of the Shari'a, knowledge of God, and the performance of miracles. . . . Sufi writings on sainthood assure us that saints exist in all countries and will continue to exist as long as the world exists; indeed they are essential for the well-being of the world" (Hoffman, 1999, p. 19; see also Hoffman, 1995).

The pool of Abraham at Urfa, southeastern Turkey. The site is sacred to Jews, Christians, and Muslims.

There is no formal mechanism or bureaucracy in Islam that identifies or "canonizes" saints; which sheikhs become sanctified is usually a matter of local recognition. Some may become widely hailed for piety and miracle-making abilities, but identification is complicated because the qualities of sainthood, *wilaya*, are sometimes believed to be hidden and only selectively and often posthumously revealed. For example, Hoffman (1999) reports that in Cairo there is a shrine erected on the site of a tomb of a small boy who, only after his death, revealed himself as a saint through a dream to a man who never knew him. The man subsequently built the shrine, which today is visited by many seeking the *baraka* or blessing of the boy saint.

As in other endeavors, sons frequently may follow in their father's foot-steps and become sheikhs. Both men and women may be recognized as having inherited their father's spiritual essence (*asrar*), but while women, in principle, can become saints, Egypt's Supreme Council of Sufi Orders does not recognize their leadership in life. Neighborhood and regional shrines of both male and female saints are important features of the landscape, places to be visited for comfort in illness and for divine assistance. While reformist or conservative purists may downplay their importance or denounce them for heterodoxy, belief in saints and sheikhs remains a major element of everyday piety.[7]

Baraka, which may be translated as "blessing or grace," is actually a very complex concept that may also mean holiness or the quality of divine blessing. Its Christian counterpart is the concept of divine grace, and, to a certain extent, the widespread secular concept of good luck. As we noted earlier, a person who possesses a great deal of *baraka* may be regarded as a saint, *walī*, or *marabout*. Both men and women may possess *baraka*, and this charismatic, presumably wonder-working power may be either inherited or acquired.

All descendants of the Prophet Muhammad or of those of his immediate family are believed to have inherited some of his *baraka*, some more so than others. But *baraka* may also be acquired by individuals especially favored by God. These individuals become living saints, who in their lives exemplify extreme piety and divine grace; they demonstrate their *baraka* through their abilities to bring good fortune, heal the sick, and make miracles. Most founders and many leaders of Sufi orders are considered saints. Saints' cults may also develop around individuals whose only distinction is to die in battle or under unusual circumstances, with their *baraka* becoming apparent postmortem. Unlike Christian saints, Muslim saints are often recognized in their lifetime, and their designation does not derive, as we have said, from a formal declaration or canonization by any religious institution. Rather it derives from communal recognition, reflecting an informal consensus among followers and members of the community.

Tombs of saints are found throughout the Middle East, both in the cities and the countryside. Usually constructed of dressed stone, these tombs frequently

---

[7] For two classic studies of Sufi orders, one historical, the other anthropological, see John Kingsley Birge (1937) and E. E. Evans Pritchard (1949).

The tomb of a seventeenth-century holy man and his family in Siirt, Turkey. The tomb is regularly visited by supplicants.

rise from fields alongside major roads to signal a halting place for passersby. Smaller whitewashed and green-domed structures may be the focus of regular visits by nearby villagers, while larger, sometimes monumental, edifices attract visitors from a wider area. On a fine day, groups of women and their children often pass the time in friendly socializing at local shrines. Indeed, it is not unusual for entire families to make seasonal outings to a favorite shrine, taking along food, which they may share with other visitors or with the beggars who are often found in the vicinity of major shrines.

These tomb-shrines are invariably differentiated from the mosques that may adjoin the particularly important shrines. Visitors seek out the tomb of the saint, circumambulate it, pray and meditate, and press bits of wax, cloth, or small pebbles on the walls of the chamber to signify special pleas to the saint. Many tombs are found near sacred springs or groves, sometimes enclosed by low walls made all the more dramatic for the lack of similar greenery in the often deforested landscape. The tombs of founders of major Sufi orders are usually located at the center of great shrine complexes.

Specialized powers may be attributed to different saints, including the ability to cure infertility in women, to treat children's diseases, to ensure success in love, or to heal the insane. More women than men seek out the *baraka* of the shrines. Perhaps because they are generally barred from participating in the formal mosque prayers, women tend to find special meaning in their relationship to saints.

In Iran, women turn to the local shrines of *imamzadehs*, male and female saints who are descendants of the 12 Imams. *Imamzadehs* are revered for their closeness to God, and their shrines are regularly visited by men and women seeking spiritual guidance and help with personal problems. A particularly popular shrine in the city of Shiraz is Qadamagh, associated with 'Abbas, the half-brother of the third imam, Hussein. Anne Bettridge (1993) describes a Saturday evening when the shrine building and the courtyard fill up with women. "Off to the side, a group of women may be praying while others are seated on the floor playing with children and exchanging news. A few women may prefer to sit alone and weep. . . . [O]utside in the courtyard people are seated on the ground eating, drinking tea, and sharing a sweet, *halva*, which they have made in fulfillment of vows" (p. 241).

The relationship between a woman and an *imamzadeh* can be a very personal one, and it is not unusual for a woman to have a lifetime relationship with a particular saint whom she believes to be especially sympathetic and responsive to her needs. Women implore, harangue, and threaten their favorite *imamzadehs* as they seek their help. As Bettridge notes, more than providing an approved setting for women to get away from home and socialize together, local shrines allow women to express their feelings and attempt to control their lives:

> The fact that women in Muslim Iran are associated with local pilgrimages is neither accidental nor incidental. Men are associated with the mosque, religious texts, reasoned theological discussions, formal ritual assemblies—in short, with intellectual aspects of religion. Women's association with local pilgrimage points out that it is bound with things of the heart, the troubling aspects of life which questions, unsettles and answers obliquely. . . . *Ziarat* [the visit] gives scope to the personal and difficult aspects of life and allows both men and women and especially women to express their emotional sides—to grieve and wail in an approved setting and to celebrate joyously with others. (p. 247)

The *baraka* associated with saints has its negative counterpart in the popular/folk concept of "ill-purpose," the evil eye or *'ayn*. This force is believed to bring sickness and misfortune and may be thought of as a form of witchcraft. Just as some people inherently possess *baraka*, others have in them the power of the *'ayn*. These people, it is believed, can cause bad luck simply by their glance. A person may deliberately direct the evil eye against enemies or their property, but he or she may also do so unwittingly through unconscious envy. To guard against the evil eye, various amulets and charms may be worn, especially by children, who are thought to be most vulnerable. Valuable animals, such as prized cattle, camels, horses, and rams, are usually protected with blue beads. A common charm worn by women is a hand made of gold, silver, or some metal filigree.

Verses from the Quran written on paper and worn about the body in lockets are believed to be especially potent, as are blue beads, amber, cowrie shells, and iron. Religious phrases such as *bismallah* (in the name of God) and *mashallah* (as God wills) adorn buses and walls and are continually on people's lips. Any undertaking, whether it is the beginning of a meal, a journey, or any other task, may invoke *bismallah*, whereas *mashallah* prefaces any praise directed at children or other family members, particularly by strangers. In this case, God's name is invoked to neutralize the likelihood of unconscious envy and the casting of the evil eye on the individual praised.

But when the evil eye is seen to afflict someone, say, a child, there is a solution—exorcism, part of many religious traditions. One form of exorcism practiced throughout the region, known in Turkish as *Kurşun Dokma* (Pouring Lead), involves threes—of breath, of prayer, of spoons—and molten lead and water. The molten lead is plunged into a pan of cold water held first over the head, then the chest, and lastly the legs of the "patient." On each occasion the exorcist (often a woman) carefully examines the shape of the reconstituted lead. Small protuberances indicate that the evil eye has certainly been cast, and bits of ash settled into the lead mean the curse has truly reached the patient's heart. The exorcist then says three prayers, pausing between each to blow gently at the patient. After the prayers, the patient is offered three spoons of the water from

Bedouin woman folk healer and her clients. Her table displays religious amulets, charms, herbs, and potions.

the pan, and as each is drunk, the exorcist throws the spoon over her shoulder. It is an especially good sign if the spoons land touching each other.

SUFISM AND SOCIOPOLITICAL ORGANIZATION

Sufi orders and Sufi-inspired mass movements take many forms and perform different functions. Some are devoted to curing the ill; others emphasize the individual mystical experience and have little public role; still others mobilize the masses into political action and, as such, seem far removed from their Sufi roots. The objectives and functions of the hundreds of orders are so diverse that some scholars question the value of lumping all of them under a single label.[8] We cannot detail here the range of variation among Sufi-inspired movements, but we have selected three cases to illustrate the vast scope of this phenomenon.

Our first case is that of the Wahabis of Saudi Arabia. After a turbulent history of violent opposition to instituted authority, Wahabism, a puritanical reformist movement, has today become the official state-sponsored doctrine of Saudi Arabia. Our second example, that of the Hamidiya-Shadhiliya order of Egypt, stands in sharp contrast. Eschewing any militant function or political stand, the Shadhiliya is a small, primarily urban-based, tightly organized order whose primary function is that of a fraternal religious club and, on occasion, a place of refuge and material support for members. The third case, that of the Nur or Fethullah Gülen Community Movement, represents Sufism in a new guise, as a contemporary social movement using all the tools of a secular age to spread their influence.

The Wahabis of Saudi Arabia

Wahabism had its origin in a special *tariqa* proclaimed by its founder, Mohammad ibn 'Abd al-Wahab (1703–1787). A student and exponent of Sufism, 'abd al-Wahab left Arabia to study and teach in Iraq and Iran. After extensive travels, he returned to his homeland and began to teach his own *tariqa* based on a highly puritanical interpretation of Islamic texts that condemned all innovation in belief and ritual subsequent to Muhammad. Among other things, it outlawed the veneration of saints and saints' tombs.

Expelled from his native region, 'Abd al-Wahab sought refuge with a tribal chief, Muhammad ibn Saud, who espoused the new doctrine and undertook its propagation. In a short time, the movement grew in influence as more and more tribes joined; some came peacefully, others were conquered in battle. By the

---

[8] It should be noted that one state in the Middle East, Turkey, in the 1920s had banned all religious brotherhoods and orders. Today there is an effective retreat from this extreme position. Sufi orders that had persisted underground since the edict are now more open in their activities, and new ones have arisen, such as the Fethullah Gülen Community Movement (discussed in this section).

beginning of the nineteenth century, the Wahabis were so strong that they attacked Karbala in Iraq, Mecca, and even Damascus. Alarmed, the Ottoman government sent a special expedition that succeeded in defeating them and forcing them to retreat to their original area in eastern Arabia.

The movement then entered a period of retrenchment and general decline until 1901, when a descendant of Muhammad ibn Saud, Abdel 'Aziz (henceforth ibn Saud), leading a small Bedouin force, succeeded in capturing the oasis of Riyadh, the present-day capital of Saudi Arabia. From his base in Riyadh, ibn Saud proceeded to enlarge and consolidate his domain, and by 1915 he had become the master of most of Arabia. In 1932, ibn Saud declared himself king of his newly formed kingdom, named Saudi Arabia after his family, and strict ultraconservative Wahabism became the only Islamic doctrine to be tolerated within its borders. Ibn Saud died in 1952, leaving a legacy of 37 sons and the nucleus of a modern government and administration. Today, ibn Saud's sons and their sons have a lock on the oil-rich country, occupying as they do all important political and economic positions. The descendants of Mohammad ibn 'Abd al-Wahab, known as āl-Sheikh, also occupy privileged positions as jurists, religious leaders, and consultants to the Saudi clan.

The great wealth derived from oil after World War II and especially since the mid-1970s, together with the massive influx of non-Saudi Arabs and other foreigners, has created social and political contradictions on a scale hard to comprehend. Wahabism, which espouses a nonmaterialistic, almost ascetic way of life, is increasingly hard to reconcile with the vast wealth and flagrant consumerism that has transformed the lives of all Saudis and has led to unprecedented riches in the hands of the royal family. While the Saudi clan retains virtually total control over all sources of political, military, and bureaucratic power, their claim to legitimacy rests, paradoxically, on their espousal and propagation of the puritanical Wahabi creed. This legitimacy is increasingly suspect in the eyes of many. The seizure of the Great Mosque in Mecca, the holiest in all Islam, by a group of Muslim zealots in 1979 bore testimony to the growing gulf between ideology and practice in Saudi Arabia. More recently, a London-based Saudi opposition group set up a Web site on which sermons of dissident Saudi *'ulama* are disseminated.[9]

The Shadhiliya Order of Egypt

The example of the Shadhiliya is best viewed in the general context of religious orders in Egyptian society. The following account is based on a book by Michael Gilsenan (1973) in which he examines the history and evolution of religious orders in Egypt, and specifically one urban *tariqa*, the Hamidiya-Shadhiliya. As Gilsenan writes, religious orders have always been an integral part of urban

---

[9] For a now classic account of the formation of the Saudi Kingdom, see H. Philby (1928). For an excellent article on the Saudi state today, see Ghassan Salame (1993, pp. 579–601).

society, and many are considered to be well within the mainstream of Sunni Islam and are tolerated by the *'ulama*. Such was the importance of these orders that their leaders came to wield great influence in the society in their dual role as educators of the young and intermediaries between the common people and the rulers, who were most often non-Egyptians: Turks, Albanians, and Circassians. Until the nineteenth century, the religious orders were very much a part of Egyptian common life, woven as they were into its social fabric.

The profound changes that transformed Egyptian society during the nineteenth century affected the Sufi orders as well. By the twentieth century, the majority of them were moribund and marginal. Gilsenan attributes the decline of the orders in Egypt to their loss of traditional functions and their concomitant inability to respond constructively to the challenges of a quickly changing social system. Rapid urbanization, the shift from subsistence farming to cash crops, and the increased dependency on world markets led to the emergence of a landless peasantry and the creation of a wage-earning class. As the state took over the function of education and trade unions slowly replaced the old craft guilds, the leaders of the Sufi orders came to lose their base of moral influence and power. They no longer played a key role in education, and their previous ties to the craft guilds ceased to be important. Their power was further undermined by their loss of revenue under land reform laws that confiscated much of their property.

The Hamidiya-Shadhiliya order, founded by Salama Musa (1867–1939), seems to have been an exception to the general decline. The order managed to grow in membership and hold its own against the competing Muslim Brotherhood, an activist religiopolitical movement that sought to establish an Islamic state based on the Shari'a. Gilsenan attributes the success of the Shadhiliya to several factors. One is that its founder was himself a member of the new bureaucracy and at the same time learned in the Islamic tradition. In establishing his order, Musa drew upon his administrative experience to create an efficient organization in which a cadre of trained and highly disciplined followers controlled each lodge. A charismatic figure and a reputed performer of miracles, Musa could simultaneously appeal to the clerical workers in the modern sector, to wage laborers, and to peasants.

In the difficult environment of urban Egypt, the order provides "elements of mutual support and benefit, of psychological and material security in a fraternal circle built on cooperation and equality" (Gilsenan, 1973, p. 206). With its strong emphasis on mutual help and personal discipline, the order offers the individual a sense of identity and security within the difficult environment of contemporary Egyptian society. The well-organized network of lodges suited the needs of workers and lower-level clerical employees, who often found themselves living away from their relatives and community in a confusing and impersonal setting.

The Nur or Fethullah Gülen Community Movement[10]

Our third example is perhaps the most intriguing. The Nur or Fethullah Gülen Community Movement emerged from obscurity only in the 1980s in Turkey, but today it is one of the fastest-growing Islamic movements in the Middle East— numbering untold thousands of adherents, managing hundreds of schools, two universities, publishing houses, a sports club, and with a presence on three continents. It is estimated that over 200 high schools are operated by Nur community adherents in Central Asia, Afghanistan, Iraq, Lebanon, Egypt, Kenya, Albania, Romania, Macedonia, Russia, the United Kingdom, Bulgaria, and the United States, not to mention over 100 schools and a private university in Turkey itself. While having deep roots in the Sufi *tariqat* tradition, leading spokesmen say that although it represents a new form of Sufism, it is not a *tariqa*. In fact, they avoid labels and names altogether and state rather that what they offer is not *tariqat* but *hakikat*, or "truth" (Kömeçoğlu, forthcoming). This is a classic example of what sociologists and political scientists call "social movements." In social movements, informal networks of individuals and groups with multiple objectives spread and coalesce until they come to acquire a collective identity, control significant resources, and coordinate activities. The Fethullah Gülen movement has its intellectual basis in the 12 volumes of *Risale-i Nur* (Treatise of Light) of Said Nursi (1877– 1960) and in the writings, sermons, and public lectures of his charismatic interpreter, Fethullah Gülen. The core adherents are drawn primarily from two sources, the elite, represented by business leaders, financiers, and professionals; and university students, small-scale merchants, and tradesmen, with the former providing resources, particularly in the early stages of the movement, and the students being the most active in propagation of the Nur doctrine, or *Nurculuk* (Turkish).

In order to understand why a movement lacking a formal organizational or institutional structure and one whose adherents need no formal initiation is seen as hugely attractive in some Muslim circles and as threatening by many secularists, followers of leftist parties, and the Islamist establishment, one has to understand just how novel the movement's approach to Islam is. The innovation of Said Nursi, referred to by his large circle of immediate followers as *Bediuzzaman*, or "The Wonder of the Age," was both to break with the Sufi *tariqat* as well as chart a path distinct from his contemporary highly politicized Islamist reformers who advocated an anti-Western struggle. He broke from Sufi tradition in that far from ignoring the external world, he urged his disciples to embrace the modern age and its scientific accomplishments while striving for

---

[10] This discussion is largely based on the unpublished analysis of Uğur Kömeçoğlu, as well as on his forthcoming article (2000), which was shared with us in galley form. We are deeply grateful for his insights and intellectual generosity (but absolve him of responsibility for any errors!); we also draw on the considerable media coverage given this movement in Turkey. For an insight into the basis of the movement's doctrine, see Şerif Mardin's (1989) authoritative account of Said Nursi's life and works. For writings by Fethullah Gülen, see his 1993 and 1995 books in English.

their inner spiritual development. He also broke from the *tariqat* tradition of teaching whereby a sheikh disseminates his esoteric knowledge verbally to a relatively small number of disciples. Said Nursi, writing often from jail or exile, communicated by typed or printed word, so that by the end of his life he had reached large numbers of people throughout the Turkish-speaking world, even though his writings were long proscribed by the authorities.

While Said Nursi was a right wing political activist in his early career, he came to believe that the quest for specifically Islamist government and the implementation of the Shari'a was futile and misplaced. He advocated inner enlightenment through reason (*akıl*) and openness to the Divine Will, and that active politics should not be allowed to impede individual religious development. One becomes a follower simply by reading his works and discussing them with others. Those who study the collected works closely and speak knowledgeably are referred to in the idiom of the movement as *şakirt* or *talebe*, that is, "students," terms that have come to distinguish a core of activist followers who spread the doctrine.

The influence of Said Nursi continued to grow after his death, but the catalyst for its explosive growth was very largely the work of Fethullah Gülen, a charismatic teacher and superb organizer. Gülen was born in 1938 in a village near the eastern city of Erzurum. Both his mother's and father's families were sayyid, and he studied Arabic and Persian with a relative who was also a senior cleric. He attended both a religious seminary, *medrese,* and the *tekke* of a Sufi order. Gülen never met Said Nursi, who died when he was 22, but at about that time he was officially appointed by the Directorate of Religious Affairs to teach in the main mosque in the western city of Edirne—one of the major clerical positions in Turkey. At this point he began expanding on the Nur metaphysical message of universal love, rationality, tolerance, and the compatibility of religious interests with the secular world. A hint of his complex worldview can be seen in this brief passage:

> Man in this world is the representative of two different powers, namely the spirit and the flesh . . . they are usually observed to conflict in such a way that the victory of one results in the defeat of the others. . . . When one sacrifices the enjoyment of material pleasures one grows perfect as long as one can stay free from selfishness and self-seeking—living only for others.

In this view one does not abandon the world or worldly concerns but struggles to make them secondary to spiritual development (Şahin, 1992, in Komeçoğlu, forthcoming).

While the doctrinal message is obviously more complex, the passage draws attention to what attracted many young intellectuals and members of the business community who were seeking to reconcile their religious beliefs with the demands of modern life. The movement's appeal was soon evident among students in secular high schools and universities and among leading business figures in the western portion of the country. During the pre-Gülen period, the Nur movement spread primarily by means of Nur-run houses, in which Said Nursi's treatises were read and studied. In the early Gülen period, these increased greatly in number, and, taking the name "houses of light" (ışık evler, a play on the fact that nur means "light" in Arabic), apartments were organized by the hundreds as residences for university students, with three to five students of the same sex rooming together and following a Nur-inspired Islamic lifestyle as they pursued their secular education, frequently at the nation's foremost universities. Some Islamists term the movement elitist because they are prominent in the best universities. A sense of cemaat, or community solidarity, was inculcated, not through explicit proselytizing but through the emulation of core followers, the şakirt or talebe, by those drawn into their intellectual, work, and social orbits. The Gülen principle was to spread the message to those who showed an interest, but in particular for adherents to behave in ways that made them role models in their behavior at work or school. Those attracted to the Nur doctrine as expounded by Gülen formed a hierarchy within the community, consisting of the şakirt or talebe at the top, the second level kardeş (brother/sister), followed by dost (friend), and, finally, the müstaid (sympathizer with the potential of becoming a "friend"). Fethullah Gülen, for all his emphasis on individual development still plays a very traditional shaykh-like role as final arbitrator on issues of doctrine, policy, and collective action.

The current, very public, and controversial phase of the Gülen movement, in Uğur Kömeçoğlu's view, started in the mid-1980s when the movement began to open high schools and university preparatory schools across the country with money donated by wealthy followers. This had a number of consequences, not the least of which was that these private schools began to earn significant revenues, enabling further expansion and the awarding of even more university scholarships. Also, even though these schools follow a strictly secular curriculum, mostly taught in English, the administrators and many of the teachers are Gülen followers who attract still more new adherents. By the end of the 1980s, with the collapse of the Soviet Union, the movement was poised to expand into the new Central Asian republics and abroad elsewhere where Muslim populations existed and where governments permitted such schools to open. Each school is expected to found sister schools, again on the Nur-Gülen principle of self-sacrifice and of making Islam's message known by deeds and socially useful behavior. University graduates, much like young members of the Church of Latter-day Saints (Mormons), are to do public service as teachers, and increasingly are performing this duty in foreign countries. One prominent financier in the movement in 1996 said that there were over 250 high schools and over 7000 young teachers abroad.

The movement has continued to grow both in numbers and public impact. In Turkey, senior government officials, including the president, have publically embraced the movement's leaders, much as the president of the United States regularly seeks out prominent religious figures. There is no doubt, too, that some officials see the movement's influence in Central Asia as in the national interest, and regard its spread among Kurdish speakers useful as well. But the movement and its leader are also sources of political contention. Turkish parties of the left are suspicious of the movement's secretive association with the business community; hard-line secularists find its appeal to Islamic values threatening; some conservative Islamists find the emphasis on rationality and the accommodation with secular modernity hard to accept—not to mention that the Nur doctrines go far beyond the traditional vision of an Islamic community. In fact, Turkish Islamic extremists have targeted a number of prominent Gülen supporters for torture and assassination, including a woman writer who was a powerful voice for an expanded role for women in Islam. And, of course, the military and other state political institutions are deeply suspicious of a movement over which they have little control. Recently, the Turkish government took steps to restrict the number of students allowed to attend the movement's Fatih University, near Istanbul. As of this writing, Fethullah Gülen is in the United States, ostensibly for medical treatment but perhaps not coincidentally at a time when there have been calls for an inquiry into his presumed influence among the police and other sectors of power.

These three cases illustrate some of the divergent ways in which Sufi *tariqas* have evolved and their quite distinct functions in different social and political contexts. Of course, Sufism is not limited to its expression in any specific *tariqa* or order, or even in any specific set of beliefs and practices. Rather, at its core it represents a shared attitude concerning the individual and his or her relationship to God.

ISLAM IN DAILY LIFE

In this and the preceding chapter, we have discussed the origins of Islam in western Arabia and its core of belief and distinguishing ritual. We have also sketched the history of its transformation into a world religion embracing different peoples and a variety of cultural traditions. We have noted its schisms and the variety of its expressions in the political and social spheres. However, this is not a book on Islamic civilization, nor is it a contemporary history of the Middle East. What we hope to convey is a sense of Islam as part of people's daily life and something of its role in Middle Eastern society. In short, we are interested in Islam primarily as a living cultural tradition.

As we noted at the beginning of Chapter 2, all too often the terms *Islam* and *Islamic Civilization* are invoked to "explain" a whole range of phenomena. These include political instability, oppression of women, economic underdevelopment, national xenophobia, and a host of supposed psychological attitudes, such as fatalism, rigid conservatism, and dependency. Such a simplistic perspective takes us back to an earlier period in history when Christians and Muslims vied with each other to control the Mediterranean and viewed each other in stereotypic religious terms.

Just as Christianity is not invoked to explain features of Western societies, such as colonialism, racism, and the Holocaust, Islam likewise cannot be considered as determining all the characteristics of societies in the Middle East. However, as with Christianity and Judaism, Islam provides a shared set of symbols and meanings that people use to identify themselves, to impart meaning to their lives, and to express certain aspirations. Islam thus remains the single most important source for the ethos that distinguishes the area and imparts to its bewildering complexity and variation a measure of unity and cultural uniformity. From this perspective, the role of the Muslim preacher, or imam, as the transmitter of religious knowledge and values assumes a special significance.[11]

Richard Antoun has pointed out that the imam acts as a

> culture broker who selects from and interprets an enormous corpus of religious ethics to a less sophisticated audience of co-religionists; but who, on the other hand . . . is constrained by and selectively incorporates the local customs accepted by his audience. (1993, p. 607)

Antoun studied religious life in a Jordanian village over a period of 30 years and analyzed the contents of the religious lessons (*dars*, pl. *durus*) given by the imam at the local mosque. The *dars* is conducted informally every Friday (before the congregational prayer) by the preacher, who sits on the floor and lectures to a circle of listeners on a topic inspired by the Quran or Hadith. The lesson lasts about 20 minutes, and listeners are free to interrupt and ask questions. In teaching Muslim ritual, ethics, and history, preachers stress the normative unity of the Muslim community, or *umma*, and underscore its common ethos, as Antoun illustrates in the following example, which we have adapted:

> In the course of one lesson, the preacher spoke of equality, and described the just leader as *al-imam al-'adil*, one who insures that everyone receives full and equal justice, and he quoted the Quran and the Hadith as his proof texts:
>
> > O Mankind! We created you from a single [pair] of a male and female. And made you into nations and tribes, that ye may know each other. (Not that ye may despise each other.) Verily, the most honored of you in the sight of God is [he who is] the most righteous of you. (Quran 49:13)
> >
> > There is no distinction of non-Arab ('ajami) over Arab except as to piety. (Hadith)

The preacher spent the remainder of the lesson describing other attributes of model Muslims whose emulation would lead to salvation.

Two weeks later the preacher again spoke of justice: "Justice involves reconciling opponents, giving honest testimony even against self and kinsmen and giving the right (*al-haqq*) to its possessor without diminishing it." The just ruler raises the case of the oppressed (as his own), and does not show partiality between his children and his wives. He again used the Hadith and the Quran as his texts:

---

[11] See also Patrick Gaffney (1994).

The sultan is the shadow of God on earth. If he does justice, he has an eternal reward and from his flock thanks. If he oppresses, sin (wizr) *falls on him, and his people must be patient. If government tyrannizes, the heavens bring drought. If the giving of alms is prohibited, the flocks perish. If fornication manifests itself, poverty and destitution appear. If the pact of trust is broken [between ruler and ruled] the unbelievers* (kuffar) *triumph.* (Hadith)

If two parties among the believers fall into a quarrel make peace between them. But if one of them transgresses beyond bounds against the others then fight ye [all] against the one that transgresses until it complies with the command of God; But if it complies, then make peace between them with justice ('adl) *and be fair* (uqsitu); *But God loves those who are fair and just.* (Quran 49:9, 614)

WOMEN AND RELIGION

Traditionally, women's religious activities have centered around all-female private gatherings to study the Quran and the Hadith and regular pilgrimages, *ziarat*, to shrines and cemeteries. In recent years, young urban women have begun to seek a more visible and active role in religion as they strive to construct a contemporary Muslim female identity and to participate in reshaping their religious tradition in the context of today's global world. While in the past women's contribution to the development of Islamic thought and ritual has been largely ignored and unrecorded, this is beginning to change:

> There is a new Islamic zeal developing in relation to women, which is evident in a female Islamic movement and involvement. Many aspects of women's life situations have become the province of Islamists by means of educational control and religious involvement. . . . This has affected the arena of traditional religious rituals, the religious socialization of the new generation, and educational opportunities for the young. (Kamalkhani, 1998, p. 178)

During the mid-1990s, Zahra Kamalkhani conducted fieldwork in an Iranian city to study the transformation that has taken place in the religious education of women since the establishment of the Islamic Republic in 1979. In the effort to reshape Iranian society, the Islamic state viewed girls' religious education as an important mechanism for the transmission of Islamic values and norms. Toward that end, the state opened a theological college in 1994 for training female preachers and ritual leaders. Today a system of Islamic universities, colleges, and schools is in place throughout Iran. This has resulted in a widespread "Islamic literacy," which increasingly is blurring the traditional boundaries between the textual and normative tradition of Islam (hitherto the province of the male religious elite) and the practical or popular understandings of Islam as a lived tradition.

> The so-called "popular" Islam often identified with the nature of beliefs among ordinary Muslims (in particular women) has become interwoven with organized higher education and re-articulated both in the local and national context. The

establishment of new theological schools and religious curricula and the exception of customary religious arenas and events has brought women more than ever into the active religious field. (p. 189)

Kamalkhani describes a new type of religious activity that has developed—an all-female meeting called *rowzeh*. At one such meeting she attended, held in a newly opened public religious hall (*hosyneh*), which had been constructed and donated to the community as *waqf* by a wealthy woman, three differently ranked female preachers presided over the well-attended meeting. One preacher instructed the women on Muslim ritual, and a second discoursed on Quran commentaries, known as the *tafsir*. The third preacher, who was a young woman in the final phase of her studies at a religious college, performed a cycle of religious lamentation songs, *noheh,* honoring one of the martyred imams.

The lamentations were broadcast on a loudspeaker and could be clearly heard outside the hall on the street. This was an obvious breach of Islamic traditional teaching, which forbids men from listening to the voices of women reciting the Quran or any other religious text. When Kamalkhani expressed her surprise about the fact that the female preacher's voice could be heard by men in the street, the young woman replied that "it was necessary to give merit to all her listeners on such a holy day," and that the religious message she preached took precedence over gender segregation and over the taboo on women's religious voices being heard in public (p. 181).

As Kamalkhani notes, the influx of religiously educated women into public arenas signals a new era in the evolution of Islamic knowledge. Highly educated and articulate female preachers and teachers attract large audiences that include women of all ages and class backgrounds; while some of these preachers may use their position to disseminate and reinforce state-approved messages, others who are politically neutral are in a position to provide alternative versions of what the role and comportment of believing Muslim women ought to be. In either case, what is important to bear in mind is the new religious space that the Islamic regime of Iran has, wittingly or not, opened up for women.

Another example of women's participation in religion comes from Turkey. As we mentioned earlier, in 1925, the Turkish government banned Sufi orders and closed their lodges and the shrines, *turbe*, of saints and renowned sheikhs. Beginning in the mid-1950s, the government began to relax its restrictions on religious orders and some shrines were allowed to reopen. Catharina Raudvere (1998) studied women's participation in the Sufi order of Halveti-Cerrahi in Istanbul during the mid-1990s. The order, founded in the eighteenth century, has a unique status in Turkey in that it is officially recognized today, albeit under the designation "Society for Traditional Turkish Music and Folklore." The following discussion is based on Raudvere's account.

In the 1960s and 1970s, the order was languishing and its membership was limited to a few older men who met weekly to perform the *zikr,* devotional prayers of remembrance. This changed in the 1980s; under the leadership of a charismatic and dynamic sheikh, and with the rising influence of Islamist movements, the order experienced a revival and expansion. The disciples of the order, *murids*, men and women, meet three times a week at the lodge, which serves as a place of devotion and social interaction. Raudvere distinguishes two groups of women members who regularly attend the *zikr* ritual at the lodge. One is made up of elderly and middle-aged women whose attendance is part of long-established family tradition. More recently, they have been joined by a group of young, educated women, university students and professionals. These women have joined the order out of personal choice, just as they have adopted the head scarf and the modest attire of a long skirt. Every Thursday night, the women enter the lodge through a separate door from the men, and go directly to their quarters on the upper balcony while men gather on the main floor. Separated by space, men and women perform the *zikr*. The women remain seated throughout while the male initiates may rise, form a spiral, and move in circles. Once a month, the women come together for a ceremony of their own without any men present. These ceremonies are led by two women appointed by the sheikh of the order. On this occasion, the devotional prayers are very emotional and are often accompanied by body movements and even dancing. After the ceremony, the women linger to talk, drink tea, and share snacks (p. 136).

The women initiates and others who participate in Sufi orders express a type of piety that is generally condemned by both Islamists and secularists in Turkey. For the Islamists, the Sufi orders are seen as encouraging "superstition" and un-Islamic behavior; the secularists, on the other hand, fear the networking and organizational capacities of the orders and view them as potential vehicles for political activity. Raudvere concludes:

> Being a young female dervish (Sufi initiate) in contemporary Istanbul is to claim both tradition and modernity. The normative discourses founded in the Koran and the Hadith offer transhistorical claims which are used to defend a variety of positions. However, in a rapidly changing social context—a steadily growing metropolis with social turbulence and political turmoil—interpretation of the holy texts is an absolute necessity to be able to construct an urban Muslim identity. . . . In the midst of this are women's lives. Nevertheless, being a religious woman is not any longer equivalent to ignorance and powerlessness. It can certainly mean resistance to authoritarian Islam. (pp. 140–141)

GENERAL OVERVIEW

We must emphasize here that Islam is not inherently a force for any particular course of action or development, whether for an authoritarian form of government or a democratic one, a socialist or a free-market economy. What Islam does, as Christianity or any universalistic faith does, is to construct an intellectual and cultural environment in which actors can choose from among myriad behavioral options. One should be wary of imputing collective traits, tendencies, and attitudes to such abstract categories as race, religion, civilization, or peoples. Islamic culture in the Middle East, however defined, is shaped by its own regionally varied history, as well as by its present realities. At this level, some scholars have found it useful to speak not of "Islam" but rather of "Islams," in order to underscore the existing variations in time and place. Just as Islamic culture in Iran is different from Islamic culture in Egypt or in Malaysia, Islam within Iran is expressed differently and plays different roles among different segments of society, whether defined in terms of region, ethnic group, or economic class.

What the anthropological perspective on Islam as culture might best offer is not further analytic distinctions, which, in effect, tend to establish normative Islam in opposition to Islam in practice. Rather, it should encourage us to see Islam as simply being what people who profess it believe and do. In this sense, Islam is neither moribund nor a relic of the past any more than are the people themselves. Islam can be as much a form of revolution as it is of conservatism, a power for justice as well as a tool for oppression. It can liberate as well as constrain. In Iran, in 1979, a despotic regime was overthrown by the unity forged by the Shi'a 'ulama among disparate segments of society through shared Islamic symbols. Today, the future of the Islamic revolution and the course of the country's development are being shaped by new interests and forces expressing a widely shared democratic impulse.

4

Communal Identities and Ethnic Groups

All contemporary societies of the Middle East have been shaped by long and varied historical processes, of which the people themselves are acutely conscious. Appeals to history often serve to validate the present as well as provide an ideological basis for unity and solidarity. Paradoxically, such historical awareness also serves to differentiate one group from another in an area and therefore contributes to cultural diversity and disunity. This diversity, sometimes visually expressed through distinctive styles of dress, ritual, and public behavior, must be properly appreciated if we are to understand Middle Eastern society. We have already seen in our discussion of Islam some of the historical processes that differentiated groups within the Islamic tradition; these differences themselves parallel, amplify, and even define group boundaries and structure intergroup relations today. In addition, there are indigenous non-Muslim populations in most countries, not to mention the Jewish state of Israel.

This diversity has been likened to a "human mosaic" in which the members of each identifiable group emphasize their common and special identity through some configuration of symbols. These symbols may be material—in the form of dress, dwelling styles, or language or dialect; of even greater significance, however, are the underlying patterns of behavior, values, and systems of belief. The recognition and acceptance of ethnic or communal differences have historically been a fundamental principle of Middle Eastern social organization. The metaphor of a human mosaic, however, has its limits. Although it may describe contemporary patterns, it offers little insight into the many processes that underlie the formation of group identities, how these change over time, and, more important, how people use them to gain access to resources and power.

Until the rise of nationalism, most polities comprised aggregates of bounded social groupings, either tribes or confessional communities, often held together by dynastic tradition. Whether joined for common purpose or held together by threat of force, the distinctive quality of the individual or localized

90

grouping was maintained through the principle of collective responsibility. It is interesting to note that more than a century of Turkish, Arab, and Iranian nationalistic movements has not succeeded in eroding the significance of more narrowly defined ethnic and tribal identity for the individual. In this chapter we discuss the broad outlines of ethnicity and the sources of individual and group identities.

Each country and region of the Middle East contains local groupings or populations that are distinct from the society as a whole and are recognized as such by themselves and others. That is to say, people recognize themselves as belonging to some unique grouping within a larger population. The elements used to signal the identity of ethnic groups include religious affiliation, language or dialect, tribal membership or shared descent, and regional or local customs.

ETHNICITY: A THEORETICAL FRAMEWORK

In considering ethnicity in the Middle East, we should keep in mind a number of points that together make up a framework for the understanding of both the phenomenon of ethnicity and ethnic group relations. *Ethnicity* refers to a social or group identity that an individual ascribes to himself or herself and that is also accepted by others. It is the basis for the formation of categories that are rooted in socially perceived differences in origin, language, and/or religion. In many respects, ethnicity resembles descent ideology: it stresses one's origins, or descent, as part of one's social identity and is usually ascribed at birth. While such an awareness of the past is a source of unity, it also emphasizes that which potentially sets one segment of the population apart from others. The Alevis of Turkey, whom we discussed earlier, are a case in point. Adhering to a mystical form of Shi'ism, they constitute a distinctive and endogamous grouping among Turkish and Kurdish speakers in Anatolia, one defined by religious practice rather than language (Shankland, 1993a and b).

Because ethnic categories are culturally defined, they can be manipulated and changed. In one situation, for example, an individual might identify him- or herself as a Kurd, while in another as a Turk or a Persian or an Arab—the politically dominant identities in the countries with large Kurdish populations. There is a high rate of bilingualism in polyglot regions, and within regional or national minorities, most males, at least, are completely at home in the politically dominant language. People may adopt the language, symbols, and codes of a special grouping to which their ties are quite remote or even nonexistent. In this sense, ethnic identity may be considered a personal strategy, a means to accomplish a desired objective. For example, in Iran, educated and well-to-do members of different non-Persian-speaking groups, such as the Qashqa'i or the Azeri, assimilated into the national elite by using Persian upper-class speech mannerisms and social codes. They, nonetheless, usually maintained their original cultural identification when with their own people. The converse also occurs; Kurdish intellectuals whose mother tongue may be Turkish, Arabic, or Persian may make of point of using Kurdish even though their fluency is less (Mango, 1995).

Ethnic identity is regularly reformulated or "reinvented" in much the same way that new nationalisms emerge, spread, and, in time, may also fade away. Still, ethnicity or local-level collective organization and identity based on notions of shared kinship, history, culture, and language, while in many respects similar to nationalism, is not simply a scaled-down or primitive representation of nationalism (Smith, 1986, p. 13). Just as nationalism, when enshrined as state ideology, proclaims the eternal unity of a land and a people, as for example, does Zionism, assertion of a distinct ethnicity can be a potent response by those whose perceived interests and identities are threatened by this same formulation of nationalism. Here, again, the Kurds of Turkey, Iran, and Iraq are a good example, as are the Palestinians. While many if not most Kurds today live outside their traditional heartlands of Kurdistan, they respond strongly to appeals phrased in ethnic terms. The most important distinction to be made between nationalism and ethnicity is how boundaries are conceptualized and operationalized. With ethnicity, the boundaries are based on perceptions of heritage and are not limited to territorial expression or claims.

Ethnic politics should not be equated with ancient, intractable animosities simply because such statements are often basic to the rhetoric of both ethnicity and nationalism. Rather, the idiom of ethnicity, like appeals to "nation" or "tribe," becomes operative in specific contexts or environments. What gives shape and continuity to political behavior might be called ideological or moral models, and these often draw on notions that are strikingly similar in tribal,

A Yomut Türkmen family en route to a wedding celebration in north central Iran.

ethnic, and national expressions: they draw upon ties of affect rooted in beliefs about morality, kinship, family, and history; and they are expressed in recognizable codes and symbols, including language and religion. However, ethnic constructions need have no territorial component nor need they be concerned with the perennial problem of nationalism—reconciling who is and who is not included. Ethnic boundaries are rooted in individual self-ascription as well as ascription by others, and so are contextual, malleable, and not based on any particular set of ideas of what distinguishes the community. The usual idioms of ethnic mobilization are "survival" and "justice," perceived collective fears and wrongs effectively creating a "we-they" divide. Thus, in at least one important respect it may be inaccurate to speak of ancient ethnic animosities and primordial ethnic hatreds, as, sadly, is so often the case with respect to the Middle East. Specific conflicts, on examination, have very specific causes however much the rhetoric of kinship, community, and culture are evoked, and a look to the past will almost invariably reveal quite different patterns of alignment and notions of community boundaries.

Even individuals who have no desire to assimilate or "pass," as it were, frequently use the codes and symbols of others to facilitate communication or simply to show respect. Of course, there are both psychological and social limits as to how people can use or manipulate ethnic or other forms of group identity. Individuals are socialized into primary groupings in ways that encourage a psychological commitment to their close relatives and to the symbols and values to which they adhere. Rarely do individuals repudiate these primary ties. Moreover, there are practical constraints on the manipulation of sources of identity. One constraint has to do with the willingness of other people to accept the use of a particular identity.

Although ethnic identity is ultimately an individual strategy, its main social significance emerges in the extent to which it serves as the basis for political or economic organization. Throughout the Middle East there was historically a strong tendency for occupational specialization to be associated with particular ethnic groups. For example, many families of the Jewish community in Isfahan traditionally specialized in fine metalwork and in trading of gold and silver; Kurds in Istanbul and Ankara, moving seasonally into the cities as temporary residents, had a near-monopoly as porters in the bazaars; most hotels and restaurants in Iraq used to be run and staffed by Assyrian Christians; most of the long-distance truck drivers and automotive mechanics of Iran were Azeri Turks, and most of the professional cooks in Egypt were Nubians. Today, this is rapidly changing, even disappearing, due to a number of factors, including mass education, mobility, and the proliferation of new occupations.

Although these days it is not possible to identify particular tasks or occupations exclusively with particular groups, there are still some general associations. For example, Gypsies are closely identified with tasks thought to be polluting or degrading, such as dealing in animal hides and public entertainment. Christians and Jews have long been associated with forms of commerce and business, which, for religious or other cultural reasons, were felt unsuitable for Muslims. Money lending or money changing and import-export activities that relied on such transactions were dominated by non-Muslims until mid-century. Only 20 percent of business enterprises enumerated in the Ottoman census of 1913–15 were Muslim-owned (Keyder, 1999). The role of non-Muslims in trade, of course, was furthered by their ability to use their contacts with core-ligionists outside the area.

What is almost universal is for each region or community to have its locally unique patterns of division of labor along ethnic lines. There are organizational advantages in having skills and trades passed from father to son, and there are advantages in closely related individuals following the same craft or line of trade. Quite apart from facilitating training, relatives are often sources of credit or capital given on the basis of personal trust and reputation. In general, communication is also easier among kin, which probably facilitates the local prominence of one or another group in a particular endeavor. Because lines of patronage and mutual support often reflect primary group ties, it is not surprising that as new jobs or employment opportunities arise, they may be filled by people sharing a social or ethnic identity.

Ethnic group membership can structure access to resources and intergroup relations. In other words, as Fredrik Barth (1969) notes very elegantly, the cultural content of ethnicity—that is, the symbols and codes that define it—can facilitate or impede the access of people to resources. In Barth's view, ethnic groups can be thought of as occupying unique places in the social landscape. The place or niche of any group is determined by what they do for a living, their social and political organization, and their relations to other groups in their environment. Further, this approach draws attention to the fact that occupational or productive specialization on the part of an entire group can be a very effective means of utilizing available resources, including labor and acquired skills.

This model emphasizes the complementarity of the roles and functions served by the different groups who interact with one another. For example, the Yörük of southeastern Turkey (see Chapter 5) have traditionally been nomadic pastoralists. They do not, however, own pastures and must acquire grazing rights from local landlords and villages. Thus, their niche is defined as much by the activities of other groups as it is by the needs of their animals and the grasses that sustain them. The Yörük exploit marginal areas and high pastures that local farmers are not equipped to fully utilize. The close lines of communication and mutual support among the Yörük make it difficult for outsiders to effectively compete with them in getting pastures, in organizing sales of animal products, and in moving flocks. Ethnicity, with its emphasis on shared unique social characteristics, thus facilitates access to certain resources, even the defense of them against others. As a result, particular resources or ways of exploiting them may become identified in many regions with particular peoples.

However, we have to keep in mind that complementarity or mutuality of benefits is only one aspect of intergroup relations. Groups frequently establish exploitative relationships with others in which ethnic identity may serve to organize and perpetuate inequality. The Shabak of northern Iraq (see Chapter 3), for example, were a caste-like grouping of agricultural sharecroppers who depended on politically and socially dominant urban Arab landlords. Differentiated by language and religious practices, the Shabak long remained a weak and exploited group. As Shabak, they were systematically denied access to better jobs outside their community and found it difficult to find anyone who would sell them land. The ethnic label of Shabak locally connoted poverty, backwardness, and low status. Should a Shabak family acquire wealth or move into town, it would rapidly try to disassociate itself from the rural community, which at times included changing language and customary practices.

Even when a high degree of economic mutuality exists among members of different groups interacting together, there may also be considerable mutual antipathy. For example, the Sulubba, Gypsy-like nomadic peoples of Arabia, formerly specialized in metalwork, music making, and entertainment. They regularly moved from one Bedouin camp to another or between villages, plying their trade. Despite close association with their hosts and clients, they were held in low esteem and were socially ostracized. Although at times the very values and attitudes held by members of a particular ethnic group toward others may engender overt hostility and conflict, this should not be overly stressed as a generalization. Mutual accommodation and tolerance are by far the more common basis for communal interaction. Lebanon, prior to the serious outbreak of interethnic violence in the mid-1970s, was held up as a paradigm of interethnic accommodation and mutual tolerance for at least two generations. Today it is once again largely free from terrorism and intercommunal fighting, having adopted an acceptable arrangement of power sharing.

We should reemphasize that ethnicity is an analytic concept used to describe or understand aspects of individual or group identity. While we speak easily of particular ethnic groups and their cultural boundaries, we have to keep in mind that the effective units of social action implied by ethnic labels are ever-changing. Whether or not a particular ethnic category of people or identifiable collectivity is meaningfully thought of as a "group" depends on a knowledge of the specific circumstances. For example, it is not useful to regard Arabs in the Middle East as an ethnic group. However, a small subpopulation of Arabic speakers within a Persian-speaking community *may* interact as a bounded group in the way that Barth suggests.

In the following sections, we look at important sources for cultural differentiation that may be utilized at any given time to define ethnic-group boundaries. These sources for differentiation constitute the raw materials for ethnic identity and group formation.

RACE

Of all the elements that may be used to define groups or social categories, phenotypic race or biological variation is the least important in the Middle East, where the vast majority of the people from Egypt to Afghanistan tend to fall within the same racial grouping, often referred to as "Mediterranean." Where a markedly differentiated population exists, such as the *'abid* or blacks of Saudi Arabia, the Nubians of Egypt, or the Türkmen of Iran (with pronounced Mongoloid features), such phenotypic differences are locally recognized but are not necessarily associated with an ethnic identity. Even though in much of the area light skin is considered a mark of beauty and high status, there is no prevailing ideology of race based on color. For example, many would describe Gypsies as a distinguishable "racial" grouping, but in fact the clues to making such an identification are largely cultural rather than phenotypic—style of dress, occupation, manner of deportment, and the like.

While slavery was historically practiced throughout the Islamic world, it was not exclusively associated with Africans or any other particular population. In the Arabian Peninsula, as might be expected by virtue of geography, most slaves were East African in origin, and their descendants still form fairly distinct groupings within Peninsular Arabian society. One remaining frontier of contention between Muslim and so-called "pagan" or animist populations runs through southern Sudan. For over 40 years there has been a struggle amounting to civil war pitting the Arabs of the north, who dominate all state institutions, against the Nilotic-speaking populations of the southern provinces, most of whom are Christian or animist. While the course of this conflict is too complex to enter into here, one sad by-product of the anarchy it has created is the resurgence of slaving involving both Christians and animists as victims.

The Ottomans recruited slaves from both Eastern Europe and the Caucasus. In general, the descendants of these slaves today do not form either racially or ethnically distinct groups. This is because many of the "slaves" were employed in high-level administrative positions and in the military. In fact, they were not slaves at all in the sense of chattel but rather were part of the sultan's entourage and administrative cadre. Once converted to Islam, such individuals served the government throughout the empire, married, and accumulated property. Slavery in this case meant little more than a "servant of the sultan." Islamic law does not privilege distinctions of race, ethnicity, class, rank, or family, and the descendants of slaves, of whatever origin, are not stigmatized, nor are the descendants of converts to Islam.

Outside of a few towns in southern Arabia, slavery in the Middle East has never been a primary means of organizing menial labor. Perhaps as a consequence, the association of class and race or ethnicity and race is not well developed in the area.[1]

---

[1] Bernard Lewis (1990, 1979).

LANGUAGE

As we have noted, under certain circumstances, linguistic differences can become ethnic markers. But, more important, language serves to establish boundaries on a much larger scale. The three major language groupings in the modern Middle East are the Semitic, Indo-European, and Altaic or Turkic linguistic families. These are broad classifications, and each encompasses a number of major languages and numerous distinctive dialects. Arabic and Hebrew are Semitic languages. Whereas Hebrew is spoken only in Israel, Arabic is the national language of the countries of North Africa, Egypt, Lebanon, Syria, Jordan, Iraq, Saudi Arabia, and the smaller states of the Arabian Peninsula. The Indo-European language family is regionally represented by the many dialects of modern Persian, Kurdish, Luri, Baluchi, and smaller groups of Greek and Armenian speakers. The major Turkic languages and dialects are western or standard Turkish of Anatolia, Azeri of Iran, Türkmen, and the languages of smaller groups of eastern Turkic speakers of Central Asian origin, such as Tatars and Kazaks. In Northwest Africa, Berber, an Afro-Asiatic language, is spoken by a large number of people, especially in the mountain and desert regions of Morocco, Algeria, Tunisia, and to a lesser extent in Libya. Berber is divided into a number of distinct, and in some cases, mutually unintelligible dialects/languages. However, Arabic is the official language throughout Northwest Africa, and the majority of the Berbers tend to be bilingual. Berber speakers, in general, do not refer to themselves as "Berber" but as "Imazighin."

Language in and of itself usually establishes only the outermost parameters to group membership, although dialect differences may precisely identify a person as to region or even tribe. In Baghdad, for example, Muslims, Jews, and Christians all speak Iraqi Arabic, a dialect distinct from colloquial Egyptian or Syrian. However, the three groups can be distinguished from one another on the basis of distinctive speech mannerisms, syntax, and grammar.

Spoken Arabic represents a number of distinct speech communities that vary regionally; those of Egypt, Syria, Iraq, and Saudi Arabia are quite distinct. Even within countries, there is regional variation, as, for example, between Lower and Upper Egypt. In the extreme southern part of the Arabian Peninsula, a small number of communities speak a highly variant dialect of Arabic identified as Southern Arabian. Nonetheless, the major dialects of Arabic are usually mutually comprehensible and all are written in one form. The rapid development of mass communication and the extension of public education are facilitating the breakdown of dialect barriers and encouraging the spread of a common standardized Arabic used in publications everywhere.

Persian, an Indo-European language, is the national language of Iran and encompasses many closely related dialects spoken as a first language by about 50 million people in Iran and by over 5 million people in neighboring Afghanistan. Persian is written in Arabic characters and, as does Turkish, has a substantial Arabic vocabulary. The infusion of Arabic is due in part to the early politicoreligious domination of Iran by the Arab Muslims and at least in equal part to the use of Arabic by medieval Persian scholars and men of letters. As with Arabic, dialect variations in Persian serve to differentiate class and regional affiliations.

The third national language in the Middle East is Turkish. Of the over 150 million Turkic-speaking peoples in the world, more than 55 million live in Turkey proper where dialectical differences are relatively minor when compared with other primary language families. Urban-rural differences in speech frequently overshadow regional differences, although certain interregional linguistic differences can be easily distinguished, for example, the Black Sea coast from the Mediterranean. Until the reforms of the Atatürk period, Turkish was written in Arabic script, but since 1928 Turkish has used the Roman alphabet. Variants of the Roman alphabet, as adapted to Turkish, are increasingly used in the Central Asian Turkic republics, marking political and cultural reorientation away from Russia.

In every state, there are important communities that speak languages other than the national languages, as well as a substantial amount of bilingualism. This gives a political dimension to language and constitutes the level at which language is most salient in defining ethnic boundaries. In Turkey, for example, about 10 million to 12 million people are native speakers of Kurdish, and many other smaller groups of people speak Armenian, Greek, Ladino (a Spanish dialect spoken by Sephardic Jews), Tatar, Circassian, or Bulgarian. Perhaps as many as 100,000 people in Turkey speak Arabic. However, only standard Turkish can be used in schools (apart from a small number of designated foreign or religious institutions) and in the courts.

At one time Kurdish newspapers, books, and records were illegal. Today in Turkey there are numerous Kurdish publications, as well as some quasi-legal TV and radio broadcasting. A national organization, the Mesopotamian Cultural Club and Press Centre, has offices throughout the country and often sponsors musical and literary events. The old euphemism "mountain Turk" is no longer used, and Kurdish identity is openly referred to in the media—although it should also be noted that new euphemisms are also employed, such as "an ethnic grouping." It remains illegal to advocate anything that the authorities might interpret as "divisive" or "separatist," which is a powerful and much resented disincentive to free speech and even musical and literary expression. However, in neighboring Iraq, where the 4 million to 5 million Kurds form an even larger minority relative to the national population, Kurdish is the language of education in districts where Kurds predominate. This has not been the case in Iran, where some 5 million Kurds live along the northwestern border. Although an Indo-European language, Kurdish is grammatically and lexically distinct from Persian. Public education is conducted exclusively in Persian, and the use of Kurdish in public media is restricted.

Like Kurdish speakers, the Baluch are also divided among a number of nation-states: Iran, Pakistan, and Afghanistan. The Baluch, who number around

3 million, speak highly localized variants of Baluchi, an Indo-European language. Located in one of the most arid mountainous zones of southwest Asia, most of the Baluch eke out a living as nomadic pastoralists, coastal fishermen, and farmers.

The presence of these large, linguistically differentiated minorities, like the Kurds, Baluch, Türkmen, or even the encapsulated Arabic-speaking communities in Turkey and Iran, has serious political implications. It is important to note that in every country there is a strong nationalist movement underwriting the use of particular languages or dialects to promote unity in the face of considerable and deeply rooted cultural diversity. For members of local populations, such as those we have noted, this often presents a major dilemma. To participate fully in the national economy, to educate their children, and to partake fully in the national culture, they have to acquire a second language and dissociate themselves to some extent from their primary communities.

Although the educated elite in most countries of the Middle East is almost always bilingual in a European language, great emphasis is placed on the promotion of a national tongue among the masses. Bilingualism in English and, to a lesser extent, French not only serves as a sign of education and status but is increasingly a necessary tool for employment in the emerging global market.

RELIGION

Although language and local dialects are significant in the differentiation of people and may delineate distinctive communities, religion is the most important single source of personal and group identity—and, by extension, social divisions. The perceived rights and obligations of one person to another are strongly tempered by whether or not the parties involved are coreligionists. The assumption that, in the final analysis, an individual will turn to and favor others of his or her faith is so pervasive as to constitute a basic principle of social interaction. Religion in its many sectarian expressions sets some of the most important limits to interpersonal behavior. Of all injunctions regarding marriage expressed by the religions of the Middle East, the one fundamental to all is that marriage be restricted to coreligionists.

This is not to say that religious ties or bonds inevitably supersede all others. In fact, class differences, tribal and ethnic divisions, and the like often take precedence over any claims of religion as people organize themselves in groups for common action. Religion is more a determinant of maximal boundaries or inclusiveness, less commonly the basis for local organization. For example, a village may be composed of both Sunni and Alevi residents (Shankland, 1993a, 1993b). This distinction is almost inevitably reflected in voluntary residential segregation. However, within each residential quarter, groups organizing for political action or other purposes are most likely to utilize more exclusive criteria for membership. Recruitment for political action is more apt to be along lines of common descent and tribal affiliation. One has only to look at the persistent conflicts in Iran between the Shi'a Azeri and Shi'a Persians, or in Iraq between the Sunni Kurds and Sunni Arabs for examples of ongoing intrasectarian conflict. Moreover, ties of close friendship, contractual partnerships, and political alliances everywhere join people across sectarian boundaries. Residence within towns and cities, while often expressing some aggregation along sectarian lines, is rarely homogeneous. In virtually every big city, Christians, Jews, and Muslims live in close juxtaposition and share apartment buildings and compounds.

Although religion cannot be evoked to explain all or even most patterns of social interaction, sectarianism continues, nonetheless, to be a factor with important political and social consequences for every country in the region. Nationalistic movements both within countries and those, like pan-Arab nationalism, which transcend state frontiers, have consistently found it difficult to reconcile sectarianism with their more encompassing national and transnational political objectives. Islamist political movements also have to contend with Muslim sectarianism.

NON-MUSLIM CONFESSIONAL COMMUNITIES: JEWS AND CHRISTIANS

Because the nature of religious distinctions in the Middle East and the development of specific confessional communities are rooted in the formative period of Islam, the tenacity of sectarianism in the political and social arenas can only be understood when considered within the historical context. Further, all successor states and governments have, one way or another, perpetuated the idea of the confessional community as part of the structure of society.

From its inception, Islam as a faith was explicitly the basis for political action; even within the lifetime of its founder it became the vehicle for the formation and organization of a new polity. The boundaries of the political community were not simply territorial but coincided with those of the religious one, or *umma*. Both the legitimacy of the ruler and the rights and responsibilities of the members derived from their common membership in the religious community; it followed that to be a full citizen was also to be a Muslim. Although over the centuries there have been many Muslim states, and although many Muslim groups have been encapsulated within non-Muslim polities, recognition of common membership in one *umma*, or Muslim community, remains a potent ideological force.

What, then, of the non-Muslims who were incorporated into the early Islamic empires and their successor states? The Prophet Muhammad regarded the Christians and Jews as "People of the Book," the recipients of a valid but incomplete, and hence imperfect, revelation. Members of both communities were allowed to practice their religion and keep their institutions and property, but on the condition that they pay a special poll tax. They were not allowed to serve in the army or assume direct authority over Muslims. As a consequence, Christians and Jews assumed a status of *Ahl al-dhimmi*, that is, tolerated clients of the Muslim community—clients who suffered certain sociopolitical liabilities in exchange for protection and the right to retain their distinctive religious identities and communal organization.[2]

While the significant distinction is between Muslim and non-Muslim, the underlying principle is more widely employed. Religious identity, even as narrowly defined by the sects that rapidly arose within Islam itself, assumes political significance. The systematic merging of social and religious identity persists and has become even further institutionalized with time, as we see, for instance, in the Coptic-Muslim social cleavage in Egypt.

Within the Ottoman Empire, the immediate political predecessor to many of the modern states with which we are concerned here, this system was particularly developed and formed a principle of the organization of the empire. In May 1453, the Ottoman armies, led by Sultan Mehmet II, captured the city of Constantinople from the Byzantines. Even though the Ottomans already ruled vast lands containing Christian subjects in Europe and Anatolia, it was only after the fall of Constantinople that they institutionalized a system of governance that came to be called the *millet*. The sultan sought the support of selected Christian religious leaders and assured the Greek Orthodox clergy that it could retain civil as well as religious authority over Orthodox Christians in the empire. In fact, he used the clergy to bring in Greek settlers to help repopulate the city, which, at the time of conquest, had been in decline.

The practice of delegating considerable authority to community and religious leaders is the basis of the *millet* system, which was later extended to the Armenians, Jews, and others. Quite apart from being an effective way of ruling non-Muslims, it had the effect of reinforcing the political and social significance of sectarian identity. Marriage, divorce, and other aspects of personal status were all regulated through the *millet*. The *millet* was also responsible for resolving many of its own internal conflicts and for paying some taxes collectively. By the nineteenth century, 17 different *millets* were recognized by the Ottoman government.

It is apparent that religious or communal divisions are basic to the structure of Middle Eastern political life and are not simply anomalies or the result of imperfect assimilation. The various Christian sects and the Jews have, over the centuries, accommodated themselves to Muslim rule, just as the Muslim majority has recognized their right to persist in a separate communal order. Likewise, within Islam itself, the various sects often maintained a separate communal order resembling that of the non-Muslim minorities.

---

[2] For an excellent study of the Christian and Jewish communities in the Middle East, see Y. Courbage and P. Fargues (1998).

Only with the advent of nationalistic ideologies in the nineteenth and twentieth centuries did this communal and sectarian compartmentalization come to be questioned and tested. The issues of what constitutes nationality and full citizenship and how to accommodate sectarian differences still have to be resolved in most of the states of the area. Interestingly, this is as true of Israel as it is of the other states. To appreciate this new dimension of Middle Eastern society and politics, we will describe briefly the historical evolution of Jewish and Christian communities in the region. We begin our discussion with the Jews, who form some of the oldest continuing ethnoreligious communities in the area.[3]

Jewish Communities

A review of the place of Jews in the Ottoman Empire is illustrative of the wider structural position of non-Muslims in society, keeping in mind that the political structure itself changed with time and that administrative practices differed regionally.[4] In 1492, on the eve of Columbus's voyage to the New World,

The Dome of the Rock mosque in Jerusalem towers above the Western Wall, a sacred site to the Jews.

[3] See Bernard Lewis (1984).

[4] The following is taken from Avigdor Levy's edited collection of recent and authoritative essays on the Jews of the Ottoman Empire (1994), as well as from Eleazar Birnbaum's excellent review of the volume (1997).

Ferdinand and Isabella of Spain issued an edict expelling all Jews from their recently unified kingdom. The Sephardim, or Jews of Spain, sought and received haven in the Ottoman Empire. Even before this influx, significant numbers of Yiddish- and Greek-speaking Jews lived in rural and urban communities throughout the empire. Heath Lowry, a historian, looking at tax records for Salonica (Thessalonika), now in northern Greece, found that the taxable Jewish population rose from zero in 1478 to 60 percent of the city in 1530 (cited in Birnbaum, 1997, p. 213). Equally interesting, he discovered a sudden decrease in their numbers in the seventeenth century paralleled by a rise in Muslim households, which, he states, "stemmed from the Jewish followers of Shabbetai Tzevi formally embracing Islam" (p. 213). (Such conversions were rare, however.) Within the Jewish community of Salonica in the sixteenth century, which was the second largest of the empire and of the world, there was a pan-congregational institution known as the *kehillah,* which represented the various congregations to the authorities for purposes of taxation, as well as running a Torah school and operating a hospital, a hospice for travelers, and an insane asylum. In commerce, crafts, the arts, and medicine, the Jews contributed greatly to the prosperity of the empire. Individual communities and congregations enjoyed considerable autonomy under rabbinical leadership. In fact, until the end of the eighteenth century the bulk of the Jewish Ladino (Spanish-speaking) population did not find it necessary to speak or to write Turkish or Greek, and the daily life in the Jewish quarter focused on annual rounds of religious ritual and celebrations

In 1835, the already de facto Jewish *millet* was formalized with the appointment by the sultan of the *haham başı,* or chief rabbi. More or less from this date, beginning with the elite merchant class, secular and reform-minded organizations began promoting the use of written Turkish, as well as education in French and the adoption of European modes of dress and deportment. By the late Ottoman period, 1911, official census registers show 375,000 Jews as citizens, although many Jewish residents of the empire were not counted as they were carrying foreign passports, as was common among non-Muslims of the period (Birnbaum, 1997, p. 450). As the empire collapsed, considerable numbers of Balkan-dwelling Jews, like their Muslim counterparts, migrated into the remaining heartland. Following the establishment of state of Israel in 1948, most Iraqi, Turkish, Syrian, Egyptian, and North African Jews moved there, although in the case of Turkey, there was some reverse migration. Today, there are about 20,000 Jews in Turkey, down from 90,000 in 1948 (de Lange, 1999).

As we have noted, until the establishment of the state of Israel in 1948, a number of fairly large Jewish communities were found throughout the Middle East. In fact, the Arab countries of Egypt, Lebanon, Syria, Iraq, and Yemen alone are estimated to have had a Jewish population of about 400,000 in the mid-1940s.[5] Now there are only about 300 Jews remaining in Syria, and fewer still in Egypt, Jordan, Iraq, and Yemen. On the whole, these communities tended to be

---

[5] *American Jewish Yearbook* (1985).

urban with a few rural exceptions, such as those in northern Iraq and Yemen. In the former, the Jews spoke a Hebrew dialect, *targum,* and were the clients of powerful Kurdish chiefs in the area. Ranging from very wealthy urban bankers and merchants with international connections to poor, small shopkeepers and artisans, the members of the urban Jewish communities reflected in their lifestyles the different cultural traditions of the areas in which they lived. While displaying great internal diversity both in language and culture, most Jewish people residing in the Middle East before World War I were either dispersed remnants of ancient Jewish communities or members, as described earlier, of mostly Sephardic populations that, fleeing Christian oppression, sought refuge in Ottoman and other Muslim lands. In places the Sephardic Jews preserved their Spanish heritage through the use of Ladino, a Spanish dialect. The Ladino-speaking Sephardim were mostly urban and were concentrated in Istanbul and Izmir in Turkey.

The 1947 Egyptian census listed 65,639 Jews, most of whom lived in Cairo, with a small group in Alexandria. Cairo, like Baghdad, also had a large indigenous Jewish population and still boasts one of the oldest synagogues in continuous existence in the world. Here, again, the Jewish community, while distinguished by class differences, resided primarily in one quarter of the city and engaged in commerce, artisanship, and peddling. The position of the Jews in Egypt, like that of the Jews in Syria and Iraq, became extremely uncomfortable during and after the 1948 War of Independence and the establishment of Israel. Moreover, many Jews were closely associated with the British, French, Italian, Greek, and other foreign communities. When nationalist sentiment became inflamed against Israel and the West, it also rose against the Jewish community, finally bringing about a mass exodus after the British, French, and Israeli invasion in 1956.

There have been Jews in Iran since ancient times, and even though their native tongue is Persian, they maintain a strong sense of separate identity fostered by close intermarriage, residential segregation, and a focus on a number of shrines and pilgrimage centers within Iran, notably in Yazd, Isfahan, and Hamadan; a major shrine is the tomb of Daniel in Shush. Following the Iranian revolution of 1979, the Jewish community in Iran came under considerable pressure, with prominent members accused in the press of ties with Israel. In 1999, 13 prominent individuals were formally indicted and charged with spying for Israel. As a result there has been considerable out-migration both to Israel and North America, although about 30,000 remain (down from 80,000 in 1979) (de Lange, 1999).

While the scope of this book does not permit for a country-by-country treatment, Israel, the world's single Jewish state, needs special attention. Of a total population of 6 million, approximately 1 million Arabs live in Israel, 76 percent of whom are Muslim and the rest Christian. Immigration is the central and unique feature of Jewish nation-building (Goldscheider, 1996). Immigration from Ethiopia and Russia has increased the Jewish population by over half a million; in contrast, Palestinian population growth is due to higher than replacement birth rates. The various Jewish communities of Middle Eastern origins form a distinctive segment of Israeli society and are collectively known as *mizrachim*, or Oriental Jews. Although they make up a large percentage of the population of Israel, they tend to be underrepresented in the upper echelons of the government, army, and bureaucracy. Furthermore, they feel unfairly disadvantaged in terms of government programs and access to jobs in comparison with the recently arrived Jews from the former Soviet Union.

Christians in the Middle East

The Christian communities in the Middle East have a long and turbulent history.[6] Originally, all Christians in the region belonged to one or another of the indigenous churches that followed the Eastern rites. Outside the Greek Orthodox church, which was the official church of the Byzantines, the others had their origin in the schismatic "heresies" of the fifth and sixth centuries. Two of the largest Christian communities, the Copts of Egypt and the Assyrian Nestorians, go back to the fifth century and the religious controversies that culminated in the Council of Chalcedon (451). The disagreements ostensibly had to do with dogma, specifically concerned with the nature of Christ. However, these secessionist movements also represented efforts by the local populations to free themselves from the cultural and political domination of the Byzantines. In fact, the oppressiveness of Byzantine rule must have greatly facilitated the early and rapid success of the Muslim armies. This was the case of the Coptic community of Egypt. Persecuted by the Byzantines who regarded their church as schismatic, the Copts welcomed the Muslim armies in the mid-seventh century. After the Muslims defeated the Byzantines, they concluded a peace treaty with the Coptic Patriarch. The Copts today constitute the single largest Christian community in the Middle East.

Rural-dwelling Copts are concentrated in Upper Egypt, where they are found in villages little different from those of their Muslim neighbors except for the presence of a small church. Copts follow their own religious calendar, with its distinctive periods of fasting and holidays. Their clergy, who are allowed to marry, wield considerable power in their communities, where they act as leaders. Like the larger Muslim community, Copts prefer arranged marriages among close relatives—for example, the marriage of a son to his father's brother's daughter. Copts speak Egyptian Arabic and are culturally very much like the Muslim Egyptians of the same social class and education.

The Assyrian Christian communities of Iraq, Syria, and Turkey, like the Copts, once constituted a *millet* within the Ottoman Empire. Although today the majority of them are probably to be found in the United States and Canada (with

---

[6] Again, see Y. Courbage and P. Fargues (1998) for an overview of the history of Christian communities in the area.

some recent immigrants to Sweden as well), enough remain in these countries to make up distinctive minorities on the Mesopotamian plains and uplands. The largest is in Iraq. In origin, most of the Assyrians were rural dwellers in the northern part of the country; today they are found throughout the cities and towns of Iraq, with the largest concentration in the capital of Baghdad.

The majority of the Assyrians belong to the Nestorian church, with a small group divided between the Catholic and Protestant churches. The Nestorian church was originally centered in southern Iraq, and its communities were scattered over a large area, some as far as Central Asia and even China. Until recently, the Assyrians, who speak an Aramaic dialect, were an agricultural people scattered in villages in the mountains of Hakkâri (on the Iraqi-Turkish border) and in the valleys east of Lake Urmia. Caught in the turbulent politics of the area following World War I, the Assyrian leaders allied themselves with the British, and Assyrians joined the British army in Iraq as special levies. With Britain's help, a group of Assyrians hoped to establish an independent state for the Assyrians in northern Iraq. However, the British shift in policy and their interest in the establishment of an Arab monarchy in Iraq combined with a divided Assyrian leadership to put a cruel end to their hopes. Not only were the Assyrians frustrated in their efforts at independence, but several hundred of them were massacred in 1933 as they tried to flee Iraq into French-held Syria.

Besides the Copts and the Assyrians, there are other Christian sects of importance in the Middle East. One such group is the Uniate churches, of which the Maronites of Lebanon make up the largest community. The term *Uniate* refers to those communities of the Eastern churches that chose to recognize the authority of the Pope and to adopt the Latin rites. They did, however, retain their own patriarchs and internal autonomy. For example, the Chaldean Christians—a group of about 160,000 in Iraq, Syria, and Iran—split from the Nestorian church in 1750 and, urged on by Dominican missionaries, joined the Catholic church and acknowledged the Pope's authority in matters of dogma. Locally recognized as an enterprising and hardworking people, the Chaldeans dominated the service sector in the cities of Iraq, especially the hotel and restaurant business. Following World War II, large numbers of them, like their Assyrian neighbors, began immigrating to the United States and Canada—a process that continues today.

It is impossible to discuss the Maronite Christians without reference to the political scene in Lebanon. The recent history of Lebanon illustrates both the consequences of those historical processes that locate politics in sectarianism and the impact of Western colonialism and international power struggles on local politics.

The Maronites of Lebanon

The Maronite Uniate church is a national one that, in the main, is limited to Lebanon. It makes up the single largest Middle Eastern Christian community outside of Egypt. Syrian in origin, the Maronites are the followers of Saint John

Maroun (d. 410), who lived and preached near Antioch in present-day Turkey. Persecuted by the Byzantines in the fifth century, they sought refuge in the mountains of northern Lebanon and later spread to north-central Lebanon, which still remains their stronghold. Ruled directly or indirectly by the Ottomans from 1516 until the establishment of the French Mandate in the 1920s, the Maronites managed to retain a measure of independence that varied largely in response to the support they received from European powers. By the second quarter of the nineteenth century, the Maronites were already closely allied with the French and had emerged as the most important local sectarian power. This brought them into conflict not only with the Ottoman authorities but, more immediately, with the Druze and other Muslim groups in their area. In 1843, following a series of uprisings in Lebanon, the Ottomans responded to European pressure to create separate sectarian governorships for the various groups they ruled. After a series of massacres between the Druze, supported by the British, and the Maronites, supported by the French, the Ottomans created, in 1864, yet another governmental apparatus, one that was essentially the basis for the present state of Lebanon. This was the governate of Lebanon, based on a system of sectarian representation with an appointed Maronite governor. The political and economic dominance of the Maronite community, institutionalized at that time, continued until tested and broken in the 1975 civil war in Lebanon.[7]

The Republic of Lebanon was proclaimed in 1926 when the constitution was promulgated, but the real reins of power remained with the French. In 1943, the various Lebanese political leaders and factions closed ranks and demanded independence. When the French ousted the president and his prime minister, the Lebanese formed a resistance government and proclaimed a National Pact, which regulated relations among the different sectarian communities, of which the Maronite was then the largest. Complete independence was not achieved until the end of 1946, when the last French soldier sailed away and Lebanon became a member of the Arab League and the United Nations.

Modern Lebanon was founded on the assumption that the various confessional groups or religious sects would be united in a single polity as corporate units holding equal rights and status in the public domain. Thus citizenship in Lebanon came to necessitate identification with one or another of the 17 recognized religious communities or sects, the 7 main ones being Maronites, Sunni Muslims, Shi'a Muslims (the largest single sect today), Greek Orthodox, Greek Catholic, Druze, and Armenian Orthodox (Gregorian). Lesser sects include the Jacobite Christians, Syrian Catholics, Armenian Catholics, Jews, and Protestants—all this in a population of little more than 3 million.

The different confessional groups in Lebanon share a common language, Arabic, and a recognition of their interdependence. No community could dominate the other without endangering the very existence of the state, which was maintained in a "precarious balance," or perhaps more aptly, "in a balance of

---

[7] See Samir Khalaf (1993).

fear." Once hailed as the model for a Middle Eastern pluralistic and democratic society, Lebanon served a key function in the area. In the past, it was a refuge for persecuted religious minorities, and in modern times it became a haven for Middle Eastern political refugees of all persuasions.

In the summer of 1975, the "precarious balance" came to an abrupt and violent end. The delicate political fabric of Lebanon began to unravel and civil war broke out. Overtly, Christian was pitted against Muslim, but some clarifying remarks are necessary to correct the oversimplistic interpretation of the "Christian-Muslim" conflict in Lebanon as having been no more than an inevitable ethnic confrontation. As with most ethnic confrontations, the one in Lebanon was symptomatic of profound political and socioeconomic dislocations, greatly exacerbated by outside forces and foreign interests.

It has been accurately noted that the catalyst for the civil war was the presence in Lebanon of a large Palestinian population, both as refugees in camps that stretched from the heart of Beirut to the southern borders and as an armed military group that constituted a state within a state. In the mid-1970s, the Palestinian presence was estimated at about half a million. The presence of the refugees put a serious strain on Lebanon's economy, and the well-armed Palestinian militia complicated the political scene both internally and at the international level. Their presence in and use of southern Lebanon as a base of operations prompted regular and severe retaliatory strikes by Israeli forces. The effect of these strikes reverberated throughout Lebanese society and further added to the strains that already existed among the different groups.

The presence of the Palestinians clearly precipitated the crisis, but there were other underlying factors. One factor had to do with the way that sectarian and ethnic groups are distributed throughout the country. Each of the 17 officially recognized sectarian or ethnic groups in Lebanon has a relatively clear regional base from which its leading families contend for power on the national scene. A second underlying cause of conflict had to do with differential access to resources. The prosperity the country experienced in the 1940s and 1950s as a result of its role as a leading trade and banking center was unequally shared among the different groups; some, like the Shi'a, were substantially excluded from the benefits of the economic growth that favored most of the Christian communities engaged in trade.[8]

Before World War II, it seems that economic disparities among the various sectarian communities were relatively muted and were channeled along well-established and generally acceptable lines. By the mid-1970s, however, the agricultural majority of the population was receiving only 15 percent of the gross national product, while the 14 percent of the population engaged in commerce and related activities received 46 percent of the GNP. The Maronites benefited disproportionately from this development. Also, although no census has been conducted since 1932, the belief was widespread that the Maronites no longer

---

[8] See Joseph Suad (1978) and Joseph Suad and Barbara Pillsbury (1978).

constituted the largest sect in the country, about 25 percent of total population, and that their political power, while reflecting their wealth, did not reflect their numbers—still another cause for resentment (Awad, 1991, p. 85).

In earlier years, sectarian identification held little implication for economic class differentiation; by 1975, such was no longer the case. In February 1975, there was a major strike by Shi'a fishermen working for Maronite boat owners; their violent protests were quickly joined by Palestinians and others. With their numbers considerably enhanced by the Palestinian refugees, the various Muslim groupings, who now made up about 65 percent of the total population, demanded a larger share of the economy and a reorganization of the political system, with increased secularization of the state and mass elections. The politically dominant Christians, fearful of losing their advantage and angered by the alien presence of the revolutionary Palestinians—Christian or Muslim—refused a drastic overhaul of the political system, and armed confrontation ensued. But it was quickly apparent that Lebanon was to become the arena for the power plays of several outside interests: American, Syrian, and Israeli, among others. The instability generated by outside intervention and acts of inter-communal violence quickly undermined the already weak central state institutions and initiated a period of civil war.

The alignments produced by the warfare were bewildering, but they are a useful reminder that conflict expressed in the rhetoric of ethnicity or religion is never as clear-cut as it may appear. Even close observers disagreed as to the underlying principles that governed the short-term alliances among the many contending parties: Shi'a allied with Palestinians; right wing Phalangist Christians were supported by the Syrian army; Israel aided (and still does to some extent) certain Christian armed militia in the south. Many who rallied supporters to their cause in terms of religious or political beliefs appeared to have little more than banditry in mind—much as was later to be the case in the breakup of Yugoslavia. It was a conflict whose destruction clearly went beyond the self-interest of any class or sect. If any interest was served in all this, it was certainly not that of the Lebanese.

After 13 years of bloody civil war that left more than 150,000 dead and 300,000 displaced, in addition to the half-million who left the country, a political accord, known as the Ta'if Agreement, was reached in 1988. The Ta'if Agreement, named after the city in which the formal deliberations were held, was drawn up under the patronage of Saudi Arabia and with the approval of Syria (and the blessing, not to mention pressure, of the United States) and put an official end to the Lebanese war but not to political conflict (Kisirwani, 1997). It stripped the Maronite presidency of most of its executive powers, formed a new and powerful council of ministers, and balanced Sunni control of the prime minister's post by making a Shi'a speaker of the parliament—in short the Maronites lost their political dominance but retained a strong confessional presence. Two years later, the massive and difficult process of reconstruction began when the Lebanese government announced a comprehensive recovery plan

Karekin I, the Catholicos of All Armenians, greeting Turkish Armenians in Istanbul

that came to be known as Horizon 2000. Lebanon today continues to deal with the problems of national reconciliation, economic recovery, and reestablishing a credible bureaucracy, among others.

The Armenians

Another Christian community in the region is that of the Armenians, with significant numbers in Turkey and Lebanon. In Lebanon, some 180,000 Armenians live mainly in the Burj Hammoud area of Beirut. Many left during the civil war for North America, Europe, or the newly independent Republic of Armenia, formed at the breakup of the USSR. While the majority belong to the Armenian Orthodox church, small groups are Roman Catholic and Protestant. The Armenians who had sought refuge in Lebanon at the end of World War I were granted citizenship in 1939 under the French mandatory regime. The Armenian population of Lebanon and the approximately 60,000 Armenian citizens of Turkey, of whom 50,000 are residents of Istanbul, are part of a diaspora that includes approximately 3.5 million in the newly independent Republic of Armenia, 1 million in the United States and Canada, and about 400,000 in France.

The Armenian community was formerly the most important and influential *millet* of the Ottoman Empire, and through its long history provided counselors to the Ottoman court and contributed actively to the commercial and intellectual life of the empire. The total Armenian population in Anatolia at the turn of the century has been estimated at about 1.8 million, with the majority living in villages in the central and eastern regions. In the steppes and mountains of Anatolia, Armenian villages were intermingled with those of Kurdish, Türkmen, and other Muslim and Christian groups. The *millet* itself was traditionally headed by a Patriarch, confirmed by the Ottoman sultan, and generally selected by influential clerics and a number of wealthy urban families.

In the nineteenth century, the Armenian *millet* was subject to the same economic and political changes that buffeted the rest of Ottoman society, including the rise of nationalism, which had sparked the separatist movements of the peninsular Greeks and Balkan Christians. Caught between the British-Russian rivalry and the desire of many Armenians for internal reform, the *millet* became faction-ridden and highly politicized. The traditional leadership was opposed by those who, calling upon the support of one or another European power, attempted to secure further political advantage or even establish an independent Armenia. Influenced by the French Revolution and especially by the 1830 and 1848 revolutionary movements in Europe, young Armenian activists founded two socialist revolutionary parties, the Hunchakian and the Dashnak. The first, founded in 1887 in Geneva, called for complete political independence; the second, founded in Tiflis in 1890, advocated reforms within the framework of the Ottoman Empire.

Reacting violently to the threat of the Armenian revolutionary movements, government-sanctioned militias attacked a number of Armenian communities. The period 1894 through 1916 was marked by much intersectarian strife, repeated attacks on Armenian villages, and anti-Armenian pogroms. European powers consistently intervened in Ottoman domestic affairs, which contributed further to the widening gap that separated Muslim and Christian communities. French, British, and Russian consulates regularly issued passports to Christian subjects of the Ottoman Empire, supplied money to dissidents, and encouraged the nationalist aspirations of the Greeks and the Armenians.

During World War I and immediately after the breakup of the Ottoman Empire, massive deportations, forced movements of populations, and even the starvation of substantial numbers ultimately resulted in the removal of nearly all Armenians from rural Anatolia. The ill-considered attempt to establish an Armenian republic in southeastern Turkey following World War I resulted in massacres and the forced migration of the last remaining rural concentration of Armenians from Turkey. Thousands fled to Lebanon and Syria. Following World War II, about 40,000 Armenians left Lebanon and Syria and immigrated to Soviet Armenia, but the rest remained in Lebanon, where today they form a strong, internally cohesive ethnic community.

MUSLIM-DERIVED SECTARIAN COMMUNITIES

Although more could be said about the nature of non-Muslim communities and their constituent social groupings, in almost every country of the Middle East we have seen something of a shared pattern. This is one of historical encapsulation rather than assimilation of communities whose outer limits are set by religion. As described in Chapters 2 and 3, there are numerous Muslim-derived communities as well. In a structural sense, they are very similar to the non-Muslim ones, forming as they do inward-looking confessional minorities. Three of the latter, mentioned earlier, are the Druze of Syria, Lebanon, and Israel, the Alawis of Syria and Alevis of Turkey, and the Shabak of northern Iran.

The Druze and the Alawis exemplify the use of distinctive Islamic ideology and practice to announce a separate identity and to maintain what amounts to closed communities within the larger society.[9] What these and others, like the 'Ibadis of Oman and the Metwali Shi'a communities of Lebanon and Syria, share is a history of political dissidence and persecution. Followers of these movements survived as weak minorities at the periphery of Islamic society; all sought refuge in rural, economically marginal, hard-to-administer areas, or "refuge zones." As a consequence, the political and social life of these communities tends to be highly involuted, inaccessible to outsiders, and hedged with secrecy. Leadership is usually in the hands of an oligarchy of religious leaders or elders. Moreover, because they are textually or scripturally based traditions, there is considerable internal diversity in belief and practice.

The spread of nationalism and the intrusion of state-wide institutions, particularly public education, have eroded some cultural boundaries that separate these sectarian groups. In Turkey, some Alevis actively participate in party politics as they seek a share of political power and economic gain, and are often sought out by secular intellectuals, particularly on the left (see Mango, 1993, 1994). In Syria the once poor and isolated Alawis or Nusairis, through their disproportionate representation in the army, managed to achieve a near-monopoly in the leadership of the country.

One case of religious dissidence, whose outcome is unique within recent Muslim history, is the Baha'i movement. In Juan Cole's masterful analysis (1999), the Baha'i faith can be interpreted as a case study in Middle Eastern modernity. Modernizing movements are almost entirely attributed to Western influences. Not so the Baha'i movement, which underwent a series of major transformations to end up as an established religion with two wings—one, the best-known and fastest-growing, emphasizing tolerance and universality, and the other, also pacific, emphasizing theocracy and scriptural literalism. The movement originated in Shiraz, Iran, in 1844, when a young man proclaimed

---

[9] See David Shankland (1993a and b) for an excellent description of Alevi communities in comparative perspective.

Street scene in Damascus with a poster of Hafiz al-Assad, the president of Syria.

himself the *Bab*, or "Gateway to Heaven," and the new manifestation of the Prophet Muhammad. He rapidly gathered a following as he preached against the corruption of the clerical and governmental establishment of the Persia of his day. In this, the movement he founded followed a familiar pattern of expressing political and social protest in the idiom of religious reform. However, once Babism, as it was called, was put down by the execution of its leader in 1850 and the brutal persecution of his followers, the movement itself was radically transformed. Baha'allah, half-brother of the founder, began to interpret Babism as a universalistic faith, trying to reconcile what he perceived to be the best of Judaism and Christianity with Islam. Ultimately, the faith he founded, Baha'ism, broke with Islam. In short, the new religion represents as big a break with its past as does any development in the history of Christianity. Today its followers are found throughout the world. One of their important temples, for example, is in Evanston, Illinois, and their spiritual leader, a descendant of Baha'allah, resides in Haifa, Israel.

Most of the small Baha'i community in the Middle East is found in Iran, where, until recently, they were relatively well-to-do, were involved in business and commerce, and reputedly had close connections to the Shah's family. Following the Islamic revolution, they again suffered persecution and were charged with apostasy and disloyalty; their numbers have continued to dwindle as many seek refuge abroad.

REGIONAL ETHNIC GROUPS

We have stressed dissidence within Islam and non-Muslim sectarianism as important sources of ethnic and cultural diversity. In addition to sectarian-defined groupings, there are important Muslim populations that are distinguished by several overlapping claims to shared identity. Foremost among these are the shared sense of history, language, and cultural heritage associated with a region or place of origin. Such groups may range from large populations with strong territorial bases, like the Baluch, the Kurds, and the Palestinians, to smaller dispersed ones, like the Circassians. The Circassians, Muslims who fled the Caucasus in the nineteenth century, are found today on the Golan Heights, in Jordan, Syria, Iraq, and western Turkey. As a small and widely dispersed people, they appear to aspire to no more of a political future than to participate in the national order of the countries in which they live. Many, perhaps most, do not retain a distinctive language.

The Balkans, too, were a source of Muslim out-migration. With the disintegration of the Ottoman Empire and the establishment of Greece, Serbia, and Bulgaria, about 1 million Muslims, some speaking Turkish, others not, moved east to remain in the diminished empire. Many of those who settled in Turkey assimilated, but some village communities persist in retaining a distinct identity (Palaczek, 1993).

Today, the Kurds, Baluch, and Palestinians are divided among a number of different nation-states. Following the collapse of the USSR, the independent republics of Azerbaijan and Turkmenistan were established, although sizable numbers of their potential citizens remain outside their frontiers in Iran. The nascent Palestinian state will also be a case where "the state disappoints the nation." Most Palestinians will undoubtedly never be found within the borders of a Palestinian state, nor will most of the territory they historically occupied. Given their numbers and long-established historical presence in their homelands, these people can be thought of as incipient nations without states. Thus it is not surprising that all of these groups have more or less active nationalistic movements seeking political expression either in independent nation-states or as recognized entities in confederated states. We will briefly consider the case of the Kurds, as they constitute the largest single regional or transnational ethnic group and one episodically involved in armed struggles.

The Kurds and Kurdistan

The Kurdish populations of Iraq, Turkey, Iran, Syria, and adjacent areas of Azerbaijan occupy a mostly highland area known historically as Kurdistan. In looking at the Kurdish populations, we see the politics of identity, religious and tribal sources of leadership, and a long history of foreign intervention and manipulation, all contributing to ongoing contention and conflict. But we also see forces at work that are transforming Middle Eastern societies in general, such as national and international labor migration, and economic and social division based on differential access to education and resources.

The Kurds were invited to the company of nation-states at the end of World War I, but never actually got through the door. In the end, the objectives of the Great Powers and the concerns of Turkey and Iran precluded statehood. The only modern Kurdish state was the short-lived Mahabad Republic, established by the Soviets during their brief post–World War II occupation of portions of Iran. While there has never been a unified Kurdish state, Kurdistan itself is also home to often sizable populations of Turks, Arabs, Persians, Lurs, and Türkmen—not to mention Armenians, whose nationalist aspirations would clash territorially with those of the Kurds. Eastern Turkey and the high plateau north of Lake Van were historically densely settled by Armenians, with Kurdish penetration relatively recent. A long history of warfare between the Persian and Ottoman empires established the present Iranian frontiers with Turkey and Iraq, while the post–World War I occupation by British forces in order to control the oil fields of Mosul and Kirkuk created the present-day Turkey-Iraq border. Since 1950, there has been large-scale migration of Kurds in Turkey, in particular to the western provinces and abroad. Approximately 750,000 Kurds live in Europe, particularly in Germany—a number augmented monthly by continued illegal migration as well as by asylum seekers. Today, the largest concentration of urban-dwelling Kurds is in Istanbul.

The region, apart from oil fields firmly under Iraqi control, has few natural resources with which to sustain development, and most outside observers would agree that rather than "exploiting" them, the nation-states in question subsidize their Kurdish regions in order to retain political control and to limit migration (Mango, 1993, p. 736). Population estimates are unreliable, but commonly used extrapolations put 10 million Kurds in Turkey, 5 million in Iran, 4 million in Iraq, 1 million in the successor states of the former USSR, and 500,000 in Syria. Kurdish is a language grouping within the Iranian family of languages and contains three main groups of dialects, Kurmanji, Sorani, and, most close to Persian, Kermanshahi. In addition, there are two smaller dialect groupings, Zaza and Gurani. Iranian Kurds of Kermanshah are mostly Shi'a, those in Turkey are Sunni, with the Zaza speakers being mostly Alevi. This linguistic and religious differentiation has been itself an obstacle to political unity and a common discourse.

While there are no uniquely or inherently Kurdish features of social organization, certain patterns stand out. The best recent anthropological source for understanding Kurdish rural society is Martin van Bruinessen (1992). He describes the tenacious survival of old loyalties, even where they come to carry new social meaning, such as in political parties and factionalism, and enduring traditional patterns of leadership in the form of tribal *aghas* (*ağa* in Turkish), usually possessing wealth in land and herds, sheikhs or religious leaders and local saints and mystics, and the families and retainers of these leaders (see Chapter 3). Even the spread of nationalism, van Bruinessen suggests, had as much to do with positions adopted by such traditional tribal leaders as Mulla Mustafa Barzani as with nationalist or Marxist ideology. Often, too, even nontribal rural-dwelling Kurds are closely associated with tribal landowners who act as patrons. Political parties in Turkey, for example, whether or not specifically associated with Kurdish identity, vie for votes in the southeast by negotiating with these traditional leaders.

Van Bruinessen describes how Kurdish national identity developed apace with other nationalisms in the late Ottoman period, and how by the end of World War II there were efforts at national autonomy underway in every country with a Kurdish population, although these populations were by no means speaking with one voice. One very prominent revolt against the Kemalist government of Turkey that still has political echoes is the February 1925 revolt led by a charismatic sheikh of the Naqshbandi order, or *tariqa*, Sheikh Said. He fused a religious appeal with nationalistic sentiment and his followers briefly controlled a number of administrative centers before being suppressed. Also related to the Naqshbandi is the Nurcu Movement founded by another sheikh,

Ruins of a seventeenth-century castle in eastern Turkey. The castle was the stronghold of Sar Sulayman, a powerful local Kurdish chieftain.

Nur Said. His writings, mostly from the 1920s, remain very popular among Kurds and others, even though by the end of his life he had rejected nationalism, per se, in favor of a modern or reformist Islamic synthesis. It is said that this was the basis for the Fethullah Gülen Community Movement, which attracts adherents from all ethnic communities, and which we described in Chapter 3.

It is beyond the scope of this book to review the complex history of the rise of Kurdish national identity and the many political forms it has taken in different countries. At the moment, the conflict in Turkey is second only to the Palestinian question as a source of instability and violence. Since 1985, when the PKK, or Kurdish Workers Party (Partiya Karkeren Kurdistan), began a campaign of violence, over 30,000 lives have been lost (20,000 of them Kurdish militants), not to mention a financial drain estimated to be 10 percent of Turkey's annual GNP. Additional costs include lost regional infrastructure and returns on investment, near total stagnation in the livestock industry, and the long-term cost to Turkey of the alienation of an important segment of its citizenry.

While the conflict has many dimensions, including contradictory visions of the future held by different segments of the Kurdish population, its origins lie in the formation of the Turkish republic itself out of the debris of the empire. The last years of empire and the subsequent struggle for independence in the face of an invasion by Greece had resulted in massive population dislocations throughout Anatolia and interconfessional strife, and had pitted competing nationalisms against each other. Against this backdrop, it is not surprising that one principle adopted by the emergent state was that Turkey was a monocultural entity, at least insofar as its Muslim populations were concerned. Greeks, Jews, and Armenians were permitted to retain their own schools and other institutions,[10] but Muslims of whatever linguistic, sectarian, or ethnic background were asserted to be of "Turkish nationality."

This national vision was entirely consistent with the prevailing nationalisms of the day and with other successor regimes of the Balkans and Greece. While this may have simplified the task of early nation-building, it has contributed to a sense of resentment and political alienation among the large Kurdish minority that has grown apace with the integration and development of the nation. The cultural diffusion of national emblems, media, and expressive culture has made many aware of what was being suppressed. Also, nationalist efforts by the Kurds of Iraq and Iran have influenced Kurdish intellectuals in Turkey. It is not that Kurds in Turkey face racial or ethnic stigmatizing and consequent social discrimination, as, for example, do Roma or Gypsies, rather their cultural heritage is suppressed or appropriated.

While the PKK, in spite of its claims, never spoke for more than a minority of Kurds, it was successful in tapping into a very widespread font of resentment (Mango, 1993, 1995; Barkey & Fuller, 1999; de Bellaigue, 1999). The often brutal military and administrative moves to suppress it served to amplify its mystique

---

[10] By the Lausanne Treaty of 1924.

and appeal beyond the relatively localized areas in which it operated. Most of the Kurdish population is now dispersed throughout the country, and the earlier objectives of the PKK for an independent (but impoverished) Kurdistan have little resonance. Since the capture, trial, and conviction of PKK leader and founder Abdullah Öcalan, in 1999, the conflict may be entering a new phase, one that focuses more on cultural and political rights, per se. The fact that many prominent Turkish politicians (about 25 percent of the current parliament), business leaders, and entertainers claim Kurdish descent, as well as the fact that territorial secession is a goal of only a tiny minority, give some hope that a transition to a culturally more inclusive society may be possible. But this would entail a significant policy reformulation, one in which Kurdish language media and culture could flourish and political parties directly address issues of Kurdish concern without fear of being banned.

GENERAL OVERVIEW

Appeals to religion, tribalism, and ethnicity in situations of conflict must be considered within specific political environments. While we can easily find instances in the Middle East where intergroup conflict occurs in the absence of strong state control, the "genie in the bottle" model, wherein politicized ethnicity or religion suddenly erupts when controls are relaxed, is not particularly helpful for understanding the situation in any country. It is, of course, true that appeals to history and assertions of a community rooted in primordial ties are crucial in forging a sense of shared identity, just as they are vital to "imagining" the nation. Nevertheless this need not imply that the political salience of any particular mode of recruitment need be continual and forceful, lying as many commentators would have it, just below the surface waiting to emerge when a powerful center weakens. Many in Turkey, Iran, Iraq, and elsewhere use this argument to justify state policy. In fact, it often obscures the fact that strong, central government control, particularly where accompanied by single-party rule or heavy-handed central administration, very often establishes the preconditions for the emergence of politicized alternatives.

Nation-building, such as experienced throughout the region since World War I, typically involved processes of centralizing power and authority, as well as the creation of modes of political discourse that exclude or marginalize some minorities. But even fairly heavy-handed imposition of limits to linguistic, religious, and cultural expression need not automatically generate communally organized political responses. Quite apart from overt coercion, which may increase the costs of responding, it is not easy for dispersed minorities to come to visualize themselves as a unified community with common interests. However, where assimilation is forced upon individuals, leaving them no realistic hope of participating in the culture of nation-state, even the extreme application of force simply fuels the political importance of identity. Violent efforts at suppressing or denigrating the symbols and codes of national minorities will likely strengthen minority opposition. Often, one suspects, in a highly centralized political environment or in the embrace of a colonial or alien regime, ethnicity (in the absence of alternative political institutions) becomes a vehicle of last resort for expressing local interests—for example, among the Palestinians of Israel. On the other hand, it is not so much that ethnicity (as a political force) is "dormant" or "suppressed"; rather, in some political environments, it is not particularly relevant.

5

Pastoralism and Nomadic Society

Among the populations of the Arab Peninsula a fundamental folk taxonomy is that of *bedu*, or nomads, as opposed to *hadar*, or settled folk of village and town. Even Ibn Khaldun, the fourteenth-century historian, utilized this distinction as the basis for a cyclical theory of dynamic change in which pastoral nomads, supposedly possessing a special vigor, solidarity, and potential for aggression, periodically overwhelm "decaying" urban regimes. Whatever the merits of this theory, nomadic pastoralists are people pursuing a way of life that, perhaps more than anything else, seems to typify the Middle East in the eyes of Westerners. The image of the mounted tribesman of the desert is all too often taken as a metaphor for all Middle Eastern peoples, perhaps as the cowboy is sometimes said to embody social values and an ethos particularly American. Reality is understandably more complex. Although the Middle East is one of the few areas of the world where substantial numbers of people have lived by specializing in animal production, agriculture is much more important by far. Pastoralism accounts for a small percentage of all food produced, and in most regions does not even supply most of the meat and dairy products consumed.

Still, nomadic pastoralism is a distinctive cultural tradition and way of life for many. More important, tribally organized nomadic-pastoral peoples have been politically and historically significant beyond their numbers. We have already seen some of the reasons for this when we sketched the events of the rise and spread of early Islam. Although we can by no means speak of the early Arab empires and city-states as exemplifying supposedly nomadic-pastoral values, we do know that the mobility and military prowess of the Arabian tribes played a significant role in early conquests of Byzantine and Persian provinces. Further, we know that the importance of Mecca as a mercantile center rested in large part on its ability to control and utilize nomadic tribes for the operation and protection of long-distance trade routes.

Who, then, are the nomadic pastoralists of the Middle East? Why do they occupy such a distinctive place in the fabric of Middle Eastern society? What problems do such peoples face in the twenty-first century, and what are their prospects? To answer these and similar questions we will look at a number of populations, including the Yörük of Turkey, the Basseri of Iran, and Al-Murra of Saudi Arabia. None of these are "typical" in the sense that they represent fixed patterns or can be taken as stereotypes. Rather, each group is a contemporary population, facing and manipulating a range of unique circumstances in attempting to solve problems common to all peoples.

In some respects, the nomads of the Middle East appear to represent the survival into the postindustrial age of an ancient and unchanging way of life. On the surface this is true enough, because some of the people we discuss continue to live in woven goat-hair tents little changed for centuries, although probably more people today use canvas tents familiar in European campgrounds and the military. Their annual routine of seasonal movement in search of grazing for their animals is as old a phenomenon as agriculture itself. But today the animals are usually moved by truck, and the watchful shepherd may well have a cell phone to keep in touch and for security. The tent groups and the tribal idiom of social organization follow principles that are described by the early chronicles of Islamic history. But as we shall see, visitors today fortunate enough to be taken into the homes of contemporary pastoralists do not find people living in the past, but families who are very much at home in today's world, coping with the many problems of contemporary society while attempting to enjoy its obvious material advantages. The Toyota truck parked outside the family home, be it a tent, a house, or a seasonal shelter, is far more common a sight today than is the mounted herdsman.

Before turning to specific people and places, let us review some of the more general observations that can be made about pastoralism in a region as complex and varied as the Middle East.

THE ECOLOGICAL BASIS FOR PASTORALISM

Although nomadic pastoralists share certain characteristics, nomadic-pastoral societies are no more like one another than are communities engaged in agriculture. Every population has a unique history and cultural heritage, including language, sectarian affiliation, and customary ways of behaving. In southeastern Anatolia, Turkish-, Arabic-, and Kurdish-speaking nomadic and sedentary groups share a common area. Likewise, in southwestern Iran a large multiethnic tribal confederation, the Khamseh, or "Five," encompasses Persian-, Turkish-, and Arabic-speaking farmers and nomadic herders. Even among groups who share a language and a common general designation, there may well be important sectarian or religious divisions. The Arabic-speaking tribes of

Khuzistan divide along lines of Sunni-Shi'a affiliations, as do some of the Kurdish pastoralists. Even with the major Türkmen tribes of north-central Iran, there is a fundamental distinction between those sections who claim sacred descent and those who do not.

The great cultural diversity among nomadic groups makes it prudent to beware of easy generalizations about nomads and their life. There are, however, a number of variables relating to pastoralism as a means of production that select for certain regularities in social and economic organization. Important variables include the degree and types of movement or nomadism that are incorporated into the system of livestock management. Other variables are related to the species of animals managed, their specific food and water requirements, and the labor it takes to herd them. Also important is how the animals are converted into the foods that the family eats and the items that they purchase—in other words, how the people make use of their animals within a larger system of exchange and trade.

The Middle Eastern landscape can be divided into three major zones of land-use potential. The first, and the most restricted in distribution, is land suited to village agriculture and urban settlement. Here, as we have already noted in Chapter 1, water is the critical variable. The second zone comprises lands almost totally unfit for human habitation—for example, the Dasht-i Kavir and the Lut deserts of Iran and the Rub' al-Khali of Arabia. The third and largest zone comprises land marginal to agriculture because of aridity or altitude. This zone, however, can be exploited with great investment of labor or on a limited seasonal basis. The desert areas seasonally support natural grasses and plants, as do the mountain slopes and high valleys and the extensive rugged steppes of Iran, Afghanistan, Iraq, and Turkey. It is in such marginal areas that pastoralism is a practical alternative or supplement to farming. Although most farmers in both the well-watered and marginal areas keep livestock for domestic use or even for sale, relatively little specialized livestock raising is engaged in by sedentary peoples. This is, of course, an important contrast between Europe and the Middle East. In Europe, as in the United States, specialized dairy farming and sedentary stock raising are important forms of land use.

The reasons why dairy farming and ranching have not evolved in the Middle East are both ecological and economic. In an arid area supporting a relatively high density of population and large concentrations of people in urban centers, it is a costly luxury to use arable land and grasses primarily to raise animals. It is far more efficient to raise cereal crops for human consumption than to attempt to convert grains and grasses into animal products. Diet in the Middle East reflects this. There is a strong emphasis on bread, together with dishes using vegetables and grains. Generally, meat is used sparingly, usually for broth and stews, although modern cuisine is, perhaps unfortunately, rapidly evolving toward more grilled or fried preparation of meat.

Animal husbandry as a major or specialized strategy pays off economically only when it increases net food production of valuable proteins. This is usually in areas where animals can be grazed on land too dry, too uneven, or too high for regular cultivation. As a consequence, grazing areas are usually tracts of wild plants where the available forage is limited. The animals must be moved regularly from pasture to pasture, often migrating over a grazing range of several hundred kilometers annually—hence the nomadic nature of the productive unit.

Sometimes farmers and nomads effect a trade-off that benefits both. In areas where farming is possible but long fallow periods are necessary to maintain soil fertility, as was traditionally the case along the Mediterranean coast and on the Syrian steppes, nomadic pastoralists may adjust their migratory schedules in order to graze their flocks on fallow fields. The advantage to the field owners is that the animals supply valuable fertilizer. This arrangement, though potentially mutual in its benefits, is by no means without serious conflict of interest. Animals often encroach on land under cultivation and may damage crops. Also villagers themselves may raise sufficient animals to fully exploit available local grazing, and nomadic pastoralists may represent a direct economic threat. Today the governments of the Middle East carefully regulate any such peasant-nomad interaction. In Turkey, for example, nomads very often may pay rental fees in order to use village lands. In Syria, the government closely controls nomadic grazing and migratory routes, as do the Iranians with regard to most of the larger nomadic tribes.

ANIMALS AND NOMADISM

One convenient way to summarize the diversity in nomadic movement and land use is in terms of two contrasting patterns: transhumance, or vertical migration, and plains, or horizontal migration. Transhumance is a pattern of animal management found in mountain areas throughout the world. It involves seasonal movement of herds between different climatic zones. In spring, the road and trails of the Zagros, Taurus, and Elburz ranges become crowded with flocks, as the nomads and villagers move their herds from the lowland winter pastures up to the mountains. In the fall, the pattern of migration is reversed, as the herds are led down the mountain ranges to spend the winter months in warmer zones. Thus, transhumant nomads usually have two major grazing areas, and their tents may remain in one place for the duration of the long grazing seasons. It has long been common in Kurdistan for families among some tribes to have permanent homes in the villages they occupy during the winter season. Although cattle are herded in some parts of the Taurus and Zagros, the majority of Middle Eastern transhumants specialize in sheep and goats. Today the basic pattern of movement persists, but most animals are transported by truck between the pastures.

Horizontal nomadism usually involves a greater movement of both herds and households. This is because different pasture zones are apt to be further apart than they would be in a mountainous area. Water, and not simply the availability of pasture, is the determinant of how many animals can be managed and where people camp. The greater distances traversed in this type of nomadism foster a greater reliance on large transport animals like camels. Nomads utilizing camels and horses have historically played an important military role in the areas where they are found. Well-mounted and knowing their terrain, they could frequently maintain a military advantage in conflict, even with the government's numerically superior troops. Further, their tribal organization facilitated territorial defense and allowed them to maintain partial, if not complete, autonomy. Even today, the Turkish-speaking Qashqa'i confederation of southwestern Iran, politically suppressed by the Shah, are again reasserting their local claims to power. Many previously forcibly sedentarized nomads are back on their migrations and as tribal groups are reclaiming their lands (Beck, 1990).

Mobility and independent action have long characterized nomadic pastoralists. In Turkey, Lâle Yalçın-Heckmann describes the Kurdish pastoralists of rugged Hakkâri Province for whom the smuggling of animals and animal products to neighboring Iraq was central to their economy (1994). Smuggling, whether animals or other contraband, is a longtime aspect of many pastoral economies, making use as it does of the nomads' ability to evade authorities (see Marx, 1999).

The type of animal or mix of species herded by pastoralists varies with the terrain and with market demands. Herded livestock includes camels, cattle, sheep, and goats. Although we often think of the camel when we speak of the Arabian Peninsula, in fact, even there, with the exception of the particularly arid wastes, the most commonly herded animals are sheep and goats. Cattle are fairly common in the extreme southern reaches of the peninsula, as well as throughout the mountainous areas of the Middle East. In Iran, a few groups, such as the Baluch, raise large numbers of camels, but for the most part, sheep and, to a diminishing extent, goats are the mainstays of nomadic-pastoral life. In highland eastern Turkey and Iran, some Kurdish tribes have specialized in cattle, but again the preponderance of pastoral production involves small animals well suited to browsing in rough, broken country.

In the arid reaches of Arabia on the margins of Rub' al-Khali, in the Gulf states, and along the southern rim of the Syrian steppe, camels were long the key to human adaptation. There the extremely rough forage, great temperature variability, and long droughts, together with the need to cover long distances between water holes, made this slow-maturing animal supremely suited to the desert habitat of the Bedouin, or more correctly, Bedu (sing. Badawi). The term *Bedu/Bedouin* is generally applied to the nomadic tribes of the desert and tends to be restricted to camel herdsmen. The Bedu/Bedouin generally claim Arab descent and are Arabic speakers.[1]

---

[1] For an excellent ethnography of a Bedouin tribe, the Rwala of the northern Arabian Desert, see William Lancaster (1997). See also Lila Abu-Lughod (1986).

The Bedouin traditionally raised camels to the near exclusion of all other animals, except for their prized racing and riding horses.[2] Sheep herders, commonly called *shawiyya*, generally keep few camels. Both groups reside year-round in black tents woven from goat hair; they follow different patterns of migration and are separated by a considerable social gulf. Camel herders consider themselves higher in rank than sheep herders, and, among themselves, some lineages are considered to be of more pure descent, *asilin,* and thus more noble than the rest. These core lineages have traditionally provided the leaders or paramount sheiks of the different tribes and confederations.

During the hot summer months of June through September, when the camels must be watered nearly daily, *asilin* camel herders of central Arabia by necessity cluster around wells and other permanent sources of water. In the other months, when moisture is available from the annual plants, the camels can go for long periods without being watered; in winter, camels are not watered at all, and the nomads range far into the arid zone. In recent years, the so-called noble tribes (*asilin*) have largely shifted to sheep, keeping only a few camels for ceremonial use, as sheep are much more marketable and trucks are now generally used for transport (Chatty, 1996).

The sheep-herding *shawiyya* who are still nomadic camp on the edge of the desert and group around wells in the summer; in winter, they take their flocks through village lands, using fallow fields made available to them after the fall harvest. Traditional dependence on sheep and goats used to limit their mobility, for these animals must be watered regularly in all seasons and are incapable of moving long distances at any appreciable speed. Today this has changed dramatically, as all use trucks to reach distant grazing areas far outside their customary ranges.

Changed also is the old pattern whereby the Bedu of the interior extracted tribute or "taxes" from their less powerful neighbors. In the past, camel-breeding Bedouin tribes of the Arabian Peninsula conformed more to our image of the "desert warrior" in that martial arts were highly regarded. The celebrated raids (*ghazzu*) carried out against the camps of other nomads or against villagers earned them a formidable reputation. The fact is that for the larger tribes raiding and warfare constituted an important part of their adaptation. Many tribal sections controlled tributary-settled populations, exacted protection money, *khuwwa,* from border villages, and received regular payments for the supervision and protection of trade routes, which often meant simply supplying guides and agreeing not to attack passing caravans. Some nomadic tribes of the desert kept slaves who were attached to the households of the wealthy.

---

[2] An interesting exception is the cattle-raising nomadic Shahra tribe of the mountainous Dhofar Province, Oman, a population who still speak a southern Arabic dialect. Nicholas Clapp, a journalist-filmmaker, gives a very rare and intriguing account of working among them (1999).

PASTORALISM AND MARKET RELATIONS

Camel herders, like all who specialize in animal husbandry, however much they may prize their independence, are still closely linked by numerous economic and social ties to the larger society. This is true for all pastoralists, whether they live and raise their animals in close proximity to villages and towns or range far into regions of no permanent settlement. Pastoralists in the Middle East raise animals for sale in markets, where they acquire most of the food they consume, not to mention clothing, cooking utensils, weapons, jewelry, and the many other items for household and personal use. The integration of the pastoralists into the larger market economy is a point that cannot be emphasized too strongly. In fact, the existence of specialized pastoralism and the number of people who can be supported in this endeavor at any given time are directly related to the ability of the pastoralists to trade with or otherwise acquire the products of sedentary communities. Moreover, these exchanges are effected, for the most part, through cash transactions.

There is recent and very impressive documentation of the balance of exchange among pastoralists and nonpastoralists in western Iran. Dan Bradburd has collected and meticulously analayzed data covering 160 years of trade and production (1996; see also 1990 and 1994). In examining a number of populations for which data were available, he was able to calculate the rate of return from a herd of 100 sheep. To his surprise, he found that the values of commodities purchased, to the extent that they had changed at all, had actually changed in favor of the pastoralists, particularly in the twentieth century. This means that in recent decades a herder could purchase more commodities than in the previous century, even though their personal consumption also increased, particularly the use of sugar, tobacco, tea, and coffee. Given this finding, Bradburd notes, one has to look to other factors in order to explain rates of sedentarization, such as government policies, the political environment, and changing employment opportunities (1996).

Two studies from the Negev point to what these other factors might be (Ginguld et al., 1997; Marx, 1999). In the northern Negev, in Israel, Bedouin persist in pastoral production, sometimes simply in order to maintain their claim to land, but also for reasons of cultural identity and, of course, to make a living. But this is increasingly difficult, not because animals are not still valuable commodities but because herding activities are greatly restricted by rules and regulations imposed by the government. While herding can be profitable utilizing cheap labor, the best economic strategy for households involves "intensifying" production through feeding livestock in addition to open grazing. Nevertheless, their access to resources is severely hampered by relations with the Israeli army, restrictive or discriminatory land-use laws and the like—in short, politics.

Bedouin leaders in the Negev have become increasingly resentful of Israeli resettlement policy. There are 120,000 Bedouin in the Negev, and the government is making strenuous efforts to move them into one of seven towns designed for them. But about half the population has resisted. "For years the authorities harassed them, evicted them from traditional pasture lands and agricultural plots, confiscating their goat herds [in the name of conservation] and destroying the houses some have built for their families," reports Clinton Bailey, Fellow of the Truman Institute for Peace at the Hebrew University (quoted in Kalman, 1999). Bailey goes on to assert, "Government denial and harassment has turned a patient, neutral and often sympathetic population into a restive, hostile and bitter one."

As Avinoam Meir (1997) documents, in 1951, enforcement by the Green Patrol, a paramilitary commando unit, of the "goat law" kept most Bedouin from grazing their goats. In 1954, the government tried to claim Negev land, and moved the Bedouin into designated areas, while, since 1966 new Israeli cities were built on tribal grazing lands. Their traditional wells, vital for the flocks, have been made a public utility, but Bedouin are denied access on the grounds that their homes are "illegal." However, the Bedouin refuse to give up claims to their traditional lands. In 1999, Talab al-Sanah, the only Bedouin member of the Knesset, was leading a legal effort to recover their losses and establish their rights (Kalman, 1999).

Since many Negev and Sinai men seek wage employment, the division of labor has shifted in an interesting way. Women and young girls increasingly tend the flocks. The Bedouin anthropologist Aref Abu-Rabia describes contemporary Bedouin pastoralism in great detail and from a personal perspective (1994). The Bedouin of the Negev today perforce pasture their flocks of sheep in the general vicinity of their homes, although in the past they were much more mobile. Generally, herding is seen as the work of men and boys, but because so many of them are seasonally employed in construction work, even young girls are involved in shepherding. In fact, women have come to feel that girls are better at caring for the sheep than are men or boys; after all, in her traditional role, a girl already was milking the ewes and devoted to the flock. Women are the first to rise in the morning and the last to go to bed; girls are taught to take advantage of being with the flocks to collect firewood, to spin wool and goat hair, and to embroider. Since two or more girls watch the herd together, this is an opportunity to practice the art of trilling—a distinctive form of singing for which Bedouin women are known. The bond of the Bedouin woman to the flock is expressed in the following song: "Oh, happy am I, the shepherdess, giving utterance to my freedom. My destiny and that of the flock are bound together" (Abu-Rabia, 1994, p. 62).

But there is a difference in male herding and the activities of young girls. Because of strict codes of family honor, young women cannot risk being in the company of unrelated males. As a consequence, they have to watch the flocks in the vicinity of their house, where they can be watched in turn by their relatives. Usually younger women go into the fields in pairs, and, while the flock is in the pasture, they sit on top of a hill so they can be seen from a distance. This watch is maintained because female seclusion is basic to their sense of family honor—a belief shared by both sexes. "Men and women constantly discuss the subject, and so heighten awareness of the women's honor" (p. 60). While restricting the activities of women, the notion of family honor does not hinder their productive roles in the domestic economy. They are central to it.

The diet and general consumption patterns of pastoralists are not substantially different from those of any other rural family except, perhaps, a higher consumption of meat and other animal products. Bread is the staple almost everywhere, and to acquire wheat or barley flour a pastoralist family must regularly sell its animals or herd products. No household in the Middle East is truly self-sufficient, and few are more specialized and hence dependent than are nomadic pastoralists.

Even before the advent of trucks, Bedouin camps in Arabia were regularly visited by two types of merchants. One class of shopkeepers, called the *Kubaisat* (after a town in southern Iraq), visited winter encampments in the desert with camels laden with such goods as cloth, sugar, rice, and small household objects. Their shops were set up in white tents—to distinguish them from the black tents of the nomads and to ensure that the merchants would not be mistakenly attacked in a sudden raid. It was considered a serious breach of the codes regulating desert warfare to assault or even rob such nontribal traders, so important was their function to the survival of the nomad pastoralists. The *Kubaisats* paid a set fee to the sheikh or leader of the tent groups for the privilege of joining the camp and being under the leader's protection.

The second type of traveling merchant in the Arabian Desert were the members of the 'Aqail tribe, who acted as agents for mercantile houses in Cairo, Damascus, Basra, and elsewhere. These agents bought camels, branded them, and took them to urban markets. Again, these merchants were protected by the established codes of war, and in the event their camels were taken in a raid, they would be returned.

Today, of course, this situation is very different, as Donald Cole, Emanuel Marx, Dawn Chatty, and other scholars of Bedouin life note. All households within each camp have jeeps or trucks, or access to them, with which they commute regularly to market towns and far-flung flocks. Among the Bedouin, mechanized transport has totally replaced reliance on the camel, and markets are readily accessible on a daily basis (Chatty, 1996). The situation is very similar among the other pastoralists of the region. Pastoralists, like ranchers in the United States, follow livestock prices closely and go to town to consult with livestock brokers and to learn the latest prices for animals. Rapid road transport gives pastoralists a choice of markets and ready access to the consumer goods of the city.

A frequent scene in many market towns near areas of pastoralism is that of herdsmen transacting business with merchants and artisans. Because each household consumes several hundred kilos of grain a year—not to mention tea, tobacco, sugar, and clothing—these transactions may involve substantial sums of money. Business is generally conducted with traders with whom very long-term relationships are established. Merchant-customer relations often include the extension of credit from one season to the next, and such relationships of mutual trust may be passed on from one generation to another.

Pastoral households, perhaps more than their sedentary counterparts, are directly dependent on others for the food they eat. This renders them particularly vulnerable to changing market prices of animal products and forces many of them to seek alternative sources of food or income. Thus, they often engage in trade, part-time farming, and other pursuits such as seasonal labor in cities or on farms. All in all, the vagaries of the marketplace are as critical as those of the weather.

Philip Salzman, who has worked extensively with the Yarah-mozadi Baluch of Iran, says that "multiple resourcefulness" would be an appropriate characterization of the Baluch adaptation—indeed, of most pastoralists (1972). The Baluch migratory cycle is determined only in part by the needs of their animals. They also move on schedule as they hire themselves out to harvest dates or till fields and even to engage in smuggling.[3] Again, one has to be careful not to confuse ethnic or tribal labels with specific economic activities even if locally they are closely linked. Bedu in Oman pursue pastoralism, agriculture, trading, and fishing; a similar range of activities is characteristic for all populations formerly closely associated with some particular way of life (Chatty, 1996).

THE STATE AND NOMADIC PASTORALISTS

We have stressed the economic aspects of pastoral adaptation in our discussion, but more is involved. No way of life is the outcome only of strictly economic pressures. Every local community interacts with adjacent groups, sometimes with those on whom it directly depends for a critical resource or item of technology. Just as often, the neighboring group is a real or potential competitor, or even hostile. The organization of any nomadic group and even its pattern of movement are also responses to its political environment—adjacent populations and the power of the encompassing government.

Governments in the Middle East are often critical in determining local patterns of land use and how local communities interact, even in areas remote from centers of power. A government may not be able to effectively administer certain territories within its national frontiers on a day-to-day basis, but usually it can intervene in local disputes in such a way as to determine their outcome. Because nomads are most commonly found in regions of low population density, remote from urban centers and in terrain difficult to control militarily, it is sometimes assumed that national politics are irrelevant. This is not and never has been the case. A recent book by an Israeli geographer and a long-term observer of the Bedouin of the Negev clearly illustrates the sociopolitical

---

[3] See also Salzman (1999) for a retrospective account.

transformation of a Bedouin population as they cope with the dual impact of Israeli policies and the changing market environment. Meir's (1997) work, as we have noted, documents the thorny relationship between the Bedouin and Israeli administrators and the processes that led to the isolation and marginalization of the Bedouin.

Modern technology has of course, greatly reduced the military advantage of mobility that pastoralists have traditionally enjoyed. Modern governments take care to maintain their monopoly over military armament, and even where tribal groups may be well armed, they are usually vulnerable to air attack and to the ability of the government to bring in large numbers of troops by truck. Such large tribal groups as the Basseri, the Türkmen, and the Qashqa'i are far from being autonomous political entities. However, even when such nomadic groups are able to keep the bureaucracy at arm's length, they still have to contend with a state that can play off one leader against another, interfere in factional disputes, and, on occasion, launch large-scale punitive expeditions.

William Irons, who has worked extensively among the Yomut Türkmen of northeastern Iran, goes so far as to say that their nomadism was largely a political response to the Iranian government's attempt to establish control over their territories. The Yomut moved their *obas,* or camps, not simply to maintain their flocks but to enhance their military capabilities vis-à-vis government troops. This strategy was also practiced by the Qashqa'i of Iran.

THE YÖRÜK OF SOUTHEAST TURKEY

The interaction of people and groups as they struggle for scarce resources, for power, or even for such elusive social rewards as prestige can be as important as the dictates of a mode of production in shaping how people will use the lands they inhabit. One case study, the Yörük pastoralists of southeastern Turkey, offers a good illustration of how changes in intergroup relations affect internal organization as well as regional patterns of land use. After a brief sketch of the modern history of the Yörük, we can begin to draw a more detailed portrait of them as people.[4]

In the Middle East, population movements have been such that we cannot say that any particular group has been there "forever." The Yörük are relative newcomers to the Gaziantep area, near the Syrian border, where they are presently the only people who specialize in animal husbandry. Although not all tribal sections arrived in the region at the same time, it is clear that none was established there before 1900. Furthermore, even though groups came to the southeast from various parts of Anatolia, all originated on the west coast, from where they dispersed in the late nineteenth and early twentieth centuries. Thus, to consider why the Yörük are where they are today may be a useful way to see

---

[4] Our discussion is based on fieldwork by coauthor Daniel Bates.

some of the problems they, and many other groups as well, faced and how they coped with them.

The Yörük, a Turkish-speaking people, were traditionally nomadic goat herders along the Aegean and western Mediterranean coasts of Turkey. Although it is not clear when they emerged as a distinct ethnic or tribal group, they are mentioned by name in twelfth-century texts. The Yörük themselves trace their origins to northern Iran and regard themselves as descended from the Türkmen. As such, they view themselves as among the earliest Turkish settlers in Anatolia. Today, of course, there are families of Yörük very proud of this ancestry, pursuing all forms of endeavor at all levels of education. For families, dispersed as they are all over the country, the notion of a tribal past is more folklore than social reality.

The Yörük, transhumant pastoralists, moved seasonally to exploit zonal and seasonal variation in wild grasses in the mountain ranges of western Anatolia, and thereby maintained herds in numbers beyond that which could be supported in any one place throughout the year. Moving in small camp groups, they would winter in the coastal plains, grazing their flocks on fallow or nonarable land. In the spring, in the classic transhumant pattern, the herds would be taken up to successively higher grazing areas. By early summer, they reached the upper pastures, called *yayla*, of the Taurus range, where they would camp until fall. At the onset of cold weather they would retrace their route downward. By then, villages on the middle and lower slopes of the seaward side of the Taurus would be finished with the grain harvest, and Yörük flocks could pass without risk of crop damage, grazing on the stubble while they enriched the fields with their droppings. The Yörük occupied a specialized niche and constituted one group among several populations engaged in different forms of land use. The Yörük were recognized by the government as having specific rights to grazing, their headmen were recognized as chiefs, analogous to village mukhtars, and in earlier periods served in military expeditions as transport and sapper troops.

The migratory schedule connected grazing areas that were seasonally available without the Yörük being subject to much direct competition with other groups. Thus their place in the regional economy was a product of different populations interacting with each other. In fact, this pattern of interaction was beneficial to all concerned. The Yörük used land that villagers could not exploit, and the nomads' flocks supplied peasants with pastoral products.

In the late nineteenth and early twentieth centuries, the western coast of Turkey became the focus for intensive agricultural development spurred by European and domestic investment and the opening of a new rail link. As the marshes were drained, areas that were formerly winter pastures for the Yörük were settled by new villages, often set up or encouraged by the government. The strategies available to the Yörük for managing their herds became more restricted. Not only was there direct competition for scarce resources but also for power among groups, as some were now supported by the government.

As a result of these pressures, particularly because of diminished pasture-land, Yörük families were obliged to change their patterns of herding and migration and even how they made a living. A substantial number of pastoral families chose to take up farming and settle in villages. Others shifted their migratory routes. Some moved to less developed but poorer areas of grazing on the coast, some to central Anatolia, and still others to southeastern Turkey. These last constitute the only large concentration of Yörük households that are still nomadic, as virtually all the remaining Yörük populations today are settled. Like many members of ethnic or tribal groupings in the Middle East, the Yörük are widely dispersed.

Those who migrated to the southeast were able to continue as nomadic pastoralists only because other nomadic populations had been forced to abandon pastures in the lowlands and high mountain valleys. By then, the government had forcibly settled local nomadic Kurdish, Arab, and Türkmen tribes. The Yörük were permitted, or even encouraged, to enter the region because they were not considered a political threat, as were the larger and more powerful Kurdish and Türkmen groups. This was part of well-established Ottoman practice of interspersing ethnic groups to prevent regional identity emerging as a salient political force.

The Yörük families who continued to be pastoralists soon shifted from goat to sheep production and established an annual routine of migration that persists today. The change in animals herded was due to governmental control of routes to mountain pastures. As these passed through forested areas, access to them was prohibited to goats in an effort to slow the rate of deforestation, which threatened still magnificent stands of pine and hardwoods. Also, today goat production almost everywhere has declined due to market forces—the urbanized population vastly prefers lamb.

The shift in emphasis from goat herding to sheep herding was not the only change in Yörük life. In 1949 and 1950, the Yörük, like other rural populations in Turkey, were greatly affected by specific national economic and political developments. A new government, concerned with rural investment and agricultural development, greatly increased the availability of agricultural credit. All-weather roads were extended into the areas of winter pastureland, and the resultant expansion of agriculture caused a decline in available pastures. Moreover, owners of fallow fields now came to charge ever-increasing fees from the nomads. Even summer pastures, most of which were located on village common land, had to be rented. These developments led once again to a large-scale settlement by Yörük households who sought alternative means of livelihood. Some became farmers and others shopkeepers and merchants in and around the city of Islahiye.

Pastoralism for those who remained nomadic now required larger herds and regular access to substantial amounts of cash and/or credit. Whereas formerly a household could support itself with 20 or 30 mature sheep, soon even 100 came to be regarded as a small herd. Today herds are rarely less that 150 for those who rely primarily on husbandry for a living. The all-cash economy favored households that could invest in veterinary care, in grain feeding, and sometimes in special canvas tents to shelter the herds in winter. Animal husbandry fast became a specialized commercial venture. In this context, it is not surprising that a number of entrepreneurial members of the tribe established mobile dairies. These dairies were moved by trucks to where the animals were grazing in spring and summer pastures. Milk from the sheep was processed daily into white cheese, packaged in tins, and sold to wholesalers in Ankara and Kayseri. Other Yörük became livestock brokers and bought and sold animals and wool. Although at no time did social and economic differentiation among the still-nomadic households approach that found in most villages, signs of stratification began to emerge. Some families were able to increase their animal holdings and other forms of wealth as others were forced into debt.

Today few if any of the Yörük remain nomadic in the sense of being tent-dwelling animal herders. Those families who still herd usually maintain a permanent home in town and hire shepherds to assist one or two family members, who truck their animals to distant pastures. In fact, Yörük herding has undergone a near-complete transformation and resembles in its use of capital and labor what is called ranching in the United States. Rather than being associated with a distinctive style of life and cultural identity, herding is now simply one of

A Yörük boy doing his homework. Today virtually all younger Yörük men and women are literate.

a number of investment strategies. In recent years, they have had to adjust to very serious political problems. In the late 1970s and 1980s, their pastures were often the scenes of violent clashes between dissident political groups and the government, and animal theft was rampant. In 1985, Kurdish separatist militants began to operate in the same area, with the same threat to security of life and property greatly hurting pastoral production. One response, fueled by rising animal prices, was to utilize more intensively the lowland and more secure pastures, renting fields for grazing on a year-round basis, and moving very little. This meant the introduction of heat-resistant breeds of animals. In the late 1990s, following the spread of irrigation throughout the southeast, investors, using urban capital, employed huge earth-movers in the lowlands to transform rocky fields into fertile fields suitable for mechanical cultivation. This, naturally, means that rents are rising.

THE BASSERI OF SOUTHWESTERN IRAN

A second case study, although conducted in the 1950s, offers insight into the social structure and patterns of leadership of a large tribal grouping in southwestern Iran; the study also provides a good sketch of the economics of production and exchange in a pastoral society. Fredrik Barth's (1961) monograph on the Basseri continues to be regarded as a classic because of the clarity with which it outlines some of the basic principles that appear to shape pastoral society and economy. Historically, the Basseri enjoyed a large measure of political autonomy, a pattern that was not uncommon for the rest of the tribal groups in southwestern Iran. Keeping in mind that Barth did his research in the mid-1950s, we will discuss some aspects of Basseri domestic and social life.

The Basseri, a Persian-speaking people in an area where there are tribes speaking Luri, Arabic, and Turkish, were the leading group in a tribal confederation called the Khamseh, which until it broke up included Arabic and Turkish tribes. The significance of this large confederation was much diminished since the reign of Reza Shah, who forcibly disarmed and settled nomadic segments in the 1930s. Although the settlement of the Basseri was virtually complete at one point, many families resumed nomadic life at the abdication of Reza Shah in 1941. At the time of Barth's fieldwork, the Basseri were fairly widely dispersed, and the tribe had many settled communities.

The Basseri nomads do not occupy an exclusive territory. As Barth put it, each of the major tribes of Fars province "owns" the rights to a route, or *il rah*, which it follows each year in its migratory cycle. Rather than owning the land through which they pass and on which they graze their flocks, the Basseri regard the *il rah* schedule as their right-of-way. The *il rah* varies yearly with the availability of passes and roads and with the sequence set by the maturation of the grasses for grazing. The intricate schedule of the Basseri yearly migration is coordinated and directed by their paramount chief, the khan.

The *il rah* of the Basseri takes them from winter pastures in the south on the arid plains or deserts to distant summer pastures at altitudes as high as 6,000 feet. The spring migration northward and upward, as well as the return down in the fall, is marked by frequent camp movement. The summer and winter grazings, however, require much less displacement. The Basseri rely primarily on sheep and goats, and like the Yörük of Turkey, keep camels, horses, and donkeys for transport.

Barth considers camp groups to be the primary communities of Basseri nomadic society, similar to hamlets and villages among peasants. What distinguishes these groups, and we might add, all nomadic camp units, is that they persist only as long as members decide to move and work together. Daily consensus is necessary on such vital issues as where to graze and how long to stay in any given area. Barth analyzes the processes by which these collective decisions are made and how the unity of the camp is maintained.

Leadership in the camp is expressed in two ways. One form of leadership is that exercised by headmen, or *katkhoda,* who are formally recognized by the paramount chief of the Basseri. A second type of leadership is informal, one held by elders called "white beards" (*riz safid*), who by consensus are thought of as natural decision makers for the community. The *katkhoda* derives authority in part from the paramount chief, or khan, and in part from the Iranian government, which plays an important role in controlling Iranian tribes. The *katkhoda* relays directives from the khan and from government and reports back to them. Daily management of the camp is in the care of its "white beards" or household heads.

At the time of Barth's study, there were 24 named *oulads,* or lineages, the largest of which had 126 tents and the smallest 13. These *oulads* themselves were grouped into larger descent segments called *tira,* of which the Basseri had 15. The *oulad* owns or controls a joint grazing area and a migratory route. Only as a recognized member of one of these lineages does one have access to pastures. The leaders (*katkhodas*) of the *oulads* report directly to the khan and are held responsible to him for the behavior of members of their specific groups. These *katkhodas,* therefore, have considerable authority in their communities.

At the top of the Basseri political hierarchy stands the paramount chief, or khan. In the 1950s, the last three generations of khans had come from one family, constituting something of a ruling dynasty within the tribe. Most members of the khan's family lived sophisticated lives as members of the Iranian national elite. The khan represented the Basseri in their dealings with the Iranian government and in conflicts with sedentary populations. Because he enjoyed great wealth in land as well as in herds, the khan moved with ease among the elite and powerful of the country. He kept houses in Shiraz, the provincial capital, and sent his children to be educated abroad. The khan possessed great power and privilege, entertained extravagantly, and at times exercised near-complete authority over his tribal subjects. Until his power was broken by the Iranian government, the ruling khan could impose fines and taxes, conduct court hearings, and order corporal punishment and even death sentences. Closely associated with the khan was a special group known as the *Darbar*. Members of this tribal segment served as the khan's private militia, servants, and companions. Even though the *Darbar* also owned flocks, tents, and property, they were considered outsiders to the Basseri tribe.

In his description of the organization of production among the Basseri, Barth concentrated on the household and on the patterns of wealth accumulation and deployment. He surveyed 32 tents of one Basseri group and found that the average household size was 5.7 people, a figure comparable to that for most of rural Iran. Most of these tents were nuclear households. The household is a property-owning unit as well as a social grouping; each depends on its own equipment and animals and generally on its own labor as well.

The average household herd consisted of about 100 sheep; a typical family could not subsist on fewer than 60 animals, at least in 1958, when the study was carried out. Barth estimated that the average household spent cash for food and other necessities amounting to no more than 40 to 50 percent of the value of its productive capital, or the mature animals. How was this high yield possible? The flocks were primarily female animals, and a mature ewe annually produces products equivalent to her total market value. Of course, all of this was not profit, as herds have to be replaced and labor hired, and animals may be lost or stolen. Still, this yield is adequate to ensure the average Basseri family a high standard of living relative to many peasant populations.

Barth described a wealthy 55-year-old man who began his career at age 15 with some 20 sheep, probably received as his share of an inheritance. His herd grew through natural increase, and soon he was able to sell approximately 20 sheep a year. With the money and with money earned from trading in animal hides, he was eventually able to buy land and settle in a village. By then his herd had grown into several hundred sheep, and he had a number of shepherds to help. This pattern of wealth accumulation, investment in land, and subsequent settlement is not unusual. Nomadic families whose herds prosper normally try to reduce their risk of sudden loss and impoverishment by investing in other resources. Many households, Barth noted, may acquire wealth and settle, only to resume nomadism several times throughout their careers. On the other hand, poor families whose herds fail settle out of necessity and hope that with time they will be able to save enough money from tenant farming and wage labor to resume pastoralism. The latter holds at least the promise of high returns. The fact that both the rich and the poor regularly leave the nomadic segment limits extreme differentiation in wealth among the pastoralists.

One limit to the accumulation of wealth in animals, Barth noted, is that animals do best in the care of their owners. Reliance on hired shepherds means higher rates of loss due to poor care or theft, and encourages the investing of surplus wealth in land. The relatively homogeneity in wealth reported among the Basseri is by no means common to other groups. Daniel Bradburd (1996) and Lois Beck (1991), working separately among the Komachi and Qashqa'i tribes, report great disparities in wealth and social class. In fact, in both societies a class of poor men is employed as shepherds by the wealthy herd owners.

Although we have no recent reports on the current status of the Basseri, Beck visited the Qashqa'i after the Iranian revolution. On the eve of the revolution, the larger tribal structure had already been greatly weakened by the state, and smaller tribal segments assumed greater responsibility for their own well-being and security. Land-reform measures, changing patterns of land use, and the availability of wage labor all contributed to restricting pastoralism and the importance of the tribe. Beck (1991) suggests that the chaos created by the 1979 revolution led to a resurgence of pastoralism as well as tribalism. In the absence of government agents, tribal leaders are reassuming some of their traditional functions.

Dan Bradburd's (1990, 1996) study of the Komanchi pastoralists in south-central Iran is a useful corrective to any temptation to view nomadic pastoralists as inherently egalitarian or as exemplifying some conflict-free tribal existence. He documents systemic differences in the wealth, social status, and general life chances of those families who, owning few animals themselves, eke out a living by herding livestock for others. The men who enter into shepherding contracts not only commit to a lengthy period of poorly rewarded labor, but their wives and children as well are at the beck and call of the employing household, a relationship Bradburd describes as structured inequality. In looking at genealogies and family histories, he found that shepherd families rarely moved into the position of herd ownership, and that, in effect, shepherd and employer moved in separate and often conflicting economic and social worlds. Another source of conflict among the Komanchi deserves mention; while kinship and marriage are rightly considered the foundation stones of tribal organizations, conflict among kin, he found, was endemic and most of it focused on disputes over marriage arrangements.

AL-MURRA OF SAUDI ARABIA

Al-Murra of the Empty Quarter of Saudi Arabia come closest to our notions of the classic desert nomad, the Bedouin (Cole, 1975). Indeed Al-Murra refer to themselves as *Bedu al-Bedu*, literally, "the nomads of the nomads." They are among the last of the great camel-herding peoples of the Arabian Peninsula.

In 1968, Donald Cole, an American anthropologist, began a two-year study that provides us with some of the best data on the contemporary Bedouin and how they fit into the society of oil-rich Saudi Arabia. Cole has since returned many times to that country and continues to report on the transformations there.

Al-Murra, a tribe of some 15,000 people, make up part of the estimated 20 percent of Saudi Arabia's total population that was still nomadic when Cole first visited them. They live in one of the most forbidding desert regions of the world. The group studied by Cole, Al Azab, keep (or kept) camels, whereas other groups of Al-Murra herd sheep and goats as well. The camel is much more than simply an animal kept for production. In Cole's words, it is "an abiding passion of the tribesman," who tell stories and make up songs and poems about their favorite camels. The camels of the tribe are famous for their milk, which is an important dietary item, along with dates, rice, and bread. Apart from milk, all these are purchased in market towns, especially at the oasis of Hofuf. Before the development and expansion of the oil economy, Al-Murra obtained most of their food through trade or tribute. Today, as members of the Saudi Reserve National Guard, Al-Murra tribesmen draw a salary from the government. Another source of cash income is from the wages received as laborers in the oil fields.

Al-Murrah claim a territory, *dira*, which extends in an arc across the west and central borders of the Rub' al-Khali. Several oases fall within the *dira*, including those of Nejran and al-Hasa. They also claim exclusive rights to a series of wells in the central part of this territory. The outer margins of the *dira* are not clearly delineated and overlap those of other tribes.

Nomadic pastoralism in Arabia relies on the yearly cycle of rainfall and on underground sources of water that supply the infrequent wells and determine what pastures can be used. During the summer months the camels are virtually untended while their owners camp near the wells. The far-ranging grazing animals come back on their own every four days for water, and at this time they are also milked. In an average year, the Al Azab group of Al-Murra travel approximately 1200 miles, which composes their annual migratory cycle. Of the two major migrations, spring and fall, the spring is the time of greater concentration of tents and hence social interaction. Feasting and celebration of marriages take place then, and the great sheikhs, or royal princes of Saudi Arabia, visit the camp and are feted.

A camp group among the Al-Murra is made up of a number of households, or *beits*. Each *beit* is thought of as possessing or sharing a unique and private domestic space, called the *dar*. Sometimes two or more *beits* will share a single *dar*, as, for example when two married brothers regularly camp and move together. The major meal of the day is eaten in common by members of the *dar*, although herding and animal care are handled by the individual households.

Each tent tends to be an autonomous social and economic grouping, free to move and to form associations with any other tent. These associations, although usually based on kinship, may also be formed through ties of friendship or convenience. Sometimes tents attach themselves to others to avail themselves of the protection that neighbors customarily extend to each other.

The fact that the *dira*, or tribal range, its wells, and its other resources are associated with distinct lineages of the Al-Murra means that most camp groups are composed of close agnatic kinspeople. Al-Murra lineage, or *fakhd*, is made up of a number of people who claim common patrilineal descent and who share certain rights and responsibilities. The *fakhd* "owns" the wells and the *dira* range and is responsible for collecting or paying blood money in the case of a murder. The herds of *fakhd* members are marked with the same brand, a geometric sign called *wasm*, which is burned into the flanks of the camel. In former days the *fakhd* was an important organization for military action, including defense as well as raiding.

A number of lineages group themselves into larger segments called *gabila*, or clans. There are seven *gabilas* within Al-Murra. Today these named groups play little role in Al-Murra life, as they own no resources in common and share no real responsibility. They serve primarily as reference groups identifying related lineages. Historically the *gabila* was important in political life. Each was headed by a leader, called *emir* to reflect his special military status. In times of large-scale warfare, the *gabila* united behind its emir, and on occasion the entire Murra grouped under the military leadership of one of the emirs.

The entire tribe, or the people of Al-Murra taken together, share a strong sense of common heritage going beyond that of descent. They speak one dialect, dress in a distinctive style, and have their own manner of furnishing their tents. Marriage is almost always within the tribal group. As they put it:

A Bedouin, his son, and their flock of sheep in the Syrian desert.

"Al-Murra, kuluna wahid, biyutuna wahid, kuluna ikhwan"—"People of the Murra are all one, our tents are one, we are all brothers."

Until the ascendancy of the Saud family in the late nineteenth century, Al-Murra was an effective military group capable of conducting raids and warfare. Today it is one reserve unit within the Saudi Arabian National Guard. In this century, the paramount leaders of the tribe, or emirs, have come from one clan. The present emir lives in a black tent (at least he did in 1970), but rarely participates in the annual migration. His complex of tents is situated not far from the town where he also keeps a house. Tribespeople can find him easily as they come and go from the town. Like the Basseri khan, he entrusts his herds to the care of his fellow tribespeople.

The emir serves as commander of the Murra Reserve Guard Unit; he distributes government salaries to the tribespeople. He also acts as arbitrator in disputes within the tribe and attempts to deal with problems such as those arising from car accidents, assaults, and murder. He intervenes in every case in which a tribesperson is held by the police, and meets with high government officials or members of the royal court to resolve such cases.

Tent life resembles that of the Yörük and the Basseri. The tent is the domain of the women, and as men increasingly leave for work in towns, women form the resident element of the household. The interior of a tent is separated into men's and women's sections. Women move freely in the men's section when guests are not present and can visit markets in the oasis towns. The division of household labor parallels that found elsewhere in the Middle East, with the

Bedouin women preparing bread, Jordan.

exception that Al-Murra men do the milking. Cole writes that Al-Murra, like the Yörük, express a strong preference for close kin marriage, the preferred one being between a man and his *bint 'amm,* or paternal uncle's daughter. Cole provides no statistics, however, on the actual occurrence of this form of marriage. Marriages are decided upon by the fathers of the couple, but negotiation may be initiated by the mothers. It is the men who have to agree upon the amount of the bride wealth, or *mahr,* which varies with the degree of kinship involved and the social status of the families.

GENERAL OVERVIEW

In our discussion of nomadic pastoralism and in our three case studies, we have touched on many aspects of nomadic life, as well as on the economic and political organization of particular pastoral communities. Throughout we have tried to avoid stereotypes and to introduce the variability and diversity that exist among nomadic-pastoral peoples. We have stressed that the pastoral peoples of the Middle East are now, and historically have been, part of a larger social and political world. Economically, they were always integrated in larger systems of exchange. Politically, they have played a historic role in the formation and overthrow of ruling dynasties. Any attempt to describe either tribalism or nomadic pastoralism as a vestige of the past is therefore misleading.

The political nature of tribalism, which is a topic quite separate from nomadic pastoralism, is taken up elsewhere. What is important to emphasize here is that tribalism among nomadic peoples, even for those like the Yörük and Basseri who have lost any semblance of political autonomy, remains an important means of expressing individual and group identity in many ways analogous to ethnicity.

We have also emphasized that pastoralists today are very much twenty-first-century people, facing the full range of problems and opportunities of modern society. To this extent their ways of making a living and their social and political organization have changed rapidly in the last few decades.

Dawn Chatty, an anthropologist, has spent 12 years studying the transformation of a small Bedouin tribe in central Oman (1996). Chatty believes that the "most far reaching development to affect nomadic pastoral tribes was the establishment of a regional infrastructure." The system of roads that was started by the French and British in the interwar period and was intended to facilitate military control of nomads quickly rendered the camel obsolete. The Bedouin responded by replacing camel herding with sheep herding. "The Bedouin's recent emphasis on sheep as the principal grazing animal and their accompanying shift from camel, as beast of burden, to truck represents a modernizing form of pastoralism." The trucks are used to transport sheep to distant markets for sale and to transport Bedouin to part-time work in nearby towns. The result of this new aspect of pastoral adaptation, which has also been reported for

Bedouin in Saudi Arabia, Iraq, Syria, and Jordan, is increased overgrazing of rangeland, a problem that is currently being addressed by the various governments in cooperation with development agencies.

Pastoralists, like all other rural people, are increasingly dependent on mechanized transport, distant sources of industrial goods, and rapid telephone (often cellular) and electronic communications for market and other information. Different peoples have, of course, responded in different ways. Some Yörük in southeastern Turkey have become small-scale ranchers, behaving in ways that directly resemble the activities of ranchers everywhere. They phone livestock brokers to get market quotes, arrange truck transport of animals, go to the banks for credit, and even sell futures in immature stock. Al-Murra, on the other hand, living in an oil-rich state, rely on government salaries and have probably decreased their reliance on their animals as an economic investment. The Bedouin of the Negev appear to regard their animal herds as a hedge against inflation and rely primarily on wage labor or farming.[5]

Is there a future for nomadic pastoralism in the Middle East? If this is taken to mean the age-old movement of flocks and tents united in a distinctive style of life, the answer is "no." Marginal fields once jointly exploited by both farmers and herders are often now put to intensive cultivation. Irrigation, modern seeds, machinery, and fertilizers make this possible. Many of the routes to mountain pastures in the Zagros, Taurus, and other ranges are now interdicted by such obstacles as national borders, zones of intensive cultivation, or political restrictions on movement. For most regions, the number of people who can camp together in any season is reduced because of the larger number of animals now needed to sustain a household, as well as diminished pasturage. This, of course, affects the nature of nomadism as a special way of life. Also, for most groups, mechanized transport means that families no longer experience large-scale migrations together and the sense of shared experience that this generates. Even with its hardships, most Yörük seem to feel that the easy sociability of camp life among tents of close friends and relatives was something to be prized. Animals continue to support people, but they are coming less and less to support distinctive communities or local cultures.

---

[5] See E. Marx (1999), Avinoam Meir (1997), William Lancaster (1997).

6

Agriculture and the Changing Village

The Middle East is one of the areas of the world in which agriculture developed earliest, some 10,000 years ago. Historically the majority of the inhabitants were rural dwellers and depended on agriculture for their livelihood. Today this situation is vastly changed. For example, in the early 1940s, an estimated 75 percent of Egyptians were rural residents directly engaged in farming. By the mid-1980s, around 35 percent of Egypt's labor force were farmers, or *fellahīn*. In 2000, the majority of the people in the region resided in urban communities and engaged in urban employment. Despite this change, agriculture remains important, and village life and society continue to be key elements in the Middle Eastern social landscape, especially as many urbanites keep village residence and treat agriculture as a part-time endeavor.

In the course of this chapter, we touch on many of the changing characteristics of rural society and economy. These include a near-complete shift to capital-intensive, privately organized farming, the increasing integration of village economies into national markets, and changes in land tenure and access to land. These processes have led to the narrowing of certain aspects of the social and cultural gaps that have historically separated urban and rural societies in the Middle East. They have also led to increased socioeconomic differentiation within rural society itself and have profound implications for the region as a whole.

While it has become commonplace to remark on the rustication of urban centers due to the influx of migrants from the countryside, the reverse is also true. Urbanization or "suburbanization" of the countryside can be seen in new styles of dwellings, patterns of consumption and home furnishings, new food items, and dress. Part of this has to do with rising income levels, not, of course, shared by all, which selectively enable improved housing and higher rates of consumption, including food items associated more with urban populations—not to mention telephones, televisions and satellite dishes, motor vehicles, and indoor plumbing. In some ways this is a reversal of the long-established pattern of extracting rural commodities and labor to sustain urban centers at the expense of rural populations. While regionally variable, most countries now exhibit high rates of investment, whether state- or market-driven, in the rural infrastructure: improved roads, electrification, and water supply, irrigation and hydroelectric projects where possible, as well as education and health care. In the oil-producing countries these investments may, in fact, far exceed anticipated, let alone realized, economic returns.

LAND USE AND RURAL SETTLEMENTS

Agriculture and patterns of rural settlement are strongly conditioned by two environmental factors: availability of water and topography. The distribution and amount of water determine the possibilities of agriculture and, hence, the distribution of peoples. Regarding topography, the question is simply whether sufficient arable land exists in plots large enough to warrant human investment in capital and labor. For example, in northeastern Iran, in an area formerly occupied by Türkmen nomads, many villages have been established in regions where few permanent settlements existed until recent times. Quite apart from the problem of political security, agriculture was limited by the fact that traditional technology did not make it worthwhile to cultivate the extensive tracts of open land that received adequate rainfall only on an irregular basis. Well-watered areas in the region were largely limited to valley bottoms, but these were usually insufficient in size to sustain a specialized agricultural population. Land drainage and modern earth-moving and cultivation technology have vastly increased the scope of agriculture. Prior to the use of modern methods, farming in these areas was an endeavor secondary to pastoralism. Such limits typified many areas recently opened to cultivation in the Middle East, but there is an opposite trend as well. Land is being lost to urban growth and industrialization; also, arable land is abandoned when it loses market viability, for example, mountain terraces where tractors cannot reach. We will return to these issues later.

Even though there might have been a high yield in some areas in certain years, the extreme unreliability of water placed limits on the size of the population and its distribution. Where water was regularly available and in sufficient quantity, as in the valleys of the Nile and the Tigris-Euphrates and in some coastal regions, intensive agrarian economies emerged. Again, the prime example is Egypt. The soil of the Nile Valley is of unusual fertility; after each annual flooding a new load of silt carried from the headwaters of the Nile in Ethiopia and Uganda is (or was, prior to the High Dam in Aswan) deposited to replenish the fields of Egypt. Productivity is extremely high, allowing multiple cropping and sustaining a dense population clustered around the riverbanks and canals.

Until the construction of the large-scale dams to control and distribute water on a year-round basis, the Egyptian peasants depended on the annual floods in a regimen dating back to the time of the Pharaohs. The old regimen consisted of dividing the fields up into shallow basins to capture the floodwaters by building earth embankments around them. One crop a year was planted, usually a winter crop, such as wheat, barley, or fodder. Summer crops like cotton, rice, maize, and millet were not well suited to basin irrigation and only spread following the introduction of continual irrigation. Cotton, the premier export crop of Egypt today, dates from the development of year-round agriculture in the mid-nineteenth century. The Aswan High Dam, completed in 1970, has extended year-long cultivation, although agriculture now requires more manufactured fertilizers.

A situation similar to that of the Nile Valley exists in patches or zones along the meandering courses of the Tigris and Euphrates rivers, which discharge their waters in April and May. Iraq's irrigation problems, however, are special. Unlike Egypt, many crops are planted prior to peak flood. The late flooding of Iraq's two major rivers mandates the impounding of the waters within their banks in order to prevent large-scale destruction of the maturing crops. Moreover, poor drainage of stagnant flood waters exacerbates the problem of soil salinity. One of the major development projects in the Middle East today is one designed to desalinate vast tracts of soil in southern Iraq that have been contaminated by years of inadequate drainage. The problem of maintaining soil quality continues to plague some of the most productive agricultural areas. All too often, irrigation agriculture has made it too easy for the farmers to overirrigate.

Water drawn from a deep well to irrigate the cotton fields of a wealthy landlord in north central Iran.

Along the southern Turkish coast, there are well-watered, densely populated agricultural areas. For example, on the broad plains around Adana, Turkey's fourth largest city, is a network of villages, all integrated into national and international markets for cotton, tobacco, and tree crops. Here land is frequently held in large, privately owned farmsteads. In coastal Turkey, the Fertile Crescent, and elsewhere, such dense settlements often occur in the same plains and valleys that were important to the city-states and empires of antiquity.

Although this pattern of land use may seem an example of continuity in the area, the facts are more complex. These same regions of Turkey, as well as those along the Tigris-Euphrates Valley that are so densely populated today, were virtually lost to agriculture in recent history. In effect, many areas of the Middle East are now being resettled. Cases in point include the central plateau of Turkey, the Syrian steppes, and parts of north and south-central Iran. Even in recent years, the expansion of irrigation is very uneven. In 1980, there were 55,360 square miles of irrigated croplands in the 16 countries of the Central Middle East; in 1984, this had declined to 53,734 square miles. However, projects in Iraq, Turkey, Egypt, and Saudi Arabia greatly increased the area irrigated throughout the 1990s (Held, 1994, pp. 99–100).

In southeastern Turkey, a massive complex of dams and canalization—the Southeast Anatolia Project; in Turkish, Güney Anadolu Projesi (GAP)—is physically reshaping the landscape; and, although not yet complete, promises continued development and change on a scale comparable to only a few water control projects in world history. When the final GAP dam on a tributary of the Tigris River is completed in 2001, the last element will be in place for near-total control of the headwaters of both the Tigris and Euphrates. Apart from the obvious political implications, this project, underway since the late 1960s, has created many new lakes and inland waterways, with the potential, already being realized, to place thousands of hectares of land under irrigation.

Even before completion, there is an upsurge in both state and market investment in land development that is greatly affecting hundreds of villages and regional cities, such as Gaziantep, Şanlıurfa, and Diyarbakır. One positive effect is rapid economic growth in these centers, often referred to in the Turkish press as Turkey's eastern "tiger" economies. The costs are also considerable; over 2,000 communities have been forced to resettle, and traditional landmarks, shrines, and historic sites have been submerged. But if managed properly and if salination is avoided, the current rapid expansion of commercial agriculture should also sustain a significant improvement in rural living standards.

High rates of population growth are obviously related to this expansion of rural resettlement and intensification of land use. However, population pressure is not the only factor. Political and economic considerations are equally important. They include the ability of governments and settled communities to maintain security and lines of communication. Even more important is the fact that the availability of urban-controlled credit and market facilities has encouraged rural investment and the transition to modern farming. This is not an entirely new phenomenon. In the past as well, rural settlement and agricultural production were closely tied to urban investment in irrigation facilities, markets, and, of course, roads.

One now classic study that illustrates how these factors are interrelated is Paul English's work on the Kirman region of central Iran (1976). English, a geographer, focused on the patterns of interdependence among the villages of the Kirman Basin and the relationship of these villages to the city of Kirman. He suggests that the dominance of the city is the key to understanding the settlement history and economy of the region. Village size and complexity decrease with distance from the regional capital of Kirman. English traced the settlement history of the region back to the installation of a Sassanian garrison center in the area around A.D. 240. This was soon followed by the establishment and spread of villages as a result of increased security and the deployment of urban capital by the land-owning elite of the city. This capital was used to build the elaborate network of underground irrigation (*qanats*) and to dig the wells that provided the water on which village agricultural life depended. Urban capital was also used to develop a carpet industry based in the villages around Kirman. English's thesis is that urban centers both create village settlements and help to keep villages relatively underdeveloped by the subsequent systematic extraction of surplus products.[1] Recent land reform measures and investment practices in many countries give more political and economic powers to local rural communities, but do not seem to be sufficient to reverse the historical pattern of urban domination. English's conclusion that Middle Eastern village life and settlement patterns are predominately shaped by forces emanating from urban centers appears to hold true.

Regional approaches to village studies can also facilitate an understanding of rural demographic processes, including migration. In a study of the Kashan region in Iran, for example, V. F. Costello (1976) found significantly higher rates of out-migration from upland hamlets, where poor soil and lack of capital inhibit intensive agriculture. Although this may be true for the Kashan region, in other areas, such as Adana in southern Turkey, mentioned earlier, some of the highest rates of out-migration come from the larger and more agriculturally productive communities. Here investment in agriculture and consolidation of holdings into larger farms have forced farmers off the land, some to become migrant laborers, others to move into cities. The point is that even though migration or movement between villages and from villages to cities is a regular phenomenon, it will vary among villages, depending in part on the location of settlements within a regional system.

While we have distinguished pastoralists from farmers in terms of our presentation, from an economic point of view many local populations had both farming and pastoral communities, such as the Baluch, Qashqai, the Türkmen, and others. Even families, as we have noted, may shift back and forth between

---

[1] For another study of a city and its hinterland in Iran, see V. F. Costello (1976).

pastoralism and farming. Emmanuel Marx (1999) gives a nice account for the Negev and, incidentally, shows how oases themselves come into being.

We usually associate the Bedouin with nomadic pastoralism, as exemplified by Al-Murra, described earlier; in reality, however, most Bedouin are sedentary farmers today. Also, many regularly alternate among herding, farming and wage labor, depending on market conditions, availability of work, and political security. In the South Sinai, for example, tribally organized Bedouin, today numbering some 10,000, in addition to herding have long been highly skilled horticulturalists, specialists in well digging, grafting and pruning fruit trees, and pollinating date palms (Marx, 1999). They not only inhabit the oases of this geographically complex and variegated region, but they create them. As Marx explains, the oasis is a human artifact, established for particular purposes. He distinguishes five varieties, including large ones, with settled year-round residents, similar to those found in North Africa and in Arabia, others established primarily for purposes of smuggling, and still others that are little more than small orchards visited only periodically by families who rely on wage labor or herding.

Although the pattern of land use has changed greatly in recent years, in large part due to the Israeli occupation (which ended in 1982), the Bedouin have a long history of horticulture, probably acquiring skills while employed by the monks of St. Catherine's monastery, which is itself a major oasis dating back to the sixth century A.D. Today, most Bedouin families have claims to orchards, even though few rely exclusively on them for income. Each tribe has a known territory within which members are free to develop sites that are not occupied. If a particular site of cultivation or oasis is left to deteriorate, it may be assumed to have been abandoned. The first step in creating an oasis is to identify the surface features which indicate that water might be present. Then a well is dug, a laborious and sometimes risky task, followed by perhaps more wells, all to be enclosed by a stone wall to indicate that the area is being developed. The final steps are to level the surface, bring in topsoil from the mountain slopes to mix with clay, and erect a counterbalanced water hoist (*shaduf*). For many families, the oasis is something of a summer home, to be visited for a few months while the fruit and vegetables raised are a welcome but secondary element in the household economy. Some 300 or more people may gather in a large oasis, but relatively few reside there throughout the year. The largest palm oases have been built or expanded in recent years using the proceeds of smuggling or tourism to employ mechanized well diggers and pumps.

THE TRADITIONAL SYSTEM OF LAND TENURE

Agricultural production, as we noted in the preceding discussion, depends on a number of key factors, among which are land, water, labor, and technology. Although all are important, because of its enduring quality and limited availability, arable land is the most regulated by law and custom. How people get access to the land they use and how they derive profit from the land they hold rights to constitute the system of land tenure. The systems found in Middle Eastern countries, while varying locally, all have a common base in Islamic law, as modified to meet local conditions and customary usage. More recently, the codification of land tenure practices in many countries has incorporated a number of European legal concepts, of which the most important is undoubtedly the registration of individual title.

There are four major categories of land rights found throughout Arabic- and Turkish-speaking areas of the Middle East. Persian categories, while essentially similar, have different terms. The Arabic terms are *mulk, miri, waqf,* and *musha'a.* We now briefly describe each and give examples of how these concepts operated in practice.

Mulk refers to freehold or private ownership. This is similar to American or European notions of private property and entails full rights of use and disposal through sale or inheritance. The concept of *mulk* extends to all kinds of property. In the Middle East private or *mulk* ownership of land is the most prevalent form of tenure. This was not the case prior to the nineteenth century, when evidence suggests that the bulk of agricultural land was ultimately the domain of the state or the ruler.

State or crown lands are generally known as *miri,* although this category subsumes a wide variety of actual practices. For example, within the Ottoman Empire two major forms of *miri* land tenure were common: the *timar* and the *iltizam.* On rich lands, the *timar* was dominant until the eighteenth century. In this system, agricultural estates were granted to individuals in compensation for services rendered to the ruling dynasty. In return, the grantee had to raise troops for the sultan's army upon demand. In theory, the land could not be passed on as an inheritance, but reverted to the state once the grantee died. In this way *timar* differs significantly from European feudal practice. The rule against inheritance was often violated; but where effective control remained with the sultan, the practice blocked the development of a stable landed aristocracy, a prominent feature in European history. Of course, inheritance patterns also limited the development of a landed aristocracy, as the Islamic law of partible inheritance broke up large estates.

In the system of *iltizam,* or tax farming, land theoretically owned by the state was turned over to tax farmers, a practice that was particularly prevalent in the Ottoman province of Egypt. The tax farmer, usually an individual in favor at the court and often a non-Muslim, paid a fixed price to the sultan for the right to tax the peasants of a particular tract of land.

Both *iltizam* and *timar* represented forms of absentee control over land, its resources, and the peasantry. The *timar* system was abolished at the beginning of the nineteenth century, and the *iltizam* soon after. The Ottoman government moved into direct collection of taxes from the peasants and attempted to encourage private ownership of land. This was done not so much to benefit the peasant as to ensure more direct control of the land, higher productivity, and increased revenues.

This process can perhaps be seen most clearly in the case of Egypt, where, beginning in 1811, the ruler Muhammad Ali embarked on a series of agrarian reforms that culminated in the Land Law of 1858. Similar reforms were instituted elsewhere in the Middle East at about the same time. These reforms were all designed to limit the power of the elite and to promote agricultural production through private ownership of land. These reforms did not arise in nineteenth-century Egypt in isolation from other forces already changing agrarian society. Even prior to initial attempts at legal land reform, private ownership of a de facto sort—that is, not based on governmental decree—was gaining ground, stimulated by rising prices of foods and food exports to Europe. Thus, in many instances legal reform was as much a consequence as a cause of shifting patterns of tenure (see Cuno, 1983).

During this period, and at least related to this transition to private ownership, Egypt experienced a very rapid transition to cash crops and an expansion of its irrigation network. This allowed those with capital to purchase land and rapidly gave rise to a new basis for social differentiation, that of landownership. The newly emergent classes may be roughly grouped into the following categories: urban-dwelling landlords who administered their estates through supervisors or agents, relatively small-hold landowners, landless tenants or sharecroppers, and landless wage laborers. Concurrent with these developments, the shift from subsistence agriculture to cash crops meant that the farmer was increasingly tied to the world market system. It is a double irony that many subsequent attempts at land reform in Egypt, as elsewhere in the Middle East, have been directed at remedying the social inequities arising from this first effort of land reform, only to be followed by re-privatization in the 1990s.

Besides the *miri* and *mulk*, a third category of land tenure is the *waqf*, which refers to an Islamic institution whereby a property is designated as a self-perpetuating trust whose income is then assigned to some end. The most usual form of *waqf* is the endowment of a charitable endeavor. Income from a piece of land, a shop, or some other property is committed to the support of a mosque, shrine, hospital, or school. For example, until recently, most of the major mosques of Istanbul were maintained by *waqf* lands in Syria, Palestine, and Egypt. The lot of the peasants who lived on these lands differed very little from that of tenant farmers anywhere else.

Another type of *waqf* is private. Individuals could designate up to one-third of their property as a trust for their descendants. This was aimed at preserving family estates by circumventing fragmentation through inheritance and alienation through sale. The net effect of the *waqf* system on land tenure and land use was to create large estates administered by bureaucrats who had no direct stake in their productivity or maintenance, not to mention reinvestment and capital improvement.

The economic inefficiency and social abuse associated with the *waqf* encouraged modern governments in the area to attempt to abolish or curb it. Land reform laws in, for example, Egypt, Iraq, Syria, Turkey, and Iran, moved forcibly to break up *waqf* estates, especially the private ones. In Egypt, one unfortunate by-product of this has been the increasing neglect and deterioration of the country's great Islamic monuments. No longer supported by their traditional *waqf* revenues, they now have to depend on an overburdened public treasury. In Iran the so-called White Revolution's attempt to break up the vast *waqf* holdings met with strenuous and ultimately successful opposition from the religious establishment. In general, though, this form of rural tenure is in decline.

The least common form of land tenure is the *musha'a*, or commons. *Musha'a* designates the common tenure and periodic redistribution of village lands. Generally speaking, *musha'a* did not exist in isolation from other forms of land tenure but in conjunction with them. For example, agricultural lands, especially orchards and irrigated fields, may be held as *mulk*, or private property, and the adjacent pastures are held in common, or as *musha'a*.

Musha'a as a significant form of agricultural land tenure is, or rather was, found primarily in the Levant, often in areas marginal to rainfall agriculture

Kurdish women preparing grape leaves for sale in the market, Diyarbakr, Turkey.

and occupied by recently settled tribal communities. Few such communities maintained this form of tenure after World War II; one of the last areas where it was prevalent was Palestine. Where most of the village lands were held as *musha'a*, it was usual to periodically redistribute fields among families according to need as well as to equalize access to better plots. Today *musha'a* is usually limited to unproductive or grazing land.

TENANCY AND ACCESS TO LAND

So far we have discussed landholding without saying much about how people actually get access to the land that supports them. One has to distinguish carefully here between those who own the land and those who actually cultivate it. Historically, the majority of Middle Eastern peasants probably belonged to the second category—that is, they cultivated land they did not own or control, and their access to land was through a number of tenancy arrangements.

Different types of tenancies have long characterized Middle Eastern agricultural relationships and persist today, despite land reform efforts. Historically, the most prevalent form of tenancy is sharecropping, whereby the cultivator provides labor, and sometimes draft animals and tools, in return for a percentage of the crop that he has raised on land belonging to someone else. The size of the share varies according to what each party provides. Sharecropping was so common a practice that the term for peasant throughout most of the area was synonymous with that of the most common form of sharecropping, the *khemmas*, or the one-fifth. In this form of sharecropping, allocation of shares was based on the five components of production: land, water, draft animals, seed, and labor. A peasant supplying only his labor would receive one-fifth of the harvest; if he provided animal power as well, he would receive two-fifths, and so on. Direct rental of land for a fixed fee was rare until very recently. Even on large estates, land was usually let out as small scattered plots in return for a share of the harvest, a practice that still persists in many villages.

Sharecropping has some advantages for both owner and tenant where yields greatly vary from one year to the next. Under this arrangement, the cultivator need not provide or maintain much equipment, draft animals, and the like; and should seed supplies be difficult to obtain locally, the cultivator could rely on the landowner to provide them. Moreover, the cost to the cultivator was automatically adjusted in terms of the annual yield. In disastrously bad years, the landlord might forgo his share in order to maintain the peasant-laborer and might even advance the peasant-laborer food supplies.

Relationships between the peasant and the landlord took the form of generalized patron-client ties. In this relationship, the landlord assumed wide responsibility for assisting and protecting the tenants. He may have interceded on their behalf with government officials, or he may have assisted them in medical and other crises. However, one must not romanticize this feudal-like relationship. In his novel about Turkish rural life, *Memed, My Hawk,* Yashar Kemal (1961) describes the misery and suffering that could result from this essentially exploitive relationship. In his portrayal, the peasant family lives in fear of dispossession, has little to show for its endless efforts, and is subject to arbitrary abuse by the landlord or his retainers. The landlords, or *aghas,* as they are called in Turkey, may exercise near-total control over the lives of those who work their land.

Where sharecropping is practiced in the absence of government regulation and supervision, it tends to be associated with an exploitive pattern that is manifested in the repeated cycle of indebtedness and poverty of the peasant. Nowhere, perhaps, was this pattern more evident than in Iran prior to the mid-1950s, when the majority of the villages were owned by a relatively small number of absentee landlords. Even as reforms in most countries moved to break up these large estates, in many instances, the introduction of modern agricultural techniques worsened the plight of many farmers. Labor, the one commodity the landless villager can supply, had become less important in the modern context, and many small holders, even when granted land by governments, could not effectively compete with those who have access to machinery.

So far our discussion of Middle Eastern agriculture and rural life has concentrated on placing the village and the agrarian economy within their larger historical and economic context. Before we take up the question of rural transformation, we shall briefly consider some aspects of the social and political organization of rural society in order to convey some idea of the ways in which rural people organize their domestic and political lives.

VILLAGE POLITICAL ORGANIZATION

Formal leadership in the village is typically vested in the office of the village headman, called *mukhtar* or *muhtar* in most Arab countries and in Turkey, *'oumda* in Egypt, and *katkhoda* in Iran (these leaders are discussed in Chapter 10). The *mukhtar* or *katkhoda* is generally elected by the heads of households and subject to confirmation by the central government, or, in some cases, he may be directly appointed by the government. The office itself is created by the state and reflects efforts to control rural populations. Thus the *mukhtar* represents the government to the villagers and only secondarily serves to bring the village interests to the attention of the central government.

On any weekday in any major Turkish town, for example, the corridors of the district governor's *kaymakamlık,* or headquarters, are filled with *mukhtars* from the surrounding villages. They come to respond to government decrees, to file reports, or to register births, deaths, and marriages. They may be accompanying conscripts as they report to military induction centers, or they may be simply responding to the complaints of their village schoolteachers, for whose well-being they are responsible. They also bring village complaints to the attention of the officials and try to gain support for themselves and their village. If the governor decides that the village streets are impassable, for example, he may require the *muhtar* to organize a work party, or, if necessary, to collect money to repair the village schoolhouse. Should disputes arise among the villagers, the *muhtar* is expected to mediate, and should open conflict erupt, to call on the assistance of the national gendarmerie. The *muhtar* is often the first and last point of call for official visitors in the village, and he must report their presence to the governor.

The real status and power of the village headman vary greatly, depending on the actual influence of the government in the countryside and the presence of competing local sources of power, such as big landlords or tribal leaders. In villages remote from urban centers, the headman may represent the government's interest less than those of the local power structure. That is, he may exemplify and exercise power in his own right or on behalf of local tribal leaders or landlords. In other communities he may be little more than a low-level government bureaucrat, wielding little power on his own and simply acting as a messenger for the national authorities. Being at the bottom of the state hierarchy, however, need not always mean a lack of power. Although Turkish *muhtars* tend to be relatively limited in the scope and effectiveness of their activities, those of Syria, Iraq, and Egypt have often been delegated considerable authority and power. They derive this, in part, from their membership in the ruling party.

The political dynamics of Middle Eastern village life are much too complex and varied to allow for easy generalizations. In an effort to clarify some of the political patterns, Robert Fernea (1970) suggests a system of classification that derives from the differences in the internal organization of villages as well as their relation to the national government. We cannot give examples of villages illustrating all of the many types Fernea suggests, but we can emphasize the significance of one distinction, that of nontribal versus the tribally organized village.

In tribally organized villages, access to power, positions of leadership, and available resources are all associated to one degree or another with membership in a named descent group. A classic example is that of the Chebayish, a tribal community in southern Iraq studied in the mid-1950s by the Iraqi anthropologist Shaker Salim (1962). Here we rely directly on Salim's fine report.

During the long period of Ottoman rule, the Chebayish, who lived in the marsh area midway between the Tigris and the Euphrates, were relatively independent. There was no government agent in the village until 1893, and the authority of the sheikh was paramount. The inhabitants of the different villages considered themselves members of a single tribe, the Beni Isad, and the population of about 11,000 was divided among nine clans. At the heart of the tribe, writes Salim, were four clans, each claiming descent from one of four brothers. The brothers themselves were thought to be the descendants of the founder of the tribe of Isad. Accordingly, the four clans held a particularly esteemed position in the tribal hierarchy, as the remaining five clans represented fragmented segments of other tribes that had been incorporated into the Beni Isad by virtue of living among them.

The four core clans were internally ranked, with one, the Ahl ish-Shaikh, being the most respected and powerful. While each clan had its own leader, or sheikh, the leader of the Ahl segment was acknowledged as being the paramount leader of the tribe.

Given this structure, what were the powers of the paramount sheikhs? According to Salim, they ruled over their followers as landowners, military commanders, and judges. Although tribal land was technically the property of the state, or *miri*, the sheikh in practice determined who used it and how much was to be allocated to his followers. Even though the sheikh received a third of the crop, it was not uncommon for him to confiscate more. In the absence of the religious courts associated with urban centers, judicial authority was the exclusive domain of the sheikh. He administered the customary law of the tribe, or *'urf*, with the occasional assistance of an informal council of notables. The executive power of the sheikh was administered by the heads of the different clans allied with him, his sons and other close relatives, and by a core of retainers and slaves.

The political autonomy of the sheikhs began to erode during the latter part of the nineteenth century. The Ottomans moved army officers and government officials into the area, and within a few decades established direct rule over most of the tribes. Indeed, everywhere in the Middle East today, the state's bureaucratic control is important, and instances of full tribal autonomy are hard to find.

How, then, did the tribes and their traditional leaders, the sheikhs, respond to the encroachment of the state? Again Salim provides a good account of tribal politics and its transformation. In pacifying the region the Ottomans attempted to work through the local leaders. While taking strenuous military action against those who resisted, they appointed friendly sheikhs and notables to administrative positions, making them responsible for the safety of travelers, the collection of taxes, and general internal order in the area. Thus, state support became the new basis for the power of the sheikhs, replacing their direct reliance on kin and armed retainers.

In 1924, the political office of the paramount sheikh was officially abolished by the newly constituted government of Iraq; however, the title of sheikh persists and is widely used today as a title of respect. To replace the sheikh, the government established the political office of *sirkal*. Although the *sirkal* serves at the pleasure of the provincial governor, in actuality *sirkals* tend to be members of the dominant lineage of the clans they represent, and sons often succeed to the office of their fathers. Thus the abolition of the sheikh's political autonomy, suppression of customary law, and intertribal warfare have all contributed to the undermining of tribal independence and the increased integration of these rural populations into the national political system. It has not, however, resulted in the disappearance of tribalism as a charter for local political and social life.

It is hard to estimate the saliency of tribal organization in village social and political life throughout the Middle East today. Certainly the exercise of local power and authority using the tribal idiom is inversely correlated with the local strength of the national government in question. In countries such as Yemen, Oman, Iran, Iraq, Syria, and Turkey, we find regions where tribal leaders wield great local influence despite state claims and administrative offices. In still other areas, where the state administrative apparatus is well entrenched, identification with a tribal name may carry significance primarily as a source of individual and group identity, but it has no direct import for leadership and political power. In southern Iraq since the Gulf War of 1990–91, the government has employed both the carrot and the stick. With rebellious groups, including marsh-dwellers like the el-Chebayish, the government has acted with extreme measures of force or terror. One unspoken rationale for the 350-mile-long Basra Canal, completed in 1993, draining the southern marshes, is to enhance political control of the area. At the same time, selected tribal leaders are courted and rewarded (see Fernea & Fernea, 1997).

NONTRIBAL VILLAGES

A Turkish village studied by Paul Stirling in the mid-1950s and revisited during the 1980s and 1990s illustrates the alternative or nontribal form of rural political organization (1965, 1993).[2] Sakaltutan, a village in the central Anatolian Plateau, was composed of 100 households and some 600 people. "Here," Stirling wrote, "people belong to their village in a way they belong to no other social group" (1965). Although this village society is differentiated by distinctions of wealth and prestige, and along lines of family and kinship, there are no sharp class boundaries or clear segmentation along lines of descent. Unlike the tribal el-Chebayish peasant, whose primary identity is with the clan, the peasant of Sakaltutan identifies with the village or any one of its family-focused political factions.

Sakaltutan, like most Turkish villages, has a territory recognized by the state as its village commons or meadowlands, which is exclusively utilized by the residents. This territory, notes Stirling, is more than simply a matter of administrative convenience; it symbolizes village communal identity. People are willing to mobilize and even fight to maintain the integrity of village communal property.

The formal political structure of Sakaltutan was that established by the state. The village was represented by the headman, who was elected by secret ballot. In addition to the headman, the village was governed by a council of elected elders, who were generally totally ignored by the villagers. Those elected gained neither prestige nor special standing. Rather, when concerted

---

[2] See also the Web site devoted to Stirling's work: http://lucy.ukc.ac.uk/tvillage/stirlingc3.htm

action was required, senior heads of households or large family groups gathered informally to make decisions. According to Stirling, the headman and the council members of Sakaltutan and neighboring communities were young or middle-aged. Senior men and individuals of great influence did not hold office themselves but controlled matters from behind the scenes. Shifting coalitions of households within the village formed factions for political action. Although these factions often had a strong basis in kinship, this was not their only organizing principle. More important than kinship was membership in a residential quarter, which included more than one kin group. What politically distinguishes Sakaltutan and other similiarly organized villages in the Middle East is the absence of high-level, overarching, and active descent groups. On visits during the 1980s and 1990s, Stirling noted that the basic household structure remained, but that materially conditions had greatly improved; the village now had electricity and running water, there was no hunger, and morbidity was down. Most men sought at least seasonal or episodic wage labor, and many had migrated to urban centers or abroad.

El-Chebayish and Sakaltutan represent two contrasting forms of village political organization, but most villages fall somewhere between, combining features of both. It is a rare village, for example, in which larger descent groups are completely absent or irrelevant. But even where these are found and are politically important, they are frequently crosscut by factions expressed in terms of residential groupings, party affiliation, and the power of the state.

A more recent village study in Turkey carried out by Carol Delaney (1991) had a very different focus than that of Stirling's now classic work. Her interest was in gender and cosmology. Out of the nearly 40,000 villages in Turkey, she selected one, like Sakaltutan, on the central Anatolian Plateau, which she refers to as Göker, home to approximately 850 people. We cannot adequately summarize here her complex and sometimes controversial theoretical framework. In sum, she shows how villagers use theories and symbols of procreation to talk about land, food, sex, interpersonal relationships, marriage, and the meaning of life. Rather than standing apart from religion, these folk constructs are intimately bound up or even enveloped in Islamic belief. The villagers, largely small-holder farmers relying on grain fields, are fairly comparable in wealth and income, with no dominant clan or landowning family. Central to Delaney's challenging thesis is an oft-repeated village metaphor to the effect that procreation is like "the seed and the soil," the male plants the seed and the woman nurtures it but makes no biological contribution. She relates how the villagers incorporate this view and related constructs, such as sexual intercourse being analagous to "plowing the field," into a larger cosmology that explains and sanctions the moral order, gender relations, and even kinship ties. As she puts it in the context of a discussion of kinship and gender: "This theory of procreation lends itself to a distinction between spiritual/essential and material/supportive, the first male and the second female" (p. 156). We return to this account in Chapter 8.

DOMESTIC ORGANIZATION

The household is the basic economic and social unit in rural societies. Termed *beit* in Arabic, *ev* in Turkish, and *hane* in Persian, this group is recognized everywhere as the individual's primary source of food, shelter, and security. Households are economic and residential units, usually composed of people related to each other in a variety of ways. Although unrelated individuals, such as servants, hired shepherds, or other retainers, may be temporarily part of the household, most commonly they identify themselves with their own families. Whereas patrilineality forms the basis for enduring, named kin groupings, the household may be thought of as a temporary kinship group that utilizes ties of marriage as well as those of descent to define its membership. Women, for example, usually do not lose their identification with their father's lineage or family: however, upon marriage, they join their husband's household or, more commonly, that of his father. This form of residence is termed *patrilocal* and is nearly universal in the rural Middle East.

Some of the variation exhibited in household organization in any village is due to the uneven distribution of resources. Households owning much land tend to be larger than those with no or very little land; they frequently include a number of married sons in addition to the head of the household, his wife or wives, and unmarried sons and daughters. Such a household may be termed *extended* and is the most frequently stipulated "ideal" or preferred form of residence in Iranian, Arab, and Turkish villages. Brothers may elect to remain together in a joint household following the death of their father if their collective property holdings are substantial, and if there are compelling economic interests in maintaining fields and herds intact. Variation in household size and organization is also due to the usual processes by which households are formed, expand, and ultimately break up. These processes can be termed the *domestic cycle*. Sons, for instance, begin life as members of their father's household; after marriage, one or more of them may continue to reside in their natal household, making it an extended one. Should their father die during this period, the brothers may elect to stay together, with the oldest assuming the role of head of household. This form of extended or joint household is relatively rare, in part because it denies at least one brother the status associated with being the head of a household. Most men aspire to head their own households and to assume the social status this responsibility confers.

The household has social continuity because sons commonly continue to reside in or near their father's household following their marriage. A new household comes into being when a man establishes his own residence after marriage. As children grow, marriages are arranged for sons whereby each brings a bride into the home for some period of time. Married sons most often live in separate rooms added on to an existing house; their common membership in the household is symbolized by their sharing one hearth or kitchen facility.

Although such a household might theoretically continue to grow to include more than two generations of married male agnates, this rarely happens. The large multigenerational *zadruga* households of some Balkan villages are seldom found in the Middle East; as noted, sons usually leave the household during their father's lifetime, and nowhere do we see a consistent pattern of brothers staying together after their father's death. As sons have children, or as frictions arise among members of an increasingly crowded household, men try to establish their own domestic units. Thus, within any village community, nuclear households are far more numerous than extended or joint households.

The growing reliance of many rural households on income derived from wage labor, with the seasonal or even full-time employment of members in urban centers, further strengthens the trend toward small, independent households. Indeed, a profound social transformation is underway in most of the rural Middle East as the capitalist market economy increasingly penetrates the countryside.

Even though small households are increasingly the norm, many villages usually have one or more households that occupy the most impressive dwellings and that stand out as major contenders for local leadership, power, and influence. They usually comprise a number of closely related adult males, usually father and sons and their dependents. This raises the issue of what the advantages are in maintaining an extended household. One advantage is that such a group provides an efficient means of organizing a reliable source of labor. This presupposes access to such resources as land where coordinated labor pays off. The large household as an economic unit can benefit from economies of scale. The division of labor is potentially quite efficient, even in the context of mechanized agriculture. For instance, one adult son might supervise animal production, while another manages the family's mechanized farm equipment, perhaps driving a family-owned tractor or combine for hire in order to secure additional income. Although mechanization tends to reduce the importance of labor relative to other inputs, skilled agricultural labor is often in short supply. Landowners have to compete with urban employers for the services of skilled drivers and mechanics. It is not feasible to turn over expensive equipment to unskilled operators. Large families possessing both land and capital frequently utilize family members directly in productive tasks. By investing in equipment they can increase the productivity of family members while they reduce their reliance on labor outside the household.

Another advantage of large, extended households is in the domain of politics. With few exceptions, the village dweller in the Middle East must cope with a relative scarcity of good land, water, and pastures. This often puts households in a competitive, even a potentially adversarial, relationship with each other. Because even closely related households may easily find themselves in competition for land or pasture, the household becomes a fundamental grouping for political action, as it serves to guarantee its members mutual security and acts in concert where property and public image are concerned. Stirling notes for Sakaltutan that neighbors might physically take over land belonging to another, and that there were continual attempts by some to extend their private fields into the village commons. The moving of field markers, diversion of water by stealth, and the trampling of grain fields by animals in search of grazing are some of the problems with which households must contend. Households without active adult males to represent their interests are vulnerable when it comes to disputes within the village. We should note, too, that when machines are involved, the traditional attitudes toward manual labor are changing. Even in well-to-do families, men may operate their own tractors or combines. This reflects what might be called a shift from peasant agriculture to farming.

The point to emphasize, however, is that regardless of the size and composition of households, and despite the many changes we have touched upon, access to resources, social status, and even one's opportunities are largely determined by familial relations.

RURAL TRANSFORMATIONS

To illustrate better some of the patterns and processes of change in the rural Middle East, we now turn our attention to Egypt. It should, however, be kept in mind that for reasons of both ecology and politics, Egypt is distinctive. Still, there are relatively good data available and, more important, Egypt was the first country of the region to initiate and experience many of the changes associated with land reform. There is a general tendency to stress the uniformities and continuities in Egyptian *fellah*, or peasant, life, but considerable regional and social variation as well as historical change are as true of Egyptian rural life as of farmers elsewhere in the region.

Mahmaud Abdel-Fadel (1975), an Egyptian economist, provides a point of departure. He writes that prior to the July 1952 revolution, owners of large estates or those with over 200 *feddans* (a *feddan* is equal to approximately one acre) made up less than 0.1 percent of the total number of landowners and possessed about 20 percent of the cultivated land. Owners of large and medium-sized estates, or those with five *feddans* or more but less than 200, possessed about 65 percent of the total cultivated land. However, in 1950, 44 percent of all rural families were landless. This compares unfavorably with 1929, when only 24 percent of rural households were without land.

Abdel-Fadel points to three major causes for this increasingly uneven distribution of agrarian wealth. First, the big landlords held a monopoly of power over land and water, which allowed them to demand exorbitant rents and dispossess tenants at will. Second, these landowners monopolized the modern credit market, forcing tenants and small landowners to turn to village moneylenders, who extorted high interest rates, often exceeding 100 percent per year. These rates often meant the ruin of small landowners and the forced sale of their land. Third, heavy speculation in rural land increased land prices beyond any corresponding increase in productivity, making it difficult for small holders to acquire more fields. (Although the focus here is on Egypt, we must note in passing that similar processes are at work elsewhere.) It is no surprise, then, that land reform was the first priority of the new regime following the Nasser Revolution of 1952.

A more recent survey of two village populations, one from Upper Egypt, the other from the delta region, provides an interesting village-level perspective that complements the earlier broad economic picture drawn by Abdel-Fadel. Nicholas Hopkins and a research team from the American University of Cairo carried out a study of animal husbandry and household economy using survey interviewing techniques (1980, 1985). We rely primarily on their findings from the larger of the two villages, Musha, in Upper Egypt near the city of Assiut.

Musha is large, even by Egyptian standards, with a population officially estimated at 35,000 and distributed among some 7000 families or households. Musha can be termed a village, however, because of its limited marketing, crafts, and commercial sectors. The bulk of the households are densely crowded in the nucleated core of the community, although recently there has been some establishment of isolated households in the fields. Members of many households reside either seasonally or permanently in the large cities to the north where they work; others may move regularly among different farming communities as seasonal agricultural laborers. People from Musha have also migrated to Saudia Arabia and Kuwait. The movement of people, both seasonally and as long-term migrants, limited access to land, and patterns of local employment are closely interrelated.

The main crops grown in the village are cotton, wheat, beans, and lentils; animal production is a significant secondary economic activity. The main livestock are buffalo, cows, sheep, and goats. Agriculture is heavily mechanized. No animals are used today to raise water to the fields or to till the land. Water is supplied from a main canal throughout the year and is passed through feeder canals, then pumped up to the fields, where it is conducted by farmer-maintained irrigation ditches to the plots under cultivation. Like many areas in Egypt, Musha has problems of waterlogging and a rising water table, which have resulted from the extension of irrigation beyond the traditional reliance on the annual flooding of the Nile.

Distribution of land, despite the long period of land reform and governmental regulation, remains unequal. At the same time, however, alternative sources of employment outside agriculture have opened up and now sustain many households. Although only approximately 10 percent of the village's households are officially considered destitute—that is, without any land or any other means of adequate support—a full two-thirds of the villagers are landless. Landless households sustain themselves by finding employment in agriculture, as laborers elsewhere, as shopkeepers, or as civil servants. About 20 percent of the households own land, but of these only 12 percent hold more than five *feddans,* the minimum thought necessary to maintain an average household.

Among those with more than five *feddans,* a handful have apparently gained great wealth from farming, some of which has been invested in urban real estate as well as in tractors, pumps, and other agricultural equipment.

An apparent paradox is that despite the large numbers of landless, even destitute, families, landlords maintain that there is a labor shortage, that labor is too costly, and that laborers are unwilling to work long hours. In contrast, workers interviewed said that it is hard to find work and still harder to live on the income they might derive from it. Hopkins notes that this debate is still unresolved in the political economy of rural Egypt (and in many other parts of the Middle East). Part of the problem has to do with the seasonality of labor demand in mechanized farming. Landowners need to hire at peak season and thus, for a short period of time, may compete with one another for workers. The ability of laborers to exploit this demand fully in the form of high wages is limited by the fact that they, too, face competition from laborers coming in from other districts. Though these ramifications go somewhat beyond Hopkins' reports, they appear reasonable. Hopkins notes, too, that because workers cannot find employment in the off-season winter months, many migrate to the city, which further aggravates the shortage of skilled farm workers. As noted, the wages and remittances of migrants have to be considered as integral to the village economy today. About 19 percent of the households surveyed by the research team had no direct involvement in farming, although they continued to be village dwellers. This, we feel, is fairly typical of villagers throughout the region, and is, if anything, an increasing trend (see Fernea & Fernea, 1997, p. 303).

Households in Musha vary considerably both in the number of people coresident and how these members are related to one another. While much of this variation has to do with the progression of the domestic cycle itself, some variation is attributable to economic factors, including migration and wage labor. Over 70 percent of the households surveyed were either nuclear (husband, wife, and unmarried offspring) or simply one-generational. The survey as a whole puts average household size at 7.6, larger than usually reported for this part of Egypt in the national census. The study notes a significant positive correlation among three interrelated variables: the amount of land owned, large animal production, and household size. Better-off households were larger and more apt to be extended in form. Moreover, animal production was economically more feasible for those with land than for others, the latter being unable to secure adequate fodder or processed animal feeds. In many respects, then, animal husbandry contributes to the wealth differential because it constitutes a form of savings and investment. Young animals are purchased when cash is available, raised, and finally sold in times of need.

We shall not attempt here to contrast Musha with the delta village investigated in the American University of Cairo project, but there is one finding that merits comment because it highlights an important aspect of the domestic economy and raises questions that might be usefully addressed in studies in other parts of the Middle East. Approximately half of the women interviewed in the delta community reported that they worked in the fields, and about 18 percent of them owned livestock in their own right. In Musha, in many respects a more prosperous village, no woman was found (or would admit to) working in the fields. Many did care for animals in their own homes, but still left their grazing and watering to the menfolk. The reasons for this contrast are not entirely clear, according to the report, and Musha sounds like an extreme case by either Egyptian or Middle Eastern standards. One reason that might account for the absence of women in agricultural labor is that Musha has a very high rate of out-migration, and many families derive income from remittances. This may enable even relatively poor families to conform to societal values, which stigmatize households whose women work outside the home. Even in the delta, where this ethic is expressed less strongly, "prosperous households limit the role of women outside the household more than poor ones do—unless that role results from success in education and a government job or its equivalent." These findings caution against assuming that new job opportunities and urban experience for males will radically alter customary patterns of female seclusion and the sexual division of labor, at least not in the short run.

In a finely nuanced article based on research in two villages south of Cairo, Elizabeth Taylor (1987) discusses the differential impact of migration on village women:[3] "The impact of migration on the position of the migrant's wife depends crucially on the type of family structure in which she is left to operate and the stage in her reproductive cycle that migration occurs." As she elaborates, these two variables set the parameters within which shifts in the role of the women occur. For a young wife living in an extended household, the absence of her husband may mean more control by her mother-in-law and an increase in her workload; the withdrawal of the migrant's labor means added work for the remaining members of the household, especially the younger women, who, in addition to their domestic tasks, will now have more agricultural tasks to perform. The implications for the wife of an independent nuclear household tend to be different, particularly where the wife is older and more mature and is able to keep control of the remittances sent by her husband and the revenue from the land. In such cases, a woman is able to operate with relative autonomy and will take on some of the roles of a head of household, including running the household and managing the land. Taylor, nonetheless, concludes that

> the temporary migration of . . . peasants has not effected any permanent change in the life styles of migrants' wives, nor in their role in production. For migration has not led to the marginalization of peasant production. . . . Revenues are invested in intensifying peasant production. This type of production still relies heavily on female household labor on the land and in animal care. The wives of the peasant migrants . . . have not withdrawn from productive activity into the secluded leisure of their home. (p. 271)

---

[3] For an assessment of the differential impact of migration on urban women in Egypt, see Homa Hoodfar (1996a).

In addition to the impact of labor migration, other changes in rural society stem from the spread of mass education and television. Kirsten Bach (1998) notes that women have always played an important role in social networking. In traditional village society, Bach reports, women and girls would meet regularly on the canal to wash clothing together, bathe children, and socialize—each representing a familial grouping much as their men would in their meetings at the mosque or teashops. Their homes, too, built of mud brick, had a broad entrance way in which family members would invite other villagers to sit and exchange conversation and small snacks. But recently, according to Bach, interpersonal relationships have begun to change significantly. Now that villages have piped water, washing is done at home, and since communications have improved, most villagers shop in nearby market towns where their children now attend school.

In Egypt one can speak of the urbanization of the countryside, just as one can speak of the ruralization of the city: factories abound and offer employment; universities and schools have been opened; rural housing is rapidly being transformed; rural people share in the recreational activities of urbanites; and many people move back and forth between village and city. Increased access to education and wage labor migration has changed rural consumption patterns. Prior to the mid-1980s, villagers had little access to, or even desire for, expensive consumer goods. Two "social fields" are now emerging; the *fellahīn* who are left behind in the new economy, and those with education and access to urban or foreign employment. This latter grouping has suddenly become very visible, building themselves red brick houses with modern kitchens and indoor bathrooms, and filled with new furniture and appliances. Patterns of consumption and income are reflected in socio-cultural cleavages. Now *fellahīn* who have money buy land not for household self-sufficiency but as an investment strategy.

Yet another dimension of the transformation of rural and, indeed, urban society is religion. Religion, both for the rural Coptic Christian minority and the Muslim majority, has always been very important. As we saw in Chapter 3, historically religious experience for Muslims focused on the local "saint" cults and mystical brotherhoods. The saints offered a spiritual analogy to the secular patron-client hierarchy in that saints could be asked to help as intermediaries with God; the brotherhoods taught ways to achieve mystical union with God (Hopkins & Westergaard, 1998, pp. 8ff). With the urbanization of the countryside and the movement of millions to urban centers in search of work, a third religious style has emerged, which Hopkins and Westergaard describe as "scriptualist" or "Islamist" (p. 9). In this approach to Islamic faith there is a strong emphasis on the strict observation of rules and codes of behavior. In some respects, this reflects the adoption by hitherto illiterate classes of society of some of the normative aspects of clerical Islam.

According to James Toth (1998), who worked in the south of Egypt in communities where militant Islamist groups are prominent, displaced or migrant farm laborers and small holders are responding to the problems they encounter in trying to survive in the city by embracing a politically active Islamism of this sort. While such Islamic groups originally recruited members from the educated population, following the economic crises of the 1980s they attracted large numbers of urban-dwelling *fellahīn*. Increasingly, the government was unwilling or unsuccessful in providing neighborhood or community social services in poor districts, a role that has come to be filled by religious organizations. This is a phenomenon found not only in other Muslim countries, but elsewhere where rural people are displaced by large-scale economic and social change.

The "structural adjustment" that Egypt, like many other countries, is undergoing in its efforts to move from a planned and heavily socialized economy to a market-driven economy is a deeply wrenching experience for those caught up in it. Detlef Müller-Mahn (1998) has estimated that 800,000 farmers lost their access to land as a consequence of "structural adjustment" reforms that came into effect in 1997, abolishing state control over rents that landowners can charge and tenants' rights to renew leases and to pass their leases on to their children. Other reforms have included an end to most crop subsidies and supports and price controls of food, land, and other commodities.

Egypt's reforms are part of a global movement pushed strongly by United States and European economic policies and implemented primarily by the World Bank and the International Monetary Fund through conditions these organizations attach to vital loans they make available to developing countries. "The dominant theme in the description of the rural Third World at the close of the twentieth century remains the story of its capitalist transformation. The theme is exemplified in rural Egypt, where the reform and removal of state controls through the program known as structural adjustment is intended to turn the land and its produce into market commodities and remake the countryside for the twenty-first century as a fully capitalist economy" (Mitchell, 1998, p. 19). It is hard to predict the long-term effects of these changes, which are meant to stimulate market production, innovation in agriculture, and extend prosperity to the countryside.

In the past, farmers had virtually hereditary title to the lands they rented, often at a nominal price. Researchers meeting in a summer rural development in Aswan in 1997 generally felt that these economic changes risk impoverishing many *fellahīn* families and will push them out of rural areas (Hopkins & Westergaard, 1998, p. 7). But at the same time, looking at data from the 1990s, they concluded that conditions of rural life in general, as measured by increased consumption, longer life expectancy, and rising rates of literacy, are gradually improving (ibid.).

One has, however, to move from the general picture to instances of specific villages and even individual men and women. Timothy Mitchell (1998), in his analysis of market relations in a sugarcane-producing village 6 kilometers north of Luxor on the Nile, revealed some interesting and paradoxical results. For the average household, bread is the main source of food. Until the introduction of free market prices for food crops—especially for wheat, which is the main food staple for fellahin small holders—almost all wheat flour was purchased in sacks as needed to prepare large loaves of 'aysh shamsi, bread leavened in the sun and baked in clay ovens at home (p. 21). Of the two thousand farm families in the village, only a dozen households grew their own wheat, and these were all those who had access to 100 or more acres of land. With the end of price control, wheat flour became prohibitively expensive for most families, and small holders rapidly took to raising their own wheat at the expense of sugarcane, their cash crop. Some families with access to only very small amounts of land put all their fields into domestic food production. The paradox from a developmental point of view is that the free market has led to a decline in the participation by many in the market as many peasants are forced to move ". . . toward increased self-provisioning and protection from the market" (p. 23).

A similar response is seen in the area of farm mechanization since the 1990s. In the village studied by Mitchell, by 1987 almost all tillage was by tractor. Once fuel subsidies were withdrawn, people turned again to camels to transport sugarcane and to buffalo for plowing. As one villager put it, a cow uses home-grown fodder and trains its own calf to eventually replace it (p. 24). At a more general level, François Ireton (1998) notes that Egypt is witnessing the end of an era in which disparities in farm size were being reduced and seeing the beginning of a period of reconcentrating landholdings.

The pattern of internal movement of population and intensification of land use is fairly widespread in the Middle East. In a study of settlement history and land use in the now heavily irrigated Marvdasht plain in Fars, north of Shiraz in Iran, Gerhard Kortum (1978) describes a long-term cyclical pattern of village expansion and subsequent decline. The organization of villages and towns closely replicates the expanded settlement systems of earlier years. While Kortum notes that settlement expansion is associated with periods of strong central government, he supplies detailed information on the locally limiting factors. Certain environmental constraints and sources of risk for farmers have remained relatively constant over the centuries: irregularity in water supplies needed for irrigation, soil salinity, breakdown of critical elements in the system of water distribution, competition from nomadic pastoralists, and political unrest have all figured in the contraction of settlements at particular times. The most recent low point throughout much of the Middle East, as in Iran, was reached toward the end of the nineteenth century.

Colonization, nomadic settlement, and investment in waterworks proceed in times of political security associated with strong state-level administration. Kortum's survey of 356 villages and 3 urban centers is remarkable for its use of archaeological and historical evidence in attempting to see the processes in settlement development that underlie the cyclical expansion of village life in the plains. His thesis is that historically the regulation and distribution of the waters of the Kur River through dams and feeder canals extended settlement into otherwise marginal areas. Inability to control the effects of salinization, plus failure to effect appropriate repairs on the critical river dams, repeatedly led to the abandonment of previously intensively farmed zones and the reversion of these lands to pasturage.

Today, the Marvdasht Plain is one of the most agriculturally developed regions of Iran, and in many areas river-supplied water is supplemented by mechanized deep wells that have significantly extended the settlement frontier and transformed village land use. Cotton is now a major cash crop. Industrialized sugar-beet production is another innovation that increases rural cash income.

The effects of capital investment in irrigation are not limited to extending settled agriculture. It has substantially altered the internal organization of production within the rural community and has changed the relationship of local communities to each other and to the marketplaces that develop to serve them. The acreage under cash cultivation tends to increase and the proportion of land cultivated for domestically used food crops or animal production decreases greatly.

In short, diversified subsistence farming has been replaced by an almost exclusively market-directed system of heavily mechanized agriculture. In the pre-irrigation system of land use, human labor constitutes one of the principal inputs or costs. In new irrigation schemes, labor inputs generally remain comparable to previous levels, while other costs rise significantly. This dramatic increase in overhead is accounted for by items that have to be purchased outside the farming communities themselves, particularly fertilizer and machine traction, not to mention the capital cost of construction. Cost of labor then shrinks by comparison to become a relatively insignificant component of the agricultural economy.

Although this might be viewed as a measure of the efficiency of this newly commercialized system of land use, it is also indicative of increasing regional, national, and, indeed, global integration and the dependence of local farmers on distant markets and sources of capital. Commitment to the marketplace and concentration on a limited range of intensively grown crops, such as cotton or sugar beets, puts the small producer, former sharecroppers, and tenants at a serious disadvantage. In the agriculturally developed Middle East, such shifts in land use have forced many to seek nonagricultural sources of employment, even when this means migration to the already swollen metropolitan centers. As we noted at the beginning of this chapter, rapidly increasing rural-to-urban migration is characteristic of the entire region.

GENERAL OVERVIEW

The transformation of agriculture through changes in land tenure, mechanization, and other capital-intensive techniques is by no means uniform or complete, even within a single country. In Egypt, mechanization is primarily directed

A Palestinian farmer gathering eggs on a community chicken farm on the West Bank, Israel.

at water management, not cultivation; even so, traditional waterwheels are occasionally still used alongside portable gasoline-driven or electric pumps. In other countries mechanization in cultivation and harvesting is more widely employed but not by all, nor is every community experiencing similar rates of investment. Indeed, families and communities are increasingly differentiated in terms of their participation in these processes of change. The introduction of new crops and techniques of production, plus access to new markets, are imposing new constraints and lines of social and economic demarcation, just as they offer new opportunities.

As we have noted, the benefits and costs of change are not borne equally. Some of the benefits may accrue to only a limited number of people in a community, while others may be widely shared—for example, better standards of health and education. For many, agricultural intensification has brought the consumer goods and styles of the city within reach. In effect, rural development has somewhat diminished the long-existing gulf between rural and urban dwellers. Television satellite dishes sprout from village homes, and in most countries it is the exceptional household that lacks a radio, TV, or refrigerator. Cars, trucks, and tractors have replaced animal transport and power in the majority of communities. The economic basis for what might be called a rural consumer economy is a commercial or market-directed agriculture often complemented by remittances sent by family members living and working elsewhere, either in the region or abroad.

Shelagh Weir (1987) describes the impact of out-migration and the sudden influx of remittances on a rural community in the highlands of Yemen. Until the early 1970s, Yemen was one of the least developed and most isolated countries in the world. This began to change dramatically in the mid-1970s, when, following the 1973–74 oil boom, Yemenis migrated to work as laborers in Saudi Arabia and the Gulf states. It is estimated that in this period as much as one-third of the Yemeni male work force was working abroad, earning high wages most of which were repatriated home.

Weir describes the rapid transformation in village life precipitated by the sudden and massive influx of cash into Al-Jabal, a small community (population 4500) with a mixed economy based on small-scale agriculture and livestock raising. The first and perhaps the key factor in subsequent changes was the construction of a motor road that linked the area to the rest of the country and introduced cars and trucks to the community. Motor transport stimulated the expansion of trade and commerce as the local demand for consumer durables, building materials, and imported foods and toiletries soared. Within a few years, what had been a small, simple weekly market had been transformed into a permanent shopping center with specialized shops and boutiques. While the influx of commodities and the change in consumer demands and tastes quickly put an end to the community's economic self sufficiency, it was greatly appreciated by the inhabitants, who experienced a marked improvement in their everyday lives. Among other things, the workload of women was greatly reduced by the import of flour mills, paraffin stoves, pressure cookers, and plastic utensils. Many found a new opportunity to earn money. The great rise in income, the availability of sewing machines, and the demand for new-style dresses opened up a new market for dressmaking. Interestingly, economic prosperity led to an inflation in the bride price (*mahr*). As Weir notes, the average brideprice in 1977 was $7000; by 1980, it had risen to $40,000 (p. 294).

Weir reports other changes, such as the shift to cash cropping, especially of the very lucrative *qat,* the mildly stimulant leaf of *Catha edulis,* which is greatly liked by the Yemenis, particularly the men. She also points to the transformation of traditional leadership patterns in the community as shopkeepers and drivers begin to challenge the authority of the tribal elders. While the sustainability and direction of change in Al-Jabal may be difficult to predict, what is clear is that the "traditional, isolated, and poor" highland community is no longer any of these.

As the case of Al-Jabal clearly illustrates, road transport now integrates most villages with major redistribution centers, thereby giving them access to metropolitan and international markets. Government and private sources of credit underwrite the acquisition of equipment and the purchase of new seed strains and chemical fertilizers. These inputs, however costly, have vastly increased productivity by allowing for shortened fallow periods, double cropping, and higher yields. In short, there is a new rural prosperity evident in the countryside, even in areas like the Nile Delta, which have long been characterized by grinding poverty.

Some of this prosperity, however, is misleading because the costs that sustain it are hidden in sprawling urban slums or in the rows of shacks lining the periphery of an otherwise wealthy-looking village. The size of the farm needed to sustain an "average family" increases rather than decreases as a consequence of integration into larger markets, and there is a more complete reliance on cash or credit to purchase the requisites of production. Families that cannot increase their holdings may fall by the wayside or be forced to move or at least seek part-time wage employment.

In Turkey, Iran, and elsewhere, villages may be virtually abandoned by the younger male populations as the men seek a livelihood outside of agriculture and leave their fields to be tilled by more prosperous neighbors. Some who move to the city do find employment and improved standards of living; many do not. This social dislocation has to be considered as a major cost of the transformation of agriculture and is increasingly a political concern for most governments of the region.

Accelerating rates of land alienation and rural out-migration have stimulated widespread speculation in land. In some countries there are few safe avenues for investment outside of real estate, including arable land, and few countries have been able to control fully rampant inflation in land values. Even where limits are imposed on acreage owned or on the transfer of land titles given by the government, these restrictions can be circumvented in practice. In many ways, these trends in the Middle East seem to recapitulate historical processes experienced in Europe and other industrialized areas of the world.

7

Cities and Urban Life

In 1959, the population of Istanbul reached the 1 million mark, a source of considerable pride as it clearly put the city among the world's major centers. In the year 2000, Istanbul's greater metropolitan population moved beyond 12 million, to the consternation of almost everyone.[1] Similarly, in 1960, Cairo's population numbered 3.7 million; by 1980, it had grown to over 9 million. Today greater Cairo boasts a population of about 14 million people! This rapid urban growth, or hyperurbanization is replicated to various degrees in every country in the region. Of course urbanism and urban life are not new in the Middle East. Urban centers in Mesopotamia and along the Nile emerged some 6000 years ago, and from that early history until now urban-dominated political and economic systems have prevailed and spread, so that today virtually all the people in the world live in the shadow of cities and urban institutions.

In the 1980s, approximately 46 percent of the people of the Middle East lived in towns of over 20,000 or more. The comparable rate of urbanization in the United States was 72 percent, and in Latin America, 50 percent. Compared to Asia and Africa, the Middle East, like Latin America, is considered a highly dynamic region in terms of population growth and urbanization. At the end of the twentieth century, the regional average urban population (on a country basis) had reached over 70 percent and is projected to increase further (see Table 7.1). Only Egypt from among the large, heavily populated countries has a rough balance between town and country dwellers. Urban dwellers are increasingly young people, with all the demands for education and employment that this implies.

---

[1] Istanbul's official population as of 1998 is just over 9 million, but taken with its sprawling suburbs, which range over three provinces, its regional population is well over 12 million. Six cities in Turkey have over 1.5 million in official population, making this country the most urbanized of the non-oil-producing states in the Middle East.

TABLE 7.1   Urban and Rural Population Estimates and Projections

Country	1997 Urban (%)	1997 Rural (%)	2020 Urban (%)	2020 Rural (%)
Bahrain	91	9	95	5
Egypt	45	55	56	44
Iran	60	40	71	29
Iraq	75	25	83	17
Israel	91	9	93	7
Jordan	72	28	81	19
Kuwait	97	3	98	2
Lebanon	88	12	93	7
Oman	79	21	93	7
Qatar	92	8	95	5
Saudi Arabia	84	16	90	10
Sudan	33	67	52	48
Syria	53	47	65	35
Turkey	72	28	85	15
United Arab Emirates	85	15	89	11
Yemen	35	65	52	48
Regional average	72	28	81	19

Source: Adapted from United Nations publication ST/ESA/SER. A/176, 1999.

The urban growth of the oil-rich Gulf states is perhaps the most phenomenal, both in its scale and speed. Whereas the Arab world as a whole is urbanizing at a rate of 4 to 4.5 percent annually, the rate of urbanization in the Gulf area is 15 to 18 percent per year; and in Kuwait and Qatar, more than 80 percent of the total population is urban dwelling. What is most fascinating, however, is that the Gulf area is on its way to becoming a series of national city-states in which the indigenous population makes up only a fraction of the total population but owns and controls most of the resources and wealth. As Galal Abdulla Moawad (1987) notes, the urbanization momentum here is due to the steady flow of Arab and non-Arab migrants. In some of these cities, over 50 percent of the population is composed of expatriate laborers, with these immigrant ethnic and national groups organized in a semi-caste fashion. Thus, in Kuwait, the largest city-state in the Gulf area, less than half of the population are natives and full Kuwaiti citizens; the rest are immigrants arranged in an occupational hierarchy that ranges from the professional-class Palestinians, Lebanese, and Egyptians, through the Indians, and down to the unskilled Baluch and Pakistani laborers. Israel's two major cities are also swollen by settlers migrating from the regions of the former USSR. It should be kept in mind, however, that the total population of these countries combined is no more than 9 million, which represents a very small segment of the population of the Middle East. The demographic weight of the region remains concentrated in the older cities—Alexandria, Cairo, Istanbul, Ankara, Tehran, Damascus, and Baghdad.

THE NATURE OF THE CITY

A city is more than a concentration of people. Cities are defined by the diversity of functions they serve and their vital roles in networks of communication. A glance at a map of any agricultural area of the Middle East illustrates this point. For example, thousands of villages and many millions of people dwell in a region whose lines of trade and communication are focused on the greater metropolitan area of Cairo with its 14 million inhabitants.

But size alone is not what is important. In Egypt today many villages number over 1000 households, or 6000 people. Some, in fact, may exceed 20,000 in population. Such large communities are locally designated as villages despite their size, not because of some arbitrary bureaucratic usage but because of the relatively narrow range of economic and political activities that take place there. In the less densely populated regions to the north and east in Turkey and Iran, settlements of 1000 households would almost inevitably be termed towns because the quality of life in them would be quite distinct from life in smaller communities. There a concentration of 5000 to 6000 people would occur in conjunction with an administrative center, a telephone or communications center, a commercial district, a high school, a police headquarters, hotels, a major mosque, a market, and probably a site of some religious significance, such as a saint's tomb or pilgrimage center. This, of course, reflects the intermediate administrative and market roles they play in the larger settlement pattern or system.

A storyteller recites an epic poem at a coffeehouse in Damascus.

A town or city comes into existence when a countryside is capable of producing food beyond its immediate requirements and can be persuaded to part with its surpluses, thus allowing an urban community to live without growing its own crops or rearing its own livestock. Needless to say, those living in the countryside may need considerable inducement to produce such surpluses. Thus some of the "services" provided by the city traditionally include the collection of taxes, the raising of armies through conscription, and the administering of city-imposed codes of law. Cities and towns, then, are distinguished not only by the marketing and manufacturing functions they serve but also by their pivotal or dominant position in a political, economic, and cultural hierarchy. The city and its hinterland form two interdependent but generally unequal components.

Urban-based regimes and city dwellers depend on the supply of vital goods from the countryside. But at the same time, families or parties from the elite, who are urban dwelling and often culturally dissimilar from rural dwellers, come to exercise great power over the countryside, concentrating wealth and erecting monumental buildings to commemorate their power. For the villagers, on the other hand, life has something of a frontier quality. They are caught between the caprices of the market and the vagaries of weather. However, like frontier people, they have options to exercise when conditions become intolerable, such as moving away, or, and in particular, moving into the city either to take refuge or to seize the opportunity to profit from periods of urban prosperity. Each day brings hundreds of newcomers to those cities perceived to offer the greatest potential for employment, which are usually already among the largest in the nation. This, of course, creates something of a snowball effect, leading to what is often termed a "mega-city" (Wikan, 1995).

As noted earlier, all this tends to impart a somewhat rural hue to Middle Eastern cities, despite the cultural gulf that may separate the educated or governing classes from the villagers. Cities continually attract rural migrants, who usually live in social settings not unlike the villages in which they grew up. Their language is flavored by rural idiom; the dress, especially of women, may retain the rustic modes of distant provinces; and their public deportment may be much constrained by rural norms of modesty and sexual segregation. The great Middle Eastern cities today, such as Tehran, Baghdad, Cairo, Istanbul, and Beirut, incorporate residential sections that are rural in everything but land use. In fact, all of these cities house between 35 and 60 percent of their population in "irregular" housing erected by newcomers themselves. Most cities were traditionally supported in terms of food by the farmlands around them, and a sizable number of people left the city each day to till fields beyond the city walls. Urban sprawl and the development of industrial zones changed this for most cities, but even in Cairo and other cities many urban dwellers, even office workers and small merchants, still retain plots or shares in fields near the city from which they derive some of the food they consume.

Janet Abu-Lughod, an American urban sociologist who has studied Cairo extensively for over 30 years, has called attention to the complex variation found in the Middle Eastern city today. This variation exists not only across an urban-rural dimension, where, within Cairo, for example, in minutes you may walk from a fully modern elegant luxury hotel to a rural-style mud-brick hut without electricity and water, but also across a time/technology dimension: "Side by side stand the modern factory and the primitive workshop, the bank and the turbaned moneylender, suggesting the persistence of a vital residue from yet another variety of urban living" (1971). While comparison can be risky, as one tends to compare ideal types, her comparative sketches of Cairo, New York, and Chicago are helpful (1990). Cairo and New York are superficially similar in the small-grained character of land use, active street life, and the diversity and mixing of peoples. Chicago, more typical of North American cities, has far less street life, highly zoned land use, and stronger racial and class segregation. Cairo is a unique urban creation, but the features Abu-Lughod points to as being shared with New York are also evident in many other Middle Eastern cities.

THE MIDDLE EASTERN CITY IN PERSPECTIVE

Is it possible to identify an " Islamic city" in contrast to other urban complexes elsewhere in the world and associate it with a religious and cultural tradition? This is the question posed by Dale Eickelman many years ago (1974) and which, despite numerous subsequent books and articles that incorporate this reference in their titles, remains unresolved. Historians and urban planners both within and outside the Islamic world seemed assured, until recently, that such an entity existed, and even strove to reproduce features of it in planned cities such as Kuwait City and, today, in Beirut.

Janet Abu-Lughod has, in our opinion, provided the best response to this question (1987). She suggests that instead of cataloging traits and then trying to match individual cases, one should ask what are the forces that shaped cities, and then what, if anything, is distinctive about cities with large Muslim populations (1987, p. 161). At first, Abu-Lughod offers her informal impressions of her visits to mixed Muslim and Hindu cities in India, where, as often in the Middle East, there is strong neighborhood association with ethnicity. She was struck by several cues, among which was the very high ratio of males to females in Muslim public space as well as much greater levels of street noise. Continuing with a review of the scholarly literature, she finds that while one cannot speak of ideal types, one finds Islamic influence expressed in subtle ways, particularly in the spatial organization of public as opposed to private areas. Historically, this is expressed, for example, in convoluted street patterns. While such patterns are found in ancient cities of Europe as well, they have been retained over a much longer period in cities of the Islamic world. In part this is due to the relatively unplanned manner in which the Middle Eastern cities often expanded into rural suburbs, developing along paths or streets which followed irregular field or garden boundaries or even the courses of twisting waterways or canals.

While Islam is clearly an important force in the changing pattern of urban life, it is by no means the only one (Duben, 1992). Cities reflect social realities, including cleavages of tribe, clan, ethnicity, and even religion, since most major cities have (or had) significant numbers of Christian and Jewish inhabitants. All of these factors are reflected in neighborhood layout and spatial barriers separating quarters in the preindustrial city. Although there was rarely jural segregation, there was a high degree of spatial segregation along lines of religion. The real impact of Islam, Abu-Lughod points out, was not to determine structure and organization but to establish certain requirements and preferences in which urban development could proceed. For example, Islam's gender ideology resulted in de facto segregation of space into male and female domains. Accordingly, building codes and customs regulated the placement of doors and windows (not to be directly facing) and heights of adjacent buildings with an eye to privacy. Edward Lane-Pool provides a nice description of an early nineteenth-century home in Cairo (quoted in Abu-Lughod, 1987, p. 167):

> (As one enters the house there) is a passage, which bends sharply after the first yard or two, and bars any view into the interior from the open door. At the end of this passage we emerge into an open court. . . . Here is no sign of life; the doors are jealously closed. The windows shrouded. . . . We shall see nothing of the domestic life of the inhabitants; for the women's apartments are carefully shut off from the court. . . . The lower rooms, opening directly off the court are those into which a man may walk with impunity and no risk of meeting any of the women. . . (another) door opens out of the court into the staircase leading to the harim rooms, and here no man but the master of the house dare penetrate. . . . When a man returns there he is in the bosom of his family, and it would need a very urgent affair to induce the doorkeeper to summon him down to anyone who called to see him.

When we think of Middle Eastern cities, it is the grand domes and minarets of the imperial capitals, Istanbul, Damascus, Cairo, and Isfahan, that come to mind. Indeed, as we have said, one often reads of the "Islamic city," sometimes with the connotation of a way of urban life both different from the European experience and possessing an overall uniformity dictated by religious tradition. We cannot ignore that which is unique about the Middle Eastern city. Nor can we deny that urbanism has been greatly affected by Islamic civilization. But we cannot generalize about a way of life as varied and changing as is urban life in the Middle East. The great metropolitan centers of Baghdad, Cairo, Istanbul, and Isfahan have long symbolized the civilization and cultural accomplishments of the Islamic world. These cities, however, are quite distinct from one another, each reflecting its own unique historical experience. Moreover, these ancient capitals bear little resemblance in their general organization and layout to new cities such as Ankara, Tehran, or Kuwait City.

When Western scholars first sought to understand the nature of these great Middle Eastern cities, they began by comparing them with the city-states of classical Greece or Christian Europe. As a consequence, much has been made of features of urban life found in the West but "lacking" in the East. Among these are the absence of municipal corporations, "free cities," city councils, and supposedly "civic mindedness." The imputed absence of civic spirit is largely a product of European ethnocentrism—witness the public buildings erected in every Middle Eastern city by private families to grace their communities. Moreover, "civic spirit" is expressed differently in different societies. This position also ignores the great variability among Middle Eastern cities. Nonetheless, there are fundamental differences distinguishing cities of the Islamic world from those of the West. We can perhaps best appreciate these by looking at how the city in the Muslim world developed and why its institutions took the shape they did.

Foremost among the factors that give a certain degree of similarity to cities in the Islamic world is how they have been affected by their shared Islamic ideology and practice, together with the administrative system that took form shortly after the original Islamic conquest (see Duben, 1992, p. 14). As S. M. Stern points out, Islamic law treats all individuals as equal. As a consequence, it does not give special recognition to any group of believers or to any corporate entities, with two notable exceptions—the co-residential family itself and the *waqf* charitable endowments.

> The right of the family to live enclosed in its house led . . . to a clear separation between public and private life; private life turned inwards, towards the courtyard and not towards the street; in the thoroughfares, the bazaars, and the mosques, a certain public life went on, policed and regulated by the ruler, active and at times rebellious, but a life where the basic units, the families, touched externally without mingling to form a civitas. (1970, pp. 25–50).

The significance of the *waqf* to city life is that it provided for the maintenance of most public urban buildings, mosques, central markets, caravanserais, baths, schools, and hospitals, not to mention lesser structures fundamental to city life, such as fountains and public water taps. In essence, the *waqf* was a major means by which rural production directly served to sustain urban institutions. The yields from *waqf* agricultural property not only maintained buildings but also paid the salaries of a class of individuals associated with them, in particular the religious functionaries. When a building was erected, its patron would endow it with income-producing property which would ensure its maintenance in perpetuity. This trust is recognized by Islamic law, and such properties have been taken over by the governments or rulers only under near-revolutionary circumstances. In Iran a major source of contention between the Shah and the Shi'a clergy had to do with the monarchy's attempts to seize rural *waqf* land and to control the considerable revenue generated from *waqf*-designated real estate.

By the twentieth century, a substantial amount of arable land in Turkey, Iran, Syria, and Egypt was held in *waqf* trusts. Even though the liquidation of much of this property has benefited the peasants, who were able to get title to fields they formerly worked as sharecroppers, many medieval Islamic buildings have suffered neglect as their revenues now come directly from the government. *Waqf*-held rural properties were a major means by which rural produce and income were channeled into cities, and the administration of these properties by urban-based religious functionaries concentrated considerable power in their hands and made of some of them a privileged class of urban notables.

As for the family, Islamic law recognizes the right of each household to privacy within its own walls. This valued privacy is expressed everywhere in domestic architecture and the use of urban space. Frequently, houses surrounded a central courtyard or compound with few outside windows, which both conformed with the need for privacy and helped solve the climatic problems of great heat in the summers and cold in the winters. Streets were narrow and twisted, designed to serve the needs of the householders rather than facilitate general traffic. The houses of the wealthy, as we have said, were traditionally divided between public rooms and private family space. Poor families, the majority everywhere, however, could usually not afford this arrangement and many people often lived crowded into one or two rooms. These, however, would not be in a distinctly "poor neighborhood" but very likely adjacent to the home of a wealthy patron, kinsman, or employer. Thus, residential patterns did not reflect socioeconomic class so much as ethnicity or occupation.

Before the twentieth century, cities in the Middle East were directly administered by the ruler or his local representatives.[2] The city was not a chartered, legal entity, nor were urban citizens distinguished juridically from rural dwellers. Provision of basic services, such as water, education, sanitation, street lighting, and security, was usually organized at the neighborhood level in ways not dissimilar to village or small-town practice. Often a public well or water source was donated as a charitable act, parents would take up subscriptions to hire a teacher or engage tutors for their children, garbage removal would be arranged by the householder, and public security was provided by a night watchman hired and supervised by the leaders of the quarter. However, this does not minimize the importance of cities as administrative or trading centers. Islam, the religion, arose in an urban setting, and its institutions and ritual practices are directed toward population concentrations and amenities associated with urban rather than rural life. Its religious leaders, or *'ulama*, simultaneously constitute an urban patrician class as well as one trained in theology, law, and administration. The Arabic word *madaniyya* means "civilization," "refinement," or "sophistication," and it comes from the same root as the word for city: *madina*.

---

[2] See Alan Duben (1992, pp. 24ff.) for a good discussion of this.

The first 100 years of Islam saw the conquest of all the lands that are presently Arabic speaking, together with Spain and most of present-day Iran. Within this broad territory were most of the great cities of Byzantium, the eastern Roman Empire, and the Sassanian Empire of Persia. Of the major metropolitan centers, only Constantinople survived in Christian hands until its conquest in 1453. Cities such as Damascus and Alexandria, with their established bureaucracies, elites, and great churches and palaces, were taken over and absorbed into the new political order. In 661, Damascus became the capital of the Umayyad Empire, which stretched from the Pyrenees to eastern Persia, and there is evidence that the existing bureaucracy, at least at the lower levels, was incorporated directly into the administrative structure of this great empire. However, the new rulers were not content to inherit the legacy of the Romans, Byzantines, and Persians. Rather, they embarked on an ambitious program of urban construction that included the creation of new cities to serve the political, economic, and religious needs of their expanding domain. Indeed, it is hard to appreciate how rapidly and thoroughly Islamic Arab civilization made its presence felt throughout the eastern Mediterranean. It did so through urban institutions and the concentration of skilled administrators and scholars living in cities. Modern urban life continues to build on these social and architectural traditions.

In existing pre-Islamic cities such as Damascus, great mosques were erected, as well as schools, palaces, and fortresses. The building of these great mosques, such as the monumental complex established on the site of the church of St. John in Damascus and the Shrine of the Dome of the Rock in Jerusalem, and the construction of thousands of lesser edifices were more than simple expressions of religious sentiment. They were a means of making political statements as they advertised the power and the presence of a new order. They also helped to legitimate the conquest where it mattered, in the centers of population. Even today, travelers coming from Europe by road find the cultural frontiers of Islam marked by the magnificent domes and minarets of the great mosque complex in Edirne (Adrianople), long the principal land route to Istanbul from the West.

Of the new cities established during the early years of Islamic rule, some were garrisons that later evolved into market and administrative centers, such as Basra in Iraq and Ardebil and Qazvin in Iran. Some evolved into major metropolitan centers, and even into national capitals. One, Al Fustat, near modern Cairo, was established as a new residential quarter upon the Arab conquest of Egypt in 641, but it soon developed into a major city and the capital of Egypt. Its successor city, Cairo, with its population of 14 million, is now one of the largest cities in the world and the leading intellectual and cultural center of the Arab world.

Clearly there are great differences in the organization and quality of life in these early Islamic cities according to how they evolved. But because there is recognizable continuity in the urban tradition, it is useful to mention some of the distinctive features of these urban centers inasmuch as they are relevant to an understanding of life today. Manuel Castells (1999) and others note that while urban sites are historically closely related to the distribution of usable water resources and arable land, they also reflect uneven flows of capital and information. The uneven distribution of cities in the Middle East reflects the uneven distribution of these key resources, as well as international trade and industry. Further, urban centers largely determine patterns of land use and production in their hinterlands through the control of capital and markets by the urban administrators. Virtually all cities have marketplaces of various sorts where rural goods are sold and urban goods and services are bought.

In addition to marketing, some cities, such as Jerusalem, Mecca, Qom, and Karbala, function primarily as religious centers of pilgrimage, and still others, such as Meshed in Iran, Konya in Turkey, and Tanta in Egypt, have major religious shrines as well as serving as trade and administrative centers.

Major differences distinguish coastal cities from those of the interior. Cities along the Mediterranean and the Aegean coasts tended to be large and cosmopolitan, reflecting their role as import-export centers serving foreign markets. Most of the African and south Indian trade entered the Middle East via the ports of Aden, Jedda, and Basra, and far-ranging dhows carried both Persian and Arab traders to East Africa. Part of this trade consisted of slaves. Today small communities of their descendants, all Muslims, can be found all along the Gulf coast. Red Sea and Gulf ports remained relatively small, as they served a far less densely settled hinterland. Until the mid-1950s, Kuwait, for instance, had a population of around 35,000, with the main industry being the seasonally active pearl fisheries. Only with oil did this Gulf city emerge as one of the largest urban centers of the region; today Kuwait has a population of over 1 million.

Some coastal cities stand out: Istanbul, Izmir, Alexandria, and Beirut were and still are international centers; until recently, little of the culture and the quality of life of their citizens was shared by other large inland cities. These cities had sizable Christian and Jewish populations and prosperous foreign communities that gave them a cosmopolitan hue. Their strongest cultural linkages, not surprisingly, were to Western Europe. Even today, after repeated efforts by nationalist governments to minimize obviously foreign influences, and despite the occasional forced movement of Christian populations, these coastal cities remain qualitatively different.

The writings of orientalists are often criticized for their ethnocentric emphasis on the shock of the exotic or the appeal of the romantic. The following excerpt captures this tendency, but also the exuberance of such early reporting for a great port city that still retains a hold on the world's imagination:

> Standing there, you can see all of Constantinople pass in an hour. . . . [A]dvancing among a mixed crowd of Greeks, Turks and Armenians may be seen a gigantic eunuch on horseback, shouting Vardah! (Make way!), and closely following him, a Turkish carriage decorated with flowers and birds filled with the ladies of a harem. . . . A Mussulman woman on foot, a veiled female slave, a Greek with her long flowing hair surmounted by a little red cap, a Maltese hidden in her black

faletta, a Jewess in the ancient costume of her nation, a negress wrapped in a many-tinted Cairo shawl, and Armenians from Trebizond, all veiled in black—a funereal apparition; these and many more follow in line as though it were a procession gotten up to display the dress of the various nations of the world. . . . Then there is the Syrian, clad in a long Byzantine dolman, with a gold-striped handkerchief wrapped around his head; the Bulgarian, in sombre-coloured tunic and fur-edged cap; the Georgian, with his casque of dressed leather and tunic gathered into a metal belt; the Greek from the archipelago, covered with lace, silver tassels, and shining buttons. From time to time it seems as though the crowd were receding somewhat, but it is only to surge forward once more in great overpowering waves of color crested with white turbans like foam, in whose midst may occasionally be seen a high hat or umbrella of some European lady tossed hither and thither by that Mussulman torrent. (Edmondo de Amicis, *Constantinople* [1896], quoted in Freely [1998], pp. 284–86)

We have already mentioned the importance of the household, its right to privacy, and how this affects domestic architecture. However, by and large, it is not the residential patterns that distinguish traditional urban life from its rural counterpart. People live in houses and family settings in cities that, with the exception of the grand houses and villas of the capitals, could be replicated in villages as well. What is distinctive about the city is the complex of buildings and institutions associated with the central mosque, the seat of government, the military installations, and the bazaar. Commonly these are in close proximity to one another; close by, too, are the major schools (*madrasas*), bathhouses (*hamams*) (with different days reserved for men and women), the courts, and the governor's compound. Until the administrative reforms of the nineteenth century, the governor's compound did not include a courthouse or federal building. Rather, the residences of officials were simultaneously their governmental offices, much as was the case with the palace of the shah or sultan, although on a far less grand scale.

The market, or bazaar or *suq* (souk), might be covered, thus forming one vast indoor shopping area, or it might be simply a section of the city's central area devoted to the sale of goods and craft manufacturing. The bazaar area contained hostels for traveling merchants and for workers coming from the villages for seasonal urban employment. Also there would be food sellers, gunsmiths, jewelers, money changers, and the like. Markets dealing in luxury items or expensive manufactured goods, such as fine cloth, gold and silverwork, copper utensils, and weapons, then as now tended to be located centrally in the city adjacent to the grand mosque and readily secured with gates and guards. Spices, condiments, and imported food items would be sold in this area as well; food staples, animals, and animal products would be sold in the less centrally located markets, or outside the city altogether.

Within the *suq*, or bazaar, crafts tended to be concentrated in particular streets or buildings, with the clamor of the metalworkers announcing their workshops to all. The close proximity of competitors, even when the competitors might be family members, served to generate one of the most valued of commercial commodities: information. Transactions were conducted with a minimum of privacy, and both buyers and sellers could size each other up. The shopper often returned to the merchant with whom he or she had a history of dealings, perhaps one who had extended credit in the past. Because similar traders were clustered together, merchants quickly gauged the demand for their items and, when bargaining with a customer, could rapidly determine the buyer's seriousness of intent as well as the prices offered by the competitors. Bargaining over the price of goods is important for both the buyer and seller. The buyer satisfies him- or herself that the price is right, while both establish or reaffirm a personal relationship that may be useful in the future.[3]

The basic units of spatial and social organization were the city quarters or neighborhoods, *mehallas*. Their inhabitants were bound together by ties of kinship, common tribal or village origins, and ethnic affiliation. Given the preference for close lineage endogamy, these overlapped. The neighborhoods often constituted distinct administrative units, each headed by its own representative, or sheikh, whose duties included collecting taxes, maintaining order, and acting as the general liaison between the inhabitants of the quarter and the governor of the city.

At certain periods and in some cities, like Baghdad, Cairo, and Aleppo, these urban neighborhoods constituted virtual "walled" mini-cities that maintained a high degree of autonomy and isolation. There were few pan-urban institutions that united them. Ira Lapidus (1973) writes that the guilds and other professional groups were very weak and that these were created primarily to meet the fiscal and regulatory needs of the state rather than the membership. The neighborhoods, or *mehallas*, were far more important. They even had their own "police" force, gangs of local youths who acted as militia enforcing public order and defending their urban turf against the encroachment of outsiders.[4] Known variously as *zu'ar* or *fahlawa*, these ganglike organizations persist even today in some cities—for example, in Cairo and Tehran—and bear more than a slight similarity to street gangs elsewhere.

Besides the kinship groups and the youth gangs, another important social grouping in the medieval city was that of the religious brotherhood. These fraternal organizations extended beyond the boundaries of the quarter, as their membership also came from the rural areas. Thus they provided an important mechanism for society-wide integration, albeit at an informal and often marginal level.

More significant perhaps, at least in terms of size and formal recognition, were the religious communities that formed around the religious elite, the

---

[3] For two excellent historical accounts of cities on the eve of modernity, see Abraham Marcus (1989) for an account of Aleppo, Syria, in the eighteenth century and Haim Gerber (1988) on Bursa, Turkey, in the years 1600–1700.

[4] Philip Khoury (1993) provides a biographical sketch of a gang leader, or *qabaday*, in Damascus, 1920–45.

'ulama and their schools of law, or madhab. These schools were organized around a core made up of the religious scholars and their students and their clientele group, consisting of the notaries and clerks in the service of the judges (qadis). Beyond this core, the different schools of law extended to include the population at large who were members of one or another madhab. In Ira Lapidus's words, the people looked to the 'ulamas for

> authoritative guidance on how to live a good Moslem life, for judicial relief, and for comfort and leadership in times of trouble. More concretely, family ties, the close association of the 'ulama with officials, merchants, and artisans, who were recruited from all quarters and classes of the population, bound the people to the schools and created communities beyond parochial quarters—communities which shared a common law, common norms in family, commercial and religious life, a common judicial authority, and common facilities such as mosques, schools, and charities. (1973, p. 50)

CITY LIFE TODAY

To what extent is city life today organized around the physical and social structures of the past? This is a difficult question to answer. Certainly, the visitor driving in from Cairo's airport will receive a mixed impression. She will pass through miles and miles of urban sprawl: shopping malls, apartment complexes, hotels, and terribly congested streets, after which she can visit the well-preserved old "Islamic" Cairo, including the old suq/bazaar and the splendid buildings of the Fatimids.

Office buildings in Dubai, United Arab Emirates.

Today all principal cities and towns have been dramatically reshaped to meet the needs of vehicular traffic, and great avenues have been laid out or simply cut through existing neighborhoods. More than just catering to new traffic patterns, today's cities serve vastly altered social, economic, and cultural needs. From Istanbul to Meshed, ancient walls and city gates that have withstood both time and armies have succumbed to urban renewal, while saints' tombs and public cisterns have become traffic circles. In Iran, under the Pahlavi regime, every town was bisected by a new highway or avenue, inevitably leading to a monument glorifying the imperial house. But the city in the Middle East today is more than a network of new streets, avenues, and highways; it is also the expression of new values and a new political order. Along the Persian Gulf, new, supermodern cities have been created with the vast revenues of oil, and they show little if any continuity with the past.

Ankara, the capital of the Turkish Republic since 1921, is a city of gray hues built on a relentless grid of avenues and streets lined with buildings whose stark, German-influenced architecture emphasizes the discipline and Western orientation of the new republican order. In fact, Ankara's government buildings borrow directly from German models, architecturally announcing a revolutionary departure from the Ottoman and Islamic past. Only the neighborhood immediately surrounding the citadel betrays the old settlement. Ankara, as well as Cairo, Tehran, Izmir, and Istanbul, now have new and expanding underground metro systems, which, while not solving these cities' horrendous traffic congestion problems, at least offer a very useful alternative mode of transport for their citizens. In every Middle Eastern capital and urban center of importance, extensive and massive apartment blocks accommodate the burgeoning professional and middle classes, in most cases rapidly replacing both the secluded villas of the old elites and the handsome townhouses built around central courtyards. In many instances, for example in Istanbul, these take the form of secluded or "gated" communities, built to provide both the amenities that the wealthy enjoy in any country, as well as security (Keyder, 1999). These, then, produce class-based residential segregation that was largely absent before.

Poor families, everywhere the majority, find housing a major problem. It is not uncommon in Cairo, for example, for families to share a single room, cooking in the stairwell, using a makeshift latrine, and drawing water from a public tap serving many buildings. The more fortunate of the urban poor may reside in shanties they built themselves, located in districts where rural migrants and others illegally occupy vacant land. The Turkish term for this form of housing, *gecekondu,* or "built in the night," evokes both the nature of the construction and the severity of the housing problem that has generated shantytowns around every metropolis, including the new wealthy cities of the Gulf. Although such homes may be superior to the village houses left behind by the migrants, they strike the established town dwellers or middle-class observers as haphazard and dilapidated, and contribute to an impression of urban seediness and decay.

All this is to say that at first glance little remains of the traditional Islamic city except for some sections in such places as Cairo, Damascus, Aleppo, Isfahan, and Istanbul. Beginning in the late nineteenth century, Middle Eastern cities witnessed a major transformation. As was the case in the United States following the American Civil War, the rapid growth and general transformation of urban centers was not simply the result of new technology and new ideas. It resulted from a radical shift in the regional economy and from the changed relationship of cities to their hinterlands. The American urban revolution resulted from the industrialization of that country and its emergent position as an exporter of finished products. The transformation and growth of the Middle Eastern city was a consequence of the decline of indigenous industry and the increasingly dependent relationship of the region on European sources of capital and technology. Most of the cities that dominate the headlines today—Tehran, Istanbul, Cairo, Beirut, to name a few—took their present form in the context of European mercantile expansion.

With the eighteenth- and nineteenth-century dominance of Europeans in Middle Eastern trade, the region ceased being a major exporter of finished products. Instead, it rapidly became a vast market for European goods, with exports largely limited to raw materials. As a result, many inland centers originally developed for trade and as sites of local industry declined rapidly, while coastal cities such as Izmir (Smyrna), Beirut, Tripoli, and Alexandria increased in population and extended their influence, in part through a new merchant class. By the mid-nineteenth century traditional crafts and industries experienced near-total destruction by foreign competition.

Historians note that almost overnight the markets of Bursa, a formerly important and thriving town inland from the Sea of Marmara, were flooded with European goods following a trade agreement that opened up Ottoman markets to foreigners. Manufactured towels and shoes, long-famed products of Bursa, were almost immediately replaced by foreign goods imported more cheaply than local craftspeople could make them (Gerber, 1988). Bursa's fate is representative of what happened to Middle Eastern manufacturing in general following the Industrial Revolution and European mercantile expansion.

Only in the latter half of the twentieth century did local industry and capital formation begin to compete with foreign products in local markets. Manuel Castells, an eminent urban theorist, views the city as a node in a global economy, part of what he terms "the information society," that arose in the 1980s as a result of restructuring of global flows of capital in conjunction with computer-driven "informationalism," not just information- or science-based, but part of a large system of interdependent flows of communication (1999, pp.145 ff). As a consequence, certain regions and even cities become pivotal—Silicon Valley, Bangalore, New York City. They bring together an educated work force, state of the art computer-based communications systems, and industrial resources.

Another example might well be Istanbul, located as it is on the eastern edge of Europe but integrated economically with Western Europe. The city is experiencing an economic renaissance as an informational center, with over 360 multinational corporations having established major offices there since 1992. Following the collapse of the Soviet Union in 1991, the huge markets of Central Asia and the Caucasus have opened up, and these multinationals find the informational infrastructure of Istanbul far superior to the faltering communications systems of Russia. Using advanced technology, these corporations determine the flow of goods and services, as well as the output of far-flung factories for large hinterlands and Istanbul's traditional hinterland in Eastern Europe and the Middle East. Beirut in the 1970s seemed poised to join the ranks of the great financial centers of the world, but 15 years of civil war left it in ruin. Today, a massive renewal program is underway to reclaim this lost promise (Makdisi, 1997).

What are some of the social and economic implications of urban growth for the countries of the region? At the present stage and given the lack of planning and control, the implications are largely negative and pose a series of major problems: over-urbanization, poor housing, declining services, and social unrest. *Hyperurbanization* is a term used to describe a situation in which more people live in cities than can be properly employed there. Urban inhabitants in the Arab world, for example, consume more than twice what they contribute to the GNP in most countries. In other words, economic development, especially industrialization, lags behind urban growth. Saad Ibrahim (1985) notes that, in 1890, when Switzerland was on the verge of its period of rapid urban growth, some 35 percent of the Swiss population resided in cities and 45 percent were employed in industry. In Egypt, in 1970, by comparison, some 45 percent of the population lived in cities, but only 18 percent were employed in industry. Urban unemployed or underemployed put a great strain on a government's budget and public services, which results in severe housing shortages and the creation of inner-city slums and suburban shantytowns.

A CAIRO NEIGHBORHOOD: A CASE STUDY

Cities cannot be understood only in terms of generalities; rather, we build our picture of urban life on the basis of specific places and the people who live there. One city we can turn to to fill in the picture is Cairo. Cairo, which we have discussed repeatedly, is, of course, a great city in its own right. But of equal importance, Cairo is viewed by the Arabic-speaking world as the intellectual capital of the Middle East and its paramount political center. As the primary city of the most populous state in the Middle East, it displays all the contradictions and problems of urban life today.

Janet Abu-Lughod's book, *Cairo, 1001 Years of the City Victorious* (1971), is the most comprehensive study of any metropolitan area in the region to date, and her work has been added to by a new generation of scholars. Abu-Lughod writes that Cairo, like any city, is more than a complex of streets, subdivisions, and landmarks; it is, in the words of Louis Wirth, a true "mosaic of social worlds." These different social worlds reflect specialized functions and diverse ways of life, which come together to constitute the social and economic fabric of the city. More than any Western city, Cairo, Abu-Lughod suggests, is a place of contrasts and contradictions as it reflects the entire spectrum of Egyptian history and society as well as the revolutionary forces within it. The population of Cairo contains large communities of *fellahīn* recently arrived from the countryside, shopkeepers residing in traditional neighborhoods, industrial workers in government-built flats, and the urban elite in their luxurious apartments overlooking the Nile.

Abu-Lughod organizes her study in terms of what she calls the urban ecology of Cairo. Accordingly, she identifies "large segments of Cairo where residents share common social characteristics and follow particular life styles that mark them off from residents of neighboring communities with whom they seldom interact" (p.183). Using census data, she delineates 13 sections that are distinct in terms of general lifestyle as expressed in dress, patterns of marriage and residence, dwelling types, literacy and education rates, and occupation. Rather than describe all 13 districts, here we briefly consider one that we feel best illustrates the continuing modern juxtaposition of the diverse elements of urban life. This is medieval Cairo, entirely encircled by more recent subdivisions today.

The central district of Cairo is essentially all that remains today of the city's medieval heritage. Within it are found some of the most impressive monuments of Cairo's Islamic past, and its covered *suqs* and winding alleys still harbor a way of life that demonstrates a resilient cultural tradition. This is also "exotic Cairo" for the foreigner and the tourist.

The southernmost extremity of medieval Cairo is marked by the citadel built by Salah el-Din, the great Kurdish warrior who recaptured Jerusalem from the Crusaders. Completed around 1193, it is now dominated by the nineteenth-century mosque of Muhammad 'Ali. At the center of the area, one can still see the remains of the ancient walls marking the site of the original city constructed toward the end of the tenth century at the orders of the Fatimid Caliph Mu'izz el-Din and named al-Qahira (the Victorious). Little remains, however, from the days of its foundation except that neighborhoods (*hara*) of medieval Cairo are still named after the great gates of the ancient Fatmid city, in particular Bab al-Futuh and Bab al-Nasr. The skyline is dotted with the domes and minarets of the many mausoleums and mosques built by subsequent dynasties that extended al-Qahira beyond its original walls.

Medieval Cairo is traversed along a north-south axis by the *qasabah*, an ancient street that marked the commercial zone at the heart of the old city. Along this street are the major markets, or *suqs*, with their shops, warehouses, inns, and workshops. Each *suq* specializes in a commodity or craft. Here among the gold, cloth, and spice markets and their teeming humanity and clamor is the famous Khan al-Khalili, the tourists' bazaar *par excellence*.

Wedged between the silent monuments of Cairo's past and the din and hustle of the busy markets live about half a million Egyptians, many trapped in poverty and neglect. For this is truly an urban slum whose inhabitants eke out a living by working here and there in the small-scale trades and informal service sectors that predominate in this part of the city.

Nawal Nadim, an Egyptian sociologist, gives a lively ethnographic description of one neighborhood in the medieval section of Cairo (1985). The *hara* al-darb al-Ahmar, the Red Alley, contains 117 families with an average size of 5.5 people. Almost all the families of the *hara* are of the nuclear type, and the 27 extended households have been formed by the addition of widows, divorcees, or other single relatives. Although the households themselves are small, the web of kinship uniting them is very far-reaching and important to their economic welfare. Housing is extremely scarce, and most families have found their residences through contacts passed on by relatives. Families within the *hara*, particularly the young generation, have intermarried, creating ties of affinity among themselves. Forty percent of the households reside in one-room dwellings, and 60 percent do not have water taps and must buy water. Twenty-one families have television sets, which they make accessible to nearly everyone else.

The occupations of the *hara* residents may be grouped into three basic categories: *al-muwazafeen* are government employees who have low status and salary; *ahl el-san'aa* are artisans and craftspeople whose incomes are the most assured among the three groups; and *ahl el-kar* are unskilled workers, occasional peddlers, and domestics.

Familial and neighborhood interaction takes place within the private and public spaces of the *hara*, which is at once a spatial and social entity. Physically, al-darb al-Ahmar is a dead-end street or alley with limited access from the larger thoroughfare. Socially, it is a community of households who regard their shared space as their collective private domain. "The passage is used for socializing with neighbors, playing games, raising poultry, cleaning household dishes as well as washing the laundry. It is not uncommon on hot summer nights, to find members of the family sleeping in the *hara* passage by their doorsteps" (Nadim, 1985, p. 220). Even in dress, the residents express a high degree of intimacy and informality that is normally considered as appropriate only within the family.

Although Nadim finds considerable variation in income among the households, and though women in particular compete with one another for status in their display of their latest purchases, there is much recognition of interdependence. Men who lose their jobs or face unexpected crises borrow from their neighbors, and there is much sharing of food and utensils among the households. Women, who ultimately control the family's purse strings, often form lending clubs among themselves, called *gamiya*. Each member of the *gamiya* regularly contributes a sum of money to a common fund that by agreement will go to a particular member once an agreed-upon amount is collected.

The members remain in the *gamiya* until each has had a chance to collect the same sum. This allows poor families access to a sum of cash that would otherwise take them a long time to save. The *gamiya* is an important way in which the poor pool their limited resources and assist each other.

In the last two decades, a number of ethnographies on gender and household in the context of contemporary Cairo have appeared.[5] These studies, which tend to focus on gender relations and the household among lower-income groups in the city, generally demonstrate the crucial role that the household plays in mediating the impact of larger socioeconomic (and political) forces on the lives of individual men and women. Their authors' detailed research into the dynamics of gender roles, division of labor, and the political economy of individual households illustrates the different coping strategies that people employ as they try to adjust to the opportunities and constraints of their rapidly changing environment. For example, Homa Hoodfar (1996b) argues that in Cairo as a result of commercialization and the decrease in public subsidies and services that accompanied the *infitah*, or "open door" policies of the 1980s (see Chapter 11), the household's need for cash has increased. This has put women in a double bind. They lost many of their domestic functions to the marketplace, and they are poorly equipped to earn cash. The result is that women are now more dependent on their husbands for support. Their weakened position is further exacerbated by the new market ideology that tends to view wage labor and cash income as the only "real" contribution to the economy of the household. One strategy women employ when faced with this dilemma is to hold onto their traditional role. Hoodfar writes:

> In order to prevent the loss of more ground to men, women actively discourage the participation of men in domestic tasks. A further response of women in this situation has been to stress their Islamic right to economic support by their husbands and to defend the traditional division of labor, which they view as the basis for interdependence of the sexes. Therefore, at least in part, the roots of women's increasing public support for the Islamization of their society should be found in the way that development and social change have devalued their contributions without offering any viable alternatives. (p. 22)

In a similar vein, Arlene Elowe McCleod (1996) argues that the adoption of the Islamic veil by lower-middle-class women who work outside the home represents their response to a similar dilemma. On the one hand, they are forced to seek employment outside the house in order to maintain their modest living standard; on the other, they have to deal with the dominant gender ideology that claims that men should be financially responsible for their families and discourages women's work outside the house. Their adoption of Islamic dress is

---

[5] See, among others, Diane Singerman (1995), Evelyn Early (1980), Andrea Rugh (1985), and Homa Hoodfar (1996). For an excellent summary of the significance of the household among the urban population of Cairo, see the Introduction in Diane Singerman and Homa Hoodfar (1996).

one way to deal with this dilemma, as it signals that they are pious Muslim women committed to the moral code of their community.

> Cairo, like many Third World urban areas, is undergoing tremendous changes; women necessarily face the ambiguities of negotiating a future within this ferment. . . . In Cairo, the ideological conflict intensifies controversy over the construction of women's identity, preventing women from realizing some of the advantages of working outside the home. How competing ideologies interact, reinforcing or contradicting each other, even within one particular class setting, is clearly important for how women will perceive and attempt to act on their options. . . . The new Muslim woman they have created may work outside the home, but she never forgets or neglects her family. (p. 47)

Uni Wikan (1985), who like Abu-Lughod has been a longtime observer of the urban poor of Cairo, adds another important note. She draws attention to the relatively crime-free environment in which the poor live. Many of the worst pathologies of Western cities are absent or muted; alcohol use is much less widespread, as is drug use; men are socialized into a commitment to get and stay married; and there is the pressure of a strong work ethic. She and others attribute lower crime levels to the influence of these Islamic values.

These sketches of life in Cairo are meant to provide some feeling for the organization and quality of life in one major city. We now turn our attention to another pervasive aspect of modern urban life, squatter settlements.

ISTANBUL SQUATTER SETTLEMENTS

Although in various periods under the Ottomans particular cities in Turkey were subject to great increases in population due to rural migrants, until World War II the newcomers were generally absorbed within the existing residential districts. Following the war, squatter settlements or shantytowns sprung up in a profusion that was alarming to the established urbanites.

The social significance of the *gecekondu*, as these settlements are called, is indicated by the fact that in 1999, over 35 percent of Istanbul's population lived in such areas. Since the beginning of such settlements, the growth of the city has enveloped many of the older *gecekondus* while new areas continue to spring up on the vastly expanded outskirts of the city. In 1960, there were 400,000 squatter homes; in 1970, 600,000; in 1980, 1,150,000; and by 1999, over 2 million such homes.[6] One interesting facet of the *gecekondu* phenomenon is how rapidly unplanned and essentially squatter-built housing becomes incorporated into the fabric of the city. As migration continues, older settlements become spatially more central relative to new ones, property values rise, and investments turn small jury-built homes into cement block or concrete structures. These in turn are usually built in anticipation of being able to add additional floors so as to

[6] Türkiye Cumhüriyet Maliye Bakanlğı Milli Emlâk Genel Müdürlüğü, *Gecekondu Raporu*, 1999.

become apartment buildings. A final stage is when the initial structure is demolished and luxury flats are built in its place.

The fact that many earlier migrants have done well in their move to the city should not disguise the fact that for most it is a wrenching experience marked by long hours of work at low wages, crowded living quarters, and all the other trials of urban poverty. One recent study looks at the human face of life in a *gecekondu*. During two years of fieldwork, Jenny White (1994) studied a number of families who had migrated from rural areas of Turkey to live in poor, working-class neighborhoods of Istanbul and who are now engaged in small-scale production. Women play a central role in producing knitted, stitched, and embroidered clothing and decorative items, either at home or on a piecework basis in family atelier workshops. Many of these goods are exported to Europe, other areas of the Middle East, and the United States, where they are sold at prices astronomically higher than the cost of their production. They are also sold through middlemen to tourists, as well as directly to friends and neighbors.

Both the women who work at home or take in piecework and the organizers of their labor (generally men) regard this work as a part of traditional female domestic activities rather than as productive labor. "For the working class women of Istanbul, labor along with honor and childbearing, is a central theme of their lives" (White, 1994, p. 7). Since the women insist that this is not "work," they do not keep track of the time spent on it; a piece of sewing or knitting is taken up and put down throughout the day by different adult women and unmarried girls, the piecework becoming integrated into their other activities. "Both piecework and the family atelier are particularly suited to the organization of women's labor . . . since the women are able to reconcile earning additional income with traditional role constraints that discourage [them] from leaving the home, making contact with strangers, and taking over the male role provider" (p. 109). In this view, "work" or a "job" is a public sector activity unsuited to women and to be engaged in only as a last resort.

In her survey, White found that 64 percent of women spent between four and seven hours a day doing paid work, mostly piecework knitting. One of the women White visited, Şengül, a Quran teacher, owns a knitting machine and produces clothing to sell to friends and neighbors. But when White pressed her as to why she was doing this knitting, she became uncomfortable and insisted that she did not do a lot of it, taking orders only from her friends and working only in spare moments between housework, taking care of the children, and entertaining relatives and neighbors. She did not see herself as "belonging to a category of people who do regular work, sell to strangers, and rely on the money earned in this way" (p. 113), although clearly her income from this labor contributed significantly to the family budget. When asked how many sweaters she made in a month, she replied, "Last month . . . I had guests from the village so I couldn't do very many. About fifteen I guess" (p. 114). Since she had previously estimated that it took her two days to make a sweater, this meant that she worked every day, a fact about which she seemed embarrassed.

In most working-class neighborhoods, there are also family-run ateliers that give out piecework to women in the neighborhood. This arrangement allows the women to work at home and to see their labor as part of their roles as women, family members, and neighbors. Women doing piecework will generally do so in the company of other women, thus making the work part of other social activities that bring them together. Hatice and her husband, Osman, run an atelier in the *gecekondu* district of Yenikent, specializing in clothes made from scraps of fine leather sewn together by crocheted panels. They have three daughters, who help out in the atelier, and one seven-year-old son. The family members prepare the leather and yarn and then give them to neighborhood women with instructions for assembly. Osman keeps a book that lists what each woman takes and what she brings back.

The idea that women's labor, either at home or in the ateliers, is not "work" allows women to contribute financially to their families while maintaining their traditionally perceived roles. Of course, the undervaluing of women's labor is also one of the major factors keeping production costs low and profits high for distributors, middlemen, merchants, and exporters.

As we might expect, great variation exists among households within *gecekondu* settlements. Some families built their own houses, while others rented, and still others purchased houses from informal contractors. Those who own their homes are soon in an enviable position in comparison to those who rent, as the value of even the smallest dwelling rises precipitously as housing continues to be very scarce. Some settlements are well supplied with water and electricity; others initially lack even such minimal urban amenities as paved streets and public water. Regularly, houses are threatened with destruction by municipal authorities. However, more often than not some form of settlement is arrived at and authorities grant titles to occupants. This is often part of the political process by which politicians vie for votes or authorities gain urban calm.

In spite of variations in wealth and sources of income among the home-steaders, all share one characteristic. Their homes were built in violation of formal codes and regulations, sometimes on land that they did not own. Now, probably, most purchase their sites, but this does not mean that they gain clear title, as the lots are rarely legally subdivided. Commonly, the land belonged to a *waqf* or to the government treasury; some sites were the disputed properties of absentee owners, while others fell within the commons of villages that used to surround the ancient city. The *gecekondu*, then, is a community that evolved in a legal vacuum and in response to problems radically different from those previously experienced by local urban populations. This is true for squatter settlements in other countries as well.

The established Istanbul urbanite usually finds *gecekondu* conditions appalling in their initial state; the village had physically and socially come to the city. Streets as the settlement begins may be little more than lanes twisting among the houses. The houses themselves initially create a ramshackle village appearance, for they were constructed at first of whatever materials came to hand, and only later, as the homesteader accumulates some capital, are they converted into small structures of cement blocks with tile or tin roofs. But remarkably soon they progress to the next stage and multistory apartment buildings begin to rise, floor by floor completed as the owners acquire more resources.

The "rural" nature of the settlement, at least in its early days, simply reflected the fact that the vast majority of the families had come from the villages. Moreover, most of the migrants had relatives, or at least people with whom they had close relations as former village neighbors or friends, within the *gecekondu*. Ties based on a shared village or even a common regional background come to be expressed as almost a form of fictive kinship, termed *hemşerilik,* or "from the same region." From all accounts the social universe that initially develops in the *gecekondu* closely parallels village or rural models (see Duben, 1992).

Continuity with rural life is expressed in patterns of household organization, marriage, and even ritual. Sons tend to bring their brides home to their father's residence after marriage, which is most likely arranged by the parents in traditional fashion. Bride-price is still often paid to the father of the bride. The marriage ceremonies of the village are maintained, and the bride is taken from her home accompanied by customary music provided by flute and drums. The wedding celebration, which in the village would be conducted over several days with guests put up in homes of friends and relatives, is transformed in the city. It takes place at a "wedding parlor," where the groom's family entertains the guests; *gecekondu* homes are too small to accommodate large parties.

But this is not a static situation. A 1999 study of a long-established *gecekondu,* Kuştepe, with most respondents to a survey coming from the Black Sea region, revealed that most adults were at least graduates of primary school and many were lycée graduates. Further, most female respondents, particularly those with primary school education, indicated that they had married by choice rather than by arrangement. Numbers of children in the household showed a marked decline paralleling increased education; over 60 percent of households had four or fewer members and the majority two or fewer children. Most were married in the 20–30 age range, which also marks a striking departure from village norms (Kazgan et al., 1999).

PLANNED DEVELOPMENT: AMMAN

Amman, the capital of Jordan, represents an interesting case in urbanization in the Arab Middle East.[7] The city, with over 1 million inhabitants, was founded by Circassian Muslim immigrants who were driven out of their homeland by

---

[7] What follows draws on Eugene Lawrence Rogan's discussion of the evolution of Amman and its present "identity crisis" (1986) except where otherwise noted.

the Russo-Turkish wars in the late nineteenth century. After arriving in the Ottoman Empire, Circassians were sent by the sultan to settle throughout the empire in order to consolidate his authority, particularly in contested regions, and, in the case of Jordan, to secure the pilgrimage routes against the raids of the Bedouin. Ancient Amman, a town that was an important entrepôt on the trade routes from the Red Sea to the Arabian Peninsula, had been sacked and totally destroyed by the Mogul invasion in 1260; for the next five centuries, a small, rural settlement existed on the ruins. Thus modern Amman was established in 1870 by a few Circassian families who used the precut masonry from the ancient settlement to construct their homes.

During the first four decades of the twentieth century, Amman grew in population and in regional importance. In 1928, it was declared the capital of the newly formed Kingdom of Transjordan (later Jordan), and by 1946, its population was estimated to have reached 26,000. Two years later, in 1948, the first massive wave of migration into the city began with the influx of Palestinian refugees fleeing the Arab-Israeli War. This was repeated with the 1967 war and the subsequent Israeli rule of the occupied West Bank. According to United Nations statistics, between 1948 and 1966, 240,000 Palestinian refugees settled in Amman. They were joined by another 100,000 in 1967. By the early 1980s, Palestinians represented 60 to 80 percent of Amman's population. In addition to the Palestinian influx, a large number of rural immigrants from Jordan's countryside were coming to the city; these people often settled in compact communities, lending a village-like atmosphere to parts of Amman. In fact, over 70 percent of Amman housing is owner-constructed, that is, not built by licensed contractors or developers (Sims, 1990).

Seteney Shami (1997) describes aspects of life in two squatter settlements in central Amman, the Wadi and the Jabal, both inhabited by Palestinians, refugees from the 1948 and 1967 wars. The Wadi settlement borders a refugee camp, while the Jabal is surrounded by a low-income neighborhood.

A baseline survey of the area revealed that the average squatter settlement household consisted of a family of 6.58 people living in a one- to two-room house made of concrete with a corrugated tin roof and enclosing a central courtyard. The house had running water and electricity, but no sewage system. Adult males worked in artisanal workshops, in construction, and as low-level government employees. Most families had at least one member working in one or another of the Gulf states and sending remittances home. Besides their domestic work, women earned some income by sewing, embroidery, or preparing food for sale in the market.

Shami's article underscores the fluidity and adaptability in the use of urban space by the inhabitants of the congested squatter areas; in particular, she illustrates how the same space is transformed from a "public" or male space into a "private" or female space, and vice versa, in the course of a day. "[P]recisely because there is a high degree of sexual segregation, the same spaces transform themselves into male and female space depending upon the time of day, the people using the space and the type of activity performed in it. This is true whether the space is an enclosed space or open one" (p. 87). Shami notes that in their efforts to negotiate the changing conditions in the squatter settlements, such as an upgrading project financed by the World Bank, to their own and their families' benefit, women employed strategies that appeared to flout the ideal of female space as private space. Dressed in their Palestinian embroidered dresses, they filled the hallways of the project's offices waiting to see the director to whom they regularly expressed their concern about some aspect or another of the project. "The presumed ideal of female seclusion was flaunted nonchalantly in these most public spaces, but in their negotiations women appealed to public officials . . . in their role as mothers, wives, and guardians of the domestic domain" (p. 96). Since the women and their families define their boundaries in terms of the kinship networks of mutual visiting and cooperation that sustain their day-to-day life, they do not recognize the legal-administrative distinctions of urban space in terms of squatter settlement, refugee camp, and low-income neighborhood.

The massive immigration of refugees and rural migrants during the 1950s and 1960s put a severe strain on housing, sanitation, and municipal services. In an effort to cope with these problems, the government of Jordan turned to Western urban planners and experts. In a short time, city services (police, post office, municipality building, etc.) that had clustered near the central mosque were relocated to the newly expanded peripheral areas. Likewise, the old *suq*, located near the central mosque, was torn down, and parking lots and new buildings with glass-fronted shops were constructed on the site. The secondary meat and vegetable *suq* was also relocated to the south of the city. By the 1970s, central Amman had been transformed into a decentralized, "modern," and characterless metropolis.

By the early 1980s, there was a widespread populist movement to impress on Amman a more "Islamic" form.[8] This movement consisted of two simultaneous but seemingly unconnected trends. The first related to the government's efforts, through legislation and ministerial councils, to preserve and restore historic sites and to establish "Islamic" guidelines for contemporary construction, both public and private. The debates and discussion raised in state councils and the media, which mirrored concerns throughout the region,[9] have raised public awareness of the issue and inspired native architects and planners to come up with distinctive solutions to the expressed problem of Amman's "identity crisis."

[8] Another interesting example is the case of Ismailia, Egypt, which was built by the Suez Canal Company in 1862 on an entirely Western urban plan, which has undergone not only extensive "Islamization" but also "secularization" (Khudori, 1999, p. 15). While new mosques are transforming the city center, the formerly sharp differentiation between "Muslim" and "non-Muslim" dwellings is disappearing, with most now taking the non-Muslim shape—that is, without the heavily shuttered windows and enclosed verandas and balconies.

[9] See Çağlar Keyder (1999) and others in this valuable edited volume.

The second trend, which has already resulted in the "physical Islamiza-tion of Amman," consisted of an accelerated rate of mosque construction throughout the city and especially in the low-income neighborhoods. The majority of these mosques, which, like mosques everywhere, function as places for communal worship, religious education, public gatherings, and social ser-vices, were built by individuals and neighborhood associations. "The mosque is the most visible (and audible) statement of communal commitment to Islam. The proliferation of mosques is thus of great consequence to efforts currently under way to impress on Amman a more Islamic form" (Rogan, 1986, p. 35).

The motives behind the government's initiative and that of the popular building of mosques are complex, ranging from political considerations (to co-opt Islamist opposition) to efforts to gain prominence and prestige in the com-munity, as well as cultural reassertion. There is no doubt, however, that the long-term result will be a slow transformation of Amman into a more Middle Eastern–Islamic city that is reflective of its inhabitants' cultural heritage.

RECONSTRUCTION BEIRUT-STYLE: "AN ANCIENT CITY FOR THE FUTURE"

The center of Beirut today is a wasteland, extending for thousands of square meters from Martyrs Square, writes Saree Makdisi (1997), who goes on to describe the remarkable way in which this ancient city is being rebuilt. What is remarkable is that the whole of this massive project is under the aegis of one pri-vate company, Solidére, which operates almost completely without govern-mental guidelines. Perhaps only in Beirut has the logic of unfettered capitalism found its full potential. The city had suffered through the terrible civil war of 1975–1990, which left 150,000 people dead, 300,000 wounded, and the heavily damaged city center an "emptied out graveyard of national dialogue and recon-ciliation" (Makdisi, 1997, p. 667). Almost more appalling is the fact that after the war, companies that were later to be reorganized as Solidére demolished more perfectly serviceable surviving buildings than had been destroyed during the entire war.

In 1984, long before the end of the war, a private company owned by the Lebanese billionaire Rafiq Hariri (who later became a postwar prime minister) began planning the reconstruction of the area, to the extent even then of large-scale demolition of sound surviving buildings. In 1990, following the Taif Peace Accord, powerful individuals from all parties and all closely connected to the government, joined as shareholders in the company now renamed Solidere, whose shares are aggressively marketed both in Lebanon and abroad. Seem-ingly, the company is largely free from public accountability or governmental regulation, its principal players being closely associated with the government. Even without specific legal guidelines, it is alleged that demolition of surviving buildings took place without much regard to property rights or even, on at least one occasion, human life (Makdisi, 1997, p. 673). In 1996, one building was brought down on the heads of squatters, killing a whole family.

> By literally bulldozing large stretches of urban space such as downtown Beirut, which is of immense historic and rehabilitative value, urban planners have now access to priceless virgin land which could not have been released by the normal exorbitant and cumbersome process of expropriation. Out of the rubble and debris of war, planners have now unparalleled opportunities to produce daring, vision-ary designs for molding or at least prefiguring the outlines of the new emergent order. (Khalaf, 1993, p. 121)

The ambitious project is largely in place, with the laying out of streets, grand avenues, and building sites covering over 1.8 million square meters, and about 600,000 square meters of land reclaimed from the sea. Two yacht basins and hotel complexes are planned on what were formerly public beaches, and about half the development will be owned by Solidere. A positive side of this project is that great attention is being paid to the opening and preservation of archaeological sites—hence the company's slogan "An Ancient City for the Future." Housing, however, will be largely out of reach for most citizens. Apart from the material aspects of the project, it is an effort to help Beirut regain its pre–civil war status as an international financial and trading center. Whether it will succeed remains an open question, but in any event the nature of the undertaking itself indicates the nature of the country's new political order.

Aseel Sawalha (1999) highlights this with reference to local responses in the face of the imposition of a global perspective in reconstructing Beirut. The

Shelled buildings in Beirut during the civil war.

planners are looking primarily at situating the new Beirut in the global order—emphasizing international chain stores, restaurants, and businesses at the expense of indigenous institutions and local values. In one example, she describes how in one district, in spite of local protests, a Hard Rock Cafe was opened directly across the street from the neighborhood mosque. The protests were not objecting to such a restaurant, with its loud Western music and service of alcohol, per se but rather its location and the fact that its employees and suppliers, not to mention its customers, had no ties to the neighborhood and provided no benefits to local residents. While not successful in keeping the restaurant out, residents have taken steps to claim and shape their cultural space by organizing historical associations and a small museum to protect their heritage. They are not rejecting the outside world but, as Sawalha puts it, "Instead, they attempt to engage the global on acceptable, that is, local terms." Time will tell how they fare in this endeavor.

GENERAL OVERVIEW

The "mega city" and the processes of "hyperurbanization" are not likely to be reversed, although the rate of change in the twentieth century cannot be maintained, at least demographically speaking. What has recently been evident and will likely continue is the amplification of contrasts between cities caught up in international flows of capital and those outside. Some cities, such as the "rentier" cities of the Gulf living on oil income, will prosper and continue to reconstitute themselves spatially but probably will not emerge as major international nodes. Provincial cities in Iran, Egypt, Syria, Jordan, and Turkey will develop within fairly limited hinterlands; Istanbul, Cairo, Alexandria, Beirut, and possibly Dubai will flourish as regional and not just national cultural and business centers. Any general assessment of the Middle Eastern city is tantamount to a sketch of all the problems and challenges of life in the Middle East. So great, in fact, has been the transformation of urban space and urban life that everywhere one hears nostalgia for the "lost" Cairo, the "lost" Beirut. The city is absolutely pivotal in the production of popular culture, as well as genres that glamorize the rural and the past. In fact, this is a major product of urban places: compact disc companies, art institutions, film and television companies—all are concentrated in just a few national and regional sites.

We can make some fairly obvious points by way of shared courses taken in urban settings. No doubt the tension between Islamists and secularists will continue apace even as de facto secularism increases in everyday life. Part of this will be visible in the increasing construction of mosques and religious edifices as "Islamic space" is established. But the everyday structures of urban life are, in most countries of the region, drifting out of the hands of religiously trained individuals and institutions. The great Egyptian novelist Naquib Mahfouz, writing of the Cairene Muslim, nicely expresses this:

He leads a contemporary [i.e., "modern"] life. He obeys civil and penal laws of Western origin and is involved in a complex tangle of social and economic transactions and is never certain to what extent these agree with or contradict his Islamic creed. Life carries him along in its current and he forgets his misgivings for a time until one Friday he hears the *imam* or reads the religious page in one of the papers, and the old misgivings come back with a certain fear. He realizes that in this new society he has been afflicted with a split personality: half of him believes, prays, fasts and makes the pilgrimage. The other half renders his values void in banks and courts and in the streets, even in the cinemas and theaters, perhaps even at home among his family before the television set. (cited in Al-Azm [1997], p. 19)

Also in thinking of "Islamic space" we should not forget that Israel has its counterparts to Islamic fundamentalists, who, not just in Hebron but in Jerusalem and elsewhere, are forcefully attempting to create Jewish space. Extreme religious Zionist organizations such as Gush Emunim have even called for the demolition of Muslim holy buildings on the Temple Mount (Champion, 1997, pp. 301ff). But, in general, without doubt what might be called "Western urban space" or "global space" is in the ascendancy.

Another very urban development is the proliferation of non-governmental organizations (NGOs), both indigenous and international. Activist organizations promoting community health, women's rights, human rights, population control, environmental protection, sports, professional and trade organizations, and many other causes are registered in the hundreds in most countries. In many instances these NGOs have come to assume functions associated with government, as for example, in Lebanon. In Turkey, in the aftermath of the 1999 earthquakes near Istanbul, NGOs were perceived to have responded much more efficiently to the emergency than state-run relief organizations such as the Red Crescent. Many, if not most of these organizations are secular, although there are ways in which such groups as the Muslim Brothers in Egypt should be seen as offering Islamic parallels. In Turkey alone there were over 57,000 legally registered NGOs in 1996, with an average of 10 new applications made in Istanbul each day (Toprak, 1996, p. 104).

The media have traditionally been under the tight control of urban-based institutions. This has not changed, but the individual consumer now has many more choices and can circumvent attempts at censorship. In Turkey, Lebanon, Israel, and Egypt, the press is very active, and even in the face of considerable hostility and risk to personal safety, reporters and publishers expose corruption and political abuse. Even in Iran many journalists are willing to confront the censors. While not "urban" per se, this sort of intellectual activity imparts a special hue to the large city not found in small towns.

Probably the terms most used, even abused, with reference to urbanization are "globalization" and the "global community," exemplified by the Internet, flows of information, multiple but limited sites producing information, and the like. Certainly every city in the Middle East is affected by global patterns of interdependence—perhaps even a product of them. But this was also largely true in the nineteenth century. What may be distinctive today with respect to global systems is the relative ease with which those who benefit from them can withdraw from the world of those excluded. But even so, this is not an absolute shift. The nineteenth-century merchant prince in Istanbul or court official in Cairo lived in walled compounds and sought refuge in club life and ocean cruises, activities as far removed as possible from the squalor of everyday urban life experienced by the majority. The urban elite today also live a life apart—again in clubs and cabarets, but more importantly by being connected to their global counterparts electronically and via the media.

One implication of globalism might appear to be that the local is doomed to be overwhelmed by the global. But in fact that is not the case, or certainly not in the Middle East. In most countries, multiple centers of power and influence continue or have actually been enhanced. As Duben (1992) has noted, local government in Turkey, Iran, and much of the Arab world has grown in importance. Today mayors and city councils play important political roles in many countries and, quite unlike in the past, represent, one way or another, local constituencies or perspectives. Even Iran has been described as having a very multivalent system of power. What global processes may do is favor one urban node over another, but local identities may be strengthened, not weakened, in the process. Small-town boosterism, chambers of commerce, and the like are increasing, not decreasing.

This, then, suggests that a dual structure is emerging, or at least being strengthened, in major cities (see Keyder, 1999)—a segment that benefits from, or is not disenfranchised by consumerism, the international flow of capital, and larger market forces and a segment that does not. As Keyder writes in respect of Istanbul, you can photograph some street scenes which you could represent as being Kabul and others as from any city in Western Europe. But, as he also notes, this polarity does not mean a lack of mutual accommodation; in fact, it could be argued that civil strife in most Middle Eastern cities is notably less than in most European or American cities.

8

Kinship, Marriage, and the Family

This chapter discusses what we feel to be the major elements of social organization based on kinship and family structure in the Middle East. Given the diverse ways of life and cultural heritages, our discussion is both broad and subject to frequent caveats and qualifications. While it is useful to draw attention to general patterns and norms of behavior, one should never apply even strongly supported norms or preferences stereotypically. Many social scientists are skeptical of efforts that purport to describe social phenomena objectively. Nevertheless, there seem to have been sufficient studies by enough observers over the years to provide cumulative data on a wide range of behavioral patterns. Needless to say, one cannot extrapolate from the general to predict the specific, nor should one essentialize such abstractions as "family," "marriage," or "society." We are convinced, however, that to understand Middle Eastern society, even its higher levels of political organization, one has to understand the nature of the primary groupings into which the individual is born and how men and women subsequently fashion and use "primordial" ties and relationships throughout their lifetimes. The relationships are perceived and expressed in the idiom of kinship or closeness (in Arabic, *qaraba*). The binary distinction here is between one who is close or kin, *qareeb,* and one who is distant or a stranger, *ghareeb.* In Iran, the same term, *ghareeb,* is applied to a nonrelative or stranger; for a relative, the term in Persian or Farsi is *khodi,* which is derived from the word *khod,* meaning "self."

There have been many attempts to characterize Middle Eastern social organization in terms of paradigms unique to Middle Eastern society, as if this region constituted a homogeneous and relatively unchanging world of its own. To that end, scholars have sought some simple and unique code that would reveal and explain social organization in the area. It is as if behavior in the Middle East cannot be understood in the same terms and concepts applicable to Europe or the rest of Asia. For example, an inordinate amount of scholarship has been devoted to the expressed preference for patrilateral parallel cousin marriage (father's brother's daughter/son). For some scholars, this rule and its extension is a metaphor for what distinguishes Middle Eastern society in general. Other scholars stress the universality of the patrilineal segmentary system in which fundamental building blocks of society are formed according to rules of descent in the male line. For still others, the code lies in a unique system of values whose core lies in deeply rooted assumptions and attitudes about human sexuality and the need to control female sexual behavior. Some trace the origin of this value complex to the Islamic heritage of the area; others relate it to longer-standing practices that revolve around basic notions of honor and shame. Although simplification is inherently attractive, and indeed is the legitimate goal of scholarship, it has to be accomplished with full cognizance of the variability and complexity of the phenomena observed.

When viewing communal organization throughout the Middle East, and indeed throughout the world, there is no doubt that the single most crucial factor underlying social relationships is that of kinship. Even in the most developed industrial societies, most individuals grow up with, co-reside with, and, in general, spend most of their time in association with people to whom they are related in one fashion or another. How people interact with one another, their expectations of behavior, and their responsibilities to others are all heavily influenced by whether they are related to one another, and if so how. This specific aspect of social organization, kinship, and the formation of groups on the basis of selected forms of kinship is our initial concern here.

TERMS OF KINSHIP

Let us begin by asking the most elementary question: How do people themselves define and classify their relatives? We have to keep in mind that such systems of classification vary greatly around the world, and that anthropologists have reduced them to a number of major types according to how people define and distinguish key relationships—parents, aunts, uncles, cousins, for example. This is more than an exercise in comparative linguistics; how people create a specific universe of relations is closely related to patterns of actual behavior. For example, the fact that the English language does not distinguish verbally between maternal and paternal cousins is indicative of the social fact that all cousins tend to stand in the same formal relationship to the speaker. In Arabic, on the other hand, as in Persian and Turkish, the speaker not only has to distinguish linguistically between the maternal and paternal cousins but also has to specify the gender of the cousin in question and his or her exact relationship to the parent in question.

This descriptive and highly specific system of kin terminology, referred to by anthropologists as the *Sudanese* type, indicates the significance of distinguishing among cousins in most Middle Eastern societies. This same system distinguishes sets of aunts and uncles from each other in terms of their links to the parents; for example, different terms are used for mother's sister and father's sister. Thus, an Arabic, Persian, or Turkish speaker may utilize as many as 16 different terms or combinations to describe immediate blood relations. This precision in referring to people is associated with the importance that is attached to distinguishing among different sets of relatives. (See Table 8.1.)

It should be kept in mind that kinship classification systems give only a little insight into the structure of social relations; they do not necessarily reveal anything of the actual content. Thus, if a Turkish male refers to one man as his father's brother, *amca*, and another as his mother's brother, *dayı*, this tells us only that these two individuals stand in different social points to the speaker. Although in both urban and rural Turkish societies, a mother's brother is generally thought of as being warm and emotionally sympathetic to his nephew or niece and one's father's brother is frequently associated with exhibiting parental authority and discipline, it does not necessarily follow that actual behavior reflects these normative expectations.

Carol Delaney (1991) describes kinship as being a system of relationships that transcends simple kinship terminology alone. Kinship behavior in the Middle East, as elsewhere, is tempered by matters of personality, expediency, and the specific context under consideration. However, the normative patterns of behavior associated with specific terms do at least set the formal frame and some of the limits for social interaction. Knowing that the terms for close relatives can be extended to more distant relatives, even to strangers under certain

TABLE 8.1   Kinship Terminology

English	Arabic	Persian	Turkish
father	'ab	pedar	baba
mother	'umm	modar	anne (ana)
father's brother	'amm	amou	amca
mother's sister	khala	khaleh	teyze
father's sister	'amma	ammeh	hala
mother's brother	khal	doyi	dayı
brother	'akh	barodar	erkek kardeş
sister	'ukht	khohar	kız kardeş
father's brother's son	'ibn 'ammi	pesar amou	amca oğlu
mother's sister's son	'ibn khalti	pesar khaleh	teyze oğlu
father's brother's daughter	bint 'amm	dokhtar amou	amca kızı
mother's sister's daughter	bint khalti	dokhtar khaleh	teyze kızı
father's sister's son	ibn 'ammti	pesar ammeh	hala oğlu
mother's brother's son	ibn khali	pesar doyi	dayı oğlu
father's sister's daughter	bint 'ammi	dokhtar ammeh	hala kızı
mother's brother's daughter	bint khali	dokhtar doyi	dayı kızı

circumstances, gives an insight into the expectations that people have of that specific relationship. For example, in the Arabic-speaking world (and in Turkey, too), the use of the term for father's brother by younger men to address older men indicates respect and deference to their authority regardless of the actual biological relationship. (Parenthetically, we may add that if used in an inappropriate context, this usage may indicate derision or patronizing. For example, in Arabic a wealthy man might address a menial servant of his as *ya 'ammi,* or "my uncle"; in this case, the term expresses the effort of the rich and powerful master to "dilute" the social gap between him and his servant.) Arab children are also encouraged to use the term *khala,* or mother's sister, when addressing their mother's female friends of similar status and age. This is to indicate both respect and yet informal intimacy.

Extending the Arabic terms *'amm* to a large circle of older males and *khala* to a large circle of older females, while at the same time restricting the usages of *'amma,* or father's sister, and *khal,* or mother's brother, to a narrower group, reflects fairly pervasive social expectations about patterns of cross-generational deference, authority, and even intimacy.

In Turkish, brothers and sisters refer to each other by terms that indicate relative birth order and, by implication, express relative expectations of authority and deference. Naturally, within any household, actual relations between brothers and sisters may bear little resemblance to a hierarchy based on age. But still, there are times when this normative ranking can or should be expressed. For example, at ceremonial meals, or when strangers are present, or when married siblings pay social visits to each other's houses, it is expected that deference will be paid to older sisters and brothers. In a discussion of family structure in a Turkish village, Paul Magnarella (1974) notes that older sisters, *abla,* become like second mothers to younger siblings, and older brothers, *ağabey,* are in many respects second fathers. Older brothers can become tyrannical in their behavior toward younger sisters as they assume the guardianship of family honor. Of course, even in a single community, people from different social classes, educational backgrounds, and so on, behave differently. However, in particular societies, it is possible to identify sets of expectations regarding proper behavior toward kinfolk. The way these expectations are met or not met in behavior can be revealing of the actual relationship among members of the family.

Thus, a basic set of Arabic terms for relatives is understood by the same 250 million speakers of that language, although this vast population encompasses a great range of social diversity and ways of life. All the same, terms take on different values and meanings in different areas and contexts. And the same word can convey different values when used in different situations. For example, the Arabic word *'amm* is used to refer to one's father's brother, as well as to address one's father-in-law, regardless of consanguinity. In certain situations, as previously described, it is also employed to signify respect for male elders or to minimize social distance. Further, one may also tease one's age-mates by calling them 'ammi.

Husbands and wives refer to one another in a variety of ways that reflect not only social class but also who is present, whether or not they are addressing each other in private, whether or not they have had children, and other factors that vary with local usage. The basic terms consist of personal names normally to be used only in private or in intimate conversation, except among the educated upper-class urbanites, where personal names are more widely used in address now. In public, a common practice among all segments of Arabic-speaking society is for spouses to refer to one another (and be referred to by others) by the name of their eldest son, for example, 'abu 'Ali or 'umm 'Ali, that is, "father of 'Ali" or "mother of 'Ali." If the couple has only daughters, the spouses are addressed by the name of the oldest girl until a son is born. Anthropologists call this practice of addressing parents in reference to their children teknonymy. Its presumed significance in the Middle East is to highlight the importance of male issue to both parents and to emphasize the responsibility of parenting in the marital bond.

Another widespread system of address is for spouses to refer to each other by the kinship term bint 'amm or ibn 'amm (father's brother's daughter/father's brother's son), particularly when wishing to stress the couple's immediate ties to one another rather than those arising from parenthood. In rural areas in much of the Arabic-speaking Middle East, husbands and wives very often simply refer to one another as marti, "my woman," and rajli, "my man," a usage disdained by educated and status-conscious individuals. Emrys Peters (1976) found that the terms used by spouses in Shi'a and Maronite villages of Lebanon differed in a slight but significant manner that reflected their different views of marriage. Husbands and wives in Shi'a villages consistently used the teknonymous system of address in private, that is, they referred to each other in terms of their children. The Maronites, on the other hand, used either personal names or kin terms such as bint 'amm, "father's brother's daughter," indicating that the spouses identified more closely with each other than with their shared children. It is because actual kinship usage is situational that it reveals much about what people expect from others and how they hope to manipulate or affect the behavior of others.

It is interesting to note here that whereas the Middle East is usually characterized as exemplifying a strong male bias with an emphasis on agnatic descent, this is not reflected in the system of kinship terminology. Whereas in many of the world's patrilineal societies, relatives on the father's side are referred to in ways that indicate a closer relationship than with the equivalent relatives on the mother's side, this is not true in the Middle East. The system of kinship terms used by most people of the area is evenhanded and can be considered as indicative of the importance that all close relatives may play in an individual's life. In other words, regardless of the political and social alignments of the moment, the core of relatives on which an individual may rely and may even manipulate is bilateral and unbounded. As the Arab proverb expresses it, "Your kin are those who stand with you when battle lines are drawn."

PATRILINEAL DESCENT AND PATRONYMIC GROUPS

Ideas of kinship do more than provide a potential network for individual action. Some forms of kinship terminology sort members of a society into groups of people who interact on a regular basis or for some purpose. Just as kinship can describe a larger, almost open-ended circle of relatives, it can also be used to establish some set of relatives apart from the others. The idea of patrilineal descent is an important principle used to distinguish among relatives and to establish potentially discrete kin groupings or categories.

Individuals are considered biologically related in equal degrees to both their father and mother, a fact reflected in the bilateral nature of kinship terms used. However, among the Arabs, the general belief is that a child inherits his or her "blood," *damm,* from both father and mother, while the nerve or sinew, *'asab,* is believed to be passed only through the father, the male line of descent. Hence, the special significance of patrilineal descent as expressed in the idiom of *'asabiyya,* translated into clan and tribal solidarity and cohesion. As such, special recognition is paid to those relatives with whom one shares a common ancestry in the male line—that is, one's father's lineal relatives. At its simplest, this is directly analogous to the way in which family names are passed on through fathers in American and English society. In general, however, patrilineal descent is much more significant than just simply a means by which family names are passed on. In both tribal and nontribal Middle Eastern societies, a number of important rights, duties, and mutual expectations are associated with close patrilineal kin. In tribal societies, these rights include rights to water, land, mutual defense, and so on (as discussed in the earlier chapter on pastoralism). In nontribal communities, an individual may depend on his or her patrikin for protection, economic assistance, and general support.

Fundamental to all Middle Eastern social groupings is the idea that inheritance rights, which often establish an individual's basic access to productive wealth, are agnatically defined. The *'asab* relationship defines primary heirs as those related to the deceased person in the ascending and descending male line. When political authority is passed through inheritance, it also follows the male line. Throughout their lifetime, women continue to partake more in their father's social status than in that of their husband. In cases of divorce or death, minor children, after they are weaned, are kept with the father or his immediate patrilateral family.

What is important is where the principle of patrilineal descent is used to form relatively small-scale groupings for social action. These can be termed extended families, patronymic groups, or shallow lineages. Although tribal organization is based on the widest extension of this principle, descent is more widely used to define small-scale groupings of the sort that characterize village, town, and city alike. This does not mean that all groups for joint action, co-residence, or other purposes are restricted to this patrilineal model. People may form groups in which the closest ties of kinship are through maternal relatives, or they may be joined by a mixture of patrilateral and matrilateral ties. Even when patrilineal groups are recognized, unrelated individuals may still join. For example, this often happens when a family settles in a village in which it has no previous patrilineal ties to the other residents. With time, facilitated by inter-marriage, the family and its descendants may well become assimilated into one of the dominant patronymic groups. In short, although the actual makeup of any given social group is apt to be varied, a consistent pattern is the primacy of the patrilineal ties in forming named groups, be they families or lineages.

THE FAMILY AND THE HOUSEHOLD

Although it is sometimes difficult to distinguish the concept of the family from that of the household, the two are not always coterminous. Families are social constructs based on marriage and consanguinity—in particular, relations of descent. It is this latter relationship that gives families continuity across genera-tions. Households, as we use the term, are the economic and residential units that may or may not correspond with the family. This analytical distinction between family and household is one made by members of Middle Eastern communities themselves, as expressed in the Arabic terms 'aila or usra for a named core of closely related kinspeople and their affines (relatives by mar-riage) and beit or dar, which refers to the smaller, co-residing group. The family was and remains the basic unit of social organization in the Middle East. This is true for rural and urban segments alike. The root of the Arabic and Turkish term for family, 'aila, means "to support," and in fact, children are referred to gen-erally as 'iyal, those to be supported or dependents. Until recently, the family in the Middle East conformed to the patriarchal model in which the father held authority and was charged with economically supporting his wife and children. The wife's main duties were confined to the household and to raising the children.

The often articulated ideal household structure among urban and rural Arabs, Turks, and Persians—an extended family made up of the father or patri-arch, his wife, one or more married sons and their families, and all the unmar-ried daughters and sons—probably was never the statistical norm. Among the 15 households making up the small settled Bedouin community in the Western Desert of Egypt, Lila Abu-Lughod (1986) reports a wide variation. The smallest was a couple and their infant and the largest consisted of 25 people who shared two adjacent houses and who "ate from one bowl."

The great variability in actual patterns of residence and in household makeup, both in terms of numbers of people and in spatial composition, does not determine the actual patterns of intensive social interaction. Very often in rural as well as urban settings, brothers or agnatic cousins cooperate in particular political or economic enterprises but reside in separate households, each rearing his own children and maintaining separate household budgets. Seteney Shami's (1997) study of two low-income neighborhoods in central Amman (discussed in Chapter 7), revealed wide variations in household composition and in the use of shared space. Shami reports that a common type is the multiple family household consisting of a conjugal couple, plus one or more married sons and their respective families. Within the dwelling space, however, there were "divisions and boundaries structured intimately by household relations. These divisions are not, as may be expected from the literature on the Middle East, divisions into male and female space. Rather each conjugal unit within the multiple-family-household has its own space, and where possible their own room" (p. 84). When conjugal families that are part of the household go away on extended trips (for example to work abroad), their rooms are locked, even though the space is badly needed by the remaining members of the household.

What is important to keep in mind is that the more inclusive unit of the family, however formed in practice, continues to be important even when residential patterns change. As Shami concludes, it is the networks of kinship and cooperation that define the people's sense of identity, "give meaning to their social relations, and sustain them through difficult and insecure economic circumstances" (p. 81).

The size and significance of publicly identifiable family groupings in the Middle East correlate closely with their resources. Rich families take pains to maintain close relations among their members and to utilize ties of kinship and marriage to reinforce, perpetuate, and advance their positions. Whereas a poor man would likely find little to draw his in-laws close to him, a rich or powerful man will probably make use of (and be used by) not only his in-laws but those created by the marriages of his children. Even where productive property is individually held, it is advantageous for members of wealthy families to act in concert. Thus, when one hears reference to the decline of the family in the Middle East, it is usually in reference to the breakup of large residential entities and not necessarily to the diminution of the viability of the kinship grouping itself.[1]

The great variability and flexibility in family and household organization are not simply a result of urban as opposed to rural society, nor is the contrast one between "modern" and "traditional" or even tribal and nontribal. These simple contrastive types tend to exist at the idealized and normative levels, whereas in reality the variation in family forms and functions occurs in response to specific socioeconomic forces that operate in a given context. This is clearly illustrated in the case of Iraq, where a severe economic embargo

---

[1] For a review article on the Arab family, see William Young and Seteney Shami (1997).

imposed by the United Nations in 1990 (following the Gulf War) has already had an impact on the family form and the division of labor among a certain sector of Iraqi society, according to Qais Al-Nouri, an Iraqi anthropologist (1997). Al-Nouri reports that the hardest-hit group are female-headed households, where a war widow is perhaps the sole provider and has no regular income. Rising food prices force these families to liquidate any property they may have, forgo family celebrations of any sort, and to withdraw their children from school so that they can be sent to work as day laborers to supplement the family's income. In extreme cases, children may be sent to beg at local religious shrines, where they hope to receive handouts from pilgrims.

Another sector that has suffered severely under the embargo is the families of civil servants, perhaps the largest wage-earning sector in Iraq. To cope with high inflation and soaring prices, this group has evolved a number of strategies of which an important one is the revival of the extended family and the multiple family household.

> Two married brothers, for example, may reside with their wives and children in the same house along with their aged parents, pooling their resources to keep up with spiraling costs. One brother may be a poorly paid government employee while the other has an independent job . . . thus the urban extended family, which was on the wane prior to the embargo, is making a comeback among government employees. (Al-Nouri, 1997, p. 103)

Those who have not been adversely affected by the embargo include major contractors and financiers and large landowners. The steep rise in commodity prices and restrictions on foreign trade have greatly profited this group, who own and control the national food industries, including dairy and meat processing, chicken farming, and fisheries. According to Al-Nouri, members of this nouveaux riches group have become famous (or, rather, infamous) for their indulgence in "casual short-term marriages," a new feature in Iraqi society and an index, perhaps, of the normative breakdown that currently prevails in that country. These short-term marriages, which may last only a few weeks, are quickly registered and as quickly dissolved because "these newly wealthy men can easily afford whatever divorce fees and alimony payments are demanded, and they feel no social constraints in their dealings with their wives" (p. 105). While the long-term implications of such arrangements, born in the context of postwar trauma and economic hardships, are difficult to assess, that they occur illustrates the adaptability of conjugal and familial arrangements and underscores the fact that in Iraq, as elsewhere, people organize and maintain themselves in familial groupings and ascribe social significance to them in proportion to the benefits that accrue from such organization.

Where there is individual access to wealth, power, and prestige, those who attain it usually attract and maintain clusters of kin around them. The poor in both rural and urban communities tend to resemble one another in that they are organized around small and unstable family groupings. The powerful in both rural and urban sectors are alike in that they frequently use part of their wealth or influence to develop and maintain large, long-lasting kin groups.

Alan Duben and Cem Behar (1991) have examined how Istanbul households were transformed between the years 1880 and 1940 in a study remarkable for its detail and scope. One important finding was that household size and fertility roughly paralleled what was happening in Western Europe, and that by the 1930s, urban populations were just reproducing themselves, while rural population growth continued unabated. In Istanbul, however, Muslim fertility declined, and "the quality of life of the children brought into the world, their health, proper socialization and education, became a major focus of the attention of parents" (p. 242). Istanbul became, in their view, the first Middle Eastern city whose population began what is known as the "demographic transition" toward low fertility, and as such was a warning to anyone who would axiomatically associate Islamic culture with high birth rates. As Andrew Mango (1993) points out, one has to see the forces that worked to shape Istanbul's dynamics in order to understand similar trends happening elsewhere in the region today. Istanbul households developed in a culture different than the Anatolian hinterland, but one that has now spread widely—a culture that favors small conjugal units, frowns on polygyny, and emphasizes marriages based on affection and compatibility (Duben & Behar, 1991, p. 246).

MIGRATION AND THE HOUSEHOLD

The transformation of Middle Eastern rural and urban life that we have described throughout this book has had a profound and differently felt impact on men and women, on rural and urban households, and even on different classes and ethnic groups. In some areas agricultural development and mechanization have generated new rural wealth and a class of landowners whose family members of both sexes benefit from access to public education and professional training. At the same time, the consolidation of small farms is driving many peasants off the land and forcing them to lead impoverished lives in urban slums. Here the real social costs may be far greater for women than for their husbands, who at least control what meager resources they live upon.

For women, one paradox is that under certain circumstances a move from a village to a town or city may increase rather than decrease some aspects of their seclusion and spatial segregation. Whereas men almost immediately adopt city dress and have more places to go for entertainment and diversion, women usually retain village dress and may even adopt the veil worn traditionally by lower-class urban women. Women in rural areas generally move relatively freely and unveiled because their neighbors are also relatives. Once in an urban setting, this is often not the case, and the women may then veil as they find themselves in public spaces and in proximity to strangers. Veiling and the seclusion of women may also indicate an upward social move, as it symbolizes the fact that the family has acquired the means to free women from work outside the home. It is only over the long term that urban residence is reflected in changed attitudes about seclusion and increased emphasis on female education

In cases where migration involves only the males of the household, the consequences for women vary, depending on such factors as age, social class, educational level, and duration of migration. Certainly communities with heavy male out-migration see a rise in de facto women-headed households, where, in the absence of adult males, the wives take charge in areas formerly the domain of their husbands. The implications of this phenomenon for family relationships are not self-evident, however. In Egypt, for example, the high rate of male migration to Saudi Arabia and the Gulf states has led to what some refer to as the "feminization of the Egyptian family." Homa Hoodfar (1996a), who studied the impact of male migration in a Cairo neighborhood, notes that whereas lower-class and uneducated women managed to improve their status within the household, better-educated, white-collar, employed wives, in contrast, lost ground to their husbands. In the latter case, where previously both husband and wife earned the same income, allowing the wife an equal voice in family decisions, the migrant husband now earned considerably more cash, undermining the wife's claim to equality. Hoodfar's conclusion is worth quoting here:

> Ironically, male migration, which has put women in the unconventional position of heading their own households, regardless of whether it resulted in more or less power for the wives, has also strengthened the more traditional marriage ideology in which the husband remains the unequivocal breadwinner and the wife financially dependent mother and homemaker. . . . Migration may have resulted in the "feminization of the Egyptian family" but it has also reaffirmed the essence of traditional gender ideology, which perpetuates the situation in which women are financially dependent on their male folk, despite some superficial changes in the realm of activities they may perform. (p. 73)

International labor migration, which is particularly important in Turkey, Egypt, Yemen, Jordan, and Lebanon, and affects both rural and urban households, has a similar impact. Women living in households with no adult males come to play wider social roles than they had formerly. Another consequence of labor migration is that women themselves may leave the countryside to join their husbands in the cities or abroad. Once there, it is not uncommon for them to take wage jobs. There are about 3 million Turkish workers and dependents in northwest European countries. Of these, well over one-third are women, many of whom arrived in Europe as spouses but soon found work outside the home. Others were recruited directly from Turkey, coming even from rural areas. In the initial phase of labor migration, many parents who would be reluctant to have a single daughter live alone in a Turkish city actively supported their daughters' seeking work abroad. Having a family member employed abroad conferred social status as well as being an important source of income. The risk of bringing shame to the family was minimized by the fact that Europe was acknowledged to have a different sexual code, one in which more independent behavior by females was accepted. This supports our contention that the codes of sexual modesty have to be understood within particular social and political contexts.

MARRIAGE

Rich or poor, large or small, almost all families in the Middle East seek to control marriage, which is viewed as essentially a union between families rather than between two individuals. Marriage is very often employed to reaffirm or strengthen existing familial ties, as well as to build new ones where none existed before. There is, in fact, a frequently expressed preference in the Arab world for marriages between first cousins and in particular between a man and his father's brother's daughter (henceforth FBD). This latter preference, which is by no means universal, is often described in the literature as a peculiarity of Middle Eastern marriage systems. The early Islamic precedent cannot be discounted in affirming the preference for FBD marriage, and even as Islam spreads today in Africa, this preference for close-cousin marriage often follows. 'Ali, cousin of the Prophet, married Fatima, the Prophet's daughter, quite likely following a well-established pre-Islamic practice. Thus, for some Muslims, such a marriage as a celebration of religious tradition is reason enough to stipulate it as an ideal.

We must , however, be wary in ascribing undue structural significance to the expressed preference for marrying a FBD, as the available studies indicate a wide range of variability in marriage practice, even within communities in which this preference is strongly voiced. Moreover, too few studies utilizing representative samples have been published to allow easy generalization about its prevalence. What we can safely say, however, is that there is a strong tendency for people in general to marry cousins, and that this practice tends to be shared by Muslims and (many) Christians alike. The Shari'a establishes the rules of exogamy, whom a person may not marry, as these prohibitions are clearly stated in the Quran as follows:

> Forbidden unto you are your mothers, and your daughters, and your sisters, and your father's sisters, and your mother's sisters, and your brother's daughters and your sister's daughters, and your foster mothers, and your foster sisters, and your mother-in-law, and your step-daughters who are under your protection (born) of your women unto whom you have gone in—but if ye have not gone in unto them, then it is no sin for you (to marry their daughters)—and the wives of your sons who (spring) from your loins. And (it is forbidden unto you) that ye should have two sisters together except what hath already happened (of that nature) in the past. Lo! Allah is ever forgiving, Merciful. (Quran 4:23)

As we have said, rates of cousin marriage vary greatly from group to group and, indeed, even among different strata of the same community. For example, in her study of marriage and property in an Arabic-speaking village in southeastern Turkey, Barbara Aswad (1971) found that a significantly higher percentage of first marriages contracted by the landowners were with the father's brother's daughter. This was in marked contrast to marriages among the poor and landless. In a sample of 473 marriages among the Yörük of southeastern Turkey, Daniel Bates (1973) found that nearly 22 percent involved women married to their father's brother's son. About 40 percent of the marriages in the same sample were between first cousins and second cousins of all sorts.

In the small settled Bedouin community of Awlad 'Ali, Lila Abu-Lughod (1986) reports a high incidence of patrilateral parallel cousin marriage; four out of the five heads of the core households (out of a total of 15) had married their father's brother's daughter. Of those who had taken a second wife, three had married a more distant paternal relative. According to Abu-Lughod, women find a number of advantages in this type of marriage. Having a paternal kinsman for a husband gives a woman more rights and sense of security since it is the duty of the paternal male kin to protect and take care of their agnatically related womenfolk. Women are also less dependent economically on their husbands, since in these cases both husband and wife often share a common patrimony. Moreover, it also means that a bride does not have to leave her close kin and familiar community to live with "strangers."

Close endogamy is common throughout the region, even among Christians, since there is a tendency for families of high status and groups controlling important resources to marry close relatives. From this wider perspective, marriage with father's brother's daughter or another close relative is simply an extreme expression of generalized endogamy, the principle that states that people should marry within their lineage, community, village, and social class. In fact, this preference for equality of status of the bride and groom is expressed in a Shari'a-based marriage rule termed *kafa'a*. Among most Muslims this rule demands that the couple be of the same or equivalent social background, but it does not spell out exactly how this equivalency is to be determined. Even though the rule of *kafa'a* is rarely invoked as a legal impediment to a marriage that has been agreed upon by the families, it does establish the basis for negotiations over the amount of bride wealth, which is often viewed as symbolic of the relative status of the families involved.

Also important to understanding marriage endogamy are patterns of inheritance, especially among people with considerable property. As we have seen, the Shari'a entitles a woman to a share of her father's property. Among poorer families in most communities, daughters are customarily excluded from claiming their share, but among the wealthy, women generally claim what is theirs. Under these circumstances, even though the formation of large patrimonial estates is precluded by partible inheritance, a cluster of close relatives can maintain continuity of control over contiguous plots of land by marrying among themselves. This helps to explain why control over marriage of women is usually a more important issue among the propertied classes than among the landless. Thus, close endogamy is one more mechanism used by local families

A traditional Yörük bride and family and contemporary Yörük newlyweds.

of note to perpetuate their position. The same strategy is also practiced by families that have claims to saintly descent and holy lineages; in other words, close endogamy functions to perpetuate material wealth and symbolic capital. Educated middle-class families are abandoning this practice as their increasingly independent-minded sons and daughters take an active role in choosing their own spouses.

In close endogamy, the created affinal or in-law ties go beyond immediate economic expediency. The renewal or reinforcement of existing relationships through intermarriage announces to the community the importance of the particular family as an enduring group. In marrying a close cousin, a man not only expresses his close association with his uncle or other relative but also affirms the fact that his own father and his father-in-law are on close terms.

There are, however, enclaves of Muslim populations who, in custom and practice, scrupulously avoid marriage with kin of any degree. They are primarily of Caucasian or Balkan origin, for example, the widely dispersed Circassians, for whom kin exogamy is a marriage requirement. In addition, in some countries, especially Turkey, the government seeks to discourage kin marriage on the grounds that it carries a genetic risk. Carol Delaney (1991) writes that the villagers she knows discount this warning, saying that they always marry close kin, and should a child be born deformed for genetic reasons, it is because the parents were inadvertently made *süt kardeş*, or blood siblings, having been nursed by the same woman.

Given the importance of affinity in expressing and maintaining social and political ties, it is not surprising that polygyny, or marriage with more than one wife, is permitted in Islam. A verse in the Quran allows the man to marry up to four wives at any time, provided he treats them equally. A later passage (4:3) seems to add another restriction on the practice: "Ye are never able to be fair and just as between women even if it is your ardent desire."[2] Among traditional propertied classes, particularly in the rural areas, a man might marry a close cousin for his first wife and take a second wife from another family, thus extending his social and political network. Again, as in the case of marriage with the father's brother's daughter, rates of polygynous marriages vary greatly from one community to another and in terms of social background and class. Apart from Saudi Arabia and the Gulf states, it is rarely encountered among urban-dwelling upper- and middle-class families. In fact, as we will see in Chapter 9, modern legislation in some countries has either forbidden it completely or has put impediments to its practice.

Comparative data are still lacking on the incidence of polygyny. It seems, however, to be most frequent among traditional landowning families in communities in which secular education is not very significant, among the sheikhs of the Gulf region and their wealthy counterparts among the tribal populations

---

[2] For an excellent discussion of the different interpretations of the Quran and the Hadith as it relates to women's status, see Barbara Stowasser (1994).

everywhere.[3] Wealthy Türkmen of northern Iran almost always keep polygy-nous households. Increasingly, however, these same families are sending their daughters to school, and polygyny will quite likely decline. Even where it is still practiced, the ability to maintain a polygynous household contributes less and less status to the male.

Monogamy, always the practice of the majority, is increasingly becoming the preferred form of marriage. This reflects social as well as economic changes in the society, among which are the decrease in infant mortality, which encourages families to have fewer children, and the increasing costs of rearing and educating children. Moreover, in every country, new values stressing romantic love and companionate marriage are disseminated by television and other media. In Egypt, for example, soap operas frequently present polygyny in a negative light and raise debates about its legitimacy. The increasing value placed on monogamy also reflects the rapidly changing status of women. No longer confined to exclu-sively domestic roles, women increasingly pursue jobs and attain status in their own right, a development that is incompatible with the personal restrictions inherent in traditional polygynous marriage. In the cities, the increased opportu-nities for women to be educated and employed outside the home further discour-age polygyny, which is increasingly viewed by educated men and women alike as exploitative of women and incompatible with modern life.

Among the Shi'a, especially in Iran, there is an alternative form of "mar-riage" termed *mut'a* or more popularly *sigheh*, the validity of which was reaf-firmed by the late Ayatollah Khomeini and even more recently by other senior clerics, sparking controversy among women's groups. Strictly forbidden by Sunni law, *mut'a*, also known as "temporary marriage," is believed to be pre-Islamic in origin. It refers to a contract between a man and an unmarried woman (who may be divorced or widowed) in which the amount of money to be paid by the man and the duration of the marriage are clearly specified. Chil-dren of such a marriage are, in principle, recognized as legitimate and may inherit from their father. Shahla Haeri (1989) states that although they are legal, women who enter into these "marriages" are, in fact, stigmatized and marginal-ized, especially since such arrangements are not registered as marriages. Iran-ian women's groups have been vocal in their opposition to the *mut'a* marriage, which they see as devaluing women, the marriage bond, and the family.

MARRIAGE ARRANGEMENTS AND WEDDING CEREMONIES

Throughout the region marriage is still customarily initiated by negotiations between families rather than the outcome of individually pursued courtship. Of

---

[3] For an interesting examination of how marriages are used to consolidate households, forge alliances, and settle disputes among a tribal population in Afghanistan, see Nancy Tapper (1991). See also Martha Mundy (1995) for the Yemen.

course, rapid changes are occurring, particularly in cities, where open forms of courtship are increasingly evident. In Cairo, male and female students at the universities attend classes together, and there is considerable socializing outside the classroom. As a consequence, marriages among the educated are very much the result of individual choice, though it is rare that any marriage will go against expressed family wishes. This pattern for the educated classes is generally true throughout the Middle East, except perhaps for Saudi Arabia. In Turkey, the freedom of courtship is widely established even among the less educated working class, but still parental approval for marriage seems the norm.

Despite the increase in individually initiated courtship in some sectors of contemporary society, the prevailing normative pattern remains that of familial negotiation and arrangements. Even when courtship results in a choice of a spouse or even in cases of elopement, the families ultimately go through the process of a formal meeting and agreement. One important part of the negotiations is the nature and amount of the *mahr,* an Arabic term that is widely used by non-Arabic speakers as well, and is usually translated as "bride wealth" or "bride price." In the Arab countries of North Africa, the *mahr* is commonly referred to as *sdaq.* The *mahr* remains significant not simply because of its possible economic value, but because it is required by Islamic law to validate any marriage contract. Thus, bride wealth is more than a folk custom carried over by force of tradition.

The *mahr* is an agreed upon sum of money or durable property that the husband agrees to pay his wife at any time prior to or during marriage or upon divorce. Technically speaking, the preponderance of legal opinion is that the *mahr* should become the property of the bride herself. In practice, where significant amounts are involved, the *mahr,* or a good part of it, often remains with her

Kurdish street musicians in Aleppo, Syria playing at a wedding party.

father or guardian. Again, there is much local variation as well as differences within communities according to social class, education, and even family reputation. In some communities or among some ethnic groups, the *mahr* may be regarded as fixed, and in any particular period, all will pay approximately the same sum. The Türkmen of Iran illustrate this approach with a tradition that bride wealth must amount to the cash equivalent of ten horses. In some rural communities in Turkey, agreement has been reached to fix bride price at a consistent and low amount, and thus to avoid the rampant inflation in the *mahr*, or *başlık* in Turkey, which afflicted many communities. In some countries such as Iran and Egypt, inflation in *mahr* payments has become a national issue debated at all levels of the society. Islamist groups often call for placing limits on the *mahr* as they decry its commercialization.

Even in communities in which a high *mahr* is the norm, some families, usually the wealthy, may make ostentatious efforts to demonstrate that the *mahr* does in fact go to their daughters in the form of jewelry, furniture, property, and so on. Among the urban elite, there is great variation in how the *mahr* is handled. In the large cities of Turkey, there is strong sentiment that the *mahr* be considered strictly symbolic, with only a token exchange or even none at all. In provincial towns or villages, however, the *mahr* may indeed involve a very substantial payment. In other countries, for example Iran, the publicly announced amounts of the *mahr* may be greatly inflated because families strive to display their status in this manner. The actual payment, on the other hand, may be only a small portion of the announced amount. Even the percentage of the *mahr* actually given the bride can vary for many reasons. Some families might give less of the *mahr* to a daughter they have put through school or formal vocational training, the implication being that the father is to be compensated for this and for the increased earning power she will bring to her husband.

A common rule regarding *mahr*, if a formal written contract is drawn up, is that about one-third of the negotiated sum is paid upon marriage, and the balance is held as security against the possibility of a future repudiation of the wife by her husband. If this is spelled out in the marriage contract, it can be considered as a form of anticipated alimony. This is common among the elite of the region, except in Turkey. Even when people frankly acknowledge that the sum may be unrealistically high or that its collection will be highly improbable, it serves in some circles as an index of social status, or at least pretension. In rural society, this practice is rarely encountered except among wealthy landowners.

Marriage arrangements among the poorer segments of the rural populations as described in ethnographic accounts often resemble a straightforward exchange of a woman for money or goods, with little pretext of providing the bride with a comparable trousseau or insurance against possible repudiation. The *mahr* here becomes a bride price, and the family is compensated for the loss of the woman's labor and childbearing potential. The money received is used to acquire a bride for a son or for any other purpose a family decides upon.

Bride wealth, however paid, is never divided among members of the extended family in the Middle East, as it is in many other parts of the world to emphasize the collective responsibility of the larger kin groups toward their members. In the Middle East the emphasis is on the primacy of the rights and obligations of the father or his surrogate and to a lesser extent of the paternal uncle toward the woman. In this sense, marriage is primarily the concern of a very restricted familial grouping, rather than the collective responsibility of such larger social entities as the lineage, clan, or village.

Traditionally, and often today, the boy's family initiates the search for a bride among "honorable and reputable" families. Steps here are informal and involve only indirect contacts. The initial steps of the negotiations fall on the women of the households. Only after agreement has been reached on all the important particulars is a formal meeting arranged, again involving female relatives of both households. At this juncture, if all goes well, the boy's side will send male intermediaries to formally request the girl's hand in marriage and to reach an understanding on the value of the *mahr*.

The next major step is an engagement ceremony, again involving women coming together and exchanging gifts. The bride-to-be symbolically indicates her respect and formal subordination to her future mother-in-law by kissing her hand publicly. This ceremony stresses the importance of the mother/daughter-in-law relationship, and the presence of the women of the two households symbolizes the union of the two kin groups. Following this, perhaps as long as a year later, a formal marriage is presided over by a religious functionary. Participants in this ceremony also include the groom, two witnesses, and a representative of the bride's family. In certain Turkish communities, as is often the case elsewhere, the bride's physical presence is not required. Both the groom and the representative of the bride are asked three times if they concur to the marriage; upon affirmative answers to each inquiry, the ceremony is complete.

Following the ceremony, the bride is transported with much to-do from her natal home to that of her father-in-law. Even if she is to reside in a separate dwelling with her new husband, she must nevertheless be taken first to her father-in-law's house, a further symbolic emphasis of the new ties between the two families. Susan Dorsky (1986) describes the arrangements and ceremonies involved in Arab weddings at a town in central Yemen, 'Amran. What follows is a brief account based on Dorsky's ethnography.

In 'Amran, parents and guardians arrange all marriages; men dominate the arrangements, although women play an important advisory role. In selecting a bride for their son, parents rank health, good temperment, and competence in household tasks as very important. While beauty is also valued, it is not considered as important as the other attributes. In theory, neither sons nor daughters can be coerced into marriage, as they have the right to refuse a match; in practice, this can be difficult. Once the match is decided, the next step involves the negotiation of the *mahr*. A portion of the *mahr* goes directly to the bride, with the larger portion going to her father and/or brothers. Dorsky writes that women strongly supported the institution of the *mahr* and saw a high amount as an affirmation of their worth and of the value of their labor.

Weddings, in general, involve two parts. The first is a private legal ritual in which a marriage contract, *'aqd* or *kitab*, is drawn up and witnessed by a judge, *qadi*, or some religious functionary; the contract represents the agreement worked out between the fathers or guardians of the groom and the bride regarding the terms of the marriage. The judge or cleric must, in principle, formally obtain the bride's consent to the marriage before the contract is signed to ensure that she is not being coerced. The second part involves the public celebration, *farah*, which follows the signing of the legal agreement

Several weeks before the wedding, female relatives of both the groom and the bride begin to prepare for the round of celebrations that mark a Yemeni wedding. Food and clothes are bought and a *muzzayyina* (female dresser-cum-entertainer) is hired; the *muzzayyina* has an important role to play at weddings. She (and often her all-female band) perform and entertain the women at the many prewedding parties that are held by the families of the bride and the groom; she also dresses and makes up the bride on the wedding day and leads her to the groom.

A few days before the wedding, the bride's father and the groom, along with several male witnesses, meet to draw up the marriage contract, after which the *fatiha*, or the first verse of the Quran, is recited. At this stage, the bride is expected to stay inside her house and do no work for the week preceding the wedding. Three days before the wedding, accompanied by her friends and relatives, she is taken to the public bath, *hamam*, where she bathes, puts on new clothes, and has her peaked bonnet removed (this bonnet is worn by all unmarried girls in rural Yemen). Upon her return home, the bride's hands and forearms are decorated with henna.

The remaining days before the wedding are punctuated with parties at the houses of both the bride and the groom. The high point of one party is the public presentation of the gifts, which are announced by the *muzzayyina*. On the wedding day, the women prepare a feast for the male guests who begin to arrive at the groom's house in the afternoon. Later that evening, the groom and his male guests depart to pray at a nearby mosque. They then return home in a slow procession through the town accompanied by youths who carry lanterns and trays with lighted candles. A professional singer leads the procession and the men sing religious chants. Ululating women and children watch from the rooftops.

Later that night, the bride is brought to the groom, who waits for her at his house. The married couple spend the next week at home in relative isolation during which they are not expected to do any work.[4]

---

[4] For a more detailed description of weddings in Yemen, albeit among a wealthier group in a small coastal town, see Anne Meneley (1996).

RESIDENCE

Residence after marriage tend to follows a regular pattern, which can be instrumental in shaping the organization of the local community, particularly where people continue to reside in close association with their relatives. The primary rule of postmarital residence in the Middle East is patrilocality, where the bride leaves her natal home to reside with her husband. He, in turn, by custom and practice, usually continues, at least for a time, to reside with his father or in close proximity to him.

As we mentioned earlier, although there is much variation in terms of the actual composition of households and of the neighborhoods they form, the incorporation of the wife into her husband's family or household is virtually universal. It is rare to find a man physically joining the household of his wife's father, although the practice of establishing a separate residence near her kin frequently occurs. It is explicitly felt in almost all sectors of Middle Eastern society that it is somewhat humiliating for a man to reside with his father-in-law because it would indicate that his family lacks social status or sufficient resources. It puts the groom in position of subservience to the authority of his father-in-law. While it is considered natural for a son to be under his father's direct or day-to-day authority, this does not extend to the father-in-law, even when the father-in-law is a close relative. Even a man's father's brother, who enjoys a generalized position of authority, is not normally considered of the same status as his own father. Furthermore, should the bride's father be forced by circumstances to move into his son-in-law's home, he would suffer a similar loss of status, as this would bring him under the authority of his son-in-law. However, if a widower were to join his son's household, he would continue to occupy at least a nominal position as head of the household and senior male.

As mentioned earlier, there is a widespread feeling that a man should avoid informal contact with his wife's parents in the first years of marriage. Such meetings as occur are likely to be ceremonial meals and visits. This avoidance clearly serves to minimize the potential friction attending the process of the transfer of responsibility for a woman from one male-defined group to another. As we might expect, the period of formality and avoidance is considerably less when close relatives intermarry.

The transfer of authority over women deserves some elaboration, as it points to some aspects of interfamily dynamics. Immediately after marriage, the husband assumes sexual rights, while his father or male surrogate assumes direct responsibility for the general well-being of the bride.[5] In this sense the bride becomes part of another household under the authority of other males of her father's generation. In fact, one often hears, in Arabic or Turkish, the new

---

[5] An interesting exception to the general rule is found among the Yomut Türkmen, where a man is expected to cohabit with his wife only some years after their marriage. Until then, she continues to live with her father, and her husband has no visiting rights.

bride referred to as "our bride" ('*aroustna* in Arabic; *gelinimiz* in Turkish) by members of the groom's family. However, the responsibility for the bride's good conduct and reputation ultimately remains with her father or brothers; only with the passage of time and with the bearing of sons is that responsibility completely relinquished. In this sense, the movement of the woman into a new family or household is seen as a gradual process of incorporation and not as a single event. As we have said, the woman never loses her identity as a member of her natal agnatic group, and she continues to partake in the social status of her father as much as or more than in that of her husband.

CONJUGAL VERSUS DESCENT TIES

Conjugal ties, however important for the formation and maintenance of households, do not supersede the jural rights stemming from descent. For example, in the event of the death or divorce of the wife, the ongoing household unit is based on the relationship of a man to his children, or even his grandchildren. Under no circumstances is it expected that children would come under the control of the woman's natal family. Further, when a woman is divorced, upon reaching a certain age (generally six years), her children revert to the custody of their father or his male kin. Unmarried children of the same father but of different mothers usually reside together and maintain close ties, being of one family. Children of different fathers but sharing the same mother rarely reside together and may not, in practice, recognize a close relationship unless their fathers are also close relatives.

The jural primacy of patrilineal ties is further evidenced in cases in which a man dies and leaves small children. They are usually taken under the custody of their father's closest male agnate, usually his father or older brother. Thus, if his widow remarries, she will most likely have to leave her children behind. Faced with this, a common but not universal practice is for the widow to marry one of her husband's brothers, if this is convenient. This practice, found among some Jewish and other non-Muslim groups as well, is known as the *levirate*.

It is obvious that there is an inherent potential for tension and even conflict between the demands arising from conjugality and the expectations and jural rights based on lineal ties. Marriage, while serving to reinforce ongoing relationships, can easily lead to contradictory demands on the loyalties and commitments of family members. The expectation everywhere is that sons should cooperate closely with their father, brothers, and close agnates. However, once married and separated from the domicile and direct authority of his father, a man may well find that he is increasingly drawn into the sphere of activities of his wife's family. This is quite understandable if we consider that the wife's sense of identification and desire to be with her natal family is as strong as that of her spouse. Women tend to prize the intimacy and relative informality of their brothers' company, and as a woman bears children she will seek to visit with her family members regularly. When disagreements or disputes arise among close agnates, it is very likely that some will increasingly turn to other relatives for support, including their wife's kin. Affines thus potentially exert a centrifugal pull on a man's loyalty; this is expressed in any number of proverbs and folk sayings to the effect that to allow one's son to "marry out" is to lose him.

The fact that close-cousin marriage is common does not necessarily resolve the potentially conflicting demands on the loyalties of the individual. Indeed, as has been suggested, it may exacerbate conflict under certain circumstances. If a man is married to a close matrilateral or even a distant agnatic relative, already existing social relationships to his wife's kinspeople may be strengthened at the expense of ties to even closer agnates. Even when a marriage is arranged among close agnates, it is not uncommon for hard feelings to be aroused in the process. There may be other closely related families who also feel that they should have been consulted, or even that their own son or daughter was slighted. In many communities, some of the most enduring intrafamilial disputes involve disagreements over marriage arrangements.

Despite the presence of a strong descent ideology and the importance of patronymic groupings and jural rights stemming from patrilineality, the individual's kin circle of interaction is quite open and flexible. Given the men's ability to shift their alliances to different sets of relatives, families that depend on shared resources such as property or political power have a great concern in regulating marriage. Families whose households rely on wages or individual sources of income are far less concerned with containing marriages within a narrow group. As the economic trend is toward increasingly individuated sources of income, we see a corollary to this in the decreasing importance of close intrafamily marriage and a corresponding increase in the significance of the conjugal bond.

We also see this expressed in the larger patterns of village and neighborhood organization and in settlement patterns. Increasingly, new households are establishing themselves whenever they can gain access to sufficient resources, even when this means moving to distant cities or settling on government-sponsored land-reclamation projects far from their natal families. Settlement patterns for many agricultural regions traditionally reflected the distribution of related patronymic groups. Today this is changing in many areas, as local governments sponsor agricultural projects and village housing and encourage movement to facilitate rural development.

GENERAL OVERVIEW

In most big cities today, the severe housing shortage and new economic realities have altered preexisting patterns of residence. In Cairo, middle- and working-class households locate wherever they are lucky enough to find accommodations.

Entire communities are built up around factories. In Baghdad, as in other Iraqi cities, the government sponsored the development of neighborhoods based on occupational groups. For example, officers, engineers, high school teachers, and so on, are entitled to house sites or apartments at special rates. In every country we see the emergence of new neighborhoods that are fairly homogeneous in terms of income and class. The increasing mobility of middle-class households and the resulting instability of newer neighborhoods have resulted in a decline in the importance of the social role of the neighbor among this sector of the population. Being a neighbor, *jar* in Arabic and *komşu* in Turkish, traditionally implied a specific set of mutual expectations and behavior. This is also true for Iran, where the term for neighbor is *hamsoyeh*. The word *soyeh* means both shade and shadow; *hamsoyeh* thus refers to people who share the same shade or shadow. One shares the cool shade with a good neighbor and falls under a dark shadow with a bad neighbor. Having a bad neighbor is considered one of the worst misfortunes in Iran (Gita Rangbaran, personal communication). The mutual support and informal visiting that characterize relations between neighbors parallel, in many regards, the responsibilities and obligations one has to close kin.

Although we have just emphasized increasing mobility, most Middle Eastern communities still reflect residential patterns based on kinship, common descent, and ethnicity. A household that depends on access to land or other local resources will in turn depend on recognition of specific rights and the support of others in the community. When conflict or disagreement arises over property rights, the matter is often settled within the community on the basis of the support each contender can muster for his claim. One tends to reside when possible near those with whom one is identified politically and socially. Most villages—indeed, traditional urban neighborhoods—are politically factionalized, and faction membership is congruent with actual residence in a particular area or neighborhood of the town or village. Even when rural people migrate to the city, they try to establish themselves near already settled kinspeople; similarly, modern housing developments also tend to reflect clear regional, ethnic, or tribal patterns. This is not that different from what we see in large American cities, where immigrants tend to cluster together with their compatriots.

In Baghdad, newly arrived migrants usually begin by living with relatives and in time, as they find jobs, move to places of their own, not far from their relatives and fellow tribesmen who act as an informal organization to assist them in their new environment. Loyalties to tribal sheikhs are maintained in the city and, paradoxically, may even be strengthened. Whereas in the countryside the tribe tended to be dispersed over a wide area, in the city its members are brought into closer daily contact and mutual dependency. The close proximity of different groups of migrants and city people reinforces the sense of ethnicity and makes the immigrants rally around their traditional leaders, who now assume new roles as spokesmen and brokers for their group vis-à-vis the government bureaucracy. Neighborhood mosques and coffee- and teahouses serve as meeting places and public forums for the migrant community.

The emphasis in this chapter has been on the uses of kinship and kinship network groups formed by patrilineal descent, marriage, and patterns of residence. We have tried to introduce the most basic elements of social organization that might be considered the building blocks of Middle Eastern society. Throughout we have stressed the principles that influence group formation and group life; in the next chapter we shift our focus to a consideration of the role and status of women in the Middle East today, a subject of considerable interest, debate, and controversy.

9

Women and the Social Order

The role and status of women in Muslim society in general and in the Middle East in particular is a complex and vexed subject, and is the focus of emotional debates and heated polemics both within Muslim societies and beyond. The political ascendancy of Islamist groups in recent years has further inflamed the issue and reinforced the Western perception that the status of Muslim women is solely determined by their religion. Even Muslim feminists from a range of perspectives have joined the fray with arguments that may be broadly grouped into two general camps, although both address Islamic issues. Some argue that the traditional Quranic and Shari'a view of women as the weak and legally subordinate sex (for example, lacking the same rationality as men) poses a serious impediment to women's full emancipation and to their achievement of equality in both the private and public domains. For them, Islamic law is an anachronism. Others counter by saying that Islam, the religion, is not the problem and that restrictions placed on women are the result of patriarchal attitudes in society, reinforced by male religious scholars who monopolize the interpretation of the Quran and the formulation of the Shari'a (Mernissi, 1991; Afkhami, 1994). Quite apart from feminists and politicians, individuals from all segments of society have opinions on this topic, as it touches virtually every aspect of the moral order. Of course, pious men and women view the Islamic codes as offering appropriate protection for women and a basis for stable family life.

The fact that there is wide variation in local custom and in adherence to Quranic precepts and religious laws indicates that the status of women has to be understood not only with reference to Islamic values and norms but also in terms of the specific socioeconomic and political contexts in which women live. Homa Hoodfar, at the beginning of her study of Cairo women and their households, puts it eloquently: "It was [with reference to many studies which look mainly to Islam to understand women's social position] Muslims, and in particular Middle Eastern people, who lived in the realm of ideology and religion, while the rest of the world lived with the economic structure" (1997, p. 15). An Egyptian Bedouin, a Syrian cabinet minister, an Iraqi architect, and an Iranian poet may have little in common besides the fact that they are at once female and Muslim. Nevertheless, there is no denying that textual and scriptural Islam has clear guidelines concerning the legal and social status and the appropriate behavior of women. This is very precisely summarized by Katerina Dalacoura (1999) as she surveys the human rights issues confronting Muslim women and the forces for and against "liberalism" rooted in Islamic thought and theory (to which we will turn in Chapter 11). In short, while looking to general patterns and modalities, we must avoid a theological reductionism or making Islam a single or even primary explanatory factor in gender relations.

Bearing this in mind, we now turn to a consideration of some of the underlying values, patterns, and institutions that distinguish this part of the world and that impart a distinctive tone to the issue of women. Our intent is to explore some of the values and codes that inform aspects of individual behavior and give meaning to the lives of people in the Middle East. We are aware that systems of meaning and values in any society are difficult to describe analytically. We all too often end up informing ourselves by means of our own values, prejudices, and biases, or by seizing upon a few points of contrast to describe a complex

Young Arab women learning needlework at a community center in Lebanon.

Iranian craftsman and young apprentices making copper plates. Boys are socialized at an early age to apprentice at the workplace.

reality. To an outsider, the Middle East presents many images, some of which tempt the unwary to make easy generalizations—for example, about male dominance, sexual segregation, and the tyranny of the codes of honor and modesty. A familiarity with the region and the peoples, their languages and cultures dispels easy stereotypes, and the challenge is to fit the wealth of observed variation in attitudes and behavior into some sort of order.

SOCIALIZATION AND SEX ROLES

Individuals are socialized within families to fulfill certain role expectations, and in the process they come to view themselves as having appropriate social identities. Studies of socialization patterns in the Middle East all emphasize early differentiation in the care and handling of boys and girls (Wikan, 1982; Delaney, 1991). A number of generalizations emerge from these studies which, although they ignore class and educational differences, still have considerable utility. For example, sons are frequently favored at the expense of daughters, and children are taught early on ways of behaving in public that are appropriate to their gender. A young girl will quickly learn that her brother has first claim to family resources, including food, living space, spending money, and clothing. A village woman with no sons is frequently pitied almost as much as a woman incapable of bearing children at all. She may, in fact, be divorced on this account, although her husband might not have community approval should he do so.

Social recognition and the inherent prestige of having sons are such that women themselves reinforce this value. They treat their sons with favoritism and indulgence. The birth of a son is usually met with celebration, that of a girl is, relatively, ignored. Later, the son's circumcision is celebrated with joy and public acclamation. No comparable event awaits a young girl; in fact, the onset of menses is considered shameful and is kept secret. In Egypt and the Sudan, where female circumcision is widely practiced, especially in rural areas, it is not viewed as an event for private or public celebration. In many rural communities, even a wedding is considered a celebration for the groom's family and may not be treated with equal enthusiasm by the bride's family. The bride is expected to be sad on her wedding day, and she often cries at leaving her father's house. A widespread custom associated with village weddings in Turkey, Iran, and many Arab countries is a ritual enactment of "bride theft." The bride is taken, a sham kidnap, by a party from the groom's family amid wails of protest by the women of her household.

In villages and working-class homes, girls are given domestic tasks and responsibilities and are placed under strict supervision from an early age; it is not unusual to see girls of six and seven already charged with the care of younger siblings. In rural homes adolescent girls serve at the command of younger brothers, much as they do later for their husbands and fathers-in-law. When guests are present, women, their daughters, and infant sons stay apart from male gatherings in the house, eating separately in seclusion; young boys are encouraged to sit quietly with the older males. Young women, even small girls, are kept constantly busy with domestic chores. The duties of the boys, such as shepherding, accompanying their fathers to market, or apprenticeship at some workshop, often take them away from the home; in contrast, as they grow older, girls find their activities increasingly restricted to the home.

Bonds of affection and emotion within the family appear to reflect these specific patterns of socialization. Boys, in particular, become very emotionally attached to their mothers, who remain throughout their lifetimes virtually the only adult women to whom they can show affection in public. Fathers are more apt to play authoritarian roles vis-à-vis their sons, with whom they generally maintain a distant and formal relationship. Daughters, on the other hand, often enjoy more relaxed and warmer interpersonal relationships with their fathers. As Abdelwahab Bouhdiba (1997) notes, albeit without reference to a specific community, the mother tends to play the role of buffer between the father and the children and interposes herself if a threat arises. She knows how to mediate, and most often she manages to get the father to yield. A true joking relationship exists between a mother and her son; even licentious or bawdy remarks or more or less indiscreet allusions to sexual taboos, despite the strict customs, are not exceptional.

Carol Delaney's study (1991) of an Anatolian village is a detailed examination of sex, gender, and sexuality. She states that in everyday village life, sex, politics, education, and religion are inextricably interwoven. Little girls learn at an early age to undervalue themselves relative to their brothers, to regard their bodies as potentially unclean and spiritually polluting, and to be ashamed (or at least to give that appearance) of their sexuality. At the onset of menarch, a girl begins to wear the head scarf, which announces that she is subject to the code of shame or *namus*, recognizes Islamic virtues, and her sexuality is under the control of her father and brothers until marriage—and even afterward. She is taught not to pray during her menses, nor to read the Quran or to visit holy tombs or shrines.

Delaney reports that villagers see little need to educate their daughters, and, moreover, regard the enterprise as dangerous to family honor. To appear in public without what is locally regarded as dress appropriate to a Muslim woman is to be "open," or *açık,* which means both visible to the stares of men and potentially open to inappropriate thoughts and impulses. Delaney describes a young girl's hair as representing "the rampant fecundity, beauty, and seductiveness of the world as well as the entanglements by which men are ensnared."

Against this backdrop, she describes a young girl who had excelled while attending the obligatory primary school, and who wanted to continue in the village middle school where attendance is voluntary.[1] Her father, reflecting wider village sentiments, was adamant that she not go on, because she would have to attend school in a uniform and without a head scarf. (In Turkey, Islamic-style head scarfs are not allowed in any public educational institution.) Once the girl was finally permitted to attend middle school, villagers began to remark publically on her breasts and sexual maturity. Some even said, when she went on to high school in a nearby town, that it was like sending a daughter into prostitution. City women who wear short dresses and otherwise ignore the code of modest dress are sometimes referred to as "naked," *çıplak.*

In general, women are brought up to find their primary ties and ultimate sources of economic security in their relationships with their fathers, brothers, and sons. A repudiated or divorced woman almost always goes back to her father's house or, should he be deceased, to that of a brother, who is legally charged with her upkeep and protection. Only very recently have some women been in a position to support themselves and maintain independent households after a divorce. Still, with the exception of some upper-class and professional women, social pressure can make it difficult for a single woman

---

[1] This is a major issue in Turkey, since in 1998 middle school attendance was made compulsory in order to strengthen secular education. This move provoked very strong, religiously motivated opposition.

to live alone and maintain her own household. However, quite apart from the fact that increasing numbers of men are participating in wage-labor migration and leaving their wives behind to manage the household, upon divorce some women are more apt nowadays to live alone. The major reason for this development is the reluctance of brothers or other male relatives to take divorced women and their children into their households. This changing attitude can be explained by the men's own changing circumstances. Not only are families increasingly dependent on wage labor, which tends to foster nuclear households, but with rapid urbanization, living space itself is at a premium.

Despite sexual segregation and a strong division of labor, the main difference between the lives of women and men in Middle Eastern societies, and one that cuts across all but the elite or emerging secularized professional classes, is that women find their lives tied much more closely to family and household, while men lead their lives in the public domain of mosque, market, and workplace. But here, too, care must be taken not to overemphasize the public-private dichotomy. Village women and men work side by side in the fields, and the street vendors of Cairo, for example, include many husband-wife teams selling foodstuffs, clothing, and trinkets. And throughout the region, widowed women act as de facto heads of households. Further, although house and property are generally considered to belong to the male head of the household, women do exercise considerable influence in decision making. Not infrequently they join in public discussions of issues affecting their families and communities, and it is a mistake to interpret overt signs of deference and reticence for powerlessness or passivity.

As we mentioned earlier, the majority of women live almost exclusively within the domestic domain, and their social roles are primarily those of mothers, wives, and daughters. Traditionally, they held no public office, nor did they work as artisans, shopkeepers, or craftspeople in the marketplace. However, women from poor urban and rural strata are often forced to work outside the home, usually as domestics or agricultural laborers in situations in which minimal contact with unrelated males is required. Those households forced to sell the labor of their womenfolk to strangers were considered low in status. A woman's labor was thought appropriately utilized only within the household, and even marketing and the provisioning of the household with goods from the marketplace was predominantly, although never exclusively, male. A woman's seclusion and avoidance of public and domestic labor were proof of her husband's success and wealth, and upper-class women occupied themselves with their children, leaving household tasks to domestics. Consequently, the most oppressive aspects of female seclusion were felt by women of families who could afford to keep them within the household but who were not wealthy enough to hire domestics and sustain the lifestyle and diversions of the wealthy.

THE POLITICS OF VEILING

The bodies of Muslim women and their public comportment have become the subject of intense political debates and confrontations masking serious issues of identity, freedom of expression, and cultural resistance to the engulfing tides of Western-style "modernity" and secularism. And the veil has become a potent symbol of Islam and the focus of questions raised within and outside the Muslim world about self-definition, traditional sex/gender systems, and the role of Islam in the public domain. The issue of veiling in the contemporary context has become an issue of politics more than an issue of religion. As a Turkish sociologist put it, "The question of veiling highlights the centrality of the gender issue to Islamist self-definition and implied Western criticism. Hence veiling is a discursive symbol that is instrumental in conveying political meanings" (Göle, 1996, p. 4).

To begin to appreciate the multiple significance of veiling , one must distinguish between the "traditional/old" veiling and the "new/Islamist" veiling.[2] Throughout history, Muslim women have traditionally worn some form of head and body covering as part of a generalized code of sexual modesty and to conform to conventional interpretations of Islam.[3] Traditional veiling assumed a number of styles that varied by country, ethnicity, tribe, social class, urban-rural residence, and level of education, among other factors. In some communities, women covered their head and breasts in an enveloping scarf, in others, they covered their whole body, including their face, in one garment. What we term "traditional veiling" was transmitted from one generation to the next, symbolically affirming continuity of an Islamic gender ideology that called for the public concealment of female sexuality and the segregation of the sexes.

The veil, and dress styles in general, became a subject of public debate in the mid-nineteenth century. This period marked the beginning of a profound social and economic transformation of the Middle East that followed the earlier encroachment of Western colonial powers into the region. The rapid transformation of Muslim societies had immediate repercussions in the cultural domain when Muslim intellectuals began to question openly the reasons for the apparent weakness and "backwardness" of their own societies in the face of European dominance. Leila Ahmed (1992) writes, "From the start the treatment and status of women were intertwined with other issues . . . including nationalism and the need for national advancement, and for political, social, and cultural reform. . . . [T]he discussion of women and reform was embedded in considerations of the relative advancement of European societies and the need for Muslim societies to catch up" (p. 128). In the later context of direct colonial

---

[2] There is a large body of literature on veiling; for a discussion of the differences between traditional and Islamist veiling, see, among others, Andrea B. Rugh (1986) and Sharifa Zuhur (1992); for a discussion relevant to Turkey, see Elisabeth Özdalga (1997).

[3] For an interesting reinterpretation of the Quranic verses on veiling, see Fatima Mernissi (1987).

domination, "The links between the issue of women and the issues of national-ism and culture were permanently forged . . . [and] the veil emerged as a potent signifier, connoting not merely the social meaning of gender but also matters of far broader political and cultural import. It has ever since retained that cargo of signification" (ibid., p. 129).

In view of the scope of this book, and the available documentation, we will take as an example the case of Egypt, which was in the forefront of develop-ments that later affected the whole of the region, to provide a sketch of some key aspects of the historical developments of "the veil issue." The British colo-nial presence in Egypt, which began in 1882, unleashed a heated debate about the status of women and stimulated a concerted call for reform and improve-ment in the position of Muslim women. Advocates of reform called for educa-tion for women, changes in the laws pertaining to polygamy and divorce, and an end to seclusion and veiling of women.[4] At the same time, critics of reform saw these demands as a betrayal of Muslim values and an affirmation of the colonialists' view of the backwardness and inferiority of Muslim societies, espe-cially as the most vocal reformers came from upper- and middle-class Egyp-tians assimilated, more or less, into Western culture.

It was in the midst of the ideological and political ferment of the first few decades of the twentieth century that the first feminist movements in the Arab Middle East were born in Egypt. The leaders of these movements came from the upper and upper-middle classes and, in general, tended to adopt secular, Western-style progressive platforms. In 1923, Huda Sha'rawi, an upper-class feminist, founded the Egyptian Feminist Union, an organization that called for women's suffrage, access to higher education, and reform in family law. In May of that year, Sha'rawi and a feminist colleague attended an international women's conference in Rome. Back in Egypt, getting off the train in Cairo, they lifted their veils and uncovered their faces to the assembled journalists. This symbolic act, which shocked the nation, ushered in a new era for women in the Middle East.

The 1940s and 1950s saw marked improvements in women's health, edu-cation, and their increased participation in the wage labor sector. At the same time, by mid-century the traditional veil had gradually disappeared among upper- and middle-class women in Egypt and throughout the region (with the notable exceptions of Saudi Arabia and the Gulf states), and was less and less commonly seen in working-class neighborhoods and small towns.

There is general agreement that the "new veiling" first appeared on uni-versity campuses in Egypt following the 1967 war and Israel's defeat of the Egyptian army. The shock of the defeat, which is commonly referred to as

[4] A leading advocate for the emancipation of women was the Egyptian Qassim Amin, whose book *Tahrir al_Mar'a* ("The Liberation of Woman"), published in 1899, is considered a landmark in the history of the movement for women's liberation in the Arab world. For an excellent historical account of the gender debate (especially in Egypt), see Leila Ahmed (1992).

al-Nakba , or "catastrophe," provided an impetus for the rise of Islamists who managed to articulate the widespread frustration and anger with the failure of the government to deal with endemic corruption, deteriorating economic standards, and wide-scale social dislocation. The Islamists called for moral regeneration through a return to "Islamic values." For women, this meant the adoption of modest dress (*al-ziyy al-islami* or Islamic dress) as the outward symbol of their new commitment to an Islamic way of life and a rejection of the corrupt values of the West. In Arabic, this form of veiling is referred to as *al-hijab*, and a woman who adopts it is called *muhajaba*. In a short time, young, often politically active women throughout the Muslim world dressed in some variation or another of the *hijab*.

There is no standardized modern *hijab* or *ziyy al-islami* throughout the Middle East; minimally it includes a loose-fitting, long-sleeved garment that covers the body and some form of head cover that usually leaves the face exposed. At its extreme, it consists of a totally enveloping black garment and full coverage of the hands and face with small slits for the eyes. The point to keep in mind is that this new style of veiling represents a modern urban innovation and is not merely a replication of traditional modes of veiling that historically prevailed in the region.[5] One perspective on this claims:

> Veiled women are not simply passive conveyers of the provincial, traditional culture; they are, rather, active self-asserting women who seek opportunities in modernism. They have come into the public scene not at the periphery, where traditions prevail, but in the urban settlements and at the universities. . . . [I]n this context, veiling symbolizes radical Islamism, which is molded on the tension between traditionalism and modernism. (Göle, 1996, p. 92)

Not all women, of course, are radical Islamists; many are simply pious. Research, conducted mainly in Egypt, indicates that the new veiling is most common among university students and young professional women from the lower middle class whose parents tend to be rural migrants. Compared to their parents, they represent an upwardly mobile generation, the first to acquire higher education and to work with men in a desegregated workplace. For these women, coming from modest, conservative backgrounds, the adoption of the new veil serves as a "practical coping strategy enabling women to negotiate in the new world while affirming the traditional values of their upbringing" (Ahmed, 1992).

From this perspective, Islamic dress signals an innovative response by a newly emerging segment of Muslim women intent on negotiating a legitimate public space for themselves, one that accommodates the contradictory demands placed on them by their faith and by the workplace (MacLeod, 1991). Moreover,

---

[5] For an interesting discussion of one type of traditional veil, the face mask, or *burqa'*, in Oman, see Uni Wikan (1982, pp. 88–108).

Three young Turkish school teachers; they are not allowed to wear full Islamist garb in the classroom.

as the women themselves admit, the adoption of Islamic dress carries certain practical advantages. It is an economical way of dressing and, as when one wears a uniform, there is less concern with competition to wear expensive, fashionable clothes. It can also save women from male harassment on the crowded streets of the cities. As one Egyptian young woman put it, "Being totally covered saves me from the approaches of men and hungry looks. I feel more free, purer, and more respectable" (quoted in K. Ask & M. Tjomsland, 1998, p. 63). Deniz Kandiyoti (1991) puts it somewhat differently, as "the partriarchal bargain": support and protection on the part of males in exchange for submissive behavior, obedience, service, and childbearing on the part of women. At the other extreme, some women adopt the garb for the same reason that any article of dress may be chosen: a desire to appear fashionable and to attract attention. Much, too, is said of the "Islamic Chic"—head-scarfed but expensively and elegantly dressed women who are not in the least "invisible."

It is clear that veiling, both in its traditional and contemporary manifestations, is a complex institution reflecting issues of gender, religion, and politics. As our brief discussion illustrates, the significance and meaning of veiling can only be understood when examined in the context of a specific time and place. For some people in the Middle East, the veil represents an elaboration and perpetuation of an archaic patriarchal order, an embarrassing relic of the past, and an impediment to progress. For others, it symbolizes a core Islamic ethos regarding sexual modesty and morality and an affirmation of a unique cultural tradition. For still others, veiling is an explicit political statement, even an expediency with which to proclaim pride of culture in the face of the assaults of the West. These disparate understandings may well be simultaneously affirmed and acted upon in any one society. During the period leading up to the Iranian revolution, middle-class college women could often be seen in the streets of Tehran wearing the head scarf and the shapeless traditional dress, or chador. While some may have newly subscribed to the religious tenets expressed by female veiling, others were simply making a political statement protesting the corruption of the Western-oriented regime of the Shah and expressing their solidarity with Iranians of all social classes. The adoption of so-called Islamic dress reflects the turbulence of an era in which social and political alienation is expressed by some in terms of Islam and by others in a quest for authenticity.

In fact, religious politics has a strong appeal for women, as Nikki Keddie (1999) agrees. It allows women to be activists in their own milieu and "to participate in the general social and ideological trends of their times, and the current trend in many parts of the world includes a rise of religious politics" (p. 6).

HONOR, SHAME, AND SEXUAL MODESTY

Beliefs about female sexuality and its control are closely related to the complex concept of individual and family honor, which is widespread throughout the Mediterranean world. "Honor," writes J. G. Pitt-Rivers, "is the value of a person in his own eyes, but also in the eyes of his society. It is his estimation of his own worth, his claim to pride, but it is also acknowledgment of that claim, his excellence recognized by society, his right to pride" (1966, p. 20).

Sources of honor are many, depending on the individual and his or her specific circumstances. They include family origin, piety, prowess, generosity, and, above all, autonomy. Wealth and power, appropriately used, can confer honor. Honor is, in brief, the ability to live up to the ideal expectations of the society. In the Middle East the most commonly used term to refer to honor is *sharaf*, a complex and diffuse concept. The most fundamental and universal component of a man's honor in the Middle East, however, is closely tied to the sexual behavior and general reputation of his womenfolk. This special aspect of honor is generally known in Arabic as *'ard* and in Turkish as *namus*.

'Ard, like *sharaf*, can be individual or collective, in that whole families, lineages, or even tribes are thought of as possessing a common "fund of honor." However, Ahmed Abou-Zeid (1966), in his study of an Egyptian Bedouin community, describes *'ard* as exclusively sexual and affected only by the conduct of women. And while *sharaf* can be acquired and augmented through correct behavior and outstanding achievement, *'ard* can only be lost and lost only through the sexual misconduct of women. Any breach of the code of sexual modesty, just as any assault on a man's general sense of pride or *sharaf*, brings

shame, *'ar,* or *'aib.* Of all sources of shame, none is felt as acutely as that occasioned by a breach of sexual mores, and throughout the Middle East the most potent curses refer to the sexual behavior of a man's mother or sister.[6] Family responses to incidents such as premarital sexual liaisons or marital infidelity range from ignoring or playing down the situation to the extreme of killing the woman.

The actual extent of these so-called "honor killings" is difficult to assess, as they are generally hushed up, and the whole subject is taboo. However, casual perusal of newspapers in the region reveals regular reports of honor killings. Jordan has recently brought the subject into the arena of public debate. In June 1999, a regional conference was held in Amman to explore ways to deal with the problem. As with the larger issue of women's status, honor killing provokes strong sentiments and divided opinions. Turkey, in the early Republican era, imposed rather more stringent penalties on those convicted of honor or revenge murders, but in more recent years this policy has apparently lapsed. Nonetheless, across the region, a new generation of young activists, lawyers, journalists, and legislators is working to toughen the laws that deal with honor killings at the same time as it is seeking to change entrenched values that link male honor to female sexual behavior. It must be kept in mind, however, that compliance with and response to this general norm depend on the individual circumstances and social standing of the people involved, as well as their general educational and cultural background.

In small communities, where a family or a household controls wealth, exercises power through local alliances, and expects public deference, the reputation of its women assumes political significance. Their behavior is read by others as an indication of the overall prestige and influence of their particular social grouping or family. For this reason, women of the traditional urban upper classes, female members of holy lineages and of well-to-do village households may in fact be more constrained in their behavior than women of poorer households.

The values of honor and shame are more than internalized psychological determinants for individual behavior. This value system operates in the social and political arenas to delineate group identity and to conserve social boundaries. In effect, it is often a statement about relative status and power. Throughout the Middle East, powerful families and groups tended to practice close endogamy, keeping their women within a close circle defined by kinship and class. The link between family honor and control over women reinforces this. While influential and powerful families might regularly recruit wives from other less influential groupings, they do not reciprocate. The taking of women is a sign of power and prestige, but the converse connotes relative weakness and lower prestige. The best anthropological study of this is Martha Mundy's study

---

[6] For an interesting discussion of notions of honor and shame as they relate to gender in a town in Oman, see Uni Wikan (1982, pp. 141–167). See also Lila Abu-Lughod (1988, especially pp. 78–117).

(1995) of marriage transactions in a Yemeni rural setting in which she illustrates the relationship among marriage, property, and the maintenance of social status.

An extreme example of the political significance of male control over women is found in Saudi Arabia today, especially among the ruling elite. Even though a strict Wahabi code of behavior applies to all Saudis, the behavior of women of the royal family and the elite is a matter of state concern. Women of the royal Saudi clan are absolutely forbidden to marry outside it, and their behavior is strictly monitored. Saudi Arabian women are generally excluded from public life; those few public offices held by women deal exclusively with women. A woman is legally considered the ward of her menfolk; she may not leave the country without her guardian's permission, be it her father, husband, or brother. She may not drive an automobile, swim at a public beach, or be seen without her veil. Strict sexual segregation prevails in banks, schools, and hospitals. Even government buildings may have a special door marked *Hareem*, "women only." Nonetheless, actual behavior is at considerable variance from the spirit of these proscriptions. For example, wealthy Saudi women traveling outside the country dress in the latest, often revealing fashions, and they dine, drink alcohol, drive, and smoke in public. At home, however, great care is taken to conform publicly to a segregated lifestyle, and great effort is made to minimize the contradiction between private lifestyle and the prevailing Wahabi ideology. This is understandable. The few occasions when public attention has been directed to breaches in the behavioral code have been dealt with a retribution so harsh as to shock non-Saudis, including other Middle Easterners. Surely part of the explanation lies in the fact that the very legitimacy of Saudi rule is, to a large measure, based on their identification with the puritanical Wahabi creed.

The ways in which notions of honor, shame, and sexual modesty are interwoven and how they influence individual behavior are difficult to describe in the abstract. How these values are expressed, manipulated, and interpreted varies greatly in time and place. Even the most commonplace, everyday activities—for example, the normal deference of women to their husbands and brothers, or the way in which children are scolded and shamed in public—may be revealing. To illustrate how these values inform specific behavior, let us consider the following brief anecdote.

Some years ago, one of the authors, Rassam, was in northern Iraq doing fieldwork in and around the city of Mosul. Having obtained her research permit, she hired a taxi and a driver, a native of a nearby village. Her notes read:

> On Tuesday morning, 'Ali my driver came to the hotel to pick me up to go to the village to begin my survey. He was dressed in the traditional garb of his region, which marked him as a rural inhabitant, a *qarawi*, or villager. I sat at the back of the taxi and we drove off. A few miles outside the city we were stopped at a military checkpoint. The soldier ignored my driver and came around to my side of the car, put his head in the window and asked where I was going. I told him that I was on my way to a village down the road, upon which he asked to see my identification papers. Discarding my protestations and ignoring my work permit, he made us

turn around and go back to the city, claiming that the road was mined and that he could not guarantee my safety. On the way back, I expressed my frustration to 'Ali and my fears that I wouldn't be able to complete my research. Upon some reflection he suggested that we try again in a day or two, but this time he would put on his suit and I should wear the *'abaya* (the shapeless black cloak worn by the more traditional women in Iraq). I agreed. When he came back two days later to pick me up he was dressed like an *affendi* (an urban gentlemen) and I was enveloped in the *'abaya*. I sat near him and we took off to the rural countryside. As we reached the checkpoint, the soldier on duty came around this time to the driver's window and asked to see his papers; he asked where we were going, and without a direct glance my way, he waved us on, and we continued on our way to the village.

The first time that Rassam set out, she was the one in the car who was socially "visible," being clearly a foreigner and a woman traveling alone in the back of a hired car dressed in Western-style clothes and without the *'abaya*. Her status was immediately recognized by the soldier, who ignored the driver and asked for her papers. Her dress identified her as a member of the urban, educated society, and the fact that she had hired a car marked her as someone of potential significance. As it transpired, the soldier chose not to assume responsibility for the presence of a strange woman in his area.

On the second attempt, by wearing the *'abaya* and sitting next to the driver, Rassam became publicly invisible; the soldier perceived her as "belonging" to the driver. Moreover, the driver, dressed in his Western-style suit, had acquired both visibility and a certain amount of social standing as well. The confrontation had now shifted to one between the two men, the soldier at the bottom of the military hierarchy and the *affendi* representing the lower bourgeoisie or those who identify with them. The woman in the car ceased to exist in any political sense. This, we might add, is one occasion when being a female anthropologist in the Middle East was an advantage. A male anthropologist would have had to show his identification papers along with those of the driver, and on being found a stranger to the area would likely have been turned back.

The code of sexual modesty is rooted in the Quran, in Shari'a, and elaborated in the Hadith, or Traditions, but is by no means an uncontested domain. While inequality between the sexes is flagrant in traditional law, the basis for the law, as Delacoura (1999) forcefully argues, is ambivalent: "Nowhere does the Koran clearly say that women must be veiled; that stoning is the punishment for adultery; or that women should be secluded or circumcised" (p. 46).[7] Essentially, female sexual modesty consists of virginity before marriage, fidelity after it, and the maintenance of a particular public comportment throughout. "Unlawful" intercourse is punishable by death, according to one sura, but many of the other so-called *ḥadd*, or required punishments, are in fact ignored in practice. If not actually veiled, women must behave as if they were—that is,

---

[7] An analogy can be found in the institution of slavery. The Quran endorsed it, as did Islamic law, but not even conservative thinkers would now argue in its favor. They argue, rather, that Quranic restrictions on slavery point to its ultimate abolition (Delacoura, 1999, p. 47).

they are expected to carry themselves in a manner that suggests that they subscribe to the "tenets of modesty." A virtuous woman is usually referred to as *mastura*, chaste or covered, as if she were invisible to the outsider and the stranger. Modesty, however, consists of much more than proper dress in public or the avoidance of illicit sexual contact. It is thought of as shaping all aspects of a woman's behavior. There is a strong connotation of the sacred attached to the image of the virtuous woman.

The word *haram*, meaning both sacred and taboo, is also applied to women. *Haram*, which can refer to a religious sanctuary such as the *ka'aba* enclosure at Mecca, is also used to describe the women of the household and their quarters in it. In some Arabic-speaking communities, the women of the household are collectively referred to as the *hareem* of its male head. The women have different claims to this status. A patriarch's daughters, for example, make up part of his *hareem* because they are sexually taboo, or *maharem*, as are his daughters-in-law. His own wife, on the other hand, is part of the *hareem* in that she dwells in the sanctity, or *haram/hurma*, of his household. It is ironic that the term *hareem* has acquired a meaning in English that is virtually the opposite of its original sense.

Islamic and Middle Eastern codes of modesty not only regulate sexuality but attempt to restrict it to the private domain of the home. Nothing so scandalizes the traditional or Islamist Middle Easterner as public displays of sexual affection and intimacy. It is interesting that in societies sometimes characterized by male vanity and dominance, men do not normally boast of sexual exploits, nor is the "Don Juan" image particularly admired. The Islamic ethos that reflects a fairly common male view emphasizes the inherent danger to the social order of unrestrained sexuality and the necessity for male control of female

Veiled women wearing the face mask, or *burqa*, in Oman.

sexual behavior. This mirrors a remarkably similar worldview found among many Mediterranean peoples, a view closely tied to the value system of honor and shame (Gilmore, 1999).

As we have noted, honor and shame are notions about social esteem (or the lack thereof) based on communal perceptions of an individual's social worth. They are ways of expressing "reputations"; those who aspire to public approbation behave so as to show concern for the opinions of others. Fundamental to this value system is the idea that men are responsible for the behavior of their kinswomen, and that a man's honor is to a large extent predicated on his ability to protect and control the women of his household. One consequence of this belief is that male-female interaction is seen as being always potentially disruptive, inasmuch as it may call into question a man's ability to control or protect the women for whom he is responsible. Romantic love can, therefore, be particularly threatening, challenging as it does male control as well as the family's reputation.

What distinguishes the Middle East is the extent to which concepts of honor and shame are the explicit basis for social action and the extent to which social institutions reflect this. The code of sexual modesty and the seclusion of women are, of course, important means of effecting male control over female sexuality and reproductive capacity. Further, they assure male control within the household and facilitate the preservation of productive property within the male descent line. Even a woman's claim to her own children is jurally secondary to that of her husband, and in the event of a divorce she loses ultimate rights to her children. Male control is often expressed in Islamic law in terms of a duty to protect women, who are perceived as weak and socially dependent on males, be they fathers, husbands, or sons.

Afsaneh Najmabadi (1999) illustrates just how powerful this sentiment can be, and how selective historical accounts are where women are concerned. An important event precipitating the Iranian Constitutional Revolution (1905–1909) was the kidnapping and sale by Sunni Türkmen raiders of young girls from villages in the province of Quchan. The plight of the "Daughters of Quchan"—an assault on honor—was used to rally broad public support for the overthrow of the regime and to ignite passionate anti-government demonstrations by men and women alike. However, once the regime collapsed, official accounts of the revolution emphasized the pivotal role of merchants and clergy in its success, with no mention of women or peasants.

Concepts of human sexuality lie at the core of the ideology that rationalizes male dominance and control. Needless to say, there is no single shared view of sexuality, nor is there any one consistent ideology that cuts across all classes and groups. Further, there is also a lack of data on sexual practices in the Middle East. At the level of the Islamic literary tradition, however, there is a great deal of material on sexuality and its role in society. This literature is frequently referred to by politicians and religious conservatives, as well as by the 'ulama. Since Fatima Mernissi (1987) and Abdelwahab Bouhdiba (1997) have ably reviewed much of this literature, we draw on their work for the following discussion.

In their exposition, the Muslim concept of sexuality is close to the Freudian concept of libido, raw instincts as being a source of energy. Sexual instincts themselves are believed to have no connotation of good or evil apart from how they serve a specific social order. The regulation of sexual drive, therefore, becomes a prerequisite in Islam to the maintenance of social order. There is intense popular concern with sexual matters, in particular female sexual behavior; women discuss sexual matters among themselves with an explicitness that may shock the unwary.

Sexual pleasure is recognized and even celebrated in literature and religious writings and is not considered to be confined to males. A woman has a right to regular sexual relations with her husband, and the achievement of sexual fulfillment is recognized as her due. Citing a tradition of the Prophet, Imam al-Ghazzali, one of the major theologians of Islam, wrote: "The Prophet said, 'No one among you should throw himself on his wife like beasts do. There should be, prior to coitus, a messenger between you and her.' People asked him, 'what sort of messenger?' The Prophet answered, 'Kisses and words'" (Mernissi, 1975, p. 10).

A research project which began in 1997 provides a rare glimpse into male views of sexuality and gender among a group of Egyptian men. Interviews with 50 men revealed a shared view that was independent of differences in age and educational levels. Nadia Wassef reports that the survey revealed a "deep-rooted anxiety over women's assumed power and strength. Men felt that they constantly needed to engage in a struggle with women to defend and assert their masculinity. Domination was the weapon of victory; sex, the battle-ground" (1999, p. 1). Respondents expressed the belief that women were sexually insatiable; women's sexuality was considered to be of such power that unless satisfied and controlled, it threatened the stability of the family and the social order. To assert their power over their wives and keep them from cheating, husbands have the duty to satisfy them. Thus "sex within marriage was considered a 'duty' and hence 'not fun' but in the context of an extra-marital or pre-marital relationship, men felt they could enjoy sex more . . . since they were not terribly concerned about their partner's pleasure" (ibid., p. 2). The respondents also said that were they to become impotent, they would divorce their wives to avoid the disgrace of the inevitable infidelity. "Most of our respondents felt that even if a woman could survive without sex for a month or two, it was inevitable that she would err, and therefore it was better for men to spare themselves the humiliation" (ibid., p. 2).

Controlling the potentially destructive force of their own sexuality is considered to require greater powers of reason and self-discipline than women are believed to possess. The code of modesty in deportment and dress and the seclusion of women serve to minimize direct male-female interaction and to limit sexual contact. By the logic of this view, one may say that these practices serve to "protect" women from the consequences of their powerful sexuality and men from succumbing to it, and that they thus contribute to the social order by minimizing conflict among the men over women. It is significant that a beautiful and seductive woman is often described in Arabic as *faten* or *fatina*, a term derived from *fitna*, a word that means social disorder or chaos, a concept not dissimilar from the Western notion of femme fatale.

This perspective portrays women as passive and yet possessed of an ability to disrupt the social order. To guard against this risk, institutions that foster male dominance and female subordination are seen as fundamental to the preservation of the social order and for the control of women's powers of disruption. Codes of female sexual modesty and segregation may be interpreted here as cultural responses to male views of female sexuality and their fears of female forms of power (see Sabbah, 1984).

Lila Abu-Lughod (1986) provides a sophisticated analysis of gender ideology among a small settled community of Bedouin, the Awlad 'Ali, in the Western Desert of Egypt. Although she is reluctant to generalize, her description is consistent with the system of values we have presented. In exploring the "moral discourse of honor and modesty," Abu-Lughod writes that sexual modesty, *hasham*, is associated with femaleness and implies dependency; maleness is associated with autonomy and independence. "Because Awlad 'Ali couch hierarchy in the language of moral worth, the association implies that male precedence is due to their moral superiority" (p. 119). She amplifies this by explaining that the Awlad 'Ali devaluation of women is rationalized by reference to their moral inferiority, which has its source in the identification of females with the "natural" domain of menstruation, procreation, and sexuality. Since menstruation is considered polluting, women are "naturally" handicapped; a menstruating woman cannot pray, enter a mosque, or touch the Quran. Furthermore, through sexuality and pregnancy, women are believed to lose control over their own bodies, and this limits their ability to attain the male ideals of independence and self mastery. "The identification of women with both menstruation and sexuality is thought to preclude them, in different ways, from achieving the moral virtue of those who uphold the honor code. It also determines the path they must take to gain respectability, the path of modesty" (p. 119). To gain and maintain honor and respect in the community, women must, therefore, obey the dictates of the code of *hasham*.

An emotionally charged subject, while regionally specific, is that of female circumcision, sometimes referred to as female genital mutilation (FGM).[8] In fact, FGM, which is most prevalent in northeastern Africa, is not practiced by the vast majority of Muslims; it is unknown among Persians, Turks, and the Arabs of the Arabian Peninsula with the exception of those of African origins, and, perhaps most significantly, there is no reference to it in the Quran. Female circumcision is nearly universally practiced in Egypt and also in the Sudan.

---

[8] A full discussion of the many issues involved in the practice of FGM is outside the scope of this book. For an excellent analysis of the issues, see Noor J. Kassamali (1998); see also Esther K. Hicks (1996).

Consequently, it often is associated by outsiders with Islam, and, indeed, some Egyptian clerics have endorsed it. But, because in Egypt it is practiced by Muslims and Christians alike, it would seem that FGM is a local custom, not a widely recognized Islamic tradition, and its practice and perpetuation are better understood in terms of the local patrilineal and patriarchal social structures in which it is embedded.

LEGAL REFORM AND PERSONAL STATUS OF WOMEN

A key area that affects the status of women both in the Middle East and in the rest of the Muslim world concerns the Shari'a-based laws of personal status and family. These laws, which regulate rights and responsibilities in the private domains of marriage, divorce, child custody, and inheritance, have a direct impact on women in their roles as daughters, wives, and mothers. In all of the countries under consideration, with the outstanding exception of Turkey, family law is formulated within the Islamic framework that, generally, translates into unequal rights for men and women in such areas as polygyny, child custody, and divorce. In fact, as many have noted, this inequality is in direct contradiction to the constitutions of the same countries that, in general, call for nondiscrimination based on sex, religion, and race. Furthermore, in all countries with an elected parliament, women have the right to vote and be elected to public office; labor laws enacted in some countries during the past few decades further guarantee women more equal treatment in the workplace.

Thus, while the last century has witnessed the progressive transformation of the legal codes that govern the political and economic domains along secular Western models (e.g., criminal and commercial laws), personal status and family laws continue to adhere to a modified and codified version of the Shari'a. As Nadia Hijab succinctly puts it, "In effect, the fact that family law has evolved within an Islamic framework means that Arab women can be equal outside the home but not within it" (1998, p. 47)—which is to say that while men and women are equal as citizens in the public domain, they are not equal within the private domain of the family.[9]

The origin, evolution, and codification of Islamic family law is far too technical and complex a subject to be presented here. In what follows, we limit ourselves to a few basic issues. We should note that, as with the more general question of the status of Muslim women (to which it is related), Islamic family law is publicly debated throughout the region. The political ascendency of Islamists in some countries has raised fears that the implementation of a very conservative version of the Shari'a as state law would erode the modest gains that women have achieved as a result of earlier legal reforms.

[9] For contemporary approaches to interpreting gender issues in the Quran, see Barbara Stowasser (1994).

In 1917, responding to changing social conditions and in their efforts to modernize, the Ottomans promulgated a new and codified family law based on the Shari'a, the Ottoman Law of Family Rights. Since then, virtually every country in the Middle East has instituted codes of personal status and family law that represent an adaptation of this Ottoman law. Going farther, in 1926, following the dissolution of the Ottoman Empire and the establishment of the Turkish Republic as a modern secular nation-state, Atatürk replaced the 1917 law with the wholesale adoption of the Swiss Civil Code. Today Turkey is the only country in the Middle East (including Israel) where one can have a civil marriage and divorce. Women have the right to retain their family names, and the law does not recognize a "head of household." As of January 2000, women in Egypt gained the right to civil divorce on the basis of "incompatibility." However, they can sue for divorce only if they forfeit all alimony and all marital property. Even with this restriction, many Islamists describe this new law as an affront to the Islamic family.

Although no other Middle Eastern country has gone as far as has Turkey in overhauling family law, we should note that Tunisia, an Arab Muslim country, boasts what is perhaps the most progressive family law formulated within the Islamic framework. The Tunisian Code of Personal Status was promulgated by the state immediately following independence from France in 1956. Among other reforms, it abolished polygyny and gave women considerable rights in divorce and child custody cases. Despite some efforts by conservative religious elements to rescind the family law, which they perceive to be too secular or un-Islamic, the Tunisian code remains a good model and a reminder of the flexibility of Quranic dicta and the role of interpreters in translating religious norms into state laws.[10]

As noted earlier, reform of personal status and family laws is an important factor in improving women's status in the Middle East. One of the earliest women's movements in the Arab world, founded in Egypt in the early 1920s, has repeatedly pressed for the abolition of polygamy and the modification of divorce laws. Today, women's organizations exist in all countries of the area, with varying degrees of political influence. Some are completely controlled by the regimes in power and are no more than government agencies; others are more autonomous, working to stimulate debate on women's issues as they campaign for legal reform and a general improvement in women's status. In 1999, the director of the United Nations Population Fund (UNPF), Atef Khalfa, underscored the importance of improving women's lives: "Educating women is key to determining the quality of life—an educated woman who has equal rights and plays her role in society will automatically choose a smaller family and better quality of life" (*New York Times*, November 19, 1999, p. A5). The UNPF puts Arab female literacy at around 55 percent, clearly linking it to the continuing high birth rates and the annual population increase of about 2.5 percent for Arab countries. Khalfa added that

[10] For an excellent article on family law in Tunisia, see Mounira Charrad (1998).

"empowering women is the key to determining the quality of life—our problem is not so much the quantity of people but the quality of life."

As many have pointed out, a major problem in this area has to do with the ambivalence that governments in the region exhibit vis-à-vis women's legal status. This is particularly clear in the case of the more secular regimes, such as Syria and Iraq, whose rhetoric calls for comprehensive social reform and full equality for women (Shaaban, 1998; Rassam, 1992). Although Islam is the official state religion according to the Syrian constitution, the ruling Ba'ath party (which came to power in 1963) describes itself as a secular party pledged to build a civil society in which men and women will have equal rights and equal opportunities under the law. Towards that end, the regime has implemented a number of programs aimed specifically at women. These include the establishment of nurseries and preschool facilities, the implementation of a compulsory education law (for ages 6 to 12), and the construction of schools in rural areas.

These efforts seem to have had an impact, and Syrian women have, in fact, made significant advances in education over the past few decades. In the early 1960s, an estimated 80 percent of rural women were illiterate; by 1992, this figure was reduced to 30.6 percent. Moreover the number of women teachers at all levels of education increased from 47 percent in 1980 to about 57 percent in 1993; at the university level, women constituted 20.75 percent of all faculty in 1990 (Shaaban, 1998, p. 104). However, as Bouthaina Shaaban points out, this impressive advance has not been matched in the political arena. In 1994, out of a total membership of 250, the Syrian parliament had only 24 women members, and by 1999 there were still no women representatives in the highest decision-making political bodies in Syria (the National Front and the Regional Leadership). But perhaps of more immediate consequence for women's lives is the reluctance of the regime to secularize the laws of personal status and to sever them from the Shari'a. This reluctance may merely be political expediency for the regime to avoid a backlash from Islamists and more conservative sectors of the population; it may also reflect the cultural perspective of the ruling elite, which defines women primarily in terms of their familial and domestic roles as custodians of the "Islamic family and tradition."[11]

Nevertheless, throughout the region reforms have been introduced that, while not necessarily aimed at equalizing the legal status of men and women within the family, are nonetheless designed to put limits on the rights of the men.[12] In Lebanon, for example, Muslim women can prevent their husbands from marrying a second wife by so stipulating in their marriage contract. In Iraq, a man must request special permission of the court in order to marry a second wife; moreover, the traditional unilateral rights of men in divorce have also

[11] For an interesting discussion of how gender and the status of women are formulated in different political discourses in Egypt, see Mesvat Hatem (1998).

[12] One of the best collections about the impact of state policies and national projects on women is Deniz Kandiyoti's edited volume (1991).

been restricted, and women given more freedom in initiating a divorce. But progress has been uneven. During the 1960s, the revolutionary Ba'ath government of Iraq formulated new laws designed to equalize inheritance shares between sons and daughters. Rumor of this proposal elicited such strong reaction from religious and conservative elements that it was quickly withdrawn. Inheritance laws are an especially difficult area for reformers to tackle because of their immediate economic impact on men.

A brief consideration of the history of legal reform affecting the status of women in Iran reveals the sensitive nature of these efforts, which are perceived as interference with the intimate and private domain of the family. In 1936, Reza Shah attempted to abolish the veil and to change certain aspects of the marriage laws to give women more freedom. He was forced to retreat in the face of strong opposition voiced by religious leaders. Despite this, over the following decades Iran saw the gradual promulgation of a number of reform-minded laws. These were introduced along with widespread efforts through the media and in the schools to propagate modern values regarding women's roles. The progressive Family Protection Act of 1967 (amended in 1973), designed to limit polygyny and to equalize the rights of spouses in divorce, was abrogated following the success of the Iranian revolution in 1979, and was replaced by Shari'a laws. In 1980, veiling was declared compulsory, and women were not permitted to wear cosmetics in public; women were removed from high-level government posts and civil service positions and were urged to confine their work to the household.

By the year 2000, although veiling and other legal handicaps remain in force,

A Bedouin woman in her new living room in Jordan.

massive socioeconomic changes already effected in Iranian society have led to a de facto enhancement of the status of women. Educated elite and middle-class women in Iran continue to participate in public life as they protest and resist the attempts of the conservative clergy to restrict their public employment. For example, one prominent woman, Shirin Ebadi, was appointed in 1997 as the first female prosecutor in Tehran; forced to resign by hard-liners, she was later elected to parliament (along with 14 other women out of 270 members) where she has been an extremely vocal defender of women's rights and of human rights in general. Her activities are personally dangerous for her, but she allows that the last 20 years have seen significant and irreversible strides forward.

In her book *Islam and Feminisms: An Iranian Case-Study* (1998), Haleh Afshar, another well-known activist, describes the struggle of Iranian women, both secular and religious, to resist the erosion of their rights and to assert themselves in the face of the more reactionary forces of the regime. She recounts the ways in which elite Islamist women have managed to become a political force in Iran and how they have succeeded in extracting important concessions from the regime by articulating their demands in terms of a reconstructed Islamic discourse that stresses justice and fairness. "Quite against the expectations of the theoreticians and the political architects of the revolution Iranian women are now at the center of the political stage. The incoming president, Ayatollah Seyed Mohammad Khatami, recognized this reality and, in his inaugural speech in August 1997, declared his commitment to furthering the cause of women in Iran" (p. 121). This obviously paid important dividends for the 2000 parliamentary election, in which women and young people generally voted for reform-minded candidates and thereby secured control of the parliament for the president.

It is important to keep in mind that radical legislation affecting gender roles and family relationships may run ahead of actual practice in some sectors of the society. Contrary to law, for example, polygynous households can be found throughout rural Turkey. In fact, recent reports from the government office of statistics indicated an increase in reported polygynous marriages; such reporting is likely to be an undercount because polygyny is illegal. Men may avoid this restriction and take a first wife using an officially registered marriage and later on, using a religious contract of no legal standing in court, take a second wife. Even members of parliament have been exposed as employing this stratagem. Such second wives may find themselves divorced without any legal claims to compensation or to their children, a tragic topic frequently treated in Turkish literature on rural life.

Nonetheless, reform of personal status and family laws does have significant long-term social impact, even when this may not be immediately apparent. Legislation passed two generations ago in Turkey is certainly one reason why Turkish women today enjoy a higher status, both within the household and outside it, compared to Arab and Iranian women. When rights are guaranteed by law, even illiterate women may seek and find help in seeing their claims adjudicated. Taking into account the obvious impediments to implementing and enforcing radical legislation, and given the gap that exists between laws on books and social practice and constraints, legal reforms in the area of personal status still have a significance for women that transcends their symbolic value.

GENERAL OVERVIEW

One important dimension of this changing situation yet to be systematically explored is how men and women are psychologically coping with the changes in their customary roles, and the attendant constellation of rights and expectations. One possible source for such an inquiry is through the analysis of contemporary novels and short stories that deal with interpersonal relations among people in different sectors of modern-day Middle East society. Apart from such general observations based on personal impressions and novels, there are few data that allow us to probe meaningfully into these areas. The intense privacy that surrounds sexuality and gender, and indeed many other personal and family matters, is an impediment to research. Even though studies of women's new economic roles and participation in public life are beginning to yield a broad picture of rapidly changing behavior, little is known about the attitudes and beliefs that accompany this change. We know little, for example, about how women of different classes and groups perceive their own lives and society, and how they cope with the restrictions imposed on their behavior.

Those few women or men who have expressed themselves on the issue in poetry, essays, or novels tend to take extreme positions. Women like the Lebanese writer Laila Ba'albaki, the Syrian Ghada al-Samman, and the Egyptian feminist Nawal Sa'adawi have all expressed anger, frustration, and impatience with the social position of women.[13] While genuine, this is unlikely to be widely experienced or shared. The few sources that portray ordinary women in the context of their familial roles and daily activities present a less dissonant and oppressive picture than we might imagine. In an often humorous and moving account of women's lives in an Iraqi village in the 1950s, Elizabeth Fernea (1965, 1998) recounts how women entertain themselves and each other, offer mutual support and solace, and manage to influence and manipulate their menfolk. At the same time, Fernea reports undercurrents of tension, even resentment experienced by the women who often chafe against the restrictions placed on their freedom of movement by the men. More recently, Abu-Lughod presents a similar portrait based on the life experiences of a small group of mostly illiterate Bedouin women in a small community in Egypt's Western Desert. The life stories and personal narratives compiled, edited, and arranged by Lila Abu-Lughod (1993) provide a glimpse into the private world of women (and men) in this marginalized rural community.[14]

---

[13] For early attempts to capture the voices of women, see the articles in Elizabeth Fernea and Basima Bezirgan (1977).

[14] For life stories of rural women in an Iranian village, see Erika Friedl (1989).

One detailed exploration of gender roles and relations is provided by the Norwegian anthropologist Uni Wikan in her study of the strictly segregated world of urban women in northern Oman (1982). Wikan presents in some detail the way that children in an Omani town are socialized into their appropriate gender roles. Beginning at age two, "boys and girls enter paths that gradually diverge and end up in very different worlds. They are ascribed different tasks and responsibilities, complementary standards of behavior, and dissimilar outlooks on life and the world. To become an Omani female . . . a girl is taught to present herself in a manner that is quiet and soft-spoken, modest and timid . . . submissive and obedient" (p. 86). A boy, while also taught similar attributes of trustworthiness and humility, is also taught to be assertive, forceful, and decisive. Later on as children enter their teens, the girls are married off, while the boys wait at least another ten years before they begin to arrange for their own marriages. "Whereas boys in their teens become masters of their own lives, girls become the subjects of a new and unknown master, their husband—and often of his mother too. Boys enter a stage of increasing freedom and experience; girls enter one of increasing work and confinement, but also of gratifying responsibilities and chances of self-actualization" (p. 87).

In the similarly segregated society of neighboring Yemen, Carla Makhlouf (1979) reports that women also form a coherent subsociety with their own values and codes of behavior, some of which are often at variance with those expressed by the men. The suggestion is that while accepting their assigned secondary status, women do not perceive it as arising from inherent "natural" inequality, nor do they take too seriously all the values expressed by the men.

Traditional systems of values and practices developed and persisted because they provided rewards to women as well as men. As more women today seek rewards and identities that are no longer encompassed within their traditional domain, the values and attitudes of both men and women will change accordingly. The trend emphasized earlier, toward smaller family size and nuclear residence, will also contribute to the enhancement of the social status of women. Given that the burden of socialization of children rests largely with the women, change in their self-images, attitudes, and expectations will no doubt affect the new generations.

Everywhere in the Middle East the traditional ideology of male domination and female segregation and confinement is under attack from within and is rapidly eroding. Although there are many countervailing forces, often present in the growing influence of Islamic and Judaic conservatism, men and women are quietly altering many of the traditional patterns of interaction both within and outside the home. Whether debated publicly or simply reflected in the practical arrangements and relationships within the household, the fact is that gender roles and family structure are rapidly changing.

10

Local Organization of Power: Leadership, Patronage, and Tribalism

Political scientists who study politics and political processes in the Middle East tend to focus on state-level institutions, national parties, state policy, and international diplomacy. By contrast, anthropologists interested in questions of authority and power tend to focus on individual villages, segments of communities, and tribal entities. The work of anthropologists has generally been more descriptive than analytical, and often details patterns of feuding, factional disputes, and different forms of social control. Less common, and much needed, is an approach that relates local patterns to the larger system of which they are a part. This chapter attempts to do just that.

Villages and tribes are almost always treated as discrete political entities with their own seats of authority and power. Taxonomies of political communities identify each type in terms of distinctive patterns of social control and leadership. It is a worthy effort, but a frustrating one. One of the problems, we feel, is that the boundaries of political communities in the Middle East, however the community is defined, can rarely be thought of as fixed. The establishment of boundaries is itself as much an outcome as a cause of political action. By "boundaries," we are not referring to the territorial national subdivisions of the state with their state-appointed administrators but to the entities that emerge for political action due to the actors themselves. In any region, loci of power are multiple and may shift regularly; thus, identification of political communities is contingent on many factors.

For some purposes, a group of families or a lineage may constitute the largest effective political community below the level of the state, whereas for others, the effective political community may be the village as a whole or even groups of villages. Sometimes dispersed tribes or parties organized for political action may form political communities for purposes of social control, loyalty, leadership, and the like. Such shifting alignments operate in urban as well as rural environments. Spatial or territorial boundaries alone do not set limits to political communities; a dispute in the Lebanese parliament between two deputies may easily lead to intervillage feuding in a remote mountain district. The assassination of a newspaper editor in Istanbul may trigger reprisals in a provincial town.

THE ENVIRONMENT OF POLITICAL BEHAVIOR

To understand the political landscape and its often bewildering shifts in loci of power and factional alignments, one has to consider the economic basis of Middle Eastern society. There are a number of important constraints that render a highly personalized and flexible system of local-level political organization advantageous. These, in turn, affect the development and stability of supralocal forms of political organization and institutions. Local populations, even individuals, by necessity cultivate and maintain multiple political and social ties with each other that allow them to cope with prevailing uncertainties of all sorts. One is tempted to say that when it comes to politics in the Middle East, there is more there than anywhere else. Let us see why this should be the case and what forms politics takes.

Until a few decades ago, when improved transportation and oil money made imported food available, the population of the Middle East was almost completely dependent on local agricultural production. Throughout history, larger urban centers relied on food produced in their immediate hinterlands. With the exception of a few Mediterranean cities, transport was limited to costly overland routes, which precluded haulage of bulk food items such as grain. At the same time, as we described in Chapter 1, the potential for agricultural production is highly variable, with sharp contrasts between productive and marginal lands, between those suitable for crops and those suitable for animal husbandry. Furthermore, within regions, members of particular communities were differentiated in terms of their access to critical resources of land and water and in terms of their place in the system of production. A great deal of exchange of food items, labor, and other services exists within village communities and, in particular, between peasants and the towns to which they are inevitably tied. This urban-rural exchange is due to the fact that no farming community is entirely self-sufficient, because tools, clothing, and numerous items of household necessity and consumption are produced by urban craftspeople. Urban populations themselves depend on extraction of food surpluses from the countryside, whether taken in the form of trade, taxes, rent, or tribute.

The result of this variability in productive potential and regional interdependence is that population is distributed unevenly, with concentrations in areas of high potential and low densities elsewhere. Rich lands and prosperous communities often abut poor areas of impoverished populations. Households and local groups often find themselves in competition for scarce resources. Peasants and pastoralists may fight for the same well, just as farmers may contend for control of vital irrigation canals. Communities, neighbors, and even relatives may frequently find themselves in competition, even as they rely on each other for help and exchange.

Environmental uncertainty is another constraint; most farming communities periodically face conditions of drought, erosion, crop and animal epidemics, and the like. This makes understandable the multiplicity of associations and the intensity with which individuals pursue social relations with others both within and outside their own neighborhoods and immediate communities. Observers of social life throughout the Middle East have been struck by the great amount of time and energy individuals spend socializing and politicking.[1] Whether it be the ubiquitous teahouses of Turkey, Iraq, or Iran, the village guesthouses of Syria, or the urban coffee shops of Egypt, clusters of men meet almost daily to reaffirm existing ties, to forge new ones, and to keep an eye on the activities of others in the community.

Another important component of the political environment today, which constitutes perhaps the most important single variable affecting everyday politics, is the pervasiveness of authoritarian leadership and highly centralized and frequently capricious state institutions. Even in countries with multiparty systems, governmental bureaucracies, not to mention the military, are part of the backdrop to everyday political behavior and cannot be ignored by the actors. This has also been true historically.[2] For one thing, shifting state policies and interventions into local politics contribute an element of uncertainty to any local political equation. Even where the state is only partly in control of territory, it still will have the ability to alter local relationships of power and authority. Moreover, it is usually in its interest to do just that in order to limit decentralizing or competing forces. Often, local leaders, be they tribal, religious, or elected, are both validated by the state and, at times, removed by state agencies. Since authoritarian structures are particularly prone to intrigue, factions, and rivalry among competing loci of power, the level of uncertainty attending state policies and practices is profoundly felt. The wise leader keeps his options open, but even the citizen at large makes political investments with caution and an eye toward possible change.

A political paradox is that authoritarian rule and a generalized local acceptance or even endorsement of hierarchical rank and status markers, not to mention deep differences in material well-being, coexist with an ethos of equality, social justice, and equity derived from Islam and, in places, tribal values

---

[1] See Shaker Salim's (1962) vivid description of the social and political significance of the tribal guesthouse in southern Iraq; see also Elizabeth Fernea and Robert Fernea (1997) for a more recent view of the same institution.

[2] Jared Diamond, in a recent book comparing the rise to power of great states and empires, attributes the fact that it was European rather than Middle Eastern or Asian civilizations that spread their might globally to the authoritarian nature of very large Eastern empires. In Europe, he argues, there were a large number of smaller, competing states, even free cities, that perforce were constantly experimenting with new technologies and modes of exploiting resources (1999).

(Lindholm, 1996). One obvious reconciliation of this contradiction is that poverty need not reflect adversely on one's character and social autonomy (ibid.). Unfortunately, it often does in reality. Wealth alone may not be a guarantor of high status where descent, honor, piety, and deportment are highly valued, but it certainly helps one build a basis from which power can be transformed into authority and status. On the one hand, values of equality are expressed in both the Quran and in folk ideology. An often cited example is in the ethos of the Bedouin. William Lancaster notes, "The Bedu system is built on the premises of equality, autonomy and the acquisition of reputation" (1977, p. 73). At the same time Arabian society has a long tradition of birth-defined rank and ascribed sanctity of person and lineage. Personal autonomy is valued but within a framework of deference to rank and explicit recognition of subordination or differential social esteem based on family or descent, occupation, and learning. These competing ideologies are also part of the political environment. Individuals constantly manipulate and exploit expectations rooted in both traditions.

Finally, we must not ignore the effect of international politics and interference on the political environment. The first Gulf War between Iran and Iraq resulted in over a million casualties and exhausted the economies of both states. The 1990–1991 war that followed Iraq's invasion of Kuwait caused over 150,000 casualties and led to deep polarization among the Arab states. Further, the series of wars with Israel, so disastrous for the Arab states, left a legacy of mistrust and recrimination that, on a popular level, views all political events as the result of conspiracies and cynical manipulation, whether they are acts of terrorism or revolution.

THE POLITICS OF SOCIABILITY

Men of influence, whether tribal sheikhs, religious leaders, landowners, or even local party officials, all host a seemingly endless stream of visitors in their homes and offices. In fact, it is not a coincidence that the same word, *majlis*, is used to refer both to national parliaments and to the daily meeting of men in the homes of local notables. Women, too, are active in their own parallel networks and patterns of visiting. Although many decisions are imposed on local communities by outsiders—for example, government agents or landowners—there is a strong emphasis on consensual action. At the level of the village, local camp, or small-town neighborhood, many, if not most, decisions affecting public life arise from long discussions, interminable negotiations, and ultimate consensus. Even gossip cannot be thought of as entirely idle. It is often a mechanism for spreading information, influencing decisions, and controlling behavior.

What does all this mean for the individual? And how does this help the household to cope with the problems of livelihood and general security? One obvious result of this intense social contact, whether in the formal men's meetings or in the informal interaction of home visiting, is to maintain a constant flow and exchange of information. People gather and discuss market prices and conditions, hazards along the road, conflicts erupting among neighbors, factors affecting crops and harvests, and, among nomads, even decisions to move camp. Further, one's very security of ownership of property or rights to use critical resources such as water and pasture may ultimately depend on one's ability to maintain an appropriate standing within the community. In emergencies arising from any number of causes, a household will draw on the different ties it has made. Regular acts of sociability serve to affirm current friendships, alliances, and commitments. In a cultural milieu in which even economic transactions are often expressed in a social idiom, it is not surprising that this is so in politics as well. Whom one visits, eats with, and is seen with are often public statements of personal and political loyalty.

A common denominator of local politics is the presence of relatively open, constantly shifting constellations of cooperating and contending households or groups. From the swollen villages of the Egyptian delta to the nomadic encampments of Baluchistan and the suburbs of Beirut, politics is strongly focused on personality and consists largely of changing networks of dyadic ties rather than a commitment to an ideology. These ties are informal "contracts" between two individuals and are based on mutual expectations of loyalty and assistance rather than on commitment to abstract principles or codes, either rules of kinship or of party politics. Even while the substance of politics is carried out in this form, it does not preclude such political structures as tribes, parties, nation-states, or whatever. It does, however, give these structures a distinctive style (see, for example, Dresch & Haykel, 1995).

MEDIATION AND PATRONAGE

The personalized approach to politics is exemplified in many ways. One widely used mechanism for social control and integration is that of mediation. *Wasta*, as it is commonly referred to in Arabic, describes the role played by intermediaries—kinsfolk, religious leaders, or political chiefs—when they intervene to repair personal breaches caused by disputes or to put people in touch with one another for some purpose. Here the *wasta*, or go-between, functions as an all-purpose broker.

Frederick Huxley (1978), in a study that remains unique, describes in detail the language and forms of mediation employed in a Lebanese village where *wasta* is used to resolve and contain conflict within the village community. It is also used, as Huxley puts it, to "tap services provided by outside sources of power (e.g., government)." Villagers who want a new road or school would begin their quest by locating someone well known to them who is also in a position to deal with the appropriate administration officials in Beirut. If the individual succeeds in assisting many villagers, he may develop a circle of clients. Ultimately, his power would come to rest not simply on his office or ability to intervene but on the number of followers upon whom he can draw.

Even politicians use personalized dyadic ties to build followings and to recruit for their causes. These ties may be considered a form of patron-client relationship, with the political figure securing loyalty in exchange for assistance in the form of mediation. In eastern Turkey it is common for politicians and wealthy landlords to enhance their popular followings through the financial sponsorship of marriages or the circumcision rituals of boys from poor families. The sponsor assumes certain responsibilities toward the boy, and the parents, in turn, assume a reciprocal obligation, which may be a vote in the next election.

Just as alliance and expectations of mutual loyalty and support are personalized, so are disagreements and disputes. Publicly expressed disagreements of almost any sort are usually considered evidence of personal animosity. When they occur among friends, they might be taken for disloyalty. Friendly disagreement is generally restricted to a small circle of intimates. Consequently, given the disruptive potential of public disagreement, strenuous efforts are made to cover up or disguise the conflicting interests that underlie compromise decisions. What might be regarded as "lying" or "hypocrisy" in some contexts is thus socially desirable, if not imperative, when it serves to avoid open challenge and possible social rupture.

STYLES OF VILLAGE POLITICS

In a comparative study of political and economic organization of two villages in southern Iran, before the Islamic revolution, Nico Kielstra (1975, 1987), a Dutch anthropologist, describes both formal and informal aspects of the local political system. Kielstra's observations can be generalized to some extent across the region. The formal political structure in Iranian villages, as elsewhere, consists of appointed and elected officials. The *katkhoda,* or headman, is appointed by the government and serves with his elected council of elders, together with a variety of titled religious functionaries, about whom we say more later. The informal world of Iranian village politics expresses itself through a number of loosely structured "conversation groups" focused on particular "opinion leaders." Kielstra describes some of these groups as dominated by young, energetic men. Most groups, however, form around older men who are influential because of their religious status or wealth. One way or another, all men of the village participate in one or more of these conversation groups, including those government officials who happen to be temporarily assigned to villages—for example, the schoolteacher or the commander of the gendarmerie. Issues that concern the village as a whole are discussed and debated in these informal groups. Although some decisions such as military conscription and the like are imposed by government authority working through the headmen, most internal village matters represent consensus or at least compromises acceptable to most sectors.

Within these Iranian villages, as with most communities, interpersonal rivalries and disputes arise over fields and house plots. Even though, as Kielstra describes, open hostilities do erupt on occasion, public expressions of personal criticism are generally muted. Individuals communicate their disagreements in private meetings and at home in conversations with relatives and close friends. These constitute a restricted and confidential communication network through which, unlike the public conversation group, a piece of gossip or a negative opinion can be passed on. Although a recipient of such information is rarely requested to pass on the gossip or personal criticism, it is expected that he or she will ultimately do so. As Kielstra puts it:

> One can always deny that one has said what is reported that he has said since no other witnesses were present. The expression "he lies" (*dorug miguyad*) does not carry heavy moral overtones in Persian. It is simply a refusal to confirm a piece of information that is passed on in the confidential communication network. (1987, p. 156)

These networks of "confidential communications" illustrate the use of intermediaries, even at the most basic household level, in communicating with neighbors and others in the village, thus minimizing the risk inherent in face-to-face confrontation. Even requests for minor favors are usually communicated indirectly, and negotiations of importance—for example, arranging a marriage—are always handled through an intermediary.

Patterns of social control and leadership at the community level take many forms, apart from the informal mechanisms of kinship, conversation groups, and systematic mediation. In general, patterns of social control reflect the overall structure of authority and power in the local society and thus vary from one community to another. For example, where government presence is strong, even minor disputes may elicit government fines and police intervention. Where government is poorly represented, even major conflicts—over land and water rights, for example—may be resolved by informal mediation, if not by force of arms.[3]

Authority, or the right to exercise legitimate power, emanates from two primary sources: the government or state, on the one hand, and the "moral order," including religion, on the other. Power, in contrast to authority, is the ability to coerce or force compliance and may stem from wealth, influential family, or leadership of armed groups (including gangsterism), as well as from the resources of the constituted government.

Even the ubiquitous office of the village headman, locally termed *'omda* (Arabic), *mukhtar* (Arabic and Turkish, meaning "chosen"), or *katkhoda* (Persian),

---

[3] For a sophisticated analysis of the sociopolitical organization of hierarchy and power in a rural region of northern Lebanon, see Michael Gilsenan (1996).

greatly varies in the exercise of authority and power. Headmen of a group of adjacent villages may run the gamut from being virtually powerless to possessing great freedom of decision making and coercion. One may be handpicked by a wealthy landlord, another the hereditary leader of a powerful lineage, and a third simply imposed on a community by the government. All bring to their position different sources of power. Kielstra writes that the elected *katkhoda* of one Iranian village visits relatives in town whenever asked by the government to register conscripts for the army, thus relegating this unpopular task to others. Where households generally have access to sufficient resources, as in small-scale freehold land tenure, the headman may simply represent the consensus of the moment, or he may have assumed a job no one else wanted. Where resources are concentrated in the hands of a few, the headman is apt to represent their interests and correspondingly will either exercise considerable power or simply be a facade for others who remain in the background but in fact hold the power.

AXES OF LOCAL POWER

Although no model exists that adequately explains variability in local power relations, we can ask what are the major axes around which authority is organized. One obvious source of authority or legitimate power is the government, which may intervene to select headmen and appoint other local officials. Most often, governments use the office of headman to incorporate selected local leaders into the national administrative hierarchy. Where the government is expanding its control, headmen may be extremely important agents for effecting change and regulating the day-to-day activities of rural people. Revolutionary Iraq and Egypt are cases in point. In both countries, many important reforms in land tenure and political mobilization were implemented through the offices of village headmen.

Alternatively, the government may select headmen from among tribal leaders or already influential families, such as great landlords, in instances where it chooses to work through established local interests. In a sense this is what happened in Israel when the Israeli government confirmed Arab clan leaders as village headmen. The effect, probably desired by the government, was to strengthen, if not revive, the traditional lineage, or *hamula,* as a significant political structure at the expense of issue-oriented politics. This approach was frequently employed by Ottoman administrators and later by colonial officials. In the mid-nineteenth century, the Ottomans settled a number of nomadic tribes in Anatolia, Syria, and Iraq by making their traditional leaders headmen and granting them title to land and other favors. The descendants of these families are often prominent among the regional elite of today.

Closely related to state-derived sources of authority is the ability of the government to intervene in local affairs through police action, law courts, and other administrative agencies. In resource-poor areas, the government may simply ignore local politics as long as open rebellion is not evident. Most commonly, however, retaining direct administrative control of rural populations is a constant concern of modern states. Political centralization, in fact, requires direct intervention by the government, and almost everywhere the administration of rural areas is the direct responsibility of ministries of the interior and the national gendarmerie.

While governments recognize headmen as officers of the state, the people themselves may view the government as an intrusion and even an illegitimate source of power. In such circumstances, headmen and other local leaders may find themselves working to keep the government at arm's length, rather than conveying local needs to their official superiors. In many instances, a regime will be recognized as a preeminent force within the village or region, but one without moral authority, as, for example, in parts of Iraq following the 1991 Gulf War.

THE MORAL BASIS OF POLITICS

What gives shape and continuity to political behavior in an area is the persistence of a number of what might be called "ideological or moral models," derived either from Islam or from community or tribal sentiment, even though, since the turn of the twentieth century, newer ideologies derived from European models have made their way into the region. One traditional model for legitimate political behavior already discussed is that derived from the concept of the Islamic community, or the *umma*. Another model, which we take up more fully in this chapter, is that of tribalism.

One important but little studied area of political life has to do with the relationship between the perceived moral order and the form of the modern state. Even historically there always existed an unresolved tension between the ideals of the Islamic community and the ruling institutions of the moment. A recurring debate over the centuries has been to define the appropriate political vehicle for Islamic ideals. Today this debate takes on renewed urgency from the fact that Islamist groups have put it on the agenda at every level of society, a topic we discuss in some detail in Chapter 11.

Since the late eighteenth century, nationalism in the Middle East has been a potent intellectual force that has closely followed developments in European political philosophy.[4] The course of nationalism as translated into political action was uneven, and until the 1940s, European agents and army officers

---

[4] There exists an extensive literature on politics in the modern Middle East, specifically on nationalism and other ideologies. For one particularly elegant and now classic analysis of the rise of nationalist thought in the region, see Şerif Mardin (1962). See also James Bill and Carl Leiden (1984). For a very personal account, see Fouad Ajami (1999).

could readily negotiate alliances with local leaders without the latter being necessarily stigmatized as traitors. It was not until World War II that the majority of
the people became citizens of states whose claims to independence rested on
nationalist ideologies, as opposed to dynastic and religious precepts.

The result has been ongoing disagreement about what constitutes proper
or moral government, a lack of consensus that transcends the differences of the
left/right political spectrum with which we are most familiar. Many people find
the contradiction between the Islamic moral basis for society and modern or
national forms of administration of great concern. The Iranian revolution,
which for a time mobilized a united front drawn from the entire society, was
possible because of the chasm that had come to separate the government of the
Shah from any recognized moral right to rule. The Shah's highly touted claim to
continuity with pre-Islamic Persian dynasties was viewed by most Iranians as a
rejection of Iran's Islamic heritage and institutions. Although Iran was an
extreme case because of the isolation of its elite class from the populace at large,
similar contradictions and tensions are evident in most countries. Turkey, the
only officially secular country of the region, is undergoing a form of popular
religious revitalization with both underground and open albeit illegal agitation
for the reestablishment of the Shari'a. All of the Arab states likewise are experiencing political unrest, much of which is expressed in the idiom of religion.
Growing opposition is becoming more vocal in its challenge to the existing
political elite, citing corruption and a betrayal of Islamic principles.

At the level of the urban neighborhood or village, where people interact
on a daily basis, we see almost everywhere the continuing influence of those
who articulate the one broadly accepted code, that of Islam. For the most part,
the activities of local religious teachers and prayer leaders are centered on providing spiritual guidance. However, the line between the religious and political
spheres of action is not always clearly defined, and such leaders are actual or
potential political actors. Even though governments use and attempt to regulate
the activities of religious leaders, such men remain alternative sources of local
authority. In Egypt, for example, as in other countries in the region, there has
been an explosion in mosque construction, funded by neighborhood groups
independently of the government. For such mosques, known as *jami'ahli* (popular mosque), the imam is funded by local donations, whereas the imams of government-sponsored mosques are salaried civil servants. In Turkey, where there
is no shortage of mosques each with its state-employed imam, it is not uncommon to see large groups of men at Friday prayers in the streets, led by a popular
preacher not in the state's employ. Nonetheless, throughout the region, governments keep the activities of religious personages under close surveillance, particularly when they are suspected of political activities.

Of course, secular political leaders or aspirants to power appeal to Islamic
values and modes of discourse. Saddam Hussein, head of an avowed secular
regime and an individual hitherto not known for his piety or religious obser-

vance, began to utilize religious symbols and appeals during and after the Gulf War (1990–1991), including sponsoring mosque construction on a large scale. In Turkey, where a multiparty parliamentary system operates in the shadow of de facto military oversight counterbalanced by strongly held religious views on the part of the majority, all parties toy with Islamic rhetoric: the secularists so as not to alienate the electorate and the Islamists very carefully so as not be barred from politics. One explicitly Islamist party, the Refah (Welfare party), used Islamic discourse to appeal to economically disadvantaged voters. However, after having won the right to lead a government, it was, at the insistence of the military, disbanded by the courts in 1998 for threatening the secular status quo. In the 1999 elections, a successor party captured the mayorships of most large cities and towns. Interestingly, many, if not most, Islamist leaders come from backgrounds involving secular higher education, especially in engineering (Roy, 1994).

This is not to say that religious personages may not have official positions within the state bureaucracy. In Saudi Arabia and the Gulf states, judges (*qadis*) are drawn from the religious establishment. In Egypt, religious teachers are paid by the state, and in Turkey, religious seminaries are run by the government, and their teachers are paid regular salaries as state employees, as are imams and

Campaign poster of the banned Islamist Party in Turkey. The young student is protesting being thrown out of school because she wears a head-scarf.

other mosque employees. Turkey, officially a secular state, is a unique secular country in that, in effect, the state recognizes, trains, and supports an exclusively Sunni, orthodox religious establishment.

Formal religious learning and sacred descent are two potential sources of politically significant authority. With a local reputation for charisma, a man may acquire a substantial following. In many respects, this is a religious version of the patron-client relationship. Fredrik Barth (1959), for instance, in a now classic study identifies two parallel but competing systems of power and authority that coexist in the same community in Swat, a district of West Pakistan. In one, secular leaders whose influence derives from landownership contend for followers; in the other, religious personages or "saints" attract followers and wield considerable power.

Whereas some religious leaders are wealthy in their own right, others rely on donations and gifts from students and disciples. Such men exercise power and influence through their roles in mediation and arbitration. Their moral prestige puts them above family or tribal sentiments, rendering them neutral in disputes. Their neutrality enables them to mediate intervillage disputes, and the fact that they may be part of a larger network of scholars or learned men facilitates intercommunity communication. As the literate in a largely illiterate society, they emerge as opinion leaders. The homes of well-known religious leaders are likely to be visited daily by a cross section of the community. The poor and the helpless come seeking aid in finding jobs or access to land; the distraught come for spiritual solace; and the wealthy to validate their social positions by public displays of piety and respect. In a study of Iranian clergy, Michael Fisher (1980) documents the way in which clergy who trained under famous scholars go on to establish their own networks of influence and prestige. It will be interesting to see how the influence of the clergy will be affected by rising levels of literacy and, more importantly, growing access to electronic sources of information. Their role as transmitters and interpreters of textual scripture must surely be diminished or, at the least, modified.

In certain communities, religious personages may form the only real source of leadership and power. In northern Iraq, for example, among both Christians and Muslim minority communities, local leadership revolves in part around the local religious representative—be he a priest, sheikh, or *pir* (Rassam, 1977; see also Van Bruinessen, 1992). Until recently the Shabak, a community of Shi'a sharecroppers near the city of Mosul, relied on their religious leaders, or *pirs*, who were simultaneously heads of mystic orders, judges, teachers, and the chief mediators between the local population and outsiders (Rassam, 1977). More commonly, however, religious leaders act as counterbalances to secular, tribal, or administrative leaders.

Among the Türkmen of north-central Iran, there are two contrasting sources of local leadership and power, each associated with a distinctive form of economic and village organization. Among the Yomut villagers, who live on the fertile plains around Gombad-I-Kavus, where cotton is the primary crop, much power is concentrated in the hands of a few tribal notables, or khans. The khans derive their power from extensive landholdings, as well as from their ability to draw on their tribal supporters. These powerful leaders, although rarely recognized as headmen, maintain close relations with offices of the Iranian government. The Göklan Türkmen, who occupy the adjacent highland area to the east, differ greatly in terms of local leadership. Lacking powerful landowning families for the most part, effective leadership is exercised by *akhunds,* men of religious learning and reputation.[5] Though generally of moderate wealth, the *akhund's* primary source of influence rests on the size of his personal following and general reputation. *Akhunds* themselves meet regularly, and their joint pronouncements on matters of community interest carry great weight.

A second source of religious prestige, as we mentioned earlier, derives from sacred descent. Even here there are gradients of prestige, with the greatest accruing to the descendants of 'Ali and the Prophet's daughter, Fatima, who are referred to in the Arab world as Ahl al-Beit. Lesser lines of holy descent are traced through other relatives of the Prophet or even his companions. This ascribed status may or may not have political saliency, depending on circumstances. Descendants of the Prophet, known as sayyids, command special recognition. Their bodies and property are inviolable, and they are thought to possess the special spiritual quality of *baraka.* Even though many may be no different from the rest of the members of the community, some manage to employ their status to gain political influence. They may become successful mediators, as they can travel without fear among hostile neighbors. Among the Türkmen of Iran, entire tribes or lineages are thought to be "holy" in this sense. They marry among themselves, and they usually reside in separate villages or in their own quarters. Not surprisingly, their communities form a regular line in the border area of two formerly hostile populations, the Yomut and the Göklan.[6]

The political power of men of holy descent, whether in southern Arabia, Iraq, or Iran, is not simply inversely proportionate to that of the central government. The influence of religious leaders in fact may be strengthened by their ability to mediate local needs within an administrative framework; and claims of holy descent are probably of most significance in circumstances in which descent itself is the primary political idiom—that is, among tribally organized populations.

What has to be borne in mind in looking at local variations in political processes are the ways that people draw upon both moral and material sources of power and translate them into political activity. A religious leader may well acquire wealth, land, and even governmental recognition. A successful secular

---

[5] Türkmen usage of this title differs sharply from the Persian, where it may be used derisively.

[6] The classic monograph on the role of holy lineages in tribal areas is that of Ernest Gellner (1979).

leader may in time acquire a moral image, or even a holy lineage through a "discovered" genealogy. Governments may encourage sayyids to go to troublesome regions to mediate disputes and thereby facilitate state control. Such a policy was followed by the Ottomans in Iraq; a number of "holy families" were invited to come from Medina and to reside in Mosul and other cities. Having come to do good, many did well, becoming large landowners whose lifestyles often appear unencumbered by sanctity.

TRIBES AND TRIBALISM

Throughout we have used the term *tribe* frequently and in different contexts. We described the political structure of the Türkmen of northern Iran, the Yörük of southeast Turkey, and Al-Murra of Arabia as tribal. We talked about the shift in political organization in southern Iraq as a tribal confederacy was absorbed into a state bureaucracy. At this juncture in our consideration of political processes, it is appropriate to take up the question of tribalism. Our organizing questions are: What makes a tribe? Under what set of circumstances do people use this form of social and political organization, and to what ends? Does tribalism as a form of social identity differ from ethnicity, and under what circumstances does it persist or dissolve? And finally, what can be identified as distinctive to the Middle Eastern version of tribalism today?

In our view, tribalism in the Middle East is best considered as one organizational principle in a dynamic and complex political environment. Other organizational principles include ethnicity, religion, and even nationalism. As Fuad Khouri (1980) puts it, "Tribalism is not a single phenomenon, an undifferentiated whole, a peripheral social system or simply a stage in the evolution of human civilization" (p. 12). It is, rather, a persistent social and political force bringing together people for many different purposes, and doing so in the context of many different, competing, or alternative principles of alignment.

Carleton Coon (1958) noted that virtually everywhere one sees the contrast between the "lands of the governed" and the "lands of insolence," where the authority of the state finds its limits defined not by national frontiers but by internal opposition.[7] In the past, powerful landlords, charismatic religious leaders, and political dissidents of all kinds mobilized followers for concerted political action, opposition, or outright rebellion. In Lebanon today, local "big men" (za'ims) continue to hold sway and divide the country among themselves into closely held fiefdoms. Their claim to leadership, apart from raw force, is often based on long-recognized claims of landownership and patronage. But perhaps

---

[7] This opposition between core areas effectively governed by the sultan and marginal areas where "anarchic" tribes prevailed has been especially elaborated for Morocco, where a historical distinction is drawn between *bled al makhzan*, the land of the governed, and *bled al siba*, the land of violence. For an overview of this, see Ernest Gellner (1979).

the most distinctive basis for local group recruitment and political action in the Middle East is that of tribalism. Time and time again the tribal idiom has been utilized to express opposition to the state itself, even to topple governments and dynasties. In fact, what most distinguishes the Middle East politically is the persistence of tribalism coexisting with the state.

As we have noted, the state in its various forms has existed for millennia in the area, but so too have alternative and complementary modes of political organization. At times tribalism has been compatible with the state and at times it has been antithetical to the interests of centralized rule. Although the tribe as a form of kinship organization has important social and economic functions, its primary significance in the history of the Middle East has been in the political arena. Ibn Khaldun, the fourteenth-century Arab historian, identifies the notion of *'asabiya*, tribal or group sentiment, as the main driving force underlying historical dynastic change.[8] *'Asabiya* is seen as the sentiment that justifies and legitimizes concerted political action; it is at once a statement of shared genealogical roots and loyalty to the group of people formed on this basis. Thus, the sense of *'asabiya*, or identification with a genealogically defined group, can be an important component of an individual's personal identity, as well as the potential basis for group recruitment.

Without going into anthropological debates and controversies regarding the notion of "tribe," for our purposes local usages suffice. A tribe is a named group claiming common descent in the patrilineal line, that is, a purportedly unbroken chain of male descendants from a common male ancestor, and using the same descent criteria to distinguish named groupings of varying degrees of inclusivity within it. These are named lineage or clan groupings above the household level, commonly referred to in the literature as "segments." We will use the term *segmentary tribe* without assuming that all tribes share a common pattern of leadership and group structure. What sets unilineal descent apart from kinship in general is that it defines groups or potential groups vis-à-vis one another; in this way unilineality can and often does become a potent political principle.

Unilineal descent is the core concept underlying tribes and tribalism in the Middle East. It creates group boundaries and establishes a framework for relating different groups to each other. The groups formed by this principle may vary greatly in size, ranging from a handful of households to a grouping of many thousands. Members of such a grouping may reside contiguously, or they may be dispersed among others. Local groups mobilized by the principle of patrilineal descent, that is, tribes or tribal segments, may control such resources as land, water, and pasture; they may act together to defend a territory or even to promote a special ideology. The actual composition of these groups will almost inevitably include people who are not biologically related or whose

---

[8] Ibn Khaldun's theory of the circulation of ruling elite is based on notions of group solidarity that anticipated Emile Durkheim's distinction between mechanical and organic solidarities.

claims to common patrilineal descent are dubious or merely putative. What is important, however, is the strength and consistency in employing the claim of common descent to mobilize and rationalize collective behavior.

TRIBAL STRUCTURE AND THE SEGMENTARY MODEL

Before we take up the dynamics of tribal politics, we should describe the commonly encountered formal components of tribal society in the Middle East. We use Arabic terms because they are widely employed, but keeping in mind that similar units of organization are distinguished by Persian-, Kurdish-, and Turkish-speaking tribal communities. The basic unit of tribal society, like that of society at large, is the individual household, *al beit*. This term encompasses the inhabitants and their dwelling, and consists of closely related persons living under the same roof or in the same compound and highly dependent on one another for their livelihoods. The Türkmen description further illustrates the meaning of household: They say the household is simply those people "whose expenses are one"; another idiom is "those who share the same cooking pot."

A number of households whose heads share an immediate patrilineal relationship to an ancestor two to five generations back constitute a second level of organization, which is often called a *fakhd,* a lineage. It is at this point that the tribal idiom defines a group that has potential political significance. Members of the same *fakhd* may share a sense of collective responsibility for property and person, and may own property in common. The households of such a group are likely to be linked to one another by a history of close interpersonal relations, including ties of marriage, and by the sharing of a common name. They also share a common reputation expressed in the code of honor. Often, but not inevitably, the *fakhds* take the name of their shared ancestor. In theory, both men and women remain identified throughout their lifetimes with the lineage into which they were born. Should women marry outside their lineages, they nevertheless consider themselves members of their father's group, and should they be repudiated or divorced, they return to it.

A number of those lineages, again claiming descent from a yet more distant common ancestor, form a larger unit, usually called *'ashira*. Using the same idea of a common ancestor, a group of *'ashiras* may form a tribe, *qabila*. In practice, both the terms *'ashira* and *qabila* are interchangeable.

It is the existence of a number of levels of organization of varying degrees of inclusiveness, all formed by the same principle of descent, that distinguishes tribal society. Moreover, these different levels of organization have different political and economic significance for the individual members of the tribe. For example, in a nomadic pastoral society like Al-Murra, those tents that camp and move together are most likely to belong to the same *fakhd*. In times of serious conflict with outsiders, more inclusive levels of tribal organization may become operant, bringing together distant relatives who would rarely see each other on a daily basis.

In forming and consolidating ever-larger groupings, there is one dominant principle, which is expressed in the Arabic proverb "I against my brother; I and my brother against my cousin; I and my brother and my cousin against the stranger." This saying expresses an ideal of how things should be in principle—namely, that closely related individuals and groups should automatically unite, and that claims of blood take precedence over other commitments. In fact, it is recognized everywhere that patterns of cooperation and alliance are not automatic. Lineages and tribes are as apt to be rent by factions and disagreements as are any other communities. The precedence of blood and the idea of solidarity derived from shared patrilineal descent are fundamental principles of organization. They constitute the norm against which behavior is measured and loyalty is judged.

The model for understanding tribal organization was first formulated in 1940 by E. Evans-Pritchard for the Nuer of Sudan and is known as the principle of segmentary lineage. It has been widely used and argued over by anthropologists interested in understanding the political processes of tribally organized

A group of Bedouin men in Jordan.

peoples in the Middle East and Africa. The segmentary lineage principle tries to answer the important question of how order is maintained in the absence of central power. It does so by positing the principle of complementary opposition, which is illustrated in the proverb just cited. According to this principle, segments of the tribe or group are expected to ally themselves or coalesce with other groups of the same level according to proximity of descent. It is assumed that all segments or lineages at the same level are roughly the same size and strength and that all individuals in the tribe are equal in status. If this were the case, then it would follow that there would always be a balance of power within the tribe, which would dampen disputes and prevent them from ramifying through the group.

Najwa Adra provides a concise description of the nature of the tribal mode of organization in central and northern Yemen, and a clear statement of how this ideology is supposed to work as a model:

> Segmentary organization provides mechanisms for the bringing together of increasingly larger groups according to need without endangering the autonomy of each segment. At each level there are distinct segments, the members of which may be called upon to cooperate with each other or with members of other segments in situations where there is a perceived need for common action. The system is held together by ideological ties of common responsibility . . . genealogy, geography, and political or administrative expediency combine to determine the loose segmentary organization of the tribes of the central and northern highland. (1985, pp. 275–286)

The stress has to be at least as much on political and administrative expediency as anything else. Paul Dresch (1984), also with reference to Yemen in particular and Arab tribes in general, notes that observers have emphasized either the tribe and its structure as an entity or the pattern of leadership. More to the point, he writes, is to see how they intersect and influence each other. If the principle of segmentation was a sufficient model in itself, tribal leadership would be a simple product of the points of fission and fusion, which it patently is not in Yemen or elsewhere (see also Dresch & Haykel, 1995). Both the actual structure of relationships among named tribal segments—that is, the formation and loss of segments with time—and leadership are one ongoing process of negotiation. While force of arms may play a role, as do geography and demography, there is much more to this process. Leadership is never axiomatic nor based on simple force. "When one examines the ethnographic record to determine what it is that Middle Eastern tribesmen are doing in political acts, one finds that they are talking to each other probably more than they are fighting, and that this has to be explained by a native model of the person as an autonomous actor in an egalitarian society, with the consequent or attendant belief that the basis of power is persuasion rather than the exercise of force" (Caton, 1987, p. 86; see also Caton, 1990).

The principle of segmentary lineage is an ideal or theoretical construct used by people to describe their own social order. It is not an accurate reflection of behavior. Complementary opposition is likewise an ideal statement expressing the primacy of kin loyalty. As Philip Salzman notes, it is also a statement about the contextual nature of loyalty and alliance (1978). It signifies that alliances among people and groups are impermanent and shifting, as allies are brought together according to the circumstances of the particular situation and especially the relationships that exist between the people involved. In a way peculiar to Middle Eastern tribal politics, professions of loyalty and alliance contain an important caveat: "subject to prior claims."

The assertion of the primacy of patrilineal ties is more often a political metaphor than a description of the substance of a particular relationship or alliance. In practice, lineages and tribal segments described in the ethnographic literature contain individuals who are not actually related to the patrilineage or who are related to it by matrilineal ties only. Similarly, as Emrys Peters (1967) and others point out, alliances among lineages do not follow the closeness of the geneaological tie. Thus, even though segmentary ideology is a model used to order or explain political relations in general, it by no means determines them.

Keeping this in mind, we can say that some variant of the segmentary lineage model of society is a shared structural element of Middle Eastern tribes. Another shared aspect of political organization is the vesting in close patrikin of the responsibility for one's social behavior, reputation, and personal security. The code of vengeance and the shared "fund of honor" express and affirm collective responsibility. Although this may appear simply to reflect the lineage model, it actually adds an important complication, one that often sets effective limits to the cohesion of patrilineal groups.

Whereas common descent is the rationale for forming large named groups, personal security lies in a circle of relatives focused not on an ancestor but on the individual himself or herself. Thus, each individual (apart from his or her siblings) will have a unique cluster of patrikin who bear primary responsibility toward him or her. Such ego-centered protection or vengeance groups are sometimes called a "sliding lineage." Unlike the descent-defined or fixed lineage, the individual's vengeance group is his or hers alone. Close relatives will, of course, have overlapping circles of kin, but some will nevertheless be more closely related to one party than to another.

The way in which this circle of kin is defined and their rights and obligations vary from tribe to tribe. For example, among the Bedouin of Arabia this group commonly includes all patrikin related to ego by no more than five intervening links of descent. In practice, this includes brothers, uncles, sons, and all first and second patrilateral cousins. This group is often referred to as the *khamsa* ("Five"), and it shares a collective responsibility. Should a man commit a homicide, vengeance could be exacted by killing any male member of his *khamsa*, although usually vengeance is directed to those most closely related to the murderer. The Yörük of Turkey similarly organize personal security in terms of a cluster of patrikin but do not define this grouping as precisely as do the Bedouin. Vengeance and collective responsibility do, however, extend to first cousins. The Türkmen of Iran term their vengeance grouping "those to whom the blood reaches," and it is defined as those who share a common patrilineal ancestor in seven or less generations.

Because most individuals within a community have unique but overlapping vengeance groups, the potential for conflict to result in serious social disruption is high. It must be said, however, that given the overlapping nature of these groups of collective responsibility, people in tribal society are usually very concerned about the behavior of their relatives, and much effort is put into defusing conflict and preventing physical violence. For example, among the Yörük, responsible relatives and friends are expected to keep men apart who are known to be on bad terms so as to minimize the chance of open conflict. Inevitably, however, this personalized system of social control sets effective limits on the size and solidarity that lineage segments can achieve and often is the reason for groups to split and reconstitute themselves as separate entities.

Demographic fluctuations, internal factioning, and infighting or even warfare can easily result in substantial differences in lineage size within a particular tribal system. When the lineage controls land or pasture, smaller declining lineages may simply be absorbed by their more powerful neighbors. When control of resources does not depend on the power of the local segment—for example, when land titles are enforced by the state—small lineages may easily coexist alongside larger ones (see Lancaster, 1997).

AUTHORITY, LEADERSHIP, AND TRIBAL SOCIETY

The question of social and economic equality within Middle Eastern tribal society is a complex one. There is great variability among tribal groups in terms of leadership patterns and social and economic differentiation, as well as in fundamental ideologies regarding social equality. For example, the Türkmen, although in many respects fiercely egalitarian, nevertheless distinguish two social categories within each lineage. Individuals are regarded as either *iğ*, "free," or *qul*, "slave," the latter being all those whose ancestry includes someone of non-Türkmen descent. All dress the same, mingle freely, enjoy the same standard of living, and are indistinguishable from one another—with the exception of a slight reluctance for free families to intermarry with slaves, although such marriages do, in fact, occur. Much more important nowadays is the pervasive economic stratification unrelated to this distinction based on access to land and other resources in a rapidly developing cash economy. This is quickly creating divergent patterns in standards of living, education, and dress. The tribal idiom of political organization does not preclude the development of socioeconomic distinctions, however much these distinctions may threaten tribal cohesion in the long run.

The case of the classic Bedouin of Arabia is more complicated. Bedouin recognized several distinct categories, even within one tribal confederation. Among the camel herders, for example, one lineage was likely to be considered of superior descent and to possess an inherent claim to fill positions of leadership for the tribe as a whole. Also, the tribe may have had a number of lineages that have no descent ties to the dominant one, but might simply have been clients, a form of second-class citizenship. At the apex were the noble lineages of the camel-herding tribes of the Arabian Peninsula, the so-called pure *bedu* or *asilin*, those of pure descent. The sheep and goat herders, or *shawiya*, enjoyed lesser status. Those *shawiya* engaged mostly in agriculture had the lowest prestige of all. These status distinctions did, to a certain extent, reflect political reality in that camel herders were the most mobile and powerful of the desert tribes. At the bottom of the social scale were the slaves and blacksmiths, who constituted a virtual caste group. Tradition claimed that Allah created the first Bedouin and the blacksmith at the same time. In Arabia, blacksmiths formed a small endogamous group and attached themselves to individual tribes.

The prevalence of inequality and social differentiation among tribal groups might seem to call into question the segmentary lineage theory, which stresses equal membership for all individuals of comparable genealogical standing. Actually, equality in esteem in principle need not entail economic equality. The question of economic equality or stratification in tribal societies cannot be viewed either in the abstract or in isolation from the larger society in which the tribe exists. For example, the Türkmen, whom we described as egalitarian in ideology, today are largely settled in agricultural villages where households may vary greatly in wealth and standards of living. This is increasingly reflected in the actual distribution of political power, as some men exert great influence.

TRIBES AND STATES

In the preceding pages, we sketched some of the principles and constituent elements of tribal organization in the Middle East. Remaining is the question of the relationship of tribes to centralized rule and the dynamics of tribalism. When do tribes emerge as important in the national political arena? What is the future of tribalism? What is the relationship of tribalism to the state?

We said earlier that a distinctive feature of tribalism in the Middle East is its integration with state forms of political organization. This is in contrast to tribalism in many parts of sub-Saharan Africa, which makes it risky for anthropologists and political scientists to extrapolate from the experiences of that region. The tenacity of the tribal idiom in the Middle East has to be understood in the context of a long tradition of urbanism and centralized rule.

Tribes are not simply coexistent with institutions of state rule and urban domination; they are an integral part of the total whole. Tribes or tribal confederations were identified throughout history with the formation of dynasties and contributed to the military and administrative cadres of a number of states. The importance of the tribal idiom in recruiting, mobilizing, and organizing people has varied historically and according to specific circumstances. But tribalism has always been a potent political force. The trend may well be, as we speculate, for tribalism in the modern state to increasingly resemble ethnicity. If this is the case, its primary significance will be less as a source of political mobilization than as a source of individual identity.

Tribalism in the Gulf states, in Arabia, and in Syria and Jordan is very different from the recent Iranian or Turkish experience. In Iran and Turkey, tribalism is regionally politically significant inasmuch as tribal identities overlap ethnic ones, as with the separatist movements among the Kurds, Baluch, and others. Moreover in southeastern Turkey, Kurdish and tribal leaders (*ağas* and sheikhs) are also large landlords owning, in some cases, entire villages. In contrast, in the Gulf and in Arabia, tribes are closely integrated into the government apparatus and are significantly represented among the ruling elite. In Jordan, too, tribal elements are prominent among the military. Egypt is the only country in which tribalism is of no political consequence; few people are tribally organized and those who are are spatially as well as socially peripheral to centers of power and population.

From time immemorial, control of rural populations has posed problems for urban-based rulers and administrators, a problem that persists even today. How can a government control far-flung and highly disparate rural populations, maintain inland trade routes, secure markets, and tax revenues? Even poor areas that do not offer a high potential in terms of revenue may nevertheless be critical in terms of trade routes and the security of adjacent zones of high productivity. Such regions are inherently costly to control and administer. A common response is to lightly garrison such areas, in which case such administration as exists will depend on local structures of power, among them tribes.

The state was often able to maintain an uneasy and incomplete hegemony through shifting its support among rival tribal leaders and local groups. Throughout their long history, the Ottomans tolerated and even encouraged tribalism, as have other governments in the region. In other areas where logistics and communication problems made tribes impossible to administer, state control consisted largely of occasional punitive expeditions and of treaties with local leaders. Such was the case in the Arabian Peninsula. Rather than even attempt to collect taxes in such areas as the Kurdish highlands and the Türkmen and Baluch regions, the state frequently paid off local tribal leaders to keep the peace. In such circumstances, tribes and their leaders were not merely the prevailing forms of political and social organization, but the only ones. This picture has, of course, changed dramatically since the 1920s, as governments now have recourse to air power. The British earned the dubious distinction of being the first to put down a tribal rebellion by air power, in Iraq in 1919. In March of 1988, the regime of Saddam Hussein bombed the Kurdish town of Halabja with poison gas, killing at least 5000 people (*Daily Telegraph*, London, March 4, 1988).

It has also, as noted in Chapter 6, diverted water from the southern marshes to control tribes there.

For rural populations everywhere, close government administration is an uncertain proposition. Although security of property and relief from banditry are obvious benefits, rapacious tax collectors, absentee landlords, conscription officers, and the like add to the burden of the peasantry and reinforce their suspicion and widespread distrust of governments and their agents. This, in turn, fosters or reinforces a dependency on local loyalties, including those of family and tribe, at the expense of political loyalty to the larger state order. Though it is not uncommon for tribal leaders to work closely with government officers and to emerge as powerful exploitative landlords in their own right, they are at the same time apt to be more responsive to local conditions and demands.[9]

The ideas sketched here can serve as the basis for a general framework for understanding state-tribal relations historically. In a very loose way, they serve as a point of departure for understanding the persistence of tribalism in the Middle East today. The framework rests on several historically recurring processes. One is the common tendency to overtax and exploit the more productive agricultural areas for the benefit of the urban population and the city elite. Another is the tendency of governments to overreach the limits of their actual power in attempting to tax and directly control peripheral areas. This may give rise to local unrest and even organized resistance. Successful local rebellions, however occasioned, frequently encourage neighboring groups to do the same and can quickly create destabilizing economic and political conditions whose effects may be widely felt. Local rebellions interrupt vital communications, occupy the military and other agencies of the state, and generally strain the resources of the government. In order to meet such challenges, governments may well institute policies of harsher taxation, which sometimes foment further unrest. For instance, in his attempt to impose direct central rule throughout Iran, Reza Shah had to engage in full-fledged warfare with a number of tribal confederacies in succession. His military success was achieved at considerable expense and left much bitterness, which proved fatal to his dynasty. Also, as noted earlier, in attempting to increase their control over the tribes of the Arabian Peninsula, the Ottomans precipitated the Wahabi movement in the mid-eighteenth century.

When tribally organized societies are faced with expanding or encroaching state control or authority, they often evidence a parallel political response in the form of stronger and more formalized leadership positions. Hitherto largely consensual and informal positions become crystallized. A good example of this is described by Lois Beck (1990, 1991) for the Qashqai. The Qashqai were part of

---

[9] For a discussion of the changing roles of tribal leaders, see Robert Fernea (1970). Also, for a very engaging revisiting of this, see Elizabeth Fernea and Robert Fernea (1997).

a largely pastoral nomadic confederacy, playing an important role in the province of Fars. Tribal leadership positions developed, roughly tracking the formation of the state in Iran in the eighteenth, nineteenth, and twentieth centuries. Emerging paramount leaders "drew their power and authority from diverse sources: their tribal bases, their state, urban, religious, and even international connections; and the rural nontribal agricultural people they governed and controlled" (1991, p. 8). Even at the level of local leadership, a headman's main role, and hence his defining purpose, was to protect his small group from the encroachments of the state and competing tribal forces.

Sometimes, the easiest way to observe political processes at work is to do so over a long period of time. Madawi Al-Rasheed's (1991) historical study of the rise and fall of a local dynasty, Al-Rasheed, in central Arabia clearly illustrates the dynamics of tribal leadership and the interconnectedness of local, regional, and even international politics in a remote region of the Middle East. The author describes her book, on which the following account is based, as "a case study of a process whereby a tribe establishes its hegemony over an oasis which became the capital of a tribal dynasty" (p. 1).

In the early nineteenth century, the Shammar, a large camel-herding Bedouin tribe, inhabited a vast desert area encompassing a cluster of oases, the largest of which, Hail, served as an entrepôt on the trade and pilgrimage routes. A tribal segment of the Shammar had settled in Hail and they were soon joined by a number of Syrian and Iraqi merchants. By the middle of the century, one of the Shammar tribal leaders, Abdullah Ibn Rasheed, had managed to consolidate his power to become paramount in Hail. Hail's strategic position provided him with control over trade and pilgrim routes, and he then exacted tribute from travelers in exchange for safe passage. Abdullah proceeded to build a castle, a prison, a mosque, and a market, transforming Hail into an urbanized town.

Like other Bedouin tribal leaders, Abdullah's authority and claim to leadership rested on a combination of factors that included descent from a prominent lineage and a personal reputation for courage, generosity, and eloquence. Having secured his power in Hail, Abdullah began to extend his authority outside the oasis by winning over other tribal leaders through generosity and diplomacy. In the process he also formed a permanent military force made up of bodyguards and ex-slaves. This "meant more political centralization, consolidation of power, increase in military hegemony, and the establishment of dynastic rule. It is important to stress that this qualitative change was accompanied by a new title to refer to political leadership." With the succession of Abdullah's eldest son, "Rashidis began to be known as amirs rather than sheikhs. The adoption of this title reflected the beginning of a process whereby a tribal 'leader' became an oasis 'ruler'" (pp. 52–53).

By the end of the nineteenth century, the emirate of the Rashidis had succeeded in extending their influence over a large part of central Arabia as far as the Syrian and Iraqi borders. However, this began to change with the rise to power of Ibn Saud, a rival leader whose capture of the town of Riyadh in 1902 marked the beginning of the end of Rashidi rule. In the decades that followed, the contest between Ibn Saud and Ibn Rasheed for control of central Arabia became embroiled in the larger political power game being played by the declining Ottoman Empire and the British. It ended when Ibn Saud, combining Wahabi religious zeal and military power, and with the help of the British, succeeded in conquering and unifying all of central Arabia. In 1932, Ibn Saud declared himself king of the newly created Kingdom of Saudi Arabia.

As we pointed out in Chapter 2, the creation of the Kingdom of Saudi Arabia in a sense also represents a case of a tribe consolidating its power over other tribes and transforming itself into a dynasty. Ibn Saud ruled the new kingdom until his death in 1952, leaving as many as 43 sons to continue his dynasty. Today, they and their sons monopolize all important positions in the country. The government is not unaware of the potential for other tribal groupings or alignments to threaten its rule. Several attempts have been made to settle the Bedouin tribes whose leaders have been, generally, co-opted with financial subsidies and service in the national guard.[10] Ironically, the Bedouin nomads, who today make up no more than 6 percent of the total Saudi population, represent the poorest segment in the kingdom.

The processes outlined here account for the frequently observed paradox that states rely on local tribes and their leaders even while they are potentially threatened by them. Indeed, a government may well enlist tribal allies to put down other tribal dissidents, a process that, even if successful, may create a stronger power base for the victorious ally tribe. Tribalism, whether the state is in political ascendency or decline, exists as an alternative form of political organization, one more closely representative of local or regional interests, and thus potentially, at least, "naturally" competitive with the state form of political organization.

GENERAL OVERVIEW

What makes the tribal idiom of political mobilization particularly potent is that it can persist even where its immediate political expression is suppressed or destroyed. The ideology of local group loyalty continues as the pattern for recruitment and organization. Its strength derives from the fact that it calls upon ties of family and kin, which run far deeper and are more enduring than other claims to loyalty. In short, tribalism is familism writ large.

Another important aspect of tribalism, quite apart from any particular political manifestation or activity of the tribe, is its role as a source of social and group identity. Even where lineages do not own property and cannot mobilize for warfare or other corporate ventures, individuals may nevertheless define their social identities by their tribal affiliations. For example, many urban

---

[10] For an excellent article on the Saudi regime, see Ghassan Salame (1993).

dwellers—especially in the Gulf states but also in the cities of Iraq, Syria, Jordan, eastern Turkey, and Iran—continue to identify themselves as members of named tribal groupings. In Baghdad, quarters of the city are named after tribes and tribal segments. Recent migrants seek out fellow tribal members for assistance.

Even where tribal forms of organization have no formal standing, populations may still maintain a strong sense of tribal identity. Associating with a particular tribe and a constituent lineage provides a person with a local history and quite likely with some specific cultural markers, such as distinctive forms of dress, dialect, and even a special cuisine. Depoliticized tribal groupings may serve as informal organizations for mutual assistance and the pursuit of social activities. Small patronymic groups, such as lineages and shallow clans, closely resemble tribes in structure, even if not explicitly recognized as part of larger, more encompassing tribal groupings. In many rural areas and small towns, as for example, in Turkey and Syria, tribes per se are politically unimportant, but patrilineages or clans of several generations' depth are often important social groupings. Many villages are divided into quarters or wards, each dominated by a core of families belonging to the same lineage. Although they acknowledge a descent relationship among most or all of the lineages in the village, they do not consider this relationship specifically significant, nor do they call themselves a tribe. What is significant here is that the same tribal principles of identity and organization are at work, albeit on a more limited scale—tribalism without tribes.

At this point we have to mention tribalism in conjunction with ethnicity. When tribalism serves primarily as a source of personal and social identity, it is virtually indistinguishable from what we would regard as cultural ethnicity in the United States, Europe, or any other pluralistic society. Even where party politics, job seeking, and patronage are concerned, the parallels between tribalism and ethnicity are obvious. Both serve as the basis for social communication and help to define a person's network. They differ, of course, in the segmentary genealogical structure of tribalism.

Tribalism and ethnicity often have historical associations arising from explicit governmental intervention. Often governments have attempted to defuse tribalism as a political force by introducing ethnically alien populations into troublesome regions. For example, in the nineteenth century the Ottomans settled many Türkmen tribes in Kurdish areas, moved Kurdish tribes into Armenian areas, and settled Circassians and Crimeans throughout Anatolia, Syria, and Jordan. The expectation was that the interspersing of ethnic groups and tribes would prevent the rise of regional movements or rebellion. Tribalism and ethnicity in such heterogeneous areas soon become almost synonymous.

With the rise of modern nation-states in the area following World War I, both tribalism and ethnicity have evolved along somewhat divergent paths. Increasingly, tribalism is functioning more as a source of personal identity rather than as a system of organizing and mobilizing people for political action. This is understandable, given the fact that modern nation-states attempt to hold a monopoly over modern weapons. Nevertheless, tribal organization persists in every country in the region. Increasingly, however, militant tribalism associated with the aspirations and strivings of national minorities seeking political rights or even independence is expressed in the more inclusive idioms of ethnicity, nationalism, and human rights.

11

Challenges and Dilemmas: The Middle East Today

We began the final chapter of the previous edition of this book by posing some basic questions having to do with the political challenges and cultural dilemmas facing people in the Middle East. What struck us in thinking about the same issues some 18 years later is how enduring the questions and problems are. Writing then, just a few years after the Iranian revolution, we asked how the forces of change are viewed by the people caught up in them. What moves Iranian city youth to political action? What underlies the virulence of Turkish civil strife? Why are movements like the Muslim Brotherhood and the Nurcu movement in Turkey, and numerous others, so threatening to current regimes? All of these specific issues are making good newspaper copy today, but with different actors and different voices. Iranian youths are again taking to the streets of major cities, but their ire now is directed not at the "Great Satan" and "Western imperialism" but at domestic structures of repression created by the revolution itself. Turkey continues to suffer civil strife, but unlike in the late 1970s, it is not driven by left versus right ideologies but by perceived cultural repression based on ethnicity or religious expression.

What, we asked then, are some of the major ideological debates, the sources of political hopes, of anger, even of rebellion? The answers, we think, now as then, devolve around political legitimacy, the role of religion in the political order, the emergence of new social formations, and changing individual aspirations. Is this to say that nothing much has changed? That the stereotypic East is doomed to replicate itself endlessly? Absolutely not; indeed, a strong case can be made that changes launched in the last two generations will result in societal transformations as profound as ever witnessed in the West.[1]

---

[1] This theme is explored by Dale Eickelman (1998); see Martin Kramer (1998) for a brief but strong refutation.

These questions, and similar ones, are remote from the usual course of anthropological inquiry; but difficult and controversial as they are, they are questions that must be addressed if we are to arrive at any understanding of Middle Eastern society today. Even a necessarily limited discussion of these issues is fundamental to any kind of synthesis of such material as we have presented in this book. The first issue we will take up concerns political legitimacy and the state. While seemingly at a remove from everyday concerns, responses to this question affect the environment in which social, economic, and political activity unfolds. How, for example, does one reconcile very different perceptions of morality and legitimacy with practical institutions of administration and decision making? What is the role of religion in legislation? Should the state manage the business of economic production and distribution, or should economic activity be privately organized and left to the marketplace? These and many other issues are directly rooted in visions of a just and moral political order.

A second set of issues that we will take up, albeit briefly, has to do with the economic forces at work and how individuals and governments must cope with them. Changing patterns of land use, agriculture, labor force composition, labor migration, and rampant urban growth are all of vital concern, but even more germane are the social divisions that arise from inequities in the distribution of economic rewards. We see the rise of new lines of economic and social segmentation in every country, which, of course, can both influence and be themselves driven by political rhetoric. The repercussions are also felt in the realms of ideology and values.

A third set of issues is the quest for cultural authenticity, continuity, and identity with the past in the face of compelling demands for increased individual autonomy and a global or transnational cultural milieu. It is hard to overestimate the extent to which authenticity and the perceived cultural impact or "hegemony" of "the West" are subjects of discussion. This is not something restricted to rarefied discussions among intellectuals but is very much a part of everyday life, touching on intimate family decisions as to what members might or might not eat, wear, and watch on TV—not to mention courtship, marriage, and lifestyle. All of these, too, have to do with individual identity—who is an Arab, a Turk, a Jew, and how one should behave.

POLITICAL LEGITIMACY, THE MORAL ORDER, AND THE STATE

One aspiration we can attribute to the diverse populations of the region is for a political and social order that, while satisfying their material needs and security, will also be congruent with their vision of a moral and just society. Needless to say, there is no agreement on the path or model to pursue. Unlike a short generation ago, the discussion today is predominantly voiced in cultural rather than strictly political or economic terms. Not very long ago, the models debated, and to varying degrees implemented, were variants on Western-derived models of modernization theory, whether Marxist or socialist, etatist, or "stages of growth." Regimes, with few if any exceptions, pursued development agendas that were imposed from the top down, with little local input. Today local voices are being raised, and listened to, even in totalitarian states. These voices use the idioms of human rights, individual rights, environmental protection, women's rights, democracy, and, of course, Islam.

The specific evolution of independence or revolutionary movements and the rise of particular nation-states are beyond the scope of our discussion. As social scientists, we are concerned here with the social implications of some of these political developments. With the exception of Iran, it was only after World War I that the present political contours of most of the region's countries emerged. Most achieved de facto sovereignty in their current boundaries only after 1945. Over this relatively short period, essentially two generations, the present bureaucracies, administrative institutions, and political apparatus were formed. In some countries, such as the now united Republic of Yemen, the recently constituted Gulf states, and Oman, the process is even more recent. In Afghanistan and Palestine, it has yet to begin.

What concerns us is not the particular events and outcomes in each country, but the fact that everywhere a succession of regimes has managed to extend state power and administrative control, even in the face of resistance and conflict. Whether constituted on the basis of a political party, monarchy, religious oligarchy, or military dictatorship, the governments in the region have progressively extended their authority and assumed new and expanded social and economic functions. As part of this process, they have taken on increased responsibilities for economic planning, administration of law, social control, and security. These are all domains that were formerly, at least in part, within the purview of religious institutions, family, tribe, or local community. Whether the slogans are those of socialism, today rare, nationalism (ubiquitous), or even religious heritage, the objective of those who govern is to consolidate state power in the face of strong centrifugal forces, whether of ethnicity, sectarianism, or regionalism. We cannot resist an aside, to be picked up later, to the effect that the policy that is now triumphant is the one least acknowledged in discourse; that is, the move to free market capitalism, privatization, and entrepreneurship.

While seemingly obvious, these processes of political centralization should not be taken for granted. They constitute the backbone of the transformation that is taking place in every country and affecting most areas of life, even if they have not been experienced to the same degree in each country, and progress has not been equally smooth. In every nation, the extension of state rule has occasioned opposition, sometimes from many quarters representing regional, class, or ethnic interests. The practical manifestations of the drive for political integration include the establishment of direct rule over villages, towns, tribes, and regions, intervention into local patterns of social control, codes of personal status, family law, and education. For example, Saudi Arabia only introduced national identification papers for women in 1999; previously, women were simply listed on their father's or husband's identity cards. Egyptian women gained the right to travel abroad without formal approval of their husbands in 2000. These are not the logical or inevitable results of gradual development; each represents areas of intense and ongoing reflection, debate, and dispute. Even something that appears as natural as extending the age of required public school attendance, as happened in Turkey in 1998, arouses strong responses. Such a law may mean that children must delay when they can contribute to the household income and may entail additional expenses (clothing and the like) for very poor people. It may also mean (depending on the country) that boys will not be able to attend religious seminaries as their parents would wish, and that young women will be forced to be in the company of unrelated young men after puberty, perhaps without the protection of Islamic garb. Changes in personal status and family laws are profound in any society, but we tend to underestimate this when the changes are in directions with which we are already familiar. Most readers of this book take women's rights for granted, but for many in the Middle East, and of all religions, any discussion of individual rights, and most especially those affecting the public behavior of women, can threaten established notions of morality, family honor, and even economic security.

State control of communications media, national systems of justice, and numerous social services also promote the primacy of state authority. With varying degrees of success, every country has instituted birth and marriage registration, identity papers, centrally directed literacy and education programs, military conscription, and regulations concerning property transfers, taxation, and the like. Governmental agencies in some countries regulate commodity prices or offer price supports for certain crops. In this fashion, the state strives to regulate even the basic systems of rural life.

Communications deserve special mention. Since the 1960s, as mass literacy increased, the importance of print media increased, and in most countries was directly or indirectly regulated; censored is perhaps more accurate. With the advent of radio and TV ownership on a near universal scale, control of these media was also the purview of the state, and they were often used relentlessly to promote the message of the regime of the moment. For example, educational and other national media are frequently utilized to disseminate the idea of a "national culture," emphasizing shared historical experience and promoting identification with the nation-state. In Yemen, for example, the last 20 years have seen great growth in government employment, and the traditional sheikhly hierarchy has been largely incorporated into the state (Mundy, 1995).

Recently, just as elsewhere in the world, technology has overtaken the censor.[2] This is a major setback for state control, but it actually does fit in with

---

[2] Martin Stokes (1999) offers a contrary opinion: Censorship and government influence in the media continue to be practiced and their impact may, he suggests, be increasing.

centralization of a different sort—global networks and transnational movements. Just as in the late 1970s, when the Shah of Iran was unable to control the flow of cassette-recorded messages, sermons, and calls to revolution coming from outside the country, today no state can police cyberspace or prevent fax communications however subversive. Satellite dishes are ubiquitous in most countries, even where supposedly outlawed. Thus, regardless of state policy, people can in effect listen to and view what they wish. This has led to a rather interesting duality. On the one hand, personal telephones, faxes, the Internet, and e-mail facilitate business and social networks within countries and cities, thereby binding closely together people who might otherwise rarely communicate—not to mention giving access to sources of "global culture." This might be seen as having a homogenizing effect on local culture. But at the same time, the same technology can be used to promote the presence, ideas, and identities of even very marginal groups or movements; one need only to browse the religious and cultural sites and Web pages on the Internet to see this. There are Web pages for any imaginable Middle Eastern political, cultural, special interest, and ethnic formation. Do these threaten the state? They may very well threaten particular regimes and governments, but on balance they may quite plausibly contribute to the emergence of a social order within existing states that emphasizes more individual autonomy.

In every country, different regions, ethnic groups, and economic classes experience the impact of political centralization differently. The government's success in exercising its authority is almost inevitably uneven geographically because some regions are strategically easier to control than others. Both facts are basic to appreciating sources of political instability, even open opposition and rebellion. Not only do certain groups, classes, or regions benefit more from national integration than others, but, in fact, the process of integration always seems to entail the suppression of some groups, or at least the benign neglect of particular regions of the country. In many countries interregional distinctions as measured in living standards and general development have been amplified rather than minimized by political integration, because the balance of political power lies in the more densely populated and industrialized portions of the country. In Turkey, for instance, this is the outcome of regional differences in ability to attract private as opposed to public investment (see Mango, 1995). The same might be said of other countries. In Yemen it reflects the historic division of the country with two major centers of power, San'a and colonial Aden. These, and a number of other cities, thrive at the expense of resource-poor and neglected hinterlands.

From the vantage point of numerous local communities, the costs of national integration are borne inequitably; governments may levy taxes, recruit conscripts, and interfere in local affairs while providing few of the services taken for granted in other regions of the country. States often arouse considerable local opposition as they intervene in matters of land adjudication and reform, family law, or secular education. Opposition may be expressed in overt action by separatist movements, for example, when the government appears vulnerable.

Even where separatist movements are not actively underway, the very process of nation building creates what might be thought of as a "fund of resentment," a latent source of civil disobedience, even rebellion. This, of course, is not unique to the Middle East but is also part of the American and European historical experience, as witnessed in civil disobedience movements and wars. In almost every country we see social fault lines that, while not likely to produce separatist movements, do mark zones of potential or actual conflict. Cases in point include the Shi'a majority in Iraq, long resentful of Sunni dominance, especially the El Chebayish population, which has borne severe oppression at the hands of the Hussein regime; the Copts in Egypt, who are episodically the targets of Muslim extremists; the Palestinians of Israel; and the Shi'a minority of Saudi Arabia—to name a few.

Since their inception in the early nineteenth century, nationalist ideologies mark a radical departure in laying the basis for a concept of "citizenship" based on membership in a territorially defined, secular state. One partial exception today is Saudi Arabia, where the concept of *umma*, as interpreted by Wahabi doctrine, continues to be the primary legitimizing ideology for the state. But even here, much power is vested in what is essentially a modern bureaucracy and secular civil service. Even after many years in power, Ayatollah Khomeini's successors in Iran have not really addressed the issue of how to reconcile the concept of *umma* with that of the nation-state. While striving for the establishment of a pan-national "Islamic state," the political expression of the *umma*, they have had, quite paradoxically, to rely on appeals to Iranian nationalism.

The conflict inherent in the often-contradictory claims of religion, ethnicity, kinship, and nationalism is rarely resolved in any country. In Turkey, a country of intense nationalism, a large Kurdish minority continues in an uneasy accommodation with the Turkish majority, while at the same time forces of religious conservatism find sympathetic audiences in all of the many ethnic groups making up Turkish society. Compounding the problem of conflicting loyalties is the fact that even secular nationalist ideologies can cut two ways. For example, even though Arab nationalism expresses the unity of all Arab speakers, when espoused by any particular leader or country as a political policy, it is likely to be divisive. This is because the appeal of this ideal is often used to promote narrower interests—for example, the primacy of one Arab country or faction over another. One reason why the appeals to Arab nationalism on the part of dictators such as Saddam Hussein or Qadafi have failed to achieve any lasting political unity or even short-term coordination is because leadership is inextricably joined to national interest.

If not nationalism, then what? Does a politicized Islam offer a genuine alternative? Against the background of only partially successful nationalist movements, and taken together with the failure of the socialist model, it is understandable that Islamic appeals have a powerful resonance. In looking at this phenomenon, variously referred to as Islamism, fundamentalism, or even neo-fundamentalism, one should keep several points in mind. First, the "clash of civilizations" model clearly does not fit with the facts on the ground. Virtually every scholar familiar with the recent developments within the Islamic world agrees that while there are shared forms of discourse and similarities in stated objectives, they mask great diversity in actual practice. There is no monolithic, determinedly anti-Western "Islam in flames" but, rather, a wide range of different and competing models—and none, including the Iranian model, with such an impressive record of accomplishment or even clarity of intellectual formulation to attract much emulation beyond its own backyard. Second, the new political formulations are not simply advocating a return to historically operant modes of governance. Political Islam is itself a product of modern nation building and contemporary world culture. Both the earlier Arab secular socialism and today's Islamic militancy exemplify this. Coming from different intellectual sources, each calls for a fundamental restructuring of society—that is, total revolution.

We cannot examine all facets of political Islam, but we can emphasize some useful distinctions. Most would agree with Olivier Roy (1994), that the origins of the contemporary proliferation of Islamic "revolutionary" movements can be traced back to two anticolonial movements of the 1930s: the Muslim Brotherhood in Egypt, founded by Hasan al Banna, and the Jamaat-i Islam party in India, founded by Abdul-Ala Maududi. Both mark a major break with tradition by rejecting their own historicity—that is, they legitimize themselves not with reference to a long history of Muslim practice and ideological development but by a supposed "return" to the original community of believers (p. 38). Social scientists often term such movements "millenarian" or "utopian." The militant Islamists differ from other conservative or "establishment" Islamic thinkers, often referred to as "fundamentalists" or, increasingly, "neo-fundamentalists," in that they call for political revolution and the restructuring of society as a prior condition for the imposition of Shari'a rule (pp. 168 ff).[3] As Ayatollah Khomeini declared in January 1989, the logic of the revolution takes precedence over the application of the Shari'a.

The Islamist movements differ from the so-called fundamentalists in two other regards. Outside of Iran, they generally are not led by clerics but by secularly educated individuals, often teachers or engineers. Further they differ with regard to the role of women. While affirming sexual segregation and Islamic codes of modesty, they nevertheless favor education for women, public sector employment, and their participation in political associations and party wings. In Turkey, for example, the Refah party and its moderate Islamist successor, the Fazilet party, used women as a major component of their neighborhood recruitment strategy. In Iran, women are visible political players across the spectrum.

---

[3] These terms are used in many, often contradictory, ways by both outside observers and Muslims.

How successful have the Islamists been? Obviously the jury is out, and there are some contradictory indicators. In Turkey, where there is an active multiparty system, albeit one existing by sufferance of the military, moderate Islamists lost electoral ground in the 1999 elections for parliament but retained mayoral control of most towns and cities. Clearly, in Turkey, as elsewhere, the Islamist appeal is not simply rural, but it is also clear that key aspects of their populist platform can be appropriated by competing parties, including extreme nationalists. In many cities in Turkey, Jordan, Egypt, and elsewhere, the Islamists proved more capable than their critics had thought them in combating urban problems, renovating public spaces, and providing services. Still, after a significant period of Islamist power, allegations of corruption and mismanagement are heard about as frequently as before.

Of course, most Islamist movements do not operate in a multiparty environment, but we can cautiously agree with Roy that generally the extreme militants are losing ground. They are viewed as having little prospect for changing society—and the idea of a return to an idealized Islamic state is quixotic. The Iranian model is not attracting many adherents because a generation of Islamist rule has achieved very little, in addition to dragging the nation into a costly war with Iraq. Their main appeal at the beginning of the twenty-first century may be similar to that of the "liberation theology" of the 1980s in South America and restricted to groups such as the Palestinian Hamas, the Hezbollah in Lebanon, the Islamic Salvation Front (FIS) in Algeria, and groups in the Caucasus and Central Asia who see themselves as actually fighting wars of liberation (see Roy, 1999; Malik, 1998).

If, as we tentatively suggest, the extreme Islamists qua activists or militants are in decline, or at least experiencing diminishing growth, where does that leave those who look to Islam for political direction? Again following Roy and others, such as Henry Munson (1998), it is possible to see two broadly defined courses of action. One, and happily the road least traveled, is that of uncompromising revolutionary zeal, such as the Taliban of Afghanistan and groups, usually Sunni, such as that of Osama bin Laden, operating under a welter of often changing names, that view almost every state as illegitimate. They are not infrequently composed of men who have fought in Afghanistan and Bosnia, and appear to follow a messianic vision in which violence toward anything perceived to be Western-derived is almost a cultural tenet—not dissimilar to the Red Army movements in Japan and Western Europe in the 1970s. Similarly, militant groups have proliferated in Russia's Caucasus region and in Central Asia. At times Islamic appeals seem little more than efforts to legitimize thuggery and warlordism. This militant and highly fragmented minority bears virtually no resemblance to conservatives or reformers in general, apart from some shared elements of rhetoric.

Much more viable as a response, and still potentially threatening to the established elite in many countries, are those who choose to work within the system to create "Islamic spaces" and social structures. That is, these groups work at the local level to challenge the established order at its legal margins by organizing neighborhoods and villages into "islands" of Islamic life—places where modest dress is perforce observed, only *halal* foods are sold and consumed, and the tempo of work and social life is guided by the rhythm of prayer, holy days, and ritual. The notion of Islamic spaces is a recurring theme in contemporary Islamic dialogue. The idea of a "cultural space," of course, is not new, and the search for it in a sense is what drove early settlement in North America by diverse European Christian sects, not to mention Orthodox neighborhoods in Jerusalem and Jewish settlements in the West Bank. In any event, in many countries such a nation is visible to varying degrees in neighborhoods, towns and villages, and even institutions such as universities or commercial enterprises that choose this route. It is also evident in what is called "reveiling"—the adoption of Islamist modest dress by women who formerly went without head scarves or whose mothers or even grandmothers had abandoned Islamic dress.

This brings us to the question of evaluating the prospects for civil society characterized by competing sources of power, popular participation, tolerance of diversity, and high levels of individual autonomy. Of course this has to be looked into at a country-by-country level or even regionally within countries. In general, one has to agree that an Islamic order or cultural space (or one created by any religion or ideology) can drastically diminish or limit freedom of choice or expression for any individual born or brought into it. In Turkey, Muslim refugees from the Balkans who have been resettled in such neighborhoods often complain strenuously that their women are harassed into outward conformity to Islamic dress and behavioral codes. But at a larger level, one can move out of such domains, if one's means allow, much as can members of closed religious or utopian communities in Europe or North America. Egypt, Lebanon, Iraq, Israel, Syria, Yemen, and Turkey are countries where a highly secularized segment of the population coexists with a visible, vocal, and politically active conservative religious population, but one that does not hold all of the reins of power. This is the critical issue: multiple sources of power. Saudi Arabia, on the contrary, remains committed to the often crude enforcement of the outward signs of a monolithic Islamic space, but one masking considerable diversity of thought and behavior on the parts of its citizens at home and abroad.

Iran is a very interesting test case for the proposition that an Islamist-dominated state can, in fact if not in word, move in the direction of increased individual autonomy and cultural freedom. While the evidence is limited, and that country is by no means an open and democratic one, at the beginning of the twenty-first century a very sizable segment of the electorate had indicated a strong desire for broader political participation and more freedom of expression. More significant is the fact that most of the reforms involving women's rights, initially repudiated after the revolution, were quietly reinstated (Zubaida, 1998). Even with regard to the Islamic institutions of rule within Iran, power is distributed among competing entities, which, while frustrating those striving for liberal reform, also prevents the imposition of total control by opponents. The dramatic trial in Tehran in late 1999 of the senior cleric reformer Abdullah Nouri is a case in point. A former vice president of the Islamic Republic, he has attracted a large following among those interested in introducing democratic reforms but is accused (and convicted) by the hard-line clerics of "apostasy" and "insulting Islam,"charges favored by the clerics to be leveled at those who challenge their monopoly on power. Clearly, the imposition of Muslim order makes many acutely aware of how their personal or even local communal vision of faith differs.

Without trying to put a favorable gloss on a mode of discourse that often uses strident stereotypic and divisive rhetoric, as well as recourse to violence, we can say that Islamists have contributed an added dimension to public debates and challenges to the often flawed status quo, which ultimately is the necessary basis for the emergence of civil society. Halim Barakat (1993) asserts that the *intifada* of the Palestinians and the 1985 uprising in the Sudan attest to the existence of a civil society in that these movements brought together teachers, professional associations, labor unions, and students to combat the excesses of authoritarian rule. While we would argue that "civil society" requires more than passing unity against oppression, he does have a useful point. By raising issues of justice, legitimate rule, and rights of expression, these movements force a discussion of human rights and of tolerance of diversity (Tibi, 1998). Also, by their challenges to the legitimacy of existing states, they make it necessary for those in power to respond, just as the Islamist rulers of Iran, too, have to validate their hegemony.

ECONOMIC TRANSFORMATIONS

Political ideology aside, the most universally employed and accepted justification for national integration is economic betterment and equity. National courses of economic transformation are highly varied due to any number of specific political factors, as well as to the availability of resources. Economic investment is unevenly distributed in every country. Nationally directed investments of all sorts are usually concentrated in particular economic sectors and geographic regions. The result on a national level resembles what on a global scale is sometimes referred to as "the development of underdevelopment." Put simply, some regions benefit at the expense of others. Industrial and commercial activities tend to be concentrated in one or two zones, often near the capital or major ports, while other regions languish. We have already seen how this is reflected in the hyper-city. Raw materials may be extracted in one region and industrially processed elsewhere where a better infrastructure is in place, and this means that employment opportunities and public services are extremely unevenly distributed.

Significant interregional disparities are seen in all the countries we are concerned with and, as is the case in other parts of the world, where these correspond with ethnic or religious cleavages, may fuel active social protest—as in Iraq, Turkey, Iran, Sudan, Yemen, and Saudi Arabia. As different regions experience different rates of economic development, the resulting inequities in such services as education, health, and availability of consumer goods, not to mention standards of living in general, stimulate interregional migration. As we have already noted, there is a high rate of rural-urban movement throughout the region. Governments aware of the political implications of this imbalance sometimes attempt to decentralize industrial development, usually without much success. In many respects, the most serious population displacements occur in the agricultural sector. Many marginal agricultural areas where further intensification is not feasible lose population as people are attracted to jobs elsewhere. This, of course, may further amplify the marginality and relative underdevelopment of such places.

And while development may be extremely rapid in some regions, with factories and workshops sprawling almost overnight into formerly agricultural lands, zoning, land use laws, and environmental standards are usually weakly enforced. As a consequence, residential and industrial areas become mixed, levels of air and groundwater pollution heightened, and transportation overstressed. Since urban growth is largely uncontrolled, expansion takes place in many cities with little attention to building codes or public amenities. The August and November 1999 earthquakes in northwestern Turkey in which over 18,000 people perished illustrate some of the unintended consequences of rapid but unregulated growth. Vast expanses of apartment blocks that collapsed had been built to poor standards, often on landfill, and in close proximity to refineries and heavy industry. Even without the devastation of the earthquake, the area, home to about 30 percent of Turkey's population and 35 percent of its manufacturing sector, was hugely congested and polluted.

Two recent books by eminent observers of Middle Eastern economic history, while differing in modes of analysis, provide the point of departure for a general overview.[4] What they suggest is that while each country has to be understood individually, there are some central tendencies. Many non-European countries, they note, followed a fairly common course of economic transformation in the twentieth century, moving first from a commodity export–based national economy to one in which industrialization and local production are encouraged in order to substitute for imports. This import-substitution phase is marked by high levels of protectionism, food subsidies, and trade barriers, but often followed ultimately by a final (and often socially wrenching) shift to an export-driven economy based on free trade, privatization, and advanced technology that utilizes an educated work force (see Owen & Pamuk, 1999, pp. xv ff). Owen and Pamuk suggest that Egypt, Israel, and Turkey follow this paradigm very closely. Iran, Iraq, Jordan, Lebanon, and Syria follow the model in a

---

[4] See Alan Richards and John Waterbury (1990) and Roger Owen and Şevket Pamuk (1999).

loose but recognizable fashion; the Gulf states, Saudi Arabia, Sudan, Yemen, and Afghanistan do not at all. Since the general trajectory of economic change is closely linked to social change and human well-being, a summary, however inadequate, is useful.

In Egypt, Israel, and Turkey, private as opposed to public sector enterprise leads the economy, and the countries are heavily involved in exports reliant on education, advanced technology, and a developed communications infrastructure. Israel has achieved levels of per capita gross domestic production (GDP) comparable to those of Western Europe and a standard of living to match, and Egypt and Turkey made marked economic strides throughout the 1990s, as measured in GDP and exports, and socially in health, housing, literacy, and overall standard of living. Iran, Iraq, and Lebanon are still affected by the economic consequences of war and political isolation. On the eve of the Gulf War, Iraq had embarked on an ambitious program of economic libralization and private investment but has essentially squandered its considerable oil wealth on costly military misadventures. Standard of living has been adversely affected for all but a few. Iran is apparently moving toward freer trade and encouragement of foreign investment with the launch of numerous foreign trade missions, and Lebanon is rebuilding its infrastructure in a environment of freewheeling capitalism. Syria set out on a course of liberalization even before Egypt and Turkey, but due to limited potential for agricultural intensification, small population size, and extremely tight political control has not experienced a comparable rate of transformation. Syria, Iraq, and Iran are sometimes termed the "fierce states" in dubious recognition of the brutality and inward-looking nature of their political regimes—which set in place environments not entirely conducive to economic experimentation and innovation. They also suffer from a "brain drain," as many educated individuals seek their livelihood abroad. The oil states are, of course, in an economic class of their own with what amounts to a "rentier" economy—that is one in which foreigners do most of the productive labor and indigenous populations rely on state subsidies to sustain relatively high levels of income and consumption.

A denominator common to all is the increasing specialization and segmentation of productive processes within national economies. This is inherent in the process of building a national economy, regardless of the path taken but is most striking in Israel, Turkey, and Egypt. By this we mean that basic productive processes, including agriculture, involve greater and greater division of labor and differentiation among spheres of activity. Although the rates and extent of industrialization per se are highly uneven, every country is experiencing economic changes whereby even long-established local crafts have become increasingly dependent on producers elsewhere, long-distance transport, electronic communications systems, and the integration of different economic sectors through markets or state agencies. Thus the productive process is increasingly segmented in that output in even small-scale manufacturing and agriculture is now dependent on material inputs from many widely scattered sources, even from abroad. Of course, the most extreme form of productive specialization is in reliance on oil exports. Thus, for every country, the regional and international economic environments are vital to domestic prosperity, and to varying degrees local economies are dependent on pivotal or key factors in the international arena—oil prices for the oil states, worker remittances for Yemen, cotton, textiles and tourism for Egypt, and so on.

As noted, in most countries today priority is being shifted to the private sector, but most, too, feel the heavy weight of past etatist policies.[5] Historically, the pattern of state-directed investment was focused on heavy industry at the expense of comparable attention to agriculture. This resulted in underdeveloped agrarian infrastructures combined with large, poorly educated and poorly housed rural populations. At the same time private investment was heavily directed toward urban real estate and unimproved farmland. Property has long been viewed as second only to gold as a secure investment in an unstable environment. Widespread trading in stocks as a means of individual investment is relatively recent but growing rapidly in many oil- and non-oil-producing countries alike—Egypt, the Gulf states, Turkey, and Iran being cases in point.

Egypt, Iran, and Turkey, not to mention Israel, have experienced higher than average growth in manufacturing, building on an earlier industrial base. Even so, Italy, by way of comparison, has five times the manufacturing of Turkey and ten times that of Iran (Richards & Waterbury, 1990). This situation has changed somewhat since this analysis, with Turkey's industrial sector expanding rapidly throughout the 1990s and with massive investment in the extension of irrigation works. There are several reasons for the emphasis on manufacturing, even apart from military considerations. One is the desire to absorb growing urban populations among whom unemployment is rampant. Another is to decrease reliance on imports, although most Middle Eastern industry is itself dependent on technology transfer. A third reason is to satisfy local markets and growing consumer demand. The major areas of export are in machinery, vehicles, consumer goods, appliances, textiles, shipbuilding, international construction, and in some instances petrochemical products, the last to take advantage of the region's oil and natural gas.

The productive shift since the 1980s, intensified through the 1990s, and following the model described earlier, has been toward an increased focus on export markets and less on the development of heavy industry. This has been paralleled in every country by a move toward privatization and a reduction in tariff barriers. The *infitah* or economic "opening," first used in Sadat's Egypt, describes the shift from state-directed to market-driven economic policies. States in the Middle East have often been termed "corporate" in that explicitly or not they were partners in a form of "social contract" with their citizens. The state, or, more specifically, the ruling establishment, directed the economy and provided basic services such as free or cheap education, abundant public sector

---

[5] See Owen and Pamuk (1999) for discussion of this on a country-by-country basis.

employment, health care, subsidized water, electricity, transport, and even food—particularly bread. In return, the citizen acquiesced in the policies of the state, however unrepresentative. This bore a more than slight resemblance to the Soviet bloc system. But with the *infitah*, the corporate state began to unravel. With the emphasis on private and even foreign investment, the state no longer directly managed the economy, and most have abandoned the idea of being the employer of last resort. Since the 1980s, every country has to varying degrees seen the proliferation of private businesses and, most striking, the emergence of national and international holding companies or conglomerates operating chains of stores and developing factories, bus and trucking firms, and other enterprises. The state, largely due to declining revenues and inefficient practice, has pulled back from many of the services provided in earlier years. While this varies by country, private banking, private insurance, and privately owned transportation systems are generally the norm, and ATM machines are ubiquitous. Some countries are privatizing health care, telecommunications, and much of the media.

One reason for this is necessity: The International Monetary Fund (IMF) has imposed conditions on borrowing countries that mandate a move away from some areas of public spending. But local leaders and businesspeople as well had become disenchanted with etatist policies, which produced little development and served mainly to perpetuate an entrenched bureaucracy. Of course, this "structural adjustment," as it is often called, has met with resistance, even violent strikes and protests, as inefficient state enterprises are sold or closed. In Egypt, efforts to eliminate food subsidies have occasioned fierce resentment. In Turkey, the closing of money-losing state-owned factories, mines, and mills has sparked unrest as well as a populist backlash.

The economic transformations upon which we have touched establish the environment in which unprecedented movement of peoples is taking place, both within national boundaries and internationally. The metropolitan areas of every country in the Middle East have experienced several decades of rapid growth, most in excess of 2.5 percent per year. Although high birth rates and declining infant mortality underlie this growth, most of the expansion of the urban population per se is due to rural migration. How this influx of people has been socially and economically accommodated has to be considered on a case-by-case basis. Apart from the oil-rich states, there is substantial urban unemployment. A growing source of social and political tension is that as unskilled rural migrants swell the potential work force, the relative value of unskilled, illiterate labor is declining. The result is that a significant segment of the urban population will remain economically and socially marginal because it lacks the skills to participate fully in the emerging economic order.

Interestingly, despite the rapid growth of the industrial sector, a number of countries have been exporting skilled workers and professionals. Turkey, Lebanon, and Egypt are foremost in this regard. Turkish and Egyptian doctors, engineers, technicians, and educators are found in significant numbers in Libya,

Oman, Kuwait, and Saudi Arabia. This is in addition to the nearly 2 million Turkish workers and their families in Europe. The case of the Palestinian people is a special one, but they, too, represent a population heavily caught up in international labor migration. Palestinians constitute a highly educated and skilled population as a whole and are found widely dispersed throughout the Arab world, filling positions ranging from skilled construction workers to employees in high administrative ranks. Yemen had almost a million workers in Saudi Arabia and the Gulf states prior to the Gulf War, most of whom were unskilled. The country is still seeing problems arising from their forced repatriation as a result of this conflict. Remittances are an important, even major, source of hard currency for these labor-exporting countries, and in Yemen, food production had become seriously neglected and been replaced by imported food made possible by the inflow of cash. Even after remittances declined, agriculture never recovered because much land has been put to the cultivation of *qat*, a mild narcotic. Turkey, largely self-sufficient in terms of food, is nevertheless sensitive to worker remittances in determining its balance of payments.

The long-term costs and consequences of the export of skilled workers and professionals is unclear, but cannot be ignored. Egypt, Turkey, and Lebanon, for example, regularly lose their best trained and most highly educated citizens in what amounts to a "brain drain." Talented professionals have migrated to Europe and North America in large numbers. On the other hand, many workers and technicians have returned to their home countries after long periods of foreign employment with capital and skills that have been used to further expand the industrial and service sectors. The increase in economic interdependency among countries of the Middle East is directly analogous to the heightened integration of regions within particular nation-states. This process of economic interdependency is quietly taking place despite the vagaries of local and international political alignments. Egypt, although no longer the political presence it once was, is still culturally and economically central in the Arab world. Turkey, though not closely allied to any other Middle Eastern country, some years ago decided to cooperate more fully economically with both the Arab bloc and Iran. At the same time, it developed close military ties with Israel. Much of Turkish industrial export today is directed to Eastern Europe and eastward to Russia, Central Asia, and Iran. All of the non-oil-exporting countries are disadvantaged by the fact that their nearest market, Western Europe, is closed to most of their potential agricultural products, and their industrial goods are usually not competitive.

SOCIAL AND CULTURAL DIMENSIONS OF CHANGE

The changing economic and political environments have their social, even moral, concomitants. We will try to synthesize what we take to be some of the major manifestations, looking at certain aspects of the social order and at what might be called the emergence of "civil society." New modes and relations of production have given rise to groups and classes of people constituted along relatively new axes. New elites and new socioeconomic classes or groupings are in the making, crosscutting preexisting social strata. Unprecedented changes are underway both in terms of what people do for a living and where they live while they do it. The growing importance of a relatively new wage-earning working and middle class that is not employed by the state is evident in almost every country. As we touched upon in Chapter 7 in discussing the transformation of urban ways of life, in every country there are new housing developments consisting of thousands of apartments designed on the European model, each usually to house a relatively small, residentially autonomous family in neighborhoods served not so much by the traditional markets and foodstalls as by supermarkets and malls. Thus every large city has its rhythm of life set by office hours and the ebb and flow of sometimes millions of commuters.

In Istanbul, a new global symbol (MacDonald's golden arches) confronts a far older one.

The environment of everyday social interactions is changing. There is a new "consumer culture," vigorously promoted in advertising and films and much discussed in the local media, in which people of even relatively modest means take for granted the availability of a huge range of domestic and foreign products. It is not surprising that peoples whose cultures had earlier perfected the great bazaars and *suqs* should embrace with such enthusiasm hypermarkets, malls, and gallerias. What is surprising perhaps is that only a generation or so ago most commerce was in the hands of non-Muslim minorities, and Muslims were often denigrated by Europeans as incapable of managing the intricacies of trade and finance.

The extent to which processes of class formation in the Middle East are similar or parallel to the European experience is highly debatable. What is incontrovertible is that new elites, indeed new social orders, based on new lines of social differentiation, are emerging. Among these are growing numbers of technically educated professionals of both sexes and especially rural and urban entrepreneurs or capitalists of a new mold. They emerge from a much wider range of backgrounds, from diverse parts of their countries, and have not been socialized, as was earlier the norm, in one of a small number of elite academies. Thus these newly prominent groupings are not easy to characterize. They may be highly trained professionals who, although working with advanced computer systems, break with the earlier expectation and espouse conservative religious values and modes of deportment; conversely, a venture capitalist whose most formative education may have been in theology may be completely comfortable in a secularized environment that provides individual autonomy. While this does not mean the demise of earlier military, administrative, and political elites, it does add a new dimension to the social equation.

One should be wary of predictions and generalizations. Sociologists and other observers have frequently written about the emergence of the middle class and the muting or even disappearance of traditional organization along ethnic, tribal, or sectarian lines. For example, in 1963, Manfred Halpern wrote:

> In the Middle East . . . the new middle class springs largely . . . from groups that had not hitherto been important, and hence had more reason and less deadweight to take advantage of new knowledge and skills. . . . The new middle class itself does not define or crystallize its character from the very outset, but only as its various strata come to intervene in the process of modernization and assume additional roles in it. It originates in the intellectual and social transformation of Middle Eastern society . . . as a secularized action group oriented towards governmental power. (p. 103)

We know now that the political saliency of the so-called "deadweight" of earlier sources of social identity remains and in some cases may even be amplified. Still, it is true that new social formations have evolved. The term *middle class*, with its European connotations, may not be entirely appropriate, as no comparable social grouping in any Middle Eastern country dominates both the state apparatus and commerce. However, these new and distinctive social formations in the Middle East share values and material aspirations that set them apart from both traditional society and the administrative "nomenclatura" of the early modern era. Further, these values and aspirations closely resemble those of West European middle classes, with an emphasis on individuated family structures and on education and a strong identification with profession or career.

The literature on class formation and sources of the new elite is highly polemical, perhaps because little empirical data are available. Moreover, the situation varies from one country to another; such factors as the basis for elite recruitment, the relative power and prestige of the vying factions, and even the extent to which a constituted elite or power group can perpetuate itself differ greatly.

In places, the new entrepreneurial class has, by its conspicuous consumption and its flaunting of traditional values, generated strong resentment not just from traditionalists but also state employees and the salaried older generation middle class. These two groups have not generally benefited in the process of the *infitah*: they are often visibly impoverished by inflation and socially marginalized as the emphasis shifts to the private sector. Only a generation ago,

Young Hezbollah women at a 1999 demonstration in Lebanon.

parents were eager for their children to enter the state work force because it offered even at the lowest ranks security and prestige. Now such positions offer very little security in the non-oil-producing countries. Relative to the private sector, state salaries and pensions are often inadequate, and health care is poor.

But for the flourishing new groups, social and consumer horizons are rapidly widening. It used to be that the conspicuous consumption of a small number of elite had considerable shock value as they threw lavish weddings, and disported themselves in casinos and expensive watering holes. Now distinctive and socially visible forms of consumption have moved beyond the merchant families and the oil-rich. Owning an automobile is taken for granted by a very significant percentage of households in the non-oil states and by almost every household in the oil-exporting ones. Perhaps even more indicative is the new phenomenon of large-scale tourism involving not just foreigners visiting the choice sites of antiquity but millions of local families taking holidays in their national resorts and abroad. So-called Islamists and traditionalists are not immune to the allure of holiday making in luxurious resorts, and have in fact established many such resorts where Islamic codes (for example, no alcohol and no mixed swimming) are enforced. From the viewpoint of changing patterns of social interaction, this is a significant development. It indicates an emphasis on familial autonomy and companionate marital relationship, puts people in touch across regions, and enhances awareness of a complex cultural history and of public spaces and the environment. It is, of course, in the end, a form of consumption that sharply differentiates those who can afford it from those who cannot.

In addition to the social consequences of unequal consumption, the social order of many countries, or at least the legitimacy of the state, is undermined by rampant corruption. Corruption does not usually take the stereotypic form of ticket fixing, or palm greasing to obtain a document or a job. Petty bribery is nowhere, in our experience, a normal part of dealing with officials. Higher-level quid pro quo, unfortunately, is. Such corruption is much more structural and embedded in the nature of state-business interactions and is socially probably more pernicious. A large (but necessarily unknown) percentage of business transactions occur off the books or in the "gray market" to avoid taxation and regulation. Most large-scale construction in most countries appears to involve regulatory breaches. Much privatized state property, including factories, shipping, and banks, have turned up in the hands of individuals with close ties to political leaders and at "fire sale" prices. This, together with such forbidden trade as arms and drugs, results in vast sums of free-floating currency that distort processes of legitimate investment and that are also available to influence high-level administrators and regulators. This form of corruption is a major problem in Turkey, Lebanon, and Egypt in particular, and undermines public confidence in state institutions. In Turkey, for example, people complain bitterly about the so-called "deep state" or the perceived collusion among business, military, and political leaders. In Iraq, and to some extent Syria, corruption takes the form of a state-sanctioned "kleptocracry." In Iran, vast sums of wealth are under the control of *waqf*, whose managers are not publically accountable. In the oil-exporting countries, the state coffers are not subject to public scrutiny.

The highly variable and frequently changing role of political parties should give pause to anyone considering a simple description of the region in terms of any one basic pattern of class formation or elite recruitment. One generalization that seems to hold true, however, is that rule by the elite of the moment, however often it changes and however it may be recruited and organized, is strongly authoritarian everywhere. Israel has followed a democratic course, but one in which the Arabs are decidedly second-class citizens; and for those Palestinians living under the occupation, authoritarian might be too mild a description of their political environment. Of the Muslim countries, only Egypt, Lebanon, and Turkey have experienced significant periods of democratic politics with independent and contending parties. Iran is a paradox in that seemingly competitive parliamentary elections coexist with deeply authoritarian structures. Apart from this, whether the legitimizing ideology is Arab socialism, dynastic loyalty, Islamic justice, or nationalism, the fact remains that power inevitably rests within a fairly narrow segment, with few avenues open for popular participation in the political process.

The twinning of what might be called "clan" and "clientship" is a major impediment to individual autonomy in politics and economics and to the emergence of a genuine civil society. "Clan" in that the most important unit of action is the family or familial network. For members of the elite classes, family contacts may be dispersed through the professions, in different businesses, and governmental agencies, and at the folk level, kin may be dispersed among occupations and villages. "Clientship" in that access to institutions, business opportunities, and bureaucratic approval, or even to clear the mundane hurdles of everyday life, works best through the agency of strategically placed intermediaries. Where the intermediary is of a higher relative status and power, he is, in effect, acting as a broker. This does not imply corruption, but it certainly facilitates quid pro quo long-term relationships that often militate against transparency and further cronyism still more. Most political parties are based on clientship.

Turning now to such long-term problems and courses of development as might be safely adduced, there are a number of issues that obviously will loom large in coming years and still others, less obvious, about which we should be aware. While all of these may have considerable potential for instability or negative consequences for quality of life, we make no effort to weigh them, since most problems are interrelated and self-amplifying. A political crisis, for example, the long anticipated change of regime in Syria or Iraq, will have unanticipated consequences in many sectors, including ethnic relations, regionalism, economic development, out-migration, and relations with neighboring countries. For Syria, for instance, it might mean that the Alawi minority is seriously disadvantaged after years of high level but resented influence; for Iraq, the Shi'a majority may succeed in asserting itself at the expense of the currently domi-nant Sunni minority. However, predictions are simply not feasible even where trends are demonstrable: We know that population is increasing everywhere and will continue to do so for the next 20 years at least; but the social conse-quences are unclear. Population increase in itself need not imply negative or positive effects on the quality of life in a particular country; that will depend on many ancillary developments in education, the economy, political structures, and other social sectors.[6]

We began this book with a discussion of water, and water remains an issue of as much as or more concern than oil reserves. Water—its availability, quality, and control—is of great concern in every country, even in those where it is most abundant and widely distributed—Turkey and Iran. It is interesting to recall that it was the collapse of the famed Marib waterworks of the Sabaeans in sixth-century Yemen, with the concomitant destruction of intensively farmed regions they supported, that according to Arab historians set in motion great waves of out-migration and tribal conflict on the very eve of the birth of Islam.[7] Today major hydraulic projects are completed or underway in Egypt, Turkey, and Iraq, and lesser ones in Israel, Iran, and Syria.

The massive Aswan Dam, brought online in 1971, provides abundant cheap electricity, as well as enhancing multiple cropping downstream. But quite apart from serious environmental problems, such as soil salinization and loss of important nutrients useful for sustaining soil fertility and fisheries, the dam essentially holds most of the population of the country hostage to its mainte-nance and defense (Abi-Aad & Grenon, 1997). Paradoxically, it may even increase the threat of drought should rains be poor in the highlands—a vast amount of water is lost to evaporation in the intense aridity of southern Egypt. The GAP project in Turkey (see Chapter 1 and Chapter 6) is even more challeng-ing to international stability. Since Turkey now controls a sizable percentage of the annual catchment of the Euphrates and Tigris rivers, and since part of the impounded waters that move downstream will have passed through irrigation works, the flow of water and its quality is a very serious area of dispute with Syria and Iraq. The Jordan River, small by comparison, is nevertheless very important to Israel, Jordan, Syria, and Palestine, and is an obvious political flash point since all parties have sharply conflicting interests. However, in both cases, the huge disparity in the military might of Turkey and Israel compared with their neighbors makes overt warfare an unlikely option.

More likely than warfare over water are large-scale disruptions and dislo-cations of population due to environmental and social impacts stemming from

---

[6] Again, Naji Abi-Aad and Michel Grenon's account (1997) of sources of instability and conflict is a good general source and analysis.

[7] A new Marib Dam has been built after more than a thousand years of desolation, and once again there is a green oasis expanding, along with newly found sources of gas and oil (see Held, 1994, p. 347).

A religious class at a Hezbollah-run school in Beirut.

water-related issues: pollution, soil salinity, and water scarcity. Every country is using more fresh water than is annually replenished by rainfall and usually using it inefficiently (see Abi-Aad & Grenon, 1997). The drilling of deep wells, in addition to depleting aquifers, lowers water tables to the extent that traditional sources and shallow wells may dry up. Unfortunately, while many countries see tourism as a potential source of hard currency, it is an industry that makes extraordinary demands on water sources. It is estimated that 100 guests in a luxury hotel use in 55 days an amount of water equivalent to that needed to feed 100 families for two years, were it applied to a 1-hectare rice field (FAO, as reported in Abi-Aad & Grenon, 1997).

We have mentioned population dynamics repeatedly in this book; perhaps the least emphasized but most important demographic factor that affects quality of life in the region as a whole is the presence of large numbers of refugees and asylum seekers. One-third of the world's refugees, over 6 million in 1992, were found in the Middle East. The same source estimated in 1999 that 3.6 million Palestinians were displaced—that is, unable to return to locales they considered home. Iran is "home" to almost 2 million refugees—mostly people fleeing from Afghanistan and Iraq and thus caring for more refugees per capita than any other country.[8] These figures, however startling, do not take into consideration

---

[8] U.S. Committee for Refugees; see also Abi-Aad and Grenon (1997).

internal movement as a result of conflict. Over 2.5 million people were so displaced in the Iran-Iraq war, and the Kurdish conflicts in Turkey and northern Iraq have similarly affected millions of people. Further, conflicts in regions contiguous to the countries we have been discussing are also serious threats to stability; fighting in Kosovo, Chechneya, Georgia, Armenia, Azerbayjan, Central Asia, Somalia and Ethopia, and Algeria are cases in point. These conflicts send flows of refugees cascading through regions far from their epicenters.

PROSPECTS FOR CIVIL SOCIETY

So what are the prospects for a new social order based on the precepts of "civil society"? While somewhat problematic as an analytic concept, the term *civil society* draws attention to the "intermediate domain between the state and the individual—a domain in which deliberation and association take place without constraint and coercion" (Sunar, 1997, p. 9). At the personal level, this is expressed in questions about the individual's rights and responsibilities regarding family, community, and nation. Much has been made in the literature on civil society of problems arising from the increased emphasis on personal autonomy, with the role of women often seen as indicative. Clearly, the extent to which one sex dominates the other is a fundamental yardstick with which autonomy can be measured: A strong form of patriarchy obviously deprives more than half of the population of individual rights.

Like most social discussion we can see a glass as half empty or half full, as we choose. First, let us take up the obvious and less optimistic perspective. There exists a general and undeniable tendency in the Middle East to discourage female employment, particularly in jobs entailing a great deal of direct male-female contact. In fact, Middle Eastern countries report the lowest rates of female participation in economic activities outside agriculture. In the last decade, according to a United Nations Development Program report (1999), women's share of the overall labor force in the Middle East and North Africa was the lowest (18.7 percent) when compared with that of East and Southeast Asia (41.2 percent), Latin America (26.3 percent), and sub-Saharan Africa (37.8 percent). In Iran, following the revolution in 1979, there was actually a decline in female labor force participation. As Haleh Afshar (1998) reports, women's employment levels fell from 13.7 percent in 1976 to 8.8 percent in 1986, and by 1996 had only climbed to 12.7 percent. Valentine Moghadam (1993) argues that in general this lag is not solely the result of the cultural restrictions placed on women. Other contributing factors include the nature of the regime in power, the development policies of the government, and the educational and class positions of women.

Turning to the positive side: Women's lives are changing in basic ways for the better. Substantial gains have been achieved in literacy, life expectancy, and health care. It is safe to say that the two factors most responsible for major changes in the patterns of women's lives, taken broadly across the region, are their access to education and entry into the wage-labor market. On the other hand, some scholars have argued that industrialization and economic development in the Third World have had a generally adverse effect on women by devaluing their domestic production, forcing them to sell their labor in the harsh environment of the marketplace without immediate benefits in terms of personal independence or control of their wages (see Hoodfar, 1997, for example). Others, and we include ourselves, see the involvement of women in wage labor as a first and necessary step to their economic independence and, if not full emancipation, at least to the improvement of their status within the family.

Moghadam (1993) examines the differential impact of paid employment on women's lives. After underscoring the diversity in state policies and developmental strategies, and taking into account the different situations of women in the region, Moghadam concludes that "since the 1960s state expansion, economic development, oil wealth, and increased integration within the world system have combined to create favorable educational and employment opportunities" (p. 66). Although benefits have spread unevenly, both she and we would argue that female education and employment are undermining patriarchal attitudes and practices. Everywhere in the Middle East the traditional ideology of male domination and strict female segregation and confinement is under attack and gradually eroding. This may be less obvious in areas where conservative or traditional dress is maintained. Nevertheless, as urbanization proceeds and employment spreads to include women, individuals quickly fall into a pattern of non-segregated interaction. Modern urban life has its own imperatives, and demands movement and public interactions regardless of ideological considerations. It is unlikely that women's participation in the wage-labor sector and the attendant transformations in gender roles and family relationships will be effectively halted or reversed.

Given the mixed scoreboard, what can we conclude with respect to the existence of or possibilities for the emergence of civil society?[9] Our point of departure is to focus on human rights since it is impossible to construe any form of civil society in the absence of human rights. Granting that the general topic goes beyond our brief here, we take the position that such rights exist distinct from any particular cultural tradition, even if the concept historically emerged, as does any concept, in a specific intellectual milieu (see Dalacoura, 1998, p. 13). Further, human rights are not the same as so-called "communal" rights or assertions that the communal order, the "authentic," or "cultural values" must prevail over the freedom of individuals. Such assertions are essentially illiberal, as they are inevitably used to empower and justify the authority of those who, however selected, speak for the "community."

---

[9] For an excellent collection of essays on this subject, specifically with reference to the Middle East, see Elisabeth Özdalga and Sune Persson (1997) and A. R. Norton (1996). See also Katerina Dalacoura (1998) for an insightful discussion of Islam and liberalism.

Clearly, our position is not one of extreme cultural relativism or post-modern arguments rooted in these modes of discourse that view behavior and values as culturally specific. Given this, we would agree with Katerina Dala-coura (1998) that a strict scriptural or textual interpretation and application of Islam is incompatible with liberalism or civil society in that one cannot deny that the Quran and Shari'a explicitly deny women rights equal to men's and prescribe obligatory and extreme punishments (*hadd*) for apostasy, adultery com-mitted by a woman, sexual contact by a Muslim woman with a non-Muslim, theft, male homosexuality, and many more. To argue, as do some Islamists, that these codes serve to protect the individual from the dangers of his or her innate drives or instincts is irrelevant. However, it is obvious that any ideology, not just Islam, based on divine texts would be equally illiberal—that is, would shackle the individual to the authority of those who interpret and apply the text.

Thus, on the face of it, the prognosis for civil society is not very good as strict textual or scriptural Islam is staunchly, even violently, advocated by many, and it is impossible to imagine a civil society in the Muslim Middle East that did not accommodate Islam. The social reality is more promising. First, many prominent Islamist thinkers, such as Abdullah Nouri and Iranian presi-dent Mohammad Khatami, are arguing for a reconciliation of Islamic law and values with contemporary social formations, in particular, with democracy. A growing number of Sunni thinkers argue that the *ijthad*, or the application of individual reason to make law and interpret Islam, is valid, even though this particular legal door was deemed closed in medieval times.[10] More important than high-level discourse is how Islam is applied and how people are actually behaving.

As noted by Amin Saikal (2000), a political scientist at the Australian National University, the election of the Muslim scholar Abdurahman Wahid as president of Indonesia sent a powerful message to Muslims everywhere, paral-leling but significantly differing from President Khatami's drive to establish an Islamic civil society and democracy in Iran. A man of great prestige, President Wahid explicitly endorses a secular system of government for his mostly Mus-lim nation.

Another welcome sign of change emphasized by Saikal is the resounding success of Al Jazeera satellite channel in Qatar, which operates entirely free of state control—one of the very few in the Arab world to do so. The channel has become one of the most popular sources of objective information in the region. Its programs have dealt with hitherto taboo topics, including the lack of democ-racy, transparency, and accountability of the ruling regimes in the area. These developments, Saikal suggests, have the "potential to change the course of Muslim politics and bring the Muslim world and the West closer together" (p. 8). This is what gives us cautious optimism. As we noted in Chapter 9, even

---

[10] See Charles Kurzman (1998) for an excellent review of the history and prospects for a liberal Islam, and why this is not a contradiction in terms.

though the Quran sanctions slavery, no one advocates or even defends it; polygyny, while sanctioned, is declining as an acceptable domestic arrangement among educated people; and the *ḥadd* punishments are not applied consistently outside of Saudi Arabia and Afghanistan. Even in Iran, the *ḥadd* punishments do not appear to be endorsed by the public in their strict sense, and jurists find ways around them. In practice, there is a quiet tendency to apply Islamic punishment contextually and according to what is thought to be the "spirit" of the law—emphasizing essentially liberal notions of justice and equity and tolerance of diversity (Kurzman, 1999). This is not to deny contrary and often strident voices, but where there is democracy or even a semblance of democracy, strident Islamist rhetoric has limited appeal. In Turkey, Islamist parties have gotten a significant share of the vote by the same means employed by other parties. They address issues of concern to the electorate, basically those of economics and social equity. The fastest-growing Islamist movement in Turkey, the Fethullah Gülen or Nurcu community movement, is not overtly political and stresses tolerance and individual self-control, piety, and self-enlightenment; and its recruits are very largely from groups with secondary or higher education. Although controversial among hard-line secularists, as far as one can tell, the movement seems entirely within the democratic tradition. Since the appeal of democracy is gradually spreading, one might cautiously hope that an Islamic liberalism is not far behind.

Glossary

The terms below are transcribed from Arabic (A), Turkish (T), or Persian (P).

ağa, agha (T)	an elder; a powerful landlord; a village leader; a tribal chieftain.
ahl al-dhimmi (A)	a designate applied to the Jews and Christians who lived within the Islamic Empire; it refers to their special status as "protected minorities."
ahl al-kitab (A)	literally "people of the book"; same as *ahl al-dhimmi.*
'aib (A)	shame; dishonor.
akhund (P)	midlevel religious cleric.
'Alawi (A)	A *Shi'a* sect whose adherents are found today in northwest Syria and parts of Iran and Iraq.
'Alevi (T)	the Turkish sect similar to 'Alawi, until recently mostly rural-dwelling and widely dispersed.
'Ali (A)	Muhammad's cousin and the husband of his only daughter, Fatima. *'Ali* is also the first imam of the Shi'a Muslims.
amir/emir (A)	a commander; the title of the caliph in his capacity as head of the Muslim community is *"amir al-mu'minin"* or "the Commander of the Faithful."
'asabiyya (A)	tribal solidarity.
'ashira (A)	a tribal segment; a group claiming common patrilineal descent.
asl/asala (A)	descent; *asala* also refers to purity of descent; authenticity.
āya (A)	Quranic verse.
āyatollah (P)	literally "sign of God"; a title bestowed on the highest ranking clerics among the Shi'a in Iran.
baraka (A)	God's blessing; divine grace.
caliph/khalifa (A)	literally "successor"; title applied to the successor of Muhammad as head of the Muslim community. In Shi'a Islam, the equivalent is *imam.*

chador (P)	an all-enveloping head-to-foot covering worn by women in Iran.
Druze (A)	a sect derived from *Ismai'ili shi'a;* adherents are found today in Lebanon, Syria, and Israel.
fallaḥ/fellaḥ (A)	a general term for peasant; someone who tills the soil.
fatiḥa (A)	the first chapter of the Quran.
fatwa (A)	a responsum; an authoritative opinion by a recognized religious scholar on some point of Islamic jurisprudence.
geçekondu (T)	literally "built overnight"; shantytown; urban quarter settled by rural migrants who build their housing.
Hadith (A)	the corpus of narratives purporting to relate the words and deeds of Muhammad as transmitted by a chain of recognized authorities.
ḥajj (A)	the pilgrimage to Mecca, incumbent on all Muslims.
ḥalāl (A)	behavior designated acceptable to God and allowed to the Muslim believer.
ḥarām (A)	behavior designated not acceptable to God and forbidden to the Muslim believer.
haram (A)	religious sanctuary.
ḥareem (A)	term referring to women in general and to women's quarters of the house in particular.
ḥasham/ ḥushuma (A)	sexual modesty.
ḥijab (A)	a cover; a barrier; a veil; the "Muslim" veil worn by women.
Hijra (A)	the emigration of Muhammad and his followers from Mecca to Medina in A.D. 622, the first year of the Muslim lunar calendar.
'id al-adha (A)	the feast of the sacrifice also known as *'Id al-Kabir:* a three-day feast that marks the end of the annual pilgrimage to Mecca celebrated by sacrificing animals to commemorate the sacrifice of Abraham. In Turkey, it is known as *Qurban Bayram.*
'id al-fitr (A)	one of the two major feasts in Islam; it marks the end of the fast of Ramadan.
iḥram (A)	the white seamless garment worn by the pilgrims at Mecca.
imam (A)	a prayer leader in a Sunni mosque; in Shi'a Islam, the term refers to a descendant of 'Ali designated to be the charismatic leader of the Muslim community.
imamzadeh (P)	a saint's shrine.
imān (A)	faith.
infitaḥ (A)	economic "opening"; nonregulated market economy.
jahiliyya (A)	"the age of ignorance"; the term used to refer to the period before Muhammad brought the message of Islam.
jami' (A)	central mosque.

jihād (A)	variously translated as "holy war" or "striving" in the way of Islam.
jizya (A)	poll tax historically paid by non-Muslim subjects in Muslim countries.
Ka'ba (A)	the sacred cube-shaped structure at the Great Mosque in Mecca; it contains a black stone considered sacred by Muslims. The Ka'ba determines the direction toward which Muslims must face when praying.
katkhoda (P)	a tribal headman, village mayor.
khalifa (A)	deputy or successor; transcribed in English as caliph.
khan (T/P)	a tribal leader.
khutba (A)	the sermon delivered at the Friday communal prayer at the mosque.
madhab (A)	Sunni school of law; sect.
madina (A)	city or town.
madrasa (A)	school; traditionally referred to a religious school for study of Muslim jurisprudence and law.
Mahdi (A)	"the rightly guided one"; refers to the absent imam whom the Shi'a expect to return and usher a period of Truth and Justice on earth.
mahr (A)	bride wealth: the money that the groom and his family give to the bride and her family as part of the marriage arrangements; in North Africa called *sdaq*.
marabout/ murabit (A)	term used in North Africa to refer to a holy man or "saint"
masjid (A)	mosque.
meḥalla (A)	neighborhood.
milla/millet (A & T)	a religious community, especially within the Ottoman system of governance.
mufti (A)	an expert on religious law or Shari'a.
mujtahid (A)	a Shi'a high-ranking cleric who has the authority to interpret Islamic law.
murīd (A)	a Sufi term applied to a student or disciple of a Sufi master.
murshid (A)	Sufi guide or master.
mut'a (A)	a temporary marriage contract among the Shi'a; also known as *sigheh* in Persia.
nabī (A)	prophet.
namūs (T)	honor; reputation.
pīr (P)	a Sufi master or teacher.
qabila (A)	tribe.
qadi (A)	religious judge.
qat (A)	*Catha edulis:* a leafy plant found in Yemen; it is chewed for its mild narcotic effect.

Quran (A)	the Muslim holy book believed to be the word of God as revealed to the Prophet Muhammad.
Ramaḍān (A)	the ninth month of the Muslim lunar calendar during which Muslims are enjoined to fast from sunrise to sunset.
rasūl (A)	messenger; used as a title of the Prophet Muhammad who is referred to as *rasūl* Allah, the Messenger of God.
ṣalāt (A)	prayer; usually refers to the ritualized five daily prayers encumbent on a Muslim.
sawm (A)	fasting; refers to the obligatory yearly one-month fast of Ramadan.
sayyid (A)	descendant of the Prophet through his daughter, Fatima, and her husband, 'Ali; term used mainly among the Shi'a.
shahada (A)	the Muslim profession or declaration of faith.
sharaf (A)	honor.
Shari'a (A)	the corpus of Islamic Law.
Sharīf (A)	a descendant of the Prophet Muhammad through his daughter Fatima; used mainly by the Sunni.
sheikh (A)	"elder"; title applied to tribal leaders, religious scholars, and heads of mystical orders.
Shi'a (A)	a major division in Islam; refers to those who supported 'Ali as the legitimate successor to Muhammad.
Şufism (A)	Islamic mysticism.
sultan (A)	ruler.
Sunna (A)	customary practice or traditions of Muhammad as reported in the Hadith; the term *Sunna* or *Sunni* also refers to the majority division in Islam.
Sunni (A)	the majority division in Islam.
sūq (A)	market; in Persian, *bazaar*; in Turkish *çarşı*.
sūra (A)	a chapter of the Quran.
ṭariqa (A)	refers to the "spiritual path" followed by a particular Sufi order; term is also used to refer to a Sufi order. In Turkish, *tarikat*.
ta'ziya (A)	the reenactment of the martyrdom of the Shi'a imam Hussein.
tekke (T)	a Sufi lodge, center for study.
tira (P)	a tribal segment.
'ulama (A)	religious scholars.
umma (A)	the Muslim community.

Wahabi (A)	a puritanical Islamic movement that began in Arabia in the eighteenth century; the official creed of the Kingdom of Saudi Arabia.
waqf (A)	religious endowment established by Muslims to support mosques, orphanages, schools, and the like.
Zaidi (A)	a Shi'a sect in Yemen.
zakāt (A)	obligatory alms tax generally fixed at an annual rate of 2.5 percent of a Muslim's net worth.
zawiya (A)	a religious meeting place or lodge; in Turkish, *tekke*.
ziara (A)	visit to a saint's shrine; in Persian, *ziarat*.
zikr (A)	"Remembrance"; recitation of God's names by Sufis.
ziyy al-islami (A)	refers to the new veiling and dress by Islamist women.

References

Abdel-Fadel, Mahmoud. 1975. *Development, Income Distribution and Social Change in Rural Egypt, 1952–70: A Study in the Political Economy of Agrarian Transition.* Cambridge: Cambridge University Press.

Abi-Aad, Naji, and Michel Grenon. 1997. *Instability and Conflict in the Middle East: People, Petroleum and Security Threats.* New York: St. Martin's Press.

Abu-Izzedin, Najla M. 1984. *The Druzes: A New Study of Their History, Faith, and Society.* Leiden: E. J. Brill.

Abukhalil, A. 1994. The Incoherence of Islamic Fundamentalism: Arab Islamic Thought at the End of the 20th Century. *Middle East Journal* 48(4) (Autumn).

Abu-Lughod, Janet. 1971. *Cairo: 1001 Years of the City Victorious.* Princeton Studies on the Near East. Princeton, NJ: Princeton University Press.

———. 1987. The Islamic City—Historic Myth, Islamic Essence, and Contemporary Relevance. *International Journal of Middle Eastern Studies* 19 (2): 155–76.

———. 1990. New York and Cairo: A View from Street Level. *International Social Science Journal* 42, 3 (125): 307–18.

Abu-Lughod, Lila. 1986. *Veiled Sentiments: Honor and Poetry in a Bedouin Society.* Berkeley: University of California Press.

———. 1993. *Writing Women's Worlds: Bedouin Stories.* Berkeley: University of California Press.

———, ed. 1998. *Remaking Women: Feminism and Modernity in the Middle East.* Princeton, NJ: Princeton University Press.

Abu-Rabia, Aref. 1994. *The Negev Bedouin and Livestock Rearing.* Providence, RI: Berg.

Abu-Zeid, Ahmed. 1966. Honour and Shame among the Bedouins of Egypt. In J. G. Peristany, ed., *Honour and Shame: The Values of Mediterranean Society.* Chicago: University of Chicago Press, pp. 243–60.

Adams, Robert McC. 1981. *Heartland of Cities: Surveys of Ancient Settlement and Land Use on the Central Floodplain of the Euphrates.* Chicago: University of Chicago Press.

Adra, Najwa. 1985. The Concept of Tribes in Rural Yemen. In Nicholas Hopkins and Saad Eddin Ibrahim, eds., *Arab Society: Social Science Perspectives.* Cairo: American University in Cairo Press, pp. 275–86.

Afkhami, Mahnaz. 1994. Women in Post Revolutionary Iran: A Feminist Perspective. In M. Afkhami, and E. Friedl, eds., *In the Eye of the Storm: Women in Postrevolutionary Iran.* Syracuse, NY: Syracuse University Press, pp. 5–19.

Afshar, Haleh. 1998. *Islam and Feminism: An Iranian Case Study.* New York: St. Martin's Press.

Ahmed, Leila. 1992. *Women and Gender in Islam: Historical Roots of a Modern Debate.* New Haven, CT: Yale University Press.

Ajami, Fouad. 1999. *The Dream Palace of the Arabs: A Generation's Odyssey.* New York: Vintage Books.

Akbar, Ahmed. 1999. *Islam Today: A Short Introduction to the Muslim World.* London: I. B. Tauris.

Akşit, Bahattin. 1993. Studies in Rural Transformation in Turkey, 1950–1990. In Paul Stirling, ed., *Culture and Economy: Changes in Turkish Villages.* Manchester, UK: Eothen Press, pp. 187–200.

Al-Azm, Sadik. 1997. Is Islam Secularizable? In E. Özdalga and S. Persson, eds., *Civil Society, Democracy, and the Muslim World.* Papers read at a conference at the Swedish Research Institute, Istanbul, 28–30 October 1996. *Swedish Research Institute in Istanbul Transactions,* vol. 7, pp. 17–23.

Algar, Hamid. 1972. The Oppositional Role of the Ulama in Twentieth Century Iran. In N. Keddie, ed., *Scholars, Saints and Sufis: Muslim Religious Institutions Since 1500.* Berkeley: University of California Press, pp. 211–31.

Al-Nouri, Qais. 1997. The Impact of Economic Embargo on Iraqi Families: Restructuring of Tribes, Socio-Economic Classes and Households. *Journal of Comparative Family Studies* 28 (Summer): 99–135.

Al Rasheed, Madawi. 1991. *Politics in an Arabian Oasis: The Rashidis of Saudi Arabia.* London: I. B. Tauris.

Altorki, Soraya, and Donald P. Cole. 1989. *Arabian Oasis City: The Transformation of 'Unayzah.* Austin: University of Texas Press.

American Jewish Yearbook. 1985. Philadelphia: Jewish Publications Society of America.

Anderson, Benedict. 1991. *Imagined Communities.* London: Verso.

Antoun, Richard. 1993. Themes and Symbols in the Religious Lesson: A Jordanian Case Study. *International Journal of Middle Eastern Studies* 25: 607–24.

Arat, Zehra F., ed. 1998. *Deconstructing Images of "The Turkish Woman."* New York: St. Martin's Press.

Arjomand, Said Amir. 1988. *The Turban and the Crown: The Islamic Revolution in Iran.* New York: Oxford University Press.

Arkoun, Mohammed. 1994. *Rethinking Islam: Common Questions, Uncommon Answers.* Boulder, CO: Westview Press.

Asad, Talal. 1993. *Genealogies of Religion: Discipline and Reasons of Power in Christianity and Islam.* Baltimore: Johns Hopkins University Press.

Ask, Karin, and Marit Tjomsland, eds. 1998. *Women and Islamization: Contemporary Dimensions of Discourse on Gender Relations.* Oxford: Berg.

Aswad, Barbara. 1971. *Property Control and Social Strategies: Settlers on a Middle Eastern Plain.* Museum of Anthropology, Anthropological Papers No. 44. Ann Arbor: University of Michigan.

Awad, Fuad. 1991. Report II: Economics of Coincidence and Disaster in Lebanon. *The Beirut Review* 1, no. 2: 82–95.

Bach, Kirsten Haugaard. 1998. The Vision of a Better Life: New Patterns of Consumption and Changed Social Relations. In Nicholas S. Hopkins and Kirsten Westergaard, eds., *Directions of Change in Rural Egypt.* Cairo: The American University in Cairo Press, pp. 184–200.

Barakat, Halim. 1993. *The Arab World: Society, Culture, and State.* Berkeley: University of California Press.

Barkey, Henri J., and Graham E. Fuller. 1999. *Turkey's Kurdish Question.* London: Rowman and Littlefield.

Barth, Fredrik. 1959. *Political Leadership among the Swat Pathans.* London School of Economics Monographs on Social Anthropology. London: Athlone Press.

———. 1961. *Nomads of South Persia: The Basseri Tribe of the Khamseh Confederacy.* Boston: Little, Brown.

———, ed. 1969. *Ethnic Groups and Boundaries: Social Organization of Cultural Differences.* Boston: Little, Brown.

Bates, Daniel G. 1973. *Nomads and Farmers: A Study of the Yörük of Southeastern Turkey.* Museum of Anthropology, An-

thropological Papers No. 52. Ann Arbor: University of Michigan.
———. 1979. The Middle Eastern Village in Regional Perspective. In Priscilla Copeland Reining and Barbara Lenkerd, eds., *Village Viability in Contemporary Society*. AAAS Selected Symposium 34. Boulder, CO: Westview Press.
———. 1994. What's in a Name? Minorities, Identity, and Politics in Bulgaria. *Identities* 1(2–3): 201–25.
Beck, Lois. 1980. Herd Owners and Herd Shepherds: The Qashqa'i of Iran. *Ethnology*, 19 (3): 345–52.
———. 1990. Tribes and the State in Nineteenth- and Twentieth-Century Iran. In Philip Khoury and Joseph Kostiner, eds., *Tribes and State Formation in the Middle East*. Berkeley: University of California Press.
———. 1991. *Nomad: A Year in the Life of a Qashqa'i Tribesman in Iran*. Berkeley, CA: University of California Press.
Bengio, Ofra, and Gabriel Ben-Dor, eds. 1999. *Minorities and the State in the Arab World*. Boulder, CO: Lynne Rienner.
Benthall, Jonathan. 1998. The Qu'ran's Call to Alms: Zakat, the Muslim Tradition of Alms-Giving. *International Institute for the Study of Islam in the Modern World Newsletter* 1, 13.
Betteridge, A. 1993. Women and Shrines in Shiraz. In Donna Lee Bowen and Evelyn A. Early, eds., *Everyday Life in the Muslim Middle East*. Bloomington: Indiana University Press, pp. 239–51.
Betts, Robert Benton. 1988. *The Druze*. New Haven, CT: Yale University Press.
Bilici, Farouk. 1998. The Function of the Alevi-Bektashi Theology in Modern Turkey. In Tord Olsson, Elisabeth Özdalga, and Catharina Raudvere, eds., *Alevi Identity: Cultural, Religious and Social Perspectives*. Papers read at a conference at the Swedish Research Institute, Istanbul, 25–27 November 1996. *Swedish Research Institute in Istanbul Transactions* vol. 8, pp. 51–63.
Bill, James, and Carl Leiden. 1984. *Politics in the Middle East*, 2nd ed. Boston and Toronto: Little, Brown.

Birge, John Kingsley. 1937. *The Bektashi Order of Dervishes*. London: Luzac.
Birnbaum, Eleazar. 1997. Review of Avigdor Levy, ed., Jews of the Ottoman Empire. *International Journal of Middle Eastern Studies* 20(3): 447–54.
Bodman, Herbert L., and Nayereh Tohidi, eds. 1998. *Women in Muslim Societies: Diversity Within Unity*. Boulder, CO: Lynne Rienner.
Bouhdiba, Abdelwahab. 1975. *La Sexualité en Islam*. Sociologie d'Aujourd'hui. Paris: PUF.
———. 1977. The Child and Mother in Arab Moslem Society. In L. C. Brown and Norman Itzkowitz, eds., *Psychological Dimensions of Near Eastern Studies*. Princeton, NJ: Darwin Press.
Bowen, Donna Lee, and Evelyn A. Early, eds. 1993. *Everyday Life in the Muslim Middle East*. Bloomington: Indiana University Press.
Bradburd, D. 1990. *Ambiguous Relations: Kin, Class and Conflict among Komachi Pastoralists*. Washington, DC: Smithsonian Institution Press.
———. 1994. Historical Bases of the Political Economy of Kermani Pastoralists: Tribe and World Markets in the Nineteenth and Early Twentieth Centuries. In Claudia Chang and Harold A. Koster, eds., *Pastoralists at the Periphery*. Tucson: University of Arizona Press, pp. 42–61.
———. 1996. Size and Success: Komachi Adaptation to a Changing Iran. In Michael Bonine and Nikki Keddi, eds., *Modern Iran: The Dialectics of Continuity and Change*. Albany: State University of New York Press, pp. 123–37.
Brand, Laurie A. 1998. *Women, the State, and Political Liberalization: Middle Eastern and North African Experiences*. New York: Columbia University Press.
Brown, Nathan J. 1997. Shari'a and State in the Modern Muslim Middle East. *International Journal of Middle Eastern Studies* 29: 359–76.
Bujra, Abdalla. 1971. *The Politics of Stratification: A Study of Political Change in a South Arabian Town*. Oxford: Oxford University Press.

Bulliet, Richard. 1994. *Islam: The View from the Edge*. New York: Columbia University Press.

Burton, Richard. 1964. *A Personal Narrative of a Pilgrimage to al-Madinah and Meccah*. New York: Dover.

Castells, Manuel. 1998. *End of Millennium*, Vol 3, *The Information Age: Economy, Society and Culture*. Oxford: Blackwell.

———. 1997. *The Power of Identity*, Vol. 2, *The Information Age: Economy, Society, and Culture*. London: Blackwell.

Caton, Steven C. 1987. Power, Persuasion, and Language: A Critique of the Segmentary Model in the Middle East. *International Journal of Middle East Studies* 19: 77–102.

———. 1990. *Peaks of Yemen I Summon: Poetry as Cultural Practice in Northern Yemeni Tribes*. Berkeley: University of California Press.

Champion, Daryl. 1997. Religious Fundamentalism: A Threat to the State of Israel? In Paul J. White and William S. Logan, eds., *Remaking the Middle East*. Oxford: Berg, pp. 297–335.

Chang, Claudia, and Harold A. Koster, eds. 1994. *Pastoralists at the Periphery*. Tucson: University of Arizona Press.

Chapman, Graham P., and Kathleen M. Baker, eds. 1992. *The Changing Geography of Africa and the Middle East*. London: Routledge.

Charrad, Mounira. 1993. *States and Women's Rights: A Comparison of Tunisia, Algeria and Morocco*. Berkeley: University of California Press.

———. 1998. Cultural Diversity Within Islam: Veils and Laws in Tunisia. In Herbert Bodman and Nayereh Tohidi, eds., *Women in Muslim Societies: Diversity Within Unity*. Boulder, CO: Lynne Reiner.

Chatty, Dawn. 1996. *Mobile Pastoralists: Development Planning and Social Change in Oman*. New York: Columbia University Press.

Chatty, Dawn, and Annika Rabo, eds. 1997. *Organizing Women: Formal and Informal Women's Groups in the Middle East*. Oxford: Berg.

Childe, V. Gordon. 1951. *Man Makes Himself*. New York: New American Library.

Clapp, Nicholas. 1999. *The Road to Ubar*. Boston: Houghton Mifflin.

Cole, Donald. 1975. *Nomads of the Nomads: The Al Murrah Bedouin of the Empty Quarter*. Chicago: Aldine.

Cole, Juan R. 1999. The Genesis of the Baha'i Faith in Middle Eastern Modernity. *International Institute for the Study of Islam in the Modern World Newsletter* 2: 9.

Combs-Schilling, M. E. 1989. *Sacred Performances: Islam, Sexuality and Sacrifice*. New York: Columbia University Press.

Coon, Carleton. 1958. *Caravan: The Story of the Middle East*. New York: Holt, Rinehart & Winston.

Costello, V. F. 1976. *Kashan: A City and Region of Iran*. Durham: Centre for Middle Eastern and Islamic Studies, University of Durham.

Courbage, Youssef. 1999. Christianity and Islam: Demography in the Middle East. *International Institute for the Study of Islam in the Modern World Newsletter*, March 1999.

———, and Philippe Fargues. 1997. *Christians and Jews in Islam*. London: New York: Tauris.

Cuno, Kenneth. 1983. The Origins of Private Ownership of Land in Egypt: A Reappraisal. In A. Hourani, P. Khoury, and M. Wilson, eds., *The Modern Middle East*. Berkeley: University of California Press, pp.195–229.

Dalacoura, Katerina. 1998. *Islam, Liberalism and Human Rights*. London: I. B. Tauris.

de Bellaigne, Christopher. 1999. Justice and the Kurds. Review of Henri J. Barkey and Graham E. Fuller, *Turkey's Kurdish Question*. *The New York Review of Books* 46(11): 19–24.

Delaney, Carol. 1991. *The Seed and the Soil: Gender and Cosmology in Turkish Village Society*. Berkeley: University of California Press.

de Seife, Rodolphe. 1995. *The Shari'a: An Introduction to the Law of Islam*. San Francisco: Austin and Winfield.

Diamond, Jared. 1999. *Guns, Germs, and Steel: The Fates of Human Societies.* New York: W. W. Norton.

Donaldson, Dwight M. 1933. *The Shi'ite Religion, A History of Islam in Persia and Iraq.* London: Luzac.

Dorsky, Susan. 1986. *Women of 'Amran: A Middle Eastern Ethnographic Study.* Salt Lake City: University of Utah Press.

Dresch, Paul. 1984. The Position of the Shaykhs Among the Northern Tribes of Yemen. *Man* (N.S.) 19 (1) (March): 31–49.

———, and Bernard Haykel. 1995. Stereotypes and Political Styles: Islamists and Tribesfolk in Yemen. *International Journal of Middle East Studies* 27: 405–431.

Duben, Alan. 1992. *The Middle East City: An Urban Management Perspective.* Istanbul: IULA-EMME, Istanbul Kent Basinevi.

———, and Cem Behar. 1991. *Istanbul Households: Marriage, Family and Fertility: 1880–1940.* Cambridge: Cambridge University Press.

Dwyer, Kevin. 1991. *Arab Voices: The Human Rights Debate in the Middle East.* Berkeley: University of California Press.

Early, Evelyn. 1980. *Baladi Women of Cairo: Playing with an Egg and a Stone.* Cairo: American University in Cairo Press.

Eickelman, Dale. 1974. Is There an Islamic City? The Making of a Quarter in a Moroccan Town. *International Journal of Middle Eastern Studies* 5 (3): 274–78.

———. 1998. Inside the Islamic Reformation. *Wilson Quarterly* 22 (1): 76–94.

———, and J. Piscatori. 1996. *Muslim Politics.* Princeton, NJ: Princeton University Press.

English, Paul. 1976. *City and Village in Iran.* Madison: University of Wisconsin Press.

Esposito, John. 1988. *The Straight Path.* New York: Oxford University Press.

———. 1992. *The Islamic Threat: Myth or Reality?* New York: Oxford University Press.

Evans-Pritchard, E. E. 1940. *The Nuer: A Description of the Modes of Livelihood and Political Institutions of a Nilotic People.* Oxford: Clarendon Press.

———. 1949. *The Sanusi of Cyrenaica.* Oxford: Clarendon Press.

Fernea, Elizabeth Warnock. 1965. *Guests of the Sheik: An Ethnography of an Iraqi Village.* New York: Doubleday.

———. 1998. *In Search of Islamic Feminism: One Woman's Global Journey.* New York: Bantam Books, Anchor Edition.

———, and Basima Quttan Bezirgan, eds. 1977. *Middle Eastern Muslim Women Speak.* Austin: University of Texas Press.

———, and Robert A. Fernea. 1997. *The Arab World: Forty Years of Change.* New York: Doubleday.

Fernea, Robert. 1970. *Shaykh and Effendi: Changing Patterns of Authority Among the El Shabana of Southern Iraq.* Cambridge, MA: Harvard University Press.

Filali-Ansary, Abdou. 1999. The Debate on Secularism in Contemporary Societies of Muslims. *International Institute for the Study of Islam in the Modern World Newsletter* 2: 6.

Fisher, Michael M. J. 1980. *Iran: From Religious Dispute to Revolution.* Cambridge, MA: Harvard University Press.

Fisher, W. B. 1978. *The Middle East: A Physical, Social and Regional Geography,* 7th ed. London: Methuen.

Flannery, Kent V. 1999. Process and Agency in Early State Formation. *Cambridge Archaeological Journal* 9(1): 3–21.

Freely, John. 1998. *Istanbul: The Imperial City.* Harmondsworth, U.K.: Penguin.

Friedel, Erika. 1991a. *Women of Deh Koh: Lives in an Iranian Village.* Harmondsworth, U.K.: Penguin.

———. 1991b. The Dynamics of Women's Spheres of Action in Rural Iran. In Nikki Keddie and Beth Baron, eds., *Women in Middle Eastern History: Shifting Boundaries in Sex and Gender.* New Haven, CT: Yale University Press.

Gaffney, P. 1994. *The Prophet's Pulpit: Islamic Preaching in Contemporary Egypt.* Comparative Studies on Muslim Societies 20. Berkeley: University of California Press.

Geertz, Clifford. 1968. *Islam Observed.* Chicago: University of Chicago Press.

Gellner, Ernest. 1979 (1969). *Saints of the Atlas.* Chicago: University of Chicago Press.

———. 1990. Tribalism and the State in the Middle East. In Philip Khoury and Joseph Kostiner, eds., *Tribes and State Formation in the Middle East.* Berkeley: University of California Press.

———. 1994. *Conditions of Liberty: Civil Society and Its Rivals.* London: Cambridge University Press.

———. and Henry Munson. 1995. Segmentation: Reality or Myth? *Journal of the Royal Anthropological Institute,* (4): 820–32.

Gerber, Haim. 1988. *Social Origins of the Middle East.* Boulder, CO: Lynne Rienner.

Gibb, H. A. R. 1958. *Mohammedanism: An Historical Survey.* New York: New American Library.

———, and H. H. Kramers, eds. 1955. *Shorter Encyclopedia of Islam.* Ithaca: Cornell University Press.

Gilmore, David. 1999. *Carnival and Culture: Sex, Symbol, and Status in Spain.* New Haven, CT: Yale University Press.

Gilsenan, Michael. 1973. *Saint and Sufi in Modern Egypt: An Essay in the Sociology of Religion.* Oxford: Clarendon Press.

———. 1993. Lying, Honor and Contradiction. In Donna Lee Bowen and Evelyn Early, eds., *Everyday Life in the Muslim Middle East.* Bloomington: Indiana University Press.

———. 1996. *Lords of the Lebanese Marches: Violence and Narrative in an Arab Society.* Berkeley: University of California Press.

Ginguld, M., A. Perevolotsky, and E. D. Ungar. 1997. Living on the Margins: Livelihood Strategies of Bedouin Herd-Owners in the Northern Negev, Israel. *Human Ecology* 25(4): 567–91.

Gleave, R., and E. Kermeli, eds. 1997. *Islamic Law: Theory and Practice.* New York: I. B. Tauris.

Goldscheider, Calvin. 1996. *Israel's Changing Society: Population, Ethnicity, and Development.* Boulder, CO: Westview Press.

Göle, Nilüfer. 1996. *The Forbidden Modern: Civilization and Veiling.* Ann Arbor: University of Michigan Press.

Gorkin, Michael. 1993. *Days of Honey, Days of Onion.* Berkeley: University of California Press.

Guillaume, Alfred. 1964. *Islam,* 2nd. ed. rev. Baltimore: Penguin.

Gülen, Fethullah. 1993. *Questions This Modern Age Puts to Islam.* Istanbul: Truestar Press.

———. 1995. *The Infinite Light.* Istanbul: Truestar Press.

Haddad, Robert. 1970. *Syrian Christians in Muslim Societies: An Interpretation.* Princeton, NJ: Princeton University Press.

Haddad, Y., and J. Esposito, eds. 1998. *Islam, Gender, and Social Change.* New York: Oxford University Press.

Haeri, Shahla. 1989. *Law of Desire: Temporary Marriage in Shi'ite Iran.* Syracuse, NY: Syracuse University Press.

Halpern, Manfred. 1963. *The Politics of Social Change in the Middle East and North Africa.* Princeton, NJ: Princeton University Press.

Hamid el-Zein, Abdul. 1977. Beyond Ideology and Theology: The Search for the Anthropology of Islam. *Annual Review of Anthropology* 6: 227–54.

Harlan, Jack. 1967. A Wild Wheat Harvest in Turkey. *Archeology* 20 (3): 197–201.

Hasluck, F. W. 1929. *Christianity and Islam Under the Sultans,* 2 vols. Oxford: Oxford University Press.

Hassanpour, Amir. 1992. *Nationalism and Language in Kurdistan, 1918–1985.* San Francisco: Mellen Research University Press.

Hatem, Mervat. 1998. Secularist and Islamic Discourses of Modernity in Egypt and the Evolution of the Post-Colonial Nation-State. In Y. Haddad and J. Esposito, eds., *Islam, Gender, and Social Change.* New York: Oxford University Press, pp. 85–100.

Held, Colbert C. 1994. *Middle East Patterns,* 2nd ed. Boulder, CO: Westview Press.

Hicks, Esther. 1996. *Infibulation: Female Genital Mutilation in Islamic Northeastern Africa.* rev. ed. New Brunswick, NJ: Transaction.

Hijab, Nadia. 1998. Islam, Social Change, and the Reality of Arab Women's Lives. In Y. Haddad and J. Esposito, eds., *Islam,*

Gender, and Social Change. New York: Oxford University Press, pp. 45–57.

Hodgson, Marshall. 1974. *The Venture of Islam: Conscience and History in a World Civilization.* Chicago: University of Chicago Press.

Hoffman, Valerie J. 1995. *Sufism, Mystics and Saints in Modern Egypt.* Columbia: University of South Carolina Press.

———. 1999. Saints and Sheikhs in Modern Egypt. *International Institute for the Study of Islam in the Modern World Newsletter* 2: 19.

Hole, Frank, Kent V. Flannery, and James A. Neely. 1969. *Prehistory and Human Ecology of the Deh Luran Plain.* Memoirs of the Museum of Anthropology, Anthropological Papers No. 1. Ann Arbor: University of Michigan.

Hoodfar, Homa. 1996a. Egyptian Male Migration and Urban Families Left Behind: Feminization of the Egyptian Family or a Reaffirmation of Traditional Gender Roles? In D. Singerman and H. Hoodfar, eds., *Development, Change, and Gender in Cairo: A View from the Household.* Bloomington: Indiana University Press, pp. 51–80.

———. 1996b. Survival Strategies and the Political Economy of Low-Income Households in Cairo. In D. Singerman and H. Hoodfar, eds., *Development, Change, and Gender in Cairo: A View from the Household.* Bloomington: Indiana University Press, pp. 1–27.

———. 1997. *Between Marriage and the Market: Intimate Politics and Survival in Cairo.* Berkeley: University of California Press.

Hopkins, Nicholas. 1980. *Animal Husbandry and the Household Economy in Two Egyptian Villages.* Report of the Rural Sociology Segment of the Project on Improved Utilization of Feed Resources of the Livestock Sector. Mimeo. Cairo: Social Research Center, American University, (May).

———. 1985. The Political Economy of Two Arab Villages. In Nicholas Hopkins and Saad Eddin Ibrahim, eds., *Arab Society: Social Science Perspectives.* Cairo: American University in Cairo Press.

———, and Saad Eddin Ibrahim. 1985. *Arab Society: Social Science Perspectives.* Cairo: American University in Cairo Press.

———, and Kirsten Westergaard, eds., 1998. *Directions of Change in Rural Egypt.* Cairo: American University in Cairo Press.

Horne, Lee. 1994. *Village Spaces: Settlement and Society in Northeastern Iran.* Washington, DC: Smithsonian Institution Press.

Hourani, Albert. 1974. *Minorities in the Arab World.* London: Oxford University Press.

———, and S. M. Stern, eds. 1970. *The Islamic City: Papers on Islamic History. 1.* Oxford: Bruno Cassirer, and Philadelphia: University of Pennsylvania Press.

Huntington, Samuel P. 1993. The Clash of Civilizations. *Foreign Affairs* 72(3) (Summer).

Huxley, Frederick. 1978. *Wasita in a Lebanese Context: Social Exchange among Villagers and Outsiders.* Museum of Anthropology, Anthropological Papers, No. 64. Ann Arbor: University of Michigan.

Ibrahim, Saad Eddin. 1985. Urbanization in the Arab World: The Need for an Urban Strategy. In Nicholas Hopkins and Saad Eddin Ibrahim, eds., *Arab Society: Social Science Perspectives.* Cairo: American University in Cairo Press, pp. 123–48.

———. 1997. From Taliban to Erbakan: The Case of Islam, Civil Society and Democracy. In E. Özdalga and S. Persson, eds., *Civil Society, Democracy, and the Muslim World.* Papers read at a conference at the Swedish Research Institute, Istanbul, 28–30 October 1996. *Swedish Research Institute in Istanbul Transactions,* vol. 7, pp. 33–43.

İlyasoğlu, Aynur. 1998. Islamist Women in Turkey: Their Identity and Self-Image. In Zehra F. Arat, ed., *Deconstructing Images of "The Turkish Woman."* New York: St. Martin's Press, pp. 241–61.

Ireton, François. 1998. The Evolution of Agrarian Structures in Egypt: Regional Patterns of Change in Farm Size. In

Nicholas S. Hopkins and Kirsten Westergaard, eds., *Directions of Change in Rural Egypt.* Cairo: The American University in Cairo Press, pp. 41–65.

Jaber, Nabila. 1997. Islam Revisited: Wo(man)hood, Nationhood, and the Legitimating Crisis of Gender Equality. In Paul J. White and William S. Logan, eds., *Remaking the Middle East.* Oxford: Berg, pp. 105–27.

Jawad, Ferida. 1999. The Triumph of Arabism: The *shu'ubiyyah* Controversy and the National Identity of Modern Iraq. Paper presented at The Third Tri-annual EURAMES-Conference, The Middle East Studies Center, University of Ghent, September 27–29, 1999.

Joseph, Suad. 1978. Muslim-Christian Conflict in Lebanon: A Perspective on the Evolution of Sectarianism. In S. Joseph and B. Pillsbury, eds., *Muslim-Christian Conflicts: Economic, Political, and Social Origins.* Boulder, CO: Westview Press, pp. 64–97.

———. 1994. Brother/Sister Relationships: Connectivity, Love, and Power in the Reproduction of Patriarchy in Lebanon. *American Ethnologist* 21: 50–73.

Kalman, Matthew. 1999. Bedouins Ask Barak to Rethink Resettling. *USA Today,* July 26, 7A.

Kamal Khani, Z. 1998. Reconstruction of Islamic Knowledge and Knowing: A Case of Islamic Practice Among Women in Iran. In Karin Ask and Marit Tjomsland, eds., *Women and Islamization: Contemporary Dimensions of Discourse on Gender Relations.* Oxford: Berg, pp. 177–95.

Kandiyoti, Deniz. 1988. Bargaining with Patriarchy. *Gender & Society* 2(3) (September): 274–89.

———, ed. 1991. *Women, Islam and the State.* London: Macmillan.

Karam, Azza M. 1998. *Women, Islamisms and the State: Contemporary Feminism in Egypt.* London: Macmillian and St. Martin's Press.

Kassamali, Noor. 1998. When Modernity Confronts Traditional Practices: Female Genital Cutting in Northeast Africa. In Herbert Bodman and Nayereh Tohidi, eds., *Woman in Muslim Societies: Diversity Within Unity.* Boulder, CO: Lynne Reiner, pp. 39–63.

Kazgan, Gülten, Hasan Kirmanoğlu, Çiğdem Çelik, and Arus Yumul. 1999. *Kuştepe araştırması 1999.* Istanbul: Istanbul Bilgi Üniversitesi Yayınları.

Keddie, Nikki, ed. 1972. *Scholars, Saints and Sufis: Muslim Religious Instructions Since 1500.* Berkeley: University of California Press.

———. 1999. Women and Religious Politics in the Contemporary World. *International Institute for the Study of Islam in the Modern World Newsletter,* March 1999.

Kemal, Yashar. 1961. *Mehmed My Hawk,* trans. Edouard Roditi. New York: Pantheon.

Kemp, Geoffrey, and Robert E. Harkavy, eds. 1997. *Strategic Geography and the Changing Middle East.* Washington, DC: Brookings Institution Press.

Keyder, Çağlar, ed. 1999. *Istanbul: Between the Global and the Local.* Lanham, MD: Rowman & Littlefield.

Khalaf, Samir. 1987. *Lebanon's Predicament.* New York: University of Columbia Press.

———. 1993. *Beirut Reclaimed: Reflections on Urban Design and the Restoration of Civility.* Beirut: Dar An-Nahar.

Khouri, Fuad. 1980. *Tribe and State in Bahrain.* Publications of the Center for Middle Eastern Studies No. 14. Chicago: University of Chicago Press.

———. 1990. *Imams and Emirs: State, Religion, and Sects in Islam.* London: Saqi Books.

Khoury, Philip. 1993. Abu Ali al-Kilaw: A Damascus Qabaday. In Edmund Burke III, ed., *Struggle and Survival in the Modern Middle East.* Berkeley: University of California Press, pp. 179–91.

Khudori, Darwis. 1999. Islamization and Secularization through Architecture: The Case of Ismailia. *International Institute for the Study of Islam in the Modern World Newsletter,* March 1999.

Kielstra, Nico. 1975. *Ecology and Community in Iran*. Amsterdam: University of Amsterdam Press.

———. 1987. Expectations and Reality in the Modernization of Two Iranian Villages. In R. Lawless, ed., *The Middle Eastern Village: Changing Economic and Social Relations*. London: Croom Helm, pp. 144–220.

Kisirwani, Maroun. 1997. The Rehabilitation and Reconstruction of Lebanon. In Paul J. White and William S. Logan, eds., *Remaking the Middle East*. Oxford: Berg, pp. 87–104.

Kömeçoğlu, Uğur. 1997. A Sociologically Interpretative Approach to the Fethullah Gülen Community Movement. MA thesis, Boğaziçi University, Istanbul.

———. 2000. Kutsal ile Kamusal: Fethullah Gülen Cenot Hareketi. In Nilüfer Göle, ed., *Islam ve Kamusal Alan*. Istanbul: Metis Press.

Kortum, Gerhard. 1978. *Die Marvdasht Ebene in Fars: Grundlagen and Entwicklung ether Alter iranischen Bewasserungslanschaft*. Kiel: Selbstverlag des Geographischen Instituts.

Kostiner, Joseph. 1990. Transforming Dualities: Tribe and State Formation in Saudi Arabia. In Philip Khoury and Joseph Kostiner, eds., *Tribes and State Formation in the Middle East*. Berkeley: University of California Press.

Kramer, Martin. 1998. The Muslim Middle East in the 21st Century. *International Institute for the Study of Islam in the Modern World Newsletter* 1: 15.

Kramer, Noah Samuel. 1963. *The Sumerians: Their History, Culture and Character*. Chicago: University of Chicago Press.

Kurzman, Charles. 1998. *Liberal Islam: A Source-Book*. Oxford: Oxford University Press.

———. 1999. Liberal Islam: Not a Contradiction in Terms. *International Institute for the Study of Islam in the Modern World Newsletter* 2: 41.

Kut, Gün. 1993. Burning Waters: The Hydropolitics of the Euphrates and Tigris. *New Perspectives on Turkey* 9: 47–74.

Lancaster, William. 1997. *The Rwala Bedouin Today*, 2nd ed. Prospect Heights, IL: Waveland Press.

Landreau, A. N., and R. S. Yohe, with D. G. Bates and Anita Landreau. 1983. *Flowers of the Yayla: Yörük Weaving of the Toros Mountains*. Washington, DC: Textile Museum.

Lapidus, Ira. 1973. The Evolution of Muslim Urban Society. *Comparative Studies in Society and History* 15(1) (January): 21–50.

Lawless, R., ed. 1987. *The Middle Eastern Village: Changing Economic and Social Relations*. London: Croom Helm.

Layish, Aharon. 1982. *Marriage, Divorce, and Succession in the Druze Family*. Leiden: E. J. Brill.

Levy, Avigdor. 1994. *The Jews of the Ottoman Empire*. Princeton, NJ: Darwin Press, and Washington, DC: Institute of Turkish Studies.

Lewis, Bernard. 1979. *Race and Color in Islam*. New York: Octagon Books.

———. 1984. *The Jews of Islam*. Princeton, NJ: Princeton University Press.

———. 1990. *Race and Slavery in the Middle East: An Historical Enquiry*. Oxford: Oxford University Press.

———. 1993. *The Arabs in History*, 6th ed. New York: Oxford University Press.

Lindholm, Charles. 1986. Kinship Structure and Political Authority: The Middle East and Central Asia. *Comparative Studies in Society and History* 28: 334–55.

———. 1995. The New Middle Eastern Ethnography. *Journal of the Royal Anthropological Institute*, 805–20.

———. 1996. *The Islamic Middle East: An Historical Anthropology*. Oxford: Blackwell.

Loeffler, Reinhold. 1988. *Islam in Practice: Religious Beliefs in a Persian Village*. Albany: State University of New York Press.

MacLeod, Arlene Elowe. 1991. *Accommodating Protest: Working Women, the New Veiling, and Change in Cairo*. New York: Columbia University Press.

———. 1996. Transforming Women's Identity: The Interaction of Household and Workplace in Cairo. In D. Singerman and H. Hoodfar, eds., *Development, Change, and Gender in Cairo: A View from the Household.* Bloomington: Indiana University Press, pp. 27–51.

Magnarella, Paul. 1974. *Tradition and Change in a Turkish Town.* Cambridge, MA: Schenkman/John Wiley.

Makdisi, Saree. 1997. Laying Claim to Beirut: Urban Narrative and Spatial Identity in the Age of Solidere. *Critical Inquiry* 23: 661–705.

Makhlouf, Carla. 1979. *Changing Veils: Women and Modernization in North Yemen.* Austin: University of Texas Press.

Malik, Jamal. 1998. Making Sense of Islamic Fundamentalism. *International Institute for the Study of Islam in the Modern World Newsletter* 1: 27.

Mango, Andrew. 1993. The Turkish Model. *Middle Eastern Studies* 29(4): 726–57.

———. 1994. *Turkey: The Challenge of a New Role.* Westport, CT: Praeger.

———. 1995. Turkey in Winter. *Middle Eastern Studies* 31(3): 620–52.

Marcus, Abraham. 1989. *The Middle East on the Eve of Modernity: Aleppo in the Eighteenth Century.* New York: Columbia University Press.

Mardin, Şerif. 1962. *The Genesis of Young Ottoman Thought.* Princeton, NJ: Princeton University Press.

———. 1989. *Religion and Social Change in Modern Turkey: The Case of Bediüzzaman Said Nursi.* Albany: State University of New York Press.

Marx, E. 1967. *The Bedouin of the Negev.* Manchester, UK: Manchester University Press.

———. 1999. Oases in South Sinai. *Human Ecology* 27(2): 341–57.

Massignon, Louis. 1922. *La Passion d'al Hosayn ibn Mansour al-Hallaj, Martyr Mystique de l'Islam,* Vol. II. Paris: P. Geuthner.

McCorriston, Joy, and Frank Hole. 1991. The Ecology of Seasonal Stress and the Origins of Agriculture in the Near East. *American Anthropologist* 93: 46–69.

McDowall, David. 1996. *A Modern History of the Kurds.* London: I. B. Tauris.

Meir, Avinoam. 1997. *As Nomadism Ends: The Israeli Bedouin of the Negev.* Boulder, CO: Westview Press.

Meneley, Anne. 1996. *Tournaments of Value: Sociability and Hierarchy in a Yemeni Town.* Toronto: University of Toronto Press.

Mernissi, Fatima. 1975. *Beyond the Veil: Male-Female Dynamics in a Modern Muslim Society.* Cambridge, MA: Schenkman.

———. 1987. *Le Harem politique.* Paris: Albin Michel.

———. 1991. *The Veil and the Male Elite: A Feminist Interpretation of Women's Rights in Islam.* Reading, MA: Addison-Wesley.

———. 1996. *Women's Rebellion and Islamic Memory.* Atlantic Highlands, NJ: Zed Books.

Meyer, Ann Elizabeth. 1998. *Islam and Human Rights: Tradition and Politics,* 3rd ed. Boulder, CO: Westview Press.

Mir-Hosseini, Ziba. 1993. Women, Marriage and the Law in Post-Revolutionary Iran. In Haleh Afshar, ed., *Women in the Middle East: Perceptions, Realities and Struggles for Liberation.* New York: St. Martin's Press.

Mitchell, Timothy. 1998. The Market's Place. In Nicholas S. Hopkins and Kirsten Westergaard, eds., *Directions of Change in Rural Egypt.* Cairo: American University in Cairo Press, pp. 19–40.

Moawad, Galal Abdulla. 1987. Urbanization and Labor Migration in the Arab Countries of the Gulf. *Journal of the Gulf and Arabian Peninsula Studies* 13(51): 189–214.

Moghadam, Valentine M. 1993. *Modernizing Women: Gender and Social Change in the Middle East.* Boulder, CO: Lynne Rienner.

———. ed. 1994. *Gender and National Identity: Women and Politics in Muslim Societies.* London: Zed Books and Oxford University Press, for the United Nations University.

Monshipouri, Mahmood. 1998. *Islamism, Secularism, and Human Rights in the Middle East.* London: Lynne Rienner.

Mottahedeh, Roy P. 1995. The Clash of Civilizations: An Islamicist's Critique. *Harvard Middle Eastern and Islamic Review* 2(2): 1–26.

Müller-Mahn, Detlef. 1998. Spaces of Poverty: The Geography of Social Change in Rural Egypt. In Nicholas S. Hopkins and Kirsten Westergaard, eds., *Directions of Change in Rural Egypt.* Cairo: The American University in Cairo Press, pp. 256–76.

Mundy, Martha. 1995. *Domestic Government: Kinship, Community, and Polity in North Yemen.* London: I. B. Tauris.

Munson, Henry, Jr. 1998. *Islam and Revolution in the Middle East.* New Haven, CT: Yale University Press.

Nadim, Nawal M. 1985. Family Relationships in a *Hara* in Cairo. In Nicholas Hopkins and Saad Eddin Ibrahim, eds., *Arab Society: Social Science Perspectives.* Cairo: American University in Cairo Press, pp. 212–23.

Najmabadi, Afsaneh. 1998. *The Story of the Daughters of Quchan: Gender and National Memory in Iranian History.* Syracuse, NY: Syracuse University Press.

Navaro-Yasin, Yael. 1999. The Historical Construction of Local Culture: Gender and Identity in the Politics of Secularism versus Islam. In Çag˘lar Keyder, ed., *Istanbul: Between the Global and the Local.* Lanham, MD: Rowman & Littlefield, pp. 59–76.

Noldeke, A. 1955. Quoted in H. A. R. Gibb and H. H. Kramers, eds., *Shorter Encyclopedia of Islam.* Ithaca, NY: Cornell University Press, pp. 360–61.

Norton, A. R., ed. 1996. *Civil Society in the Middle East.* Leiden: E. J. Brill.

Olson, E. A. 1985. Muslim Identity and Secularism in Contemporary Turkey: The Headscarf Dispute. *Anthropological Quarterly* 58: 161–89.

Olsson, Tord, Elisabeth Özdalga, and Catharina Raudvere, eds. 1998. *Alevi Identity: Cultural, Religious and Social Perspectives.* Papers read at a conference at the Swedish Research Institute, Istanbul, 25–27 November 1996. *Swedish Research Institute in Istanbul Transactions,* vol. 8.

Owen, Roger, and Şevket Pamuk. 1999. *A History of Middle East Economies in the Twentieth Century.* Cambridge, MA.: Harvard University Press.

Özdalga, Elisabeth, and Sune Persson, eds. 1997. Civil Society and Its Enemies: Reflections on a Debate in the Light of Recent Developments Within the Islamic Student Movement in Turkey. In E. Özdalga and S. Persson, eds., *Civil Society, Democracy, and the Muslim World.* Papers read at a conference at the Swedish Research Institute, Istanbul, 28–30 October 1996. *Swedish Research Institute in Istanbul Transactions,* vol. 7, pp. 73–83.

———. 1997. *Civil Society, Democracy, and the Muslim World.* Papers read at a conference at the Swedish Research Institute, Istanbul, 28–30 October 1996. *Swedish Research Institute in Istanbul Transactions,* vol. 7.

Palaczek, Gabriele. 1993. Labour Migration Among Bursa Muhacirs: Some Wider Implications. In Paul Stirling, ed., *Culture and Economy: Changes in Turkish Villages.* Manchester, U.K.: Eothen Press, pp. 95–114.

Peters, Emrys L. 1967. Some Structural Aspects of the Feud Among the Camel-Herding Bedouin of Cyrenaica. *Africa* 37(3) (July): 261–81.

———. 1976. Aspects of Affinity in a Lebanese Maronite Village. In J. G. Peristany, ed., *Mediterranean Family Structure, Cambridge Studies in Social Anthropology* 13. New York: Cambridge University Press, pp. 62–63.

Philby, H. 1928. *Arabia of the Wahabis.* London: Constable.

Pitt-Rivers, J. 1966. Honour and Social Status. In J. G. Peristany, ed., *Honour and Shame: The Values of Mediterranean Society.* Chicago: University of Chicago Press, pp. 19–78.

Rahman, Fazlur. 1979. *Islam,* 2nd ed. Chicago: University of Chicago Press.

Rassam, Amal. 1974. Ethnicity, Cultural Discontinuity, and Power Brokers in Northern Iraq: The Case of the Shabak. *American Ethnologist* 1(1) (February): 207–18.

———. 1977. Al-taba'iyya: Power, Patronage, and Marginal Groups in Northern Iraq. In E. Gellner and J. Waterbury, eds.,

Patrons and Clients in Mediterranean Societies. London: Duckworth, pp. 156–66.

——. 1992. Political Ideology and Women in Iraq: Legislation and Cultural Constraints. *Journal of Developing Societies* 8: 80–96.

Raudvere, Catharina. 1998. Female Dervishes in Contemporary Istanbul: Between Tradition and Modernity. In Karin Ask and Marit Tjomsland, eds., *Women and Islamization: Contemporary Dimensions of Discourse on Gender Relations.* Oxford: Berg, pp. 125–47.

Redman, Charles L. 1999. *Human Impact on Ancient Environments.* Tempe: Arizona State University Press.

Richards, Alan, and John Waterbury. 1990. *A Political Economy of the Middle East: State, Class and Economic Development.* Boulder, CO: Westview Press.

Rodinson, Maxime. 1971. *Muhammad.* New York: Pantheon Press.

Rogan, Eugene Lawrence. 1986. Physical Islamization in Amman. *Muslim World* 76(1) (January): 24–42.

Roy, Olivier. 1994. *The Failure of Political Islam,* trans. Carol Volk. Cambridge, MA: Harvard University Press.

——. 1999. The Radicalization of Sunni Conservative Fundamentalism. *International Institute for the Study of Islam in the Modern World Newsletter* 2: 7.

Rugh, Andrea. 1985. *The Family in Egypt.* Cairo: American University in Cairo Press.

——. 1986. *Reveal and Conceal: Dress in Contemporary Egypt.* Syracuse, NY: Syracuse University Press.

Sabbah, Fatna A. 1984. *Woman in the Muslim Unconscious,* trans. Mary Jo Lakeland. Elmsford, NY: Pergamon Press.

Said, Edward W. 1979. *Orientalism.* New York: Vintage Press.

——. 1997. *Covering Islam: How the Media and the Experts Determine How We See the Rest of the World.* New York: Random House.

Salame, Ghassan. 1993. Political Power and the Saudi State. In A. Hourani, P. Khoury and M. Wilson, eds., *The Modern Middle East.* Berkeley: University of California Press, pp. 579–601.

Salim, Shaker. 1962. *Marsh Dwellers of the Euphrates Delta.* London: Athlone Press.

Salzman, Philip. 1972. Multi-Resource Nomadism in Iranian Baluchistan. In William Irons and Neville Dyson-Hudson, eds., pp. 60–68, *Perspectives on Nomadism.* Leiden: Brill.

——. 1978. Does Complementary Opposition Exist? *American Anthropologist* 80(1): 53–70.

——. 1994. Baluchi Nomads in the Market. In Claudia Chang and Harold A. Koster, eds., *Pastoralists at the Periphery.* Tucson: University of Arizona Press, pp. 165–74.

——. 1999. *The Anthropology of Real Life: Events in Human Experience.* Prospect Heights, IL: Waveland Press.

Saqqaf, Abdulaziz Y., ed. 1987. *The Middle East City: Ancient Traditions Confront a Modern World.* New York: Paragon House.

Savas, İlkay. 1997. İslam and Civil Society. In E. Özdalga and S. Persson, eds., *Civil Society, Democracy and the Muslim World.* Papers read at a conference at the Swedish Research Institute, Istanbul, October 28–30, 1996. Swedish Research Institute in Istanbul Transactions, vol. 7, pp. 9–16.

Sawalha, Aseel. 1999. The Reconstruction of Beirut: Local Responses to Globalization. *City and Society* (Fall): 1–13.

Schimmel, Annemarie. 1975. *Mystical Dimensions of Islam.* Chapel Hill: University of North Carolina Press.

Shaaban, Bouthaina. 1998. Persisting Contradictions: Muslim Women. In Dawn Chatty and Annika Rabo, eds., *Organizing Women: Formal and Informal Women's Groups in the Middle East.* Oxford: Berg, pp. 81–99.

Shah, Idris. 1964. *The Sufis.* New York: Doubleday.

Shami, Seteney. 1997. Domesticity Reconfigured: Women in Squatter Areas of Amman, Syria. In Herbert L. Bodman and Nayereh Tohidi, eds., *Women in Muslim Societies: Diversity Within Unity.* London: Lynne Rienner, pp. 101–19.

Shankland, David. 1993a. Alevi and Sunni in Rural Anatolia: Diverse Paths of

Change. In Paul Stirling, ed., *Culture and Economy: Changes in Turkish Villages*. Manchester, UK: Eothen Press, pp. 46–64.

———. 1993b. Alevi and Sunni in Rural Turkey: Diverse Paths of Change. Ph.D. thesis, Cambridge University.

Sims, David. 1990. Owner-Builder Housing in Jordan. *Habitat International* 14(1): 123–35.

Singerman, D. 1995. *Avenues of Participation: Family, Politics, and Networks in Urban Quarters of Cairo*. Princeton, NJ: Princeton University Press.

———, and Homa Hoodfar, eds. 1996. *Development, Change, and Gender in Cairo: A View from the Household*. Bloomington: Indiana University Press.

Smith, Anthony. 1986. *The Ethnic Origins of Nations*. Oxford: Basil Blackwell.

Spencer, C. S. 1998. A Mathematical Model of Primary State Formation. *Cultural Dynamics* 10: 5–20.

Stavropoulos, Pam. 1997. Dichotomy and Complementarity: Tenets of Islam and Their Interrelationship. In Paul J. White and William S. Logan, eds., *Remaking the Middle East*. Oxford: Berg, pp. 41–58.

Stern, S. M. 1970. The Constitution of the Islamic City. In Albert Hourani and S. M. Stern, eds., *The Islamic City: Papers on Islamic History. 1*. Oxford: Bruno Cassirer, and Philadelphia: University of Pennsylvania Press, pp. 25–50.

Stewart, Frank. 1994. *Honor*. Chicago: University of Chicago Press.

Stirling, Paul. 1965. *Turkish Village*. New York: John Wiley.

———, ed. 1993. *Culture and Economy: Changes in Turkish Villages*. Manchester, UK: Eothen Press.

Stokes, Martin. 1999. Sounding Out: The Culture Industries and the Globalization of Istanbul. In Çağlar Keyder, ed., *Istanbul: Between the Global and the Local*. Lanham, MD: Rowman & Littlefield, pp. 121–39.

Stowasser, Barbara F. 1994. *Women in the Qur'an: Traditions and Interpretation*. New York: Oxford University Press.

Suad, Joseph, and Barbara Pillsbury, eds. 1978. *Muslim-Christian Conflicts: Eco-*

nomic, Political and Social Origins. Boulder, CO: Westview Press.

Sunar, İlkay. 1997. Civil Society and Islam. In E. Özdalga and S. Persson, eds., *Civil Society, Democracy, and the Muslim World*. Paper read at a conference at the Swedish Research Institute, Istanbul, 28–30 October 1996. *Swedish Research Institute in Istanbul Transactions*, vol. 7, pp. 9–15.

Tapper, Nancy. 1991. *Bartered Brides: Politics, Gender, and Marriage in an Afghan Tribal Society*. Cambridge Studies in Social and Cultural Anthropology 74. Cambridge: Cambridge University Press.

Tapper, Richard, ed. 1994. *Islam in Modern Turkey: Religion, Politics and Literature in a Secular State*. London: I. B. Tauris.

Taylor, Elizabeth. 1987. Egyptian Migration and Peasant Wives. In R. Lawless, ed., *The Middle Eastern Village: Changing Economic and Social Relations*. London: Croom Helm, pp. 253–71.

Tibi, Bassam. 1997. The Cultural Underpinning of Civil Society in Islamic Civilization: Islam and Democracy—Bridges Between the Civilizations. In E. Özdalga and S. Persson, eds., *Civil Society, Democracy, and the Muslim World*. Paper read at a conference at the Swedish Research Institute, Istanbul, 28–30 October 1996. *Swedish Research Institute in Istanbul Transactions*, vol. 7, pp. 23–31.

———. 1998. *The Challenge of Fundamentalism: Political Islam and the New World Order*. Berkeley: University of California Press.

Toprak, Binnaz. 1996. Civil Society in Turkey. In A. R. Norton, ed., *Civil Society in the Middle East*. Leiden: E. J. Brill, pp. 87–119.

Toth, James. 1998. Beating Plowshares into Swords: The Relocation of Rural Egyptian Workers and their Discontent. In Nicholas S. Hopkins and Kirsten Westergaard, eds., *Directions of Change in Rural Egypt*. Cairo: The American University in Cairo Press, pp. 66–87.

van Bruinessen, Martin. 1992. *Agha, Shaikh and State: The Social and Political Structures of Kurdistan*. London: Zed Books.

Wassef, Nadia. 1999. Asserting Masculinities: FGM in Egypt Revisited. *Middle East Women's Studies Review* 14 (3): 1–3.

Watt, W. Montgomery. 1961. *Muhammad: Prophet and Statesman.* London: Oxford University Press.

Weir, Shelagh. 1987. Labor Migration and Key Aspects of Its Economic and Social Impact on a Yemeni Highland Community. In R. Lawless, ed., *The Middle Eastern Village: Changing Economic and Social Relations.* London: Croom Helm, pp. 290–312.

White, Jenny B. 1994. *Money Makes Us Relatives: Women's Labor in Urban Turkey.* Austin: University of Texas Press.

White, Paul J., and William S. Logan, eds. 1997. *Remaking the Middle East.* Oxford: Berg.

Wikan, Uni. 1982. *Behind the Veil in Arabia: Women in Oman.* Chicago: University of Chicago Press.

———. 1985. Living Conditions Among Cairo's Poor: A View from Below. *Middle East Journal* 39(1): 7–26.

———. 1995. Sustainable Development in the Mega-City: Can the Concept Be Made Applicable? *Current Anthropology* 36: 635–55.

Wright, H. T. 1998. Uruk States in Southwestern Iran. In G. M. Feinman and J.

Marcus, eds., *Archaic States.* Santa Fe, NM: School of American Research, pp. 173–97.

Yalçın-Heckmann, Lâle. 1994. Ethnic Islam and Nationalism among the Kurds in Turkey. In Richard Tapper, ed., *Islam in Modern Turkey: Religion, Politics and Literature in a Secular State.* London: I. B. Tauris, pp. 102–20.

Yann, Richard. 1995. *Shi'ite Islam: Polity, Ideology, and Creed. Studies in Social Discontinuity.* Cambridge, MA: Blackwell.

Young, William, and Seteney Shami. 1997. Anthropological Approaches to the Arab Family: An Introduction. *Journal of Comparative Family Studies; Special Issue; The Arab Family* 28 (Summer).

Yumul, Arusyak. 1992. Religion, Community and Culture: The Turkish Armenians. Ph.D. Thesis, Oxford University.

Zubaida, Sami. 1998. Muslim Societies: Unity or Diversity? *International Institute for the Study of Islam in the Modern World Newsletter* 1: 1.

Zuhur, Sherifa. 1992. *Revealing Reveiling: Islamist Gender Ideology in Contemporary Egypt.* Albany: State University of New York.

Photo Credits

Index